JOHN CHANDLER ob
of Nottingham and we
industry. He later beca
at Brighton Technical
Basingstoke Technical
for O-level and A-leve
Wolsey Hall, Oxford.

RICK WILKINSON is a graduate of the University of Southampton. He gained a Ph.D. for his research work in Organic Chemistry. He has taught at Winchester Tutorial College, coaching GCE candidates, and is currently lecturer in Physics and Chemistry at Basingstoke Technical College.

key facts

GCE A-Level Passbooks

APPLIED MATHEMATICS, E. M. Peet, B.A.

BIOLOGY, H. Rapson, B.Sc.

CHEMISTRY, J. E. Chandler, B.Sc. and R. J. Wilkinson, Ph.D.

ECONOMICS, R. Maile, B.A.

GEOGRAPHY, R. Bryant, B.A., Ph.D., R. Knowles, M.A. and J. Wareing, B.A., M.Sc.

MODERN BRITISH AND EUROPEAN HISTORY, R. Maples, B.Ed., M.A. and M. A. Wright, M.A.

PHYSICS, J. R. Garrood, M.A., Ph.D.

PURE MATHEMATICS, R. A. Parsons, B.Sc. and A. G. Dawson, B.Sc.

PURE AND APPLIED MATHEMATICS, R. A. Parsons, B.Sc. and A. G. Dawson, B.Sc.

GCE A-Level Passbook

Chemistry

J. E. Chandler, B.Sc.

and

R. J. Wilkinson, Ph.D.

key facts

Published by Charles Letts and Co Ltd
London, Edinburgh and New York

Diary House, Borough Road, London SE1 1DW
Reprinted 1985
Made and printed by Charles Letts (Scotland) Ltd
ISBN 0 85097 510 7

Contents

Introduction

This book is intended for students taking the examinations for the General Certificate of Education at Advanced Level (both traditional and Nuffield type courses). In addition it will prove useful to students taking Technical Education Council courses in Chemistry to level III.

The contents take into account the majority of topics listed in the various syllabuses of the regional examining boards at this level, including aspects of qualitative and quantitative analysis. S.I. (International System) units and nomenclature are used throughout.

Qualifications in Chemistry are of considerable importance both in their own right and in many fields including biology, medical and veterinary sciences, engineering and allied subject areas. An understanding of Chemistry to the level of this text is important to enable a student to study to undergraduate level in these fields.

Acknowledgements
To Janet for her hard work in typing and checking the manuscript and for her tolerance and encouragement during the writing of this book.

Thanks also to Julia for her support and encouragement.

Chapter 1
Atomic and Molecular Mass Determination; Colloids

Relative atomic mass, A_r, (formerly known as atomic weight) is defined as the average mass of the atoms of an element on a scale on which one atom of ^{12}C isotope of carbon has a mass of 12 units.

$$\text{Relative atomic mass, } A_r = \frac{\text{mass of one atom of element} \times 12}{\text{mass of one atom of } ^{12}\text{C}}$$

Mass spectrometer

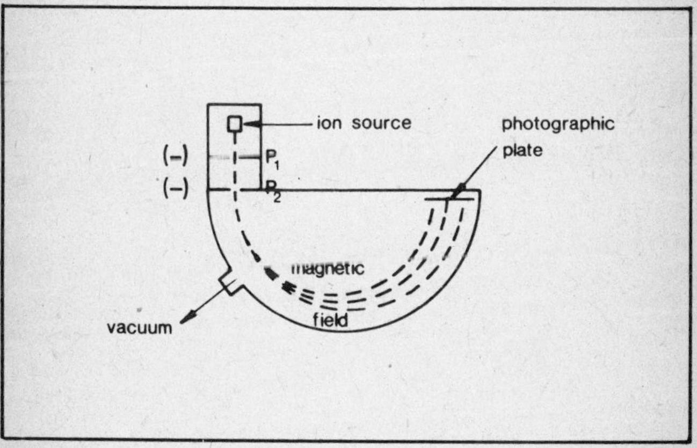

Figure 1. Mass spectrometer

The mass spectrometer has now superseded all previous methods for measuring atomic mass. The sample is introduced into the spectrometer and ionized either by electron bombardment, electric discharge or by direct heating. The ionized atoms are then accelerated by applying a high negative potential to the plates P_1 and P_2. The slit in P_2 produces a fine beam of ions all moving with the same velocity. The beam then enters a uniform magnetic field which deflects the ions in a circular path. The radius of the path depends on the mass and charge of the ion. At 180° to the original beam direction the ions fall onto a photographic plate producing a series of lines corresponding to the different charges on the ions. The photographic plate is calibrated using a sample of ^{12}C and by comparing the positions of the lines the atomic mass can be found. Alternatively electronic detectors can be used. The whole apparatus is kept under high vacuum.

Relative molecular mass, M_r, (formerly known as molecular weight) of an element or compound is defined as the average mass of its molecules on a scale on which one atom of the ^{12}C isotope of carbon has a mass of 12 units.

The relative molecular mass of a compound is also equal to the sum of the relative atomic masses of the atoms in the molecule. However relative molecular mass is normally used to derive molecular formulae and not vice versa.

Molecular masses of gases and vapours

A **mole** is the amount of substance which contains the same number of particles (i.e. atoms, molecules, ions etc.) as there are atoms in 12 grams of ^{12}C. This means that the mass in grams of a mole of compound is its relative molecular mass. **Avogadro's hypothesis** states that equal volumes of gases at the same temperature and pressure contain the same number of molecules, from which it is found that **one mole of all gases at s.t.p. occupies 22·4 dm³.**

Hence: relative molecular mass of a gas (or vapour) = mass in grams of 22·4 dm³ of the gas measured at s.t.p.

Molecular masses are more conveniently found from the **relative or vapour density** of a gas. Relative density of a gas is defined as the ratio of the masses of equal volumes of the gas and hydrogen measured under identical conditions.

$$\text{Relative density} = \frac{\text{mass of one volume of gas}}{\text{mass of one volume of hydrogen}}$$

$$= \frac{\text{mass of } n \text{ molecules of gas}}{\text{mass of } n \text{ molecules of hydrogen}}$$

(Avogadro's theory)

$$= \frac{\text{mass of 1 molecule of gas}}{\text{mass of 1 molecule of hydrogen}}$$

(dividing by n)

$$= \frac{\text{mass of 1 molecule of gas}}{\text{mass of 2 atoms of hydrogen}}$$

(since hydrogen is diatomic)

$$= \tfrac{1}{2}(\text{relative molecular mass})$$

$$\text{Relative density} = \frac{M_r}{2} \quad \left(= \frac{M_r}{2{\cdot}016} \text{ more exactly}\right)$$

Regnault's method This method of finding relative molecular mass is by direct weighing of a gas in a bulb of about 1 dm^3 volume. 1. The bulb is evacuated and weighed (M_1). 2. The bulb is filled with the gas at a known temperature and pressure and reweighed (M_2). 3. The bulb is filled with water and weighed (M_3). $M_3 - M_1$ is the mass of water and hence the volume of gas filling the bulb. This volume is reduced to s.t.p. and since the mass of gas, ($M_2 - M_1$), is known then M_r the mass of 22·4 dm^3 of the gas can be found. Corrections for the upthrust of air on the bulb improve the accuracy.

Dumas' method This method is suitable for volatile liquids and solids which vaporize on heating. A bulb with a fine capillary neck is used.

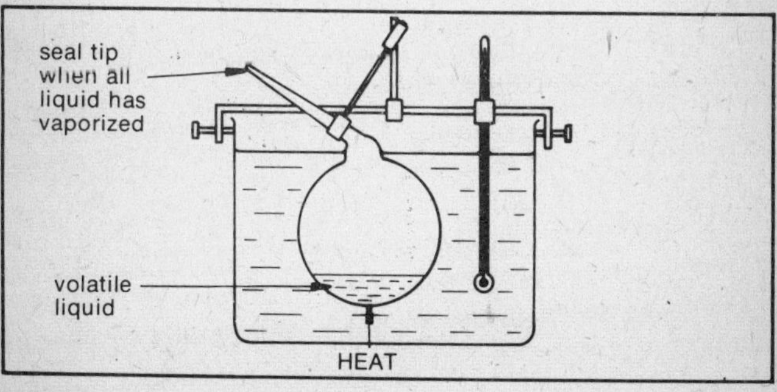

Figure 2. Dumas' bulb

1. The bulb is weighed full of air, (M_1). 2. Some of the liquid is introduced into the bulb. 3. The liquid is vaporized by immers-

ing the bulb in a bath at least 10°C above the boiling point of the liquid. The vapour fills the bulb completely, the excess vapour which escapes expelling the remaining air. 4. The tip of the bulb is sealed and when cool the bulb is weighed (M_2). 5. The tip of the bulb is broken under water, which rapidly fills the bulb due to the vacuum caused by the condensed vapour. The mass of the bulb and water is found (M_3). The volume of the bulb is found from ($M_3 - M_1$). By multiplying this by the density of air the mass of air in the bulb can be found. Then mass of bulb = M_1 − mass of air in bulb = M_4. The mass of vapour in the bulb = $M_2 - M_4$. The temperature of the heating bath is measured and the volume of vapour (volume of bulb) is corrected to s.t.p. From the mass and volume of vapour the mass of 22·4 dm^3 (M_r) can be found.

Example A bulb of volume 1·33 dm^3 and mass 107·08 g when filled with air, has a mass of 112·1 g when filled with tetrachloromethane vapour. The temperature of the heating bath was 373 K. Find the rel. mol. mass of CCl_4 if the lab. temp. is 293 K, atmospheric pressure is 750 mm Hg and the density of air at s.t.p. is 1·293 g dm^{-3}.

$$\text{vol. of air in bulb at s.t.p.} = \frac{1{\cdot}33 \times 750 \times 273}{760 \times 293} = 1{\cdot}22\ \text{dm}^3$$

mass of air = 1·22 × 1·293 = 1·58 g

True mass of bulb = 107·08 − 1·58 = 105·5 g

mass of vapour = 112·1 − 105·5 = 6·6 g

$$\text{The volume of vapour at s.t.p.} = \frac{1{\cdot}33 \times 750 \times 273}{760 \times 373} = 0{\cdot}961\ \text{dm}^3$$

The mass of 0·961 dm^3 is 6·6 g

$$\text{mass of } 22{\cdot}4\ \text{dm}^3 = \frac{6{\cdot}6 \times 22{\cdot}4}{0{\cdot}961} = 154\ \text{g}$$

$$\therefore \quad M_r = 154$$

Diffusion or effusion method Graham's law of diffusion (p. 30) is

$$\frac{R_1}{R_2} = \sqrt{\frac{\rho_2}{\rho_1}}$$

where R_1, R_2, are the rates of diffusion and ρ_1, ρ_2 the densities of two gases.

$$\text{Relative density} = \frac{\text{density of gas}}{\text{density of hydrogen}}$$

$$\frac{R_1}{R_2} = \sqrt{\frac{d_2}{d_1}} \quad \text{where } d_1, d_2 \text{ are relative densities}$$

To find the relative density of a gas its rate of effusion is usually found. Effusion is the passage of a gas under pressure through a small orifice; the same law applies as for diffusion. The rates of effusion for two gases, one of known M_r, are compared by finding the time taken for them to effuse through the same apparatus under identical conditions. The rate of effusion is inversely proportional to the times taken, t_1, t_2.

$$\frac{R_1}{R_2} = \frac{t_2}{t_1} = \sqrt{\frac{d_2}{d_1}}$$

From this expression the unknown relative density, and hence molecular mass, can be found.

Abnormal relative densities of vapours

Association Occasionally substances have abnormally high relative densities. Often the relative density is double the expected value. This is due to molecules dimerizing in the vapour state, e.g.

$$2FeCl_3 \rightleftharpoons Fe_2Cl_6; \qquad 2AlCl_3 \rightleftharpoons Al_2Cl_6$$

Thermal dissociation Vapours which show much lower relative densities than expected are probably undergoing thermal dissociation. Many compounds split up at high temperatures and recombine on cooling

$$NH_4Cl \rightleftharpoons NH_3 + HCl$$

$$PCl_5 \rightleftharpoons PCl_3 + Cl_2$$

$$N_2O_4 \rightleftharpoons 2NO_2$$

On complete dissociation the volume of vapour is doubled while the mass remains the same and so the relative density is halved. The value of the relative density enables the **degree of dissociation**, α, to be determined.

For all the above systems, if α is the fraction of molecules dissociating, the number of moles at equilibrium is given by, e.g.

$$N_2O_4 \rightleftharpoons 2NO_2$$

$$1-\alpha \quad 2\alpha \qquad \text{moles}$$

The total number of moles present at equilibrium will be

$$1-\alpha+2\alpha=1+\alpha$$

For a given mass of vapour the density is inversely proportional to the volume or number of moles present.

$$\frac{\text{density undissociated}}{\text{density dissociated}}=\frac{1+\alpha}{1}$$

$$\therefore \quad \alpha=\frac{\text{density undissociated}}{\text{density dissociated}}-1$$

Molecular masses of solids: Colligative properties

When a non-volatile solid is dissolved in a liquid

1. the vapour pressure of the liquid is lowered
2. the boiling point is raised
3. the freezing point is lowered
4. osmosis can occur.

These colligative properties are used to determine molecular weights of compounds. The laws relating to these properties apply only to **non-electrolytes** in **dilute solutions.**

1. Lowering of vapour pressure It is found that **the relative lowering of vapour pressure of a solution is equal to the mole fraction of solute.** This is an alternative statement of **Raoult's law** (see p. 33). The lowering of vapour pressure depends on the **number of particles** of solute (dissolved substance) and not on the type of molecule (provided there is no ionization).

Mathematical statement:

$$\frac{p^0-p}{p^0}=\frac{n}{N+n}\simeq\frac{n}{N} \quad \text{(dilute solution)}$$

where p^0 and p are the vapour pressures of solvent and solution respectively and n and N are the number of moles of solute and solvent respectively. An explanation on kinetic theory grounds is that the dynamic equilibrium which exists between the solvent and its vapour is upset by the presence of involatile solute molecules. A **dynamic equilibrium** is achieved when the rate of molecules evaporating from the liquid is equal to the rate of molecules condensing from the vapour. These rates attain equilibrium at a constant temperature. The involatile solute can only occupy the liquid state and hinders the evaporation rate. The condensation rate remains constant and a new equilibrium is reached with less molecules in the vapour and a lower vapour pressure.

By measuring the relative lowering of vapour pressure of a solution the weight of one mole of non-volatile solute can be determined. This is achieved by passing a stream of dry air through the solution and then the pure solvent and measuring the loss in weight of each.

Example A solution contains 6·3 g urea in 45 g of water. When air was bubbled successively through this solution and then pure water the loss in weight of the solution was 1·112 g and of the water 0·0469 g. Find the molecular weight of urea.

$$\text{Loss in weight of solution} \propto p = 1{\cdot}112\ \text{g}$$

$$\text{Loss in weight of water} \propto p^0 - p = 0{\cdot}0469\ \text{g}$$

$$\text{Total loss in weight} \propto p^0 = 1{\cdot}112 + 0{\cdot}0469\ \text{g}$$

Hence $$\frac{p^0 - p}{p^0} = \frac{0{\cdot}0469}{1{\cdot}1589} = \frac{n}{N+n} = 0{\cdot}0405$$

If M_r is the relative molecular mass of urea then n, number of moles of solute

$$= \frac{6{\cdot}3}{M_r}$$

and N, number of moles of solvent

$$= \frac{45}{18}$$

$$\therefore \quad \text{mole fraction, } \frac{n}{N+n} = \frac{6{\cdot}3/M_r}{45/18 + 6{\cdot}3/M_r} = 0{\cdot}0405$$

$$\therefore \quad M_r = 60$$

2. Elevation of boiling point

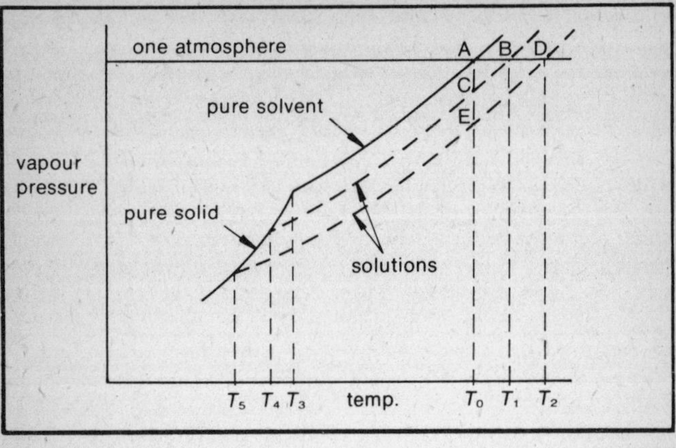

Figure 3

A liquid boils when its vapour pressure is equal to the external pressure. Figure 3 shows the lowering of vapour pressure produced by adding an involatile solute to a solvent. It can be seen that the solutions must be raised to higher temperatures (T_1, T_2) before the saturated vapour pressure is equal to atmospheric pressure (i.e. boiling point). For dilute solutions the solution curves are parallel to the solvent curve and ABC and ADE are similar triangles.

Thus $$\frac{AB}{AD} = \frac{AC}{AE}$$

But AB and AD correspond to the elevation of boiling point and AC and AE correspond to the lowering of vapour pressure. Hence

$$\frac{\text{elevation of b.p. for solution 1}}{\text{elevation of b.p. for solution 2}} = \frac{\text{lowering of s.v.p. for 1}}{\text{lowering of s.v.p. for 2}}$$

but the lowering of v.p. is proportional to the concentration of solute. Therefore, **the elevation of boiling point of a solvent is proportional to the molar concentration of solute**. This can also be shown experimentally and is true provided there is no dissociation or association of the solute. The elevation of boiling point is **independent of the type of solute, it depends only on the number of particles present.**

The elevation of boiling point produced by one mole of solute contained in 100 g (or 1000 g) of a solvent is termed the **ebullioscopic** (or elevation of boiling point) **constant** and has the symbol K. The relative molecular mass (M_r) of m grams of solute in w grams of solvent can be calculated from the following formula

$$M_r = \frac{m \times 100 \times K}{w \times t} \qquad (1.1)$$

(100 is replaced by 1000 if values of K are quoted per 1000 g of solvent.)

The value of K can be found experimentally or from the expression

$$K = \frac{RT^2}{100L} \qquad (1.2)$$

where T = boiling point, L = latent heat of vaporization of the solvent and R = the molar gas constant.

Example Calculate the molecular weight of sulphur if 1·38 g dissolved in 63 g of carbon disulphide (K = 23·7°C/100 g) raises its boiling point by 0·203°C.

From equation 1.1

$$M_r = \frac{1{\cdot}38 \times 100 \times 23{\cdot}7}{63 \times 0{\cdot}203}$$

$$M_r = 256 \ (= S_8)$$

3. Depression of freezing point The graph in fig. 3 shows that the lowering of vapour pressure also lowers the freezing point ($T_3 \rightarrow T_4$ and T_5). It can be shown that **the freezing point depression is proportional to the molar concentration of solute,** for dilute solutions of involatile solutes which do not associate or dissociate. The depression of freezing point produced by dissolving one mole of solute in 100 g of solvent is termed the **cryoscopic** (or depression of freezing point) **constant**, symbol K (°C/100 g).

It may be found experimentally or from equation 1.2 where T = melting point and L = latent heat of fusion of the solvent.

The depression of freezing point (t) is related to relative molecular mass by the same formula as for elevation of boiling point.

$$M_r = \frac{m \times 100 \times K}{w \times t}$$

where K is the cryoscopic constant, m = grams of solute, w = grams of solvent.

Rast's method for determining relative molecular masses using camphor

The cryoscopic constant for camphor is very high (396°C per 100 g) and consequently if freezing point depressions are measured in camphor the thermometer used only has to be accurate to 0·1°C or even 1°C. A known weight of solute and of camphor are melted in a test tube and thoroughly mixed. After solidification the mixture is ground to a powder and a little is placed in a capillary tube. The tube is attached to the bulb of a thermometer and the melting point determined by heating in an oil bath. The melting point of pure camphor is found by a similar method and the depression of freezing point is thus obtained.

Example Calculate the weight of ethylene glycol, (ethan-1,2-diol) which, when dissolved in 4 litres of water, would just prevent the formation of ice at −10°C. (K for water = 18·6°C/100 g.)

Ethylene glycol has the formula $CH_2.(OH).CH_2.OH$ and the relative molecular mass is 62. The weight of solvent is 4000 g. If m is the mass of ethylene glycol then from equation 1.1

$$62 = \frac{m \times 100 \times 18{\cdot}6}{4000 \times 10} \qquad \therefore \quad m = 1333{\cdot}3\text{ g}$$

4. Osmosis is the passage of solvent molecules through a **semi-permeable membrane.** These membranes contain pores of a size which allow passage of small solvent molecules but prevent the passage of larger solute molecules. Examples are pig's bladder, cellophane and parchment. If a concentrated solution, contained in a tube sealed by a semi-permeable membrane, is immersed in the pure solvent, then solvent will diffuse into the solution raising the liquid level in the tube, and thus creating a hydrostatic pressure. Eventually the hydrostatic pressure prevents further osmosis. The pressure required to prevent osmosis is termed the **osmotic pressure,** Π.

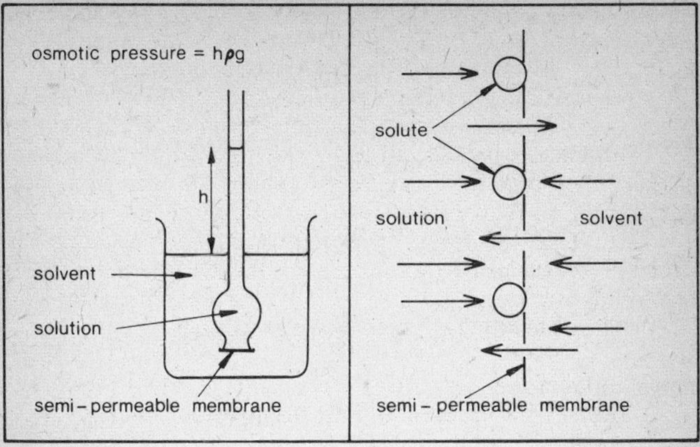

Figure 4

The kinetic theory explanation of osmosis considers the diffusion of solvent molecules through the semi-permeable membrane. Diffusion from solution to solvent is reduced by the presence of solute particles while solvent to solution diffusion is unaltered. The equilibrium can only be restored by increased pressure on the solution side which will increase the diffusion rate.

Berkeley and Hartley's method for measuring osmotic pressure

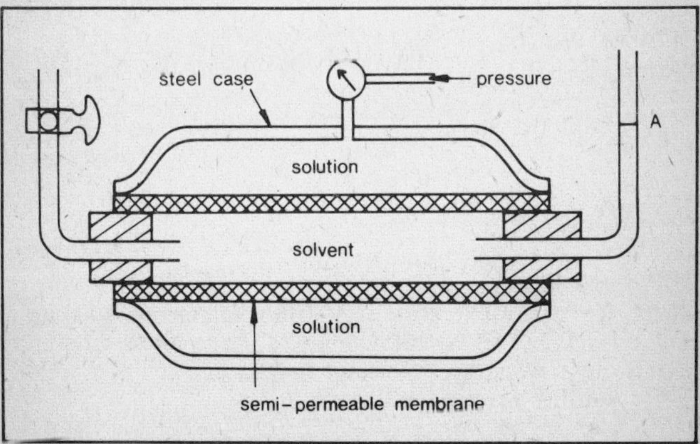

Figure 5

The principle of the method is shown in fig. 5. The solvent is placed inside the porous pot which has a semi-permeable membrane of copper hexacyanoferrate(II) deposited inside it for strength. This is achieved by placing solutions of copper sulphate inside and potassium hexacyanoferrate(II) outside the pot. An anode is placed in the copper sulphate and a cathode in the outer solution. The current causes the ions to migrate through the porous pot where the membrane of $Cu_2Fe(CN)_6$ deposits. The solvent in the porous pot diffuses into the solution placed inside the outer steel jacket. The pressure on the solution is increased until osmosis is prevented (the level at A will be steady) and the pressure recorded.

Laws of osmotic pressure Pfeffer and Van't Hoff showed that the osmotic pressure was proportional to the molar concentration of solution and to absolute temperature.

$$\Pi \propto CT$$

where C = molar concentration (mol dm^{-3}).

There is an analogy between dilute solutions and gases. The solute molecules behave as gas molecules occupying a space (the solvent).

Concentration is inversely proportional to volume

hence

$$C \propto \frac{1}{V}$$

$$\Pi \propto \frac{1}{V} \qquad \left(\text{cf. Boyle's law } P \propto \frac{1}{V}\right)$$

and

$$\Pi \propto T \qquad (\text{cf. Pressure law } P \propto T)$$

Thus osmotic pressure problems may be solved either by using the equation

$$\Pi V = nRT \qquad (\text{cf. } PV = nRT)$$

where Π = osmotic pressure, V = the volume of solvent in dm^3, n = number of moles of solute, T = absolute temperature and R = the molar gas constant (0·0821 dm^3 atm deg^{-1} mol^{-1}) or by using the expression

$$\frac{\Pi_1}{C_1T_1} = \frac{\Pi_2}{C_2T_2} \qquad \left(\text{cf. } \frac{P_1V_1}{T_1} = \frac{P_2V_2}{T_2}\right)$$

where $\Pi_2 = 1$ atmosphere which is the osmotic pressure of a solution of 1 mole in 22·4 dm^3 (C_2) at 273 K (T_2) and Π_1, C_1, and T_1 refer to the measured solution.

Osmotic pressure measurements, although not very accurate, are extremely useful for finding very large molecular weights such as those of proteins or plastics. These cannot easily be determined by other methods.

Example 40 g of a substance dissolved in one dm^3 of benzene gives an osmotic pressure of 265 Pa at 27°C. Find the molecular weight of the substance. Atmos. press. = $1{\cdot}013 \times 10^5$ Pa.

$$\frac{\Pi_1}{C_1T_1} = \frac{\Pi_2}{C_2T_2}$$

Let M_r be the relative molecular mass of the substance.

$$C_1 = \frac{40/M_r}{1} \text{ mol dm}^{-3}$$

and

$$\frac{265}{40/M_r \times 300} = \frac{1{\cdot}013 \times 10^5}{1/22{\cdot}4 \times 273}$$

$$\therefore \quad M_r = 3{\cdot}76 \times 10^5$$

Van't Hoff factor In all measurements of colligative properties the results depend on the number of particles of solute. If association or dissociation (ionization) occurs then the observed value will deviate from the calculated value.

The Van't Hoff factor, $i = \dfrac{\text{observed value}}{\text{calculated value}}$ (of colligative property)

If i is bigger than 1 ionization or dissociation has occurred (more particles than predicted) and if less than 1 association has occurred (less particles than predicted). For example, ethanoic acid in benzene only produces half the expected depression of freezing point. This is because the acid dimerizes. Potassium bromide in water however produces twice the expected depression because at low concentration it ionizes fully.

Molecular masses of liquids:
Steam distillation

The total vapour pressure above a mixture of liquids is equal to the sum of the individual vapour pressures at that temperature. It is independent of the amount of each liquid. Since a liquid boils when its saturated vapour pressure equals atmospheric pressure a mixture of immiscible liquids will boil below the boiling point of either pure constituent. A mixture of water and aminobenzene (aniline) for example boils at 98·5°C. At this temperature the vapour pressure of water is 93·3 kPa and that of aminobenzene is 8 kPa giving a total of 101·3 kPa (1 atmosphere). On distilling a mixture of the two liquids both will be carried over in the vapour in proportion to their partial vapour pressures. The relative masses of liquid in the distillate, m_1, m_2 is given by

$$\frac{m_1}{m_2} = \frac{p_1 M_{r_1}}{p_2 M_{r_2}}$$

where p_1, p_2 and M_{r_1}, M_{r_2} are respectively the vapour pressures and relative molecular masses of the two liquids.

Colloids

Colloidal solutions are somewhere in between a true solution and a suspension. The particle size is too small to be seen, even by a microscope, but the properties of colloids are different from solutions. The particles of a colloid lie between 10^{-5} and 10^{-7} cm in diameter. Settlement of the particles is slow and effectively prevented by slight convection currents.

Classification of colloid systems This depends on the physical state of the solvent, which is known as the **dispersion medium,** and the solute, known as the **dispersed phase**. The dispersion medium is a continuous phase, the dispersed phase consists of separate particles.

Dispersion medium	Dispersed phase	Name
gas	liquid	mist or fog
gas	solid	smoke
liquid	gas	foam
liquid	liquid	emulsion
liquid	solid	sol
solid	gas	gel or foam
solid	liquid	gel

Preparation of colloids Colloids are divided into two classes: **Lyophilic** which are solvent loving and **lyophobic** which are solvent hating. Lyophilic sols naturally form colloidal solutions when dispersed phase and dispersion medium are brought together. They are termed reversible since they can be coagulated and reformed easily. Lyophobic sols are irreversible, there is no interaction between dispersed phase and dispersion medium, and once coagulated cannot be reformed.

There are two general methods of production: dispersion methods when larger particles are broken down to colloidal size and condensation or aggregation methods when molecular size particles group together to form colloids.

Dispersion methods

1. Peptization This is the process of bringing precipitates into the colloidal state by addition of small quantities of electrolytes, often containing a common ion. The ions absorb onto the precipitate particles and cause a breakdown of the aggregates by electrostatic repulsion. Silver chloride can be peptized by hydrochloric acid or silver nitrate solutions and iron(III) hydroxide by iron(III) chloride.
2. Bredig's arc This method forms colloidal solutions of metals by passing an electric arc between two metal electrodes held below the surface of the dispersion medium. The system is kept cool to prevent coagulation.
3. Colloid mill Dispersed phase and dispersion medium are passed through metal rollers which rotate in opposite directions and are very close together. This method is used to make oil in water and water in oil creams for cosmetics.

Aggregation methods These methods are much more common and involve reactions like double decomposition which cause precipitation, under conditions which prevent particle growth up to suspension size. Typical examples:

1. Sulphur sols can be prepared by passing hydrogen sulphide into a solution of sulphur dioxide

$$2H_2S + SO_2 \rightarrow 3S + 2H_2O$$

or by acidification of dilute sodium thiosulphate solution

$$Na_2S_2O_3 + 2HCl \rightarrow 2NaCl + SO_2 + H_2O + S$$

2. Arsenic(III) sulphide sol can be prepared by passing

hydrogen sulphide through a solution of arsenic(III) oxide

$$As_2O_3 + 3H_2S \rightarrow As_2S_3 + 3H_2O$$

3. Gold (or silver) sols are prepared by reducing a dilute solution of the metal chloride (or nitrate) with organic compounds such as tannic acid (or an aldehyde).

Properties of colloids

1. **Dialysis** is used to separate colloids from crystalloids, due to their different rates of diffusion through a permeable membrane. Crystalloids such as salts, alcohol, sugars etc. diffuse much more readily than colloids because of their significantly smaller size. If a mixture of colloids and crystalloids, contained in a vessel fitted with a permeable membrane, is put into a second vessel through which distilled water is 'flowing', after a while all the crystalloid will be found to have been removed from the first container leaving the colloid behind. This principle is used in the artificial kidney machine.

2. **Optical properties** If a beam of light is passed through a colloidal solution its path can be seen from the side. This is due to reflection by the colloid particles. It is called the **Tyndall effect**. If the cone of light is viewed by a microscope points of light scattered by individual particles can be seen to be in constant random motion. This is **Brownian motion** and is due to collisions between colloid particles and solvent molecules.

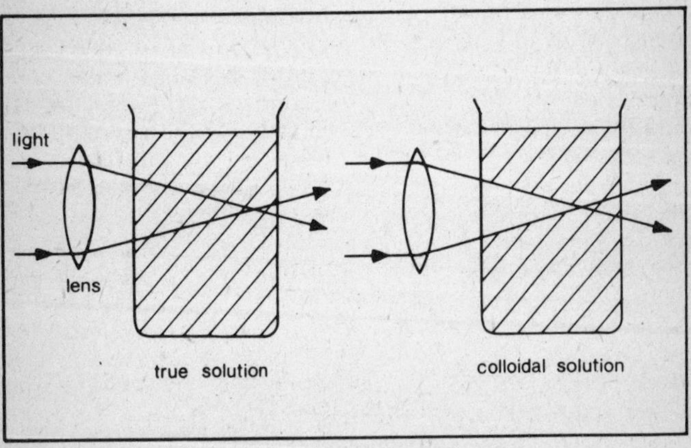

Figure 6. Tyndall effect

3. Electrophoresis Colloids are electrically charged, a property which gives them their stability. This charge can be shown by electrophoresis.

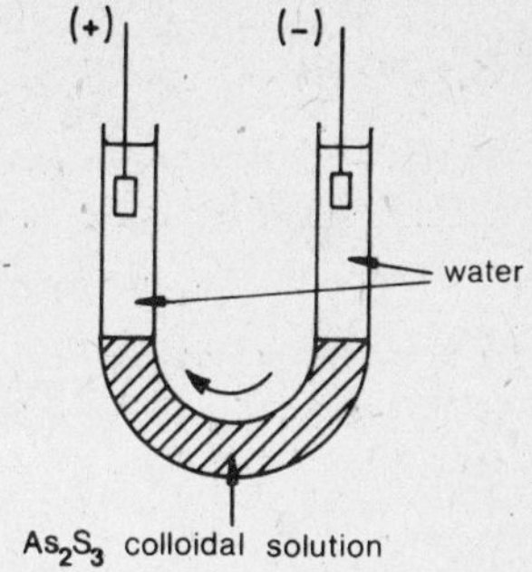

Figure 7. Electrophoresis

A sol, for example, arsenic(III) sulphide is carefully poured into a 'U' tube so that it runs under a layer of distilled water; electrodes are then introduced into the water. The colloid particles move towards the positive electrode showing that As_2S_3 sol is negatively charged. Iron(III) hydroxide and aluminium hydroxide sols carry positive charges. When the colloid particles reach the electrode they lose their charge and coagulate. The charge on the colloid particles keeps them from aggregating. Because colloidal solutions are electrically neutral the solvent particles must carry equal but opposite charges to the colloid particles. The dispersion medium moves in the opposite direction to the dispersed phase in electrophoresis. The colloidal particles absorb ions from the solvent leaving a layer of oppositely charged ions surrounding it. This is called a **Helmholtz double layer.**

Coagulation of colloids Colloids can be stabilized or coagulated by the addition of electrolytes. To coagulate a colloid an ion must be introduced which is of opposite charge to the colloid. The higher the charge on the ion the more effective it is. Aluminium sulphate is used in 'styptic' pencils to coagulate blood. Mixing colloids of opposite charge also causes coagulation. If a lyophilic colloid is added to a lyophobic colloid of the same charge the increased stability of the lyophilic colloid may help to stabilize the lyophobic one. This is called **protective action.**

Key terms

Relative atomic mass, A_r

$$= \frac{\text{average mass of an atom of the element} \times 12}{\text{mass of one atom of carbon-12}}$$

Relative molecular mass, M_r

$$= \frac{\text{av. mass of one molecule of a compound} \times 12}{\text{mass of one atom of carbon-12}}$$

A mole is the relative molecular mass of a substance in grams.

$$\text{amount in moles} = \frac{\text{mass in grams of substance}}{\text{relative molecular mass}}$$

One mole of any gas occupies $22{\cdot}4\,\text{dm}^3$ at s.t.p.

Relative density $= \dfrac{M_r}{2}$

Graham's law of diffusion $\dfrac{R_1}{R_2} = \sqrt{\dfrac{\rho_2}{\rho_1}}$

R_1, R_2 are the rates of diffusion of two gases under identical conditions and ρ_1 and ρ_2 are their densities.

$$\alpha\text{, fraction of moles dissociating} = \frac{\text{density undissociated}}{\text{density dissociated}} - 1$$

Raoult's law The relative lowering of vapour pressure of a solution is equal to the mole fraction of solute.

$$\frac{p^0 - p}{p^0} = \frac{n}{N + n} \simeq \frac{n}{N}$$

p^0 and p are the vapour pressures of solvent and solution respectively and n and N are the number of moles of solute and solvent.

Elevation of b.p. is proportional to the concentration of solute.

$$M_r = \frac{m \times 100 \times K}{w \times t}$$

M_r = rel. mol. mass, m = mass of solute, w = mass of solvent,

K = ebullioscopic constant (elevation of b.p. produced by one mole of solute in 100 g of solvent) and t = temperature rise.
Depression of f.p. is proportional to the conc. of solute. Same formula as above with K = cryoscopic constant (depression of f.p. produced by one mole of solute in 100 g of solvent).
Osmosis Osmotic pressure (Π) is proportional to the concentration (C) of solute and the Kelvin temperature (T).

$$\Pi = nRCT$$

C is in moles dm^{-3}, $R = 0{\cdot}0821\ dm^3\ atm\ deg^{-1}\ mol^{-1}$, n = number of moles of solute, and T = kelvin temperature.

or
$$\frac{\Pi_1}{C_1T_1} = \frac{\Pi_2}{C_2T_2}$$

Van't Hoff factor, $i = \dfrac{\text{observed value of colligative property}}{\text{calculated value of property}}$

$i = 2$ for complete dissociation of a binary electrolyte
$i = \frac{1}{2}$ for dimerization of solute

Steam distillation $$\frac{m_1}{m_2} = \frac{p_1M_{r_1}}{p_2M_{r_2}}$$

where m_1 and m_2 are the masses, p_1, p_2 the vapour pressures and M_{r_1}, M_{r_2} the relative molecular masses of the two vapours being distilled.
Colloids: dispersion medium = continuous phase
dispersed phase = separate particles
A lyophilic sol is solvent loving and is reversible.
A lyophobic sol is solvent hating and is irreversible.
Preparation methods
Peptization Aggregates of the precipitate are broken down by absorption of an electrolyte containing a common ion.
e.g. AgCl is peptized by the addition of HCl
Bredig's arc Electric discharge.
A Colloid mill uses two contra-rotating plates to grind materials down to a size such that they will remain dispersed as a colloid.
Aggregation methods The colloid is formed directly by double decomposition, reduction etc., e.g.

$$As_2O_3 + 3H_2S \rightarrow \underset{\text{colloidal}}{As_2S_3} + 3H_2O$$

Tyndall effect Scattering of light beam by colloids.
Electrophoresis The movement of colloidal particles in an electric field.

Chapter 2
Chemical and Physical Equilibria

Physical equilibria

The gas laws

1. Boyle's law The volume (V) of a given mass of gas is inversely proportional to its pressure (P) at constant temperature (see fig. 8).

$$V \propto 1/P \quad \text{or} \quad PV = \text{constant}$$

2. Charles' law The volume (V) of a given mass of gas is directly proportional to the Kelvin temperature (T) at constant pressure.

$$V \propto T \quad \text{or} \quad V/T = \text{constant}$$

This law may also be stated: At constant pressure the volume of a given mass of gas expands by 1/273 of its volume at 0°C for every 1°C rise in temperature. The factor 1/273 is the coefficient of cubical expansion of a gas and should be the same for all gases. By extrapolation of a graph of gas volume against temperature it is found that gases should have zero volume at −273°C. This temperature is called absolute zero and is theoretically the lowest possible temperature (see fig. 8).

Thermodynamic or kelvin scale of temperature The kelvin scale of temperature (K) begins at absolute zero (−273°C) and proceeds in intervals of degrees centigrade:

$$\text{kelvin temperature} = {}^\circ\text{C} + 273$$

It must be used in all thermodynamic and gas law calculations.

Ideal gas equation Combining the two gas laws it is found that

$$\frac{PV}{T} = \text{constant}$$

alternatively

$$\frac{P_1V_1}{T_1} = \frac{P_2V_2}{T_2}$$

This equation is used in converting gas volumes after changes in pressure and temperature. The **units of pressure and volume** are not important but they **must be the same on both sides of the equation. Temperature must be in Kelvin**

For n moles of gas the equation is written

$$PV = nRT$$

where R, the molar gas constant, is a constant for all gases. The equation only applies to perfect or ideal gases.

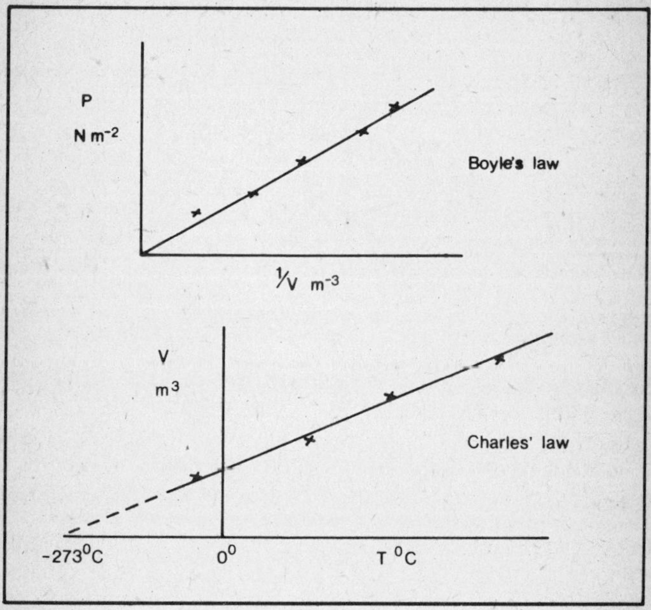

Figure 8. Boyle's law and Charles' law

s.t.p. stands for standard temperature and pressure. These are 273 K (0°C) and 1 atmosphere (760 mm Hg or 101 325 N m^{-2} (Pa)) pressure. Volumes of gases at s.t.p. are often required since 22·4 dm^3 of any gas at s.t.p. occupies one mole.

Calculation of molar gas constant At s.t.p. one mole of gas occupies 22·4 dm^3.

$$PV = nRT$$

if $n = 1$ $$R = \frac{PV}{T}$$

standard temperature and pressure = 273 K, 101 325 N m^{-2}

$$\therefore \quad R = \frac{101\,325\ \text{N m}^{-2} \times 0{\cdot}0224\ \text{m}^3}{273\ \text{K}} = 8{\cdot}31\ \text{J mol}^{-1}\ \text{K}^{-1}$$

Dalton's law of partial pressures Provided the gases do not react, the pressure of a mixture of gases is equal to the sum of the partial pressures of each constituent. The partial pressure of a constituent is the pressure it would exert if it occupied the whole space alone and can be found by multiplying the mole fraction of a gas in a mixture by the total pressure. If N_A and N_B are the number of moles of two gases A and B which are mixed together at a pressure P then:

$$\text{mole fraction of } A = \frac{N_A}{N_A + N_B}$$

$$\text{mole fraction of } B = \frac{N_B}{N_A + N_B}$$

$$\text{partial pressure of } A,\ P_A = N_A/(N_A + N_B) \times P$$

$$\text{partial pressure of } B,\ P_B = N_B/(N_A + N_B) \times P$$

and $$P = P_A + P_B \qquad \text{(Dalton's law)}$$

Graham's law of diffusion The rates of diffusion (effusion) of different gases (under identical conditions) are inversely proportional to the square roots of their densities. For two gases 1 and 2

$$R_1/R_2 = \sqrt{\rho_2/\rho_1}$$

where R_1 and R_2 are the diffusion rates and ρ_1 and ρ_2 are the densities. Use is made of differences in rates of diffusion to separate some gaseous mixtures.

Phase equilibria

Any physically and chemically distinct part of a system is called a **phase**. A mixture of water and ice is a two phase system, so is a mixture of monoclinic and rhombic sulphur. Two phase systems may consist of two solids, two liquids, solid and liquid, solid or liquid and gas. Since gases are miscible in all proportions they only ever form one phase.

Components of a system are the minimum number of chemically distinct constituents necessary to describe the composition of each phase of a system. It is the total number of distinct chemical constituents minus the number of distinct chemical reactions between them. A mixture of calcium carbonate, calcium oxide and carbon dioxide contains three separate compounds but it is a two component system as any one can be considered to arise from reaction between the other two.

$$CaCO_3 \rightleftharpoons CaO + CO_2$$

One component systems: Water In discussing phase equilibria three variables – temperature, pressure and concentration are considered. For a one component system however the concentration of each phase remains constant and is not considered. As there are only two variables the water phase equilibrium can be represented by a graph of T v p (fig. 9).

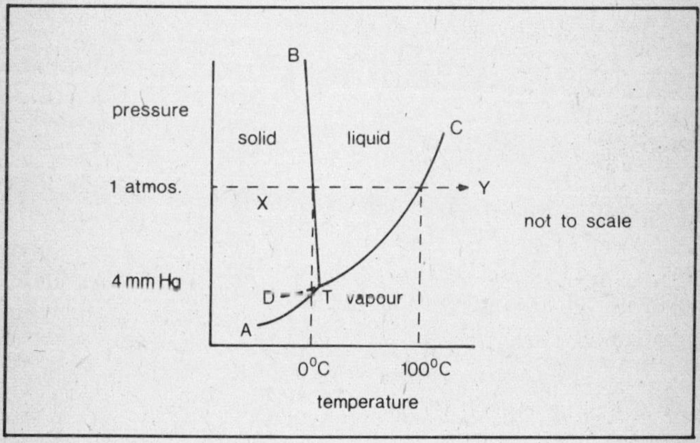

Figure 9. Phase diagram for water

In the diagram the line TC represents the conditions under which water and vapour co-exist in equilibrium. This is the saturated vapour pressure curve. There is a unique saturated vapour pressure for each temperature, which means that there is only **one degree of freedom**. A similar condition applies to the solid–vapour equilibrium (sublimation) AT and the solid–liquid equilibrium TB. Within the areas bounded by these curves the single phase, marked, may exist which has two degrees of freedom. There are a range of pressures and temperatures for which each phase may be stable. Only one set of conditions exists for all three phases to be in equilibrium, 0·0075°C and 4 mm Hg pressure. This point, *T*, is the **triple point** (or invariant point). To have ice, water and its vapour in equilibrium at 0°C is impossible unless another component (e.g. air) is introduced. The point *C* is the **critical point**. Above this pressure or temperature a gas can no longer be liquefied by decreasing the temperature or increasing the pressure alone. The dotted line TD shows super cooling of liquid water. The line XY shows the transfer from ice to water (0°C) and then from water to steam (100°C) at one atmosphere pressure. At a pressure below the triple point **sublimation** would occur (solid ↔ vapour). Note that the line BT (solid ↔ liquid) slopes backwards, increasing pressure lowers the melting point of ice. This is fairly unusual since only antimony and bismuth show similar behaviour and for most systems BT would slope forwards.

Allotropy: Sulphur and phosphorus

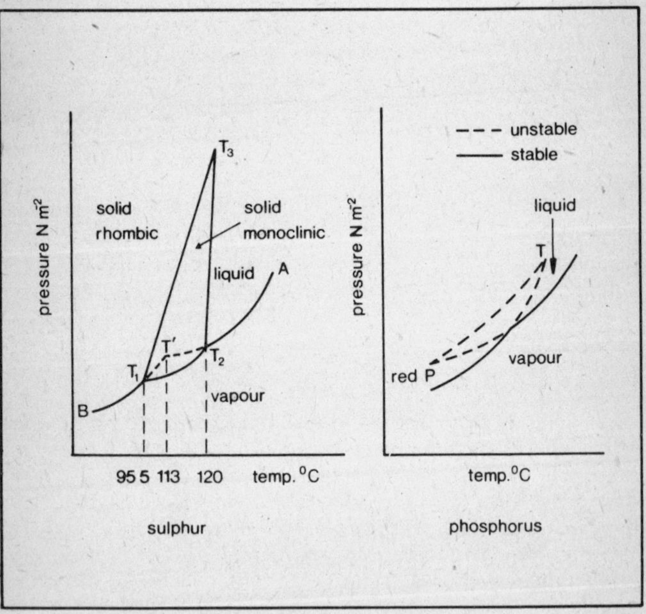

Figure 10. Allotropy of sulphur and phosphorus

The sulphur diagram, fig. 10, shows the type of allotropy known as **enantiotropy**; both forms, monoclinic and rhombic, can be stable under suitable conditions. Up to T_1 (95·5°C) rhombic sulphur is stable; at this triple point rhombic, monoclinic and vapour can co-exist. T_2 and T_3 are the other stable triple points. T' is an unstable triple point for rhombic, liquid and vapour; it can be realized by rapid heating of rhombic sulphur as the conversion between solid forms is slow. The phosphorus diagram is an example of **monotropy**. Only one form (red phosphorus) is stable. In monotropy the transition point for the solid forms (T) is above the melting point. White phosphorus can only be made by condensing the vapour.

Multi-component systems – Solutions

Solutions of gases in liquids Provided that a gas does not combine chemically with a liquid then the solubility of a gas generally decreases with increase in temperature. This is in accordance with Le Chatelier's principle (p. 45) as heat is usually evolved when a gas dissolves. Pressure has a marked effect on the solubility of gases. **Henry's law** states that the mass of gas dissolved by a given volume of solvent at a constant temperature is directly proportional to the pressure. Solubility of a gas in a liquid is usually given in terms of an absorption coefficient (α) which is the maximum volume of gas (reduced to s.t.p.) which can be dissolved by 1 cm^3 of liquid at a given temperature.

Solutions of liquids in liquids – fully miscible For liquids which mix completely over all ranges of composition the vapour pressure of each constituent is given by **Raoult's law**: **the vapour pressure of a constituent in an ideal solution is equal to the vapour pressure exerted by the pure constituent at that temperature, multiplied by the mole fraction by which it is present.** Mole fraction is a convenient way of expressing concentration and is defined as the number of moles of a constituent divided by the total number of moles present in the mixture, i.e. for two components

mole fraction of A, $\quad X_a = N_a/(N_a + N_b)$

where N_a, N_b are the number of moles of A and B respectively, and

mole fraction of B, $\quad X_b = 1 - X_a$

Raoult's law can be expressed mathematically as

$$P_A = X_a P^0_A$$

where P_A is the vapour pressure of A over the liquid mixture, X_a is the mole fraction of A in the liquid mixture, P^0_A is the vapour pressure of pure A at that temperature. By Dalton's law the total vapour pressure above a mixture of liquids will be the sum of the partial pressures.

Total pressure, $P = P_A + P_B$

Figure 11a shows the variation in v.p. with composition above a mixture of two ideal liquids at constant temperature.

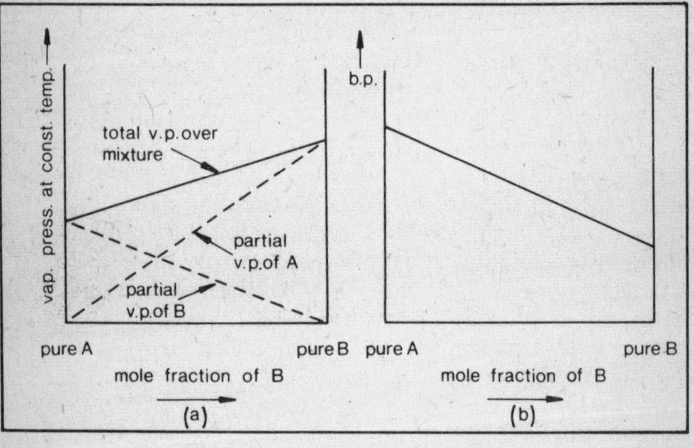

Figure 11

An ideal liquid mixture is one in which the intermolecular forces in both liquids are almost identical. Mixtures such as benzene/methylbenzene, propan-1-ol/propan-2-ol, which are of very similar compounds, approximate to ideal liquid mixtures.

Figure 11b shows the corresponding variation in boiling point for the pair of liquids at constant pressure. Liquid A has a lower vapour pressure than pure B at the given temperature and consequently will have to be raised to a higher temperature than B before the corresponding vapour pressure reaches atmospheric pressure and the liquid boils. Boiling point/composition curves are mirror images of vapour pressure/composition curves.

Deviations from Raoult's law Two types of deviation are recognized. **Positive deviation** is characterized by the total vapour pressure being higher than that calculated for an ideal solution. This occurs when the molecules are held by weaker binding forces in the mixture than in the pure liquids. This is often the case when very polar molecules are mixed with non-polar molecules. In the pure liquid the polar molecules have to escape the strong intermolecular attractive forces and thus have a low vapour pressure but when mixed with non-polar molecules the attractive force is lessened and there is an increased tendency to escape.

Less common is **negative deviation** which results in a lower vapour pressure above a mixture of liquids than would be expected. In this case molecules experience a greater attractive force within the liquid mixture than in the pure liquid. It occurs when two compounds have a very strong attraction for each other or when actual compound formation happens.

Liquids which show a positive deviation from Raoult's law often show an increase in volume and an absorption of heat on mixing. In the extreme cases immiscibility results. Liquids showing negative deviations tend to contract and evolve heat on mixing (the bonds being formed are stronger than those being broken). Figure 12 shows vapour pressure-composition curves for positive and negative deviations.

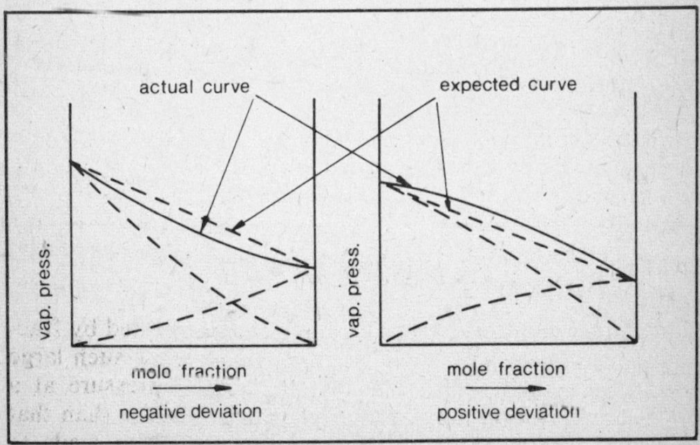

Figure 12. Vapour pressure – composition curve

Boiling point-composition curves are drawn to show the composition of both the vapour and liquid at each temperature. When a mixture of two liquids boils the vapour given off is always richer in the more volatile component. For example, in figure 13 the lower curve shows the boiling points of various propanone/water mixtures and the upper curve shows the composition of the vapour distilling off. If a mixture A boils then the distillate is shown at A′. When this condenses it will boil at a temperature shown by B giving a vapour of composition B′. When this condenses and is reboiled C′ is reached. The distillate becomes richer in the more volatile component, propanone. As this is removed the liquid in the distillation flask becomes richer in the less volatile component, water, and the temperature rises to 100°C. To fully separate a mixture of propanone and water a fractionating column is required. The vapour ascends the column condensing and re-evaporating becoming steadily richer in the more volatile component. The less volatile component descends the column as a liquid.

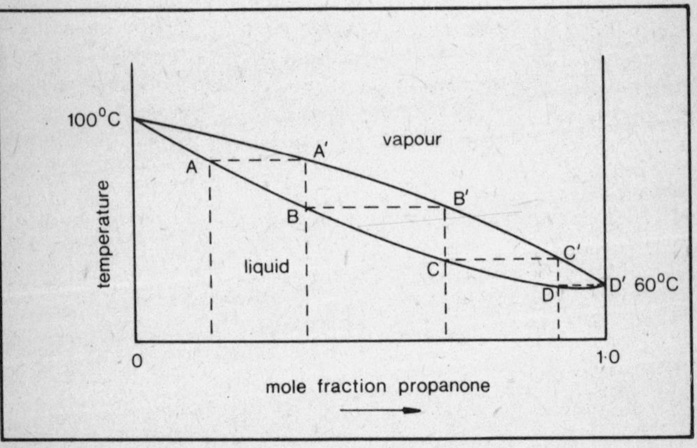

Figure 13. Boiling point – composition curve

Some liquid mixtures cannot be completely separated by fractional distillation. These are mixtures which show such large deviations from Raoult's law that the vapour pressure at a certain composition may be greater than or smaller than that of either pure component. In the former case this leads to mixtures showing a **minimum boiling point**, and in the latter case a **maximum boiling point mixture** results. A system showing a large enough positive deviation to lead to a minimum boiling mixture is aqueous ethanol (fig. 14a). When a liquid mixture containing less than 95·5% ethanol is distilled the vapour produced contains 95·5% ethanol eventually leaving pure water behind. Distilling a mixture with more than 95·5% ethanol produces the same composition vapour leaving pure ethanol behind. This constant boiling mixture is referred to as an **azeotrope**. Figure 14b shows the nitric acid and water system which in common with the other mineral acids has a maximum boiling mixture. If a mixture of composition less than 38% nitric acid is boiled pure water distils off and the residue becomes richer in nitric acid until the azeotrope remains, boiling steadily at 122°C. For mixtures above 38% HNO_3 pure acid distils off eventually leaving the azeotrope.

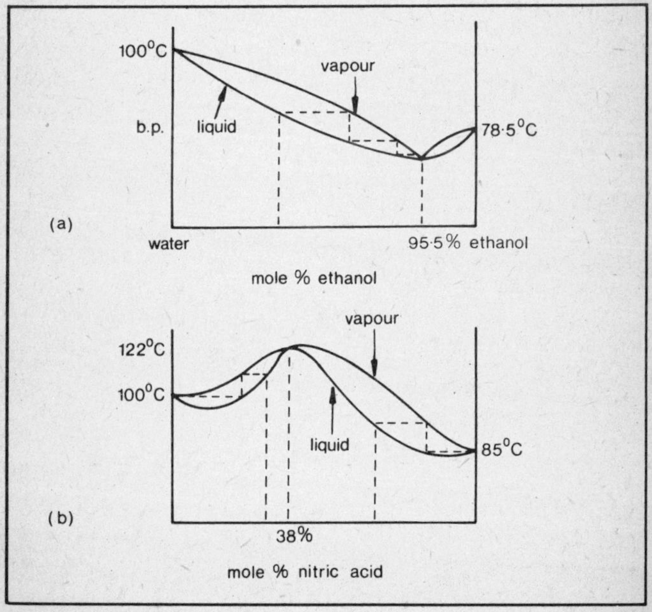

Figure 14

To obtain pure ethanol the remaining water must be removed chemically (by calcium oxide), by adsorption (silica gel) or by distilling with a small quantity of benzene. The latter results in a low boiling azeotrope of water, benzene and ethanol, which removes the water, and a binary azeotrope of benzene and ethanol, which removes excess benzene leaving pure ethanol.

Solutions of liquids in liquids – partially miscible An example of partially miscible liquids is phenol and water. If they are mixed two liquid layers form, a saturated solution of phenol in water above a saturated solution of water in phenol. If the mixture is warmed the mutual solubilities are increased so that more phenol dissolves in the water and more water in the phenol until a single layer forms. A graph showing the variation of miscibility with temperature may be constructed by preparing a range of mixtures of phenol and water, which are then heated until one layer forms. The temperature is noted, then the sample is cooled and the temperature noted at the first sign of turbidity. The two temperatures are averaged and plotted against composition of the mixture. Figure 15 shows the phenol–water graph. Within the closed curve two layers exist while conditions represented outside the curve always result in a single phase. The temperature, *T*, above which all mixtures are fully miscible is called the upper consolute temperature. Much less common are systems which have a lower consolute temperature. This only occurs when solubility increases with a decrease in temperature. A few systems even show an upper and lower consolute temperature.

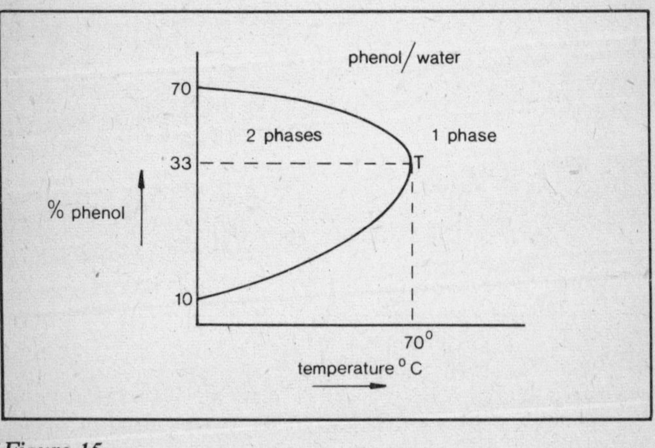

Figure 15

Solutions of solids in solids – Eutectics Pure substances generally have sharp melting points. Addition of another substance lowers the melting point and extends the temperature range between the first appearance of solid and complete solidification. Lead and tin are metals which are completely miscible in the liquid state. Adding tin to lead lowers the melting point of lead and adding lead to tin lowers the melting point of tin. If the two curves of composition against melting point are drawn they must meet (fig. 16). The point X on the graph shows a 30% tin–70% lead mixture at 350°C. As the mixture cools it remains molten until it reaches the point L. At this point it begins to solidify by depositing crystals with a high percentage of lead (given by S). Because lead has been deposited the remaining liquid has a higher proportion of tin and so the freezing point is lowered. The line AE shows the variation of freezing point with liquid composition. The composition of the crystals which are deposited is given by AC. If a mixture of composition Y is cooled it will deposit tin rich crystals, of composition given by the line BD, at the point L′. The liquid becomes richer in lead and follows the line BE. At E both lead rich and tin rich crystals are deposited together and the composition of the liquid remains constant. The freezing point therefore also remains constant. This mixture is called the **eutectic mixture**. The temperature is called the eutectic temperature. Other metal alloys may have more complex phase diagrams involving compound formation.

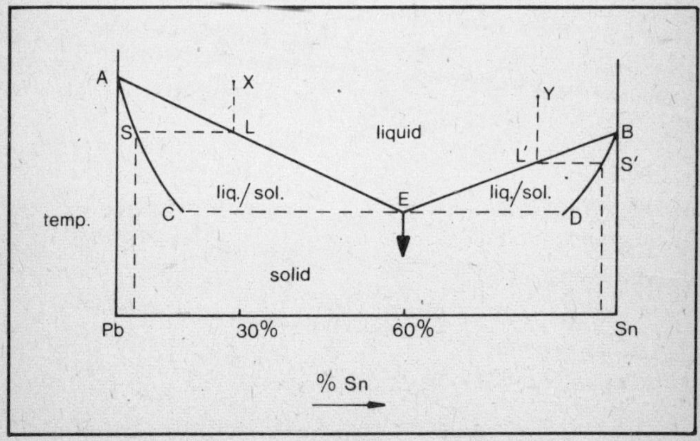

Figure 16

Distribution of a solute between immiscible solvents When a substance is added to two immiscible liquids in each of which it is soluble an equilibrium is eventually reached with the substance distributed between the two solvents. It is a dynamic equilibrium with solute molecules continually passing between the two layers. Equilibrium is achieved more quickly if the layers are agitated (this increases the area of contact).

The distribution law (Nernst's law) The ratio of the concentrations of a solute distributed between two immiscible solvents is a constant, provided the temperature remains constant and the molecular state of the solute is the same in both solvents.

$$\frac{\text{Concentration of solute in solvent } A}{\text{Concentration of solute in solvent } B} = K$$

***K* is the partition or distribution coefficient**

Solvent extraction It can be shown by the distribution law that it is more efficient to extract an organic compound from aqueous solution using three or four aliquots of an organic solvent than to use all the solvent in one extraction.

Distribution with association in one solvent It has already been mentioned that ethanoic acid dimerizes in some organic solvents. Consider the case of ethanoic acid distributed between benzene and water (fig. 17). In benzene the equilibrium is between single acid molecules and the dimer.

$$\frac{[(CH_3COOH)_2]_{\text{benzene}}}{[CH_3COOH]^2_{\text{benzene}}} = K_1 \tag{2.1}$$

$$[CH_3COOH]^2_{\text{benzene}} = \frac{1}{K_1} \cdot [(CH_3COOH)_2]_{\text{benzene}}$$

The equilibrium across the water–benzene interface is between the single ethanoic acid molecules.

$$\frac{[CH_3COOH]_{\text{benzene}}}{[CH_3COOH]_{\text{water}}} = K_2$$

substituting for $[CH_3COOH]_{\text{benzene}}$ in equation 2.1 we obtain

$$\frac{[(CH_3COOH)_2]^{1/2}_{\text{benzene}}}{[CH_3COOH]_{\text{water}}} = K$$

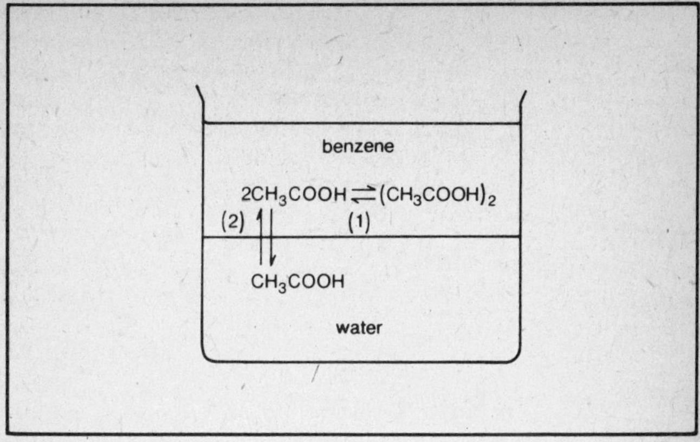

Figure 17

If ethanoic acid is entirely associated in benzene then the total concentration may be substituted for the concentration of dimer.

$$K = \frac{[CH_3COOH]^{1/2}_{benzene}}{[CH_3COOH]_{water}}$$

Similarly if a substance polymerizes further in a particular solvent then its concentration in that solvent is reduced to $\frac{1}{3}, \frac{1}{4}, \ldots$ etc.

Chemical equilibria

Reversible reactions and equilibrium Many chemical reactions can be considered to be reversible. That is to say that the reaction can take place in both directions. The reacting molecules can combine together to give products and the products can react to give the reactants.

$$\text{reactants} \rightleftharpoons \text{products}$$

The rate of reaction depends on the concentration of the reacting species. At the start of the reaction the forward rate (reactants to products) is high but as the reactants disappear this rate falls and the backward rate (products to reactants) increases. Eventually the two rates become equal and no further change in the concentration of products and reactants can be detected. The reaction has effectively ceased although in fact it has reached a state of dynamic equilibrium. The equilibrium position of a reaction may be altered by varying the conditions of temperature and pressure. Some reactions appear to go to completion although in fact the concentration of reactants may simply be too small to measure and the equilibrium is displaced to the extreme right (product side). Equilibrium can only be set up in a 'closed' system (i.e. one in which matter cannot be exchanged with the surroundings).

The equilibrium law The law governing equilibrium is an empirical one. It is a relationship arising from data taken from experimental studies. The data from two such studies are reproduced below:

1. The hydrogen iodide equilibrium

equilibrium concentration of H_2 in mol dm^{-3}	equilibrium concentration of I_2 in mol dm^{-3}	equilibrium concentration of HI in mol dm^{-3}	$\frac{[HI]}{[H_2][I_2]}$	$\frac{[HI]^2}{[H_2][I_2]}$
$4{\cdot}56 \times 10^{-3}$	$0{\cdot}74 \times 10^{-3}$	$13{\cdot}54 \times 10^{-3}$	$4{\cdot}01 \times 10^{-3}$	54·3
$3{\cdot}56 \times 10^{-3}$	$1{\cdot}25 \times 10^{-3}$	$15{\cdot}59 \times 10^{-3}$	$3{\cdot}50 \times 10^{-3}$	54·6
$2{\cdot}25 \times 10^{-3}$	$2{\cdot}34 \times 10^{-3}$	$16{\cdot}85 \times 10^{-3}$	$3{\cdot}20 \times 10^{-3}$	53·9
$0{\cdot}48 \times 10^{-3}$	$0{\cdot}48 \times 10^{-3}$	$3{\cdot}53 \times 10^{-3}$	$15{\cdot}3 \times 10^{-3}$	54·1
$0{\cdot}50 \times 10^{-3}$	$0{\cdot}50 \times 10^{-3}$	$3{\cdot}66 \times 10^{-3}$	$14{\cdot}6 \times 10^{-3}$	53·6
$1{\cdot}14 \times 10^{-3}$	$1{\cdot}14 \times 10^{-3}$	$8{\cdot}41 \times 10^{-3}$	$6{\cdot}47 \times 10^{-3}$	54·4

The above table shows the equilibrium concentrations of hydrogen, iodine and hydrogen iodide when they are reacted together in heated closed vessels at constant temperature. It will be noticed that the values of $\frac{[HI]^2}{[H_2][I_2]}$ are almost constant ([ ] indicate equilibrium concentration in mol dm^{-3}).

This relates to the stoichiometric equation for the reaction

$$H_2 + I_2 \rightleftharpoons 2HI$$

2. The ethyl ethanoate equilibrium

When an acid and an alcohol are reacted together in the presence of a mineral acid an ester and water are formed. When an ester and water are heated together the reverse process can occur.

$$\underset{\text{acid}}{CH_3COOH} + \underset{\text{alcohol}}{C_2H_5OH} \underset{\text{hydrolysis}}{\overset{\text{esterification}}{\rightleftharpoons}} \underset{\text{ester}}{CH_3COOC_2H_5} + \underset{\text{water}}{H_2O}$$

The following results were obtained when different amounts of ester and water were reacted together, at constant temperature, and the mixture analyzed when equilibrium had been reached.

equilibrium amounts (mol)				
ethyl ethanoate	water	ethanoic acid	ethanol	$\frac{[CH_3COOH][C_2H_5OH]}{[CH_3COOC_2H_5][H_2O]}$
0·231	0·079	0·065	0·065	0·232
0·204	0·118	0·082	0·082	0·279
0·150	0·261	0·105	0·105	0·282
0·090	0·531	0·114	0·114	0·272

The values in the final column are again almost constant (the variation is due to difficulties in knowing the exact water content). For this system the constant, K_c, averages to 0·27.

$$\text{Therefore } K_c = 0{\cdot}27 = \frac{[CH_3COOH]_{eqm.}[C_2H_5OH]_{eqm.}}{[CH_3COOC_2H_5]_{eqm.}[H_2O]_{eqm.}}$$

This also relates to the stoichiometric equation.

Many other systems support the general **equilibrium law** that for a reaction represented by

$$aA + bB \rightleftharpoons cC + dD$$

$$K_c\text{, equilibrium constant} = \frac{[C]^c[D]^d}{[A]^a[B]^b}$$

K_c is the constant expressed in concentrations and may or may not have units depending on the number of terms in the expression. $[A]$, $[B]$, $[C]$, and $[D]$ indicate equilibrium concentrations in mol dm^{-3}.

For reactions involving gases it is often better to use an equilibrium constant expressed in terms of pressure instead of concentration. The concentration of a gas is proportional to its partial pressure (mole fraction of gas times total pressure).

For the reaction $aA + bB \rightleftharpoons cC + dD$

$$K_p\text{, pressure equilibrium constant} = \frac{(p_C)^c \times (p_D)^d}{(p_A)^a \times (p_B)^b}$$

where p_A, p_B, p_C, p_D are partial pressures of A, B, C, D. Solids have constant partial pressure. Both K_c and K_p remain constant and only vary with temperature. They can be used to predict equilibrium concentrations in reactions.

Example 4·6 g of ethanol and 6·0 g of ethanoic acid were kept at a constant temperature until equilibrium was reached. 2 g of acid were found to remain. In a second experiment 9·2 g of alcohol, 3·6 g of acid, 1·1 g of ethyl ethanoate and 9·0 g of water were mixed and allowed to attain equilibrium. What was the composition of the resulting mixture?

	C_2H_5OH	$+ CH_3COOH$	$\rightleftharpoons CH_3COOC_2H_5$	$+ H_2O$
initial amount (mol)	$\frac{4\cdot6}{46} = 0\cdot1$	$\frac{6\cdot0}{60} = 0\cdot1$	0	0
equilibrium amount (mol)	0·033	$\frac{2}{60} = 0\cdot033$	0·067	0·067

Note that 2 g of acid remained which is 0·033 moles. Therefore $0\cdot1 - 0\cdot033 = 0\cdot067$ moles must have reacted. Hence 0·067 moles of each product are formed and 0·067 moles of alcohol must also have reacted.

equilibrium conc. (mol dm^{-3})	$\frac{0\cdot033}{V}$	$\frac{0\cdot033}{V}$	$\frac{0\cdot067}{V}$	$\frac{0\cdot067}{V}$

$$K_c = \frac{[CH_3COOC_2H_5][H_2O]}{[CH_3COOH][C_2H_5OH]} = \frac{0\cdot067^2}{0\cdot033^2} = 4\cdot0$$

Provided the second reaction is carried out at the same temperature K_c remains constant.

	C_2H_5OH	$+ CH_3COOH$	$\rightleftharpoons CH_3COOC_2H_5$	$+ H_2O$
initial amount (mol)	$\frac{9\cdot2}{46} = 0\cdot2$	$\frac{3\cdot6}{60} = 0\cdot06$	$\frac{1\cdot1}{88} = 0\cdot0125$	$\frac{9\cdot0}{18} = 0\cdot5$

If x moles react then at equilibrium

concentration (mol dm^{-3})	$\frac{0\cdot2 - x}{V}$	$\frac{0\cdot06 - x}{V}$	$\frac{0\cdot0125 + x}{V}$	$\frac{0\cdot5 + x}{V}$

$$K_c = 4 = \frac{(0\cdot0125 + x)(0\cdot5 + x)}{(0\cdot2 - x)(0\cdot06 - x)}$$

$$3x^2 - 1\cdot5525x + 0\cdot04175 = 0$$

solving by the formula, $x = 0\cdot49$ or $0\cdot029$ moles.

The first value for x is impossible since the initial amounts of acid and alcohol were less than 0·49 moles. If 0·029 moles have reacted the equilibrium composition is:

$0{\cdot}2 - 0{\cdot}029 = 0{\cdot}171$ moles alcohol, $0{\cdot}06 - 0{\cdot}029$
$= 0{\cdot}031$ moles acid,
$0{\cdot}0125 + 0{\cdot}029 = 0{\cdot}0415$ moles ester and $0{\cdot}5 + 0{\cdot}029$
$= 0{\cdot}529$ moles water

Factors affecting chemical reactions in equilibrium. Le Chatelier's principle This principle enables qualitative predictions to be made about the effects of pressure, concentration, and temperature on equilibrium position. Le Chatelier's principle states that if a constraint is applied to a system in equilibrium, the equilibrium position changes so as to nullify the constraint.

1. Effect of pressure change Pressure will only affect gaseous reactions in which there is a volume change in going from reactants to products. Increasing the pressure on a gas increases the concentration (see also p. 46, 47).

2. Effect of concentration change Increasing the concentration of a reactant or product will drive the equilibrium away from that species. For the reaction $A + B \rightleftharpoons C + D$,

$$K_c = \frac{[C][D]}{[A][B]}$$

If other factors remain constant then K_c is a constant and if, for example, the concentration of A is increased then to keep K_c constant the concentrations of C and D increase. Therefore to force reactions to give a greater yield of product the concentration of the cheaper reactant may be greatly increased. Similarly reactions can be forced to completion by continually removing one of the products, the concentration of that product is kept low in the equilibrium expression and reaction continues.

3. Effect of temperature Equilibrium constants are temperature dependent. For an exothermic reaction K decreases with increasing temperature and so the concentration of products decreases. For endothermic reactions increasing temperature increases the yield of product. This can also be argued from Le Chatelier's principle. Exothermic reactions produce heat in going from reactants to products; raising the temperature (adding heat) is a constraint to the equilibrium; the reaction can remove the constraint by absorbing the heat in proceeding from products to reactants.

4. Effect of catalysts Catalysts affect forward and backward rates equally and have no affect on equilibrium position but they do enable equilibrium to be reached more quickly.

Examples
1. The Haber process

$$\underset{4\ \text{volumes}}{N_2 + 3H_2} \rightleftharpoons \underset{2\ \text{volumes}}{2NH_3} + \text{heat} \quad (\Delta H = -46{\cdot}2\ \text{kJ})$$

The reaction between nitrogen and hydrogen to yield ammonia is accompanied by a decrease in volume and is exothermic. If the reaction is carried out under high pressure then the equilibrium is forced to the right as the formation of ammonia lowers the volume and, by Le Chatelier's principle, tries to relieve the pressure. The pressures used vary from 450 to 1000 atmospheres. By Le Chatelier's principle the formation of ammonia should be favoured by low temperature. However this reduces the rate of reaction and in practice high temperatures (about 500°C) are used which produce a reduced yield but at a much higher rate. A catalyst of finely divided iron is used.

2. Contact process

$$\underset{3\ \text{volumes}}{2SO_2 + O_2} \rightleftharpoons \underset{2\ \text{volumes}}{2SO_3} \quad (\Delta H = -395\ \text{kJ})$$

As with the Haber process, by Le Chatelier's principle increased yield is favoured by increased pressure (since the volume of product is less than that of reactants), and by low temperature (the reaction is exothermic). In practice the reaction is carried out at 1 atmosphere (since the volume change is not large enough to justify the expense of high pressure vessels) and about 450°C (since a fast rate is more important than a high yield).

Heterogeneous equilibrium In heterogeneous equilibria the concentrations of all pure solid and pure liquid phases can be assumed to be constant.

Examples 1. The calcium carbonate system

$$CaCO_{3(s)} \rightleftharpoons CaO_{(s)} + CO_{2(g)}$$

$$K_c = \frac{[CaO][CO_2]}{[CaCO_3]}$$

but [CaO] and [$CaCO_3$] are constant

$$\therefore \quad K_c = [CO_2]$$

or

$$K_p = p_{CO_2}$$

It follows that for any given temperature there is a constant concentration and therefore constant partial pressure of carbon dioxide in equilibrium with calcium carbonate and calcium oxide. In the manufacture of lime, chalk is roasted in a current of air to remove the carbon dioxide and force the reaction to go to completion.

2. The iron steam system

$$3Fe_{(s)} + 4H_2O_{(g)} \rightleftharpoons Fe_3O_{4(s)} + 4H_{2(g)}$$

$$K_c = \frac{[H_2]^4[Fe_3O_4]}{[Fe]^3[H_2O]^4}$$

which reduces to

$$K = \frac{[H_2]^4}{[H_2O]^4} \text{ or } K = \frac{[H_2]}{[H_2O]} = p_{H_2}/p_{H_2O}$$

The ratio of partial pressures of steam and hydrogen is constant for all proportions of iron and iron oxide at a given temperature.

Key terms

Ideal gas equation

$$PV = nRT \quad \text{or} \quad \frac{P_1V_1}{T_1} = \frac{P_2V_2}{T_2}$$

where P is pressure, V is volume, T is temperature in kelvin, n is number of moles and R is the molar gas constant.

Dalton's law of partial pressures Provided the gases do not react, the total pressure of a mixture of gases is the sum of the partial pressures. Partial pressure is the mole fraction of a constituent times the total pressure.

Graham's law of diffusion The rates of diffusion (or effusion) of different gases under identical conditions are inversely proportional to the square roots of their densities.

$$R_1/R_2 = \sqrt{\rho_2/\rho_1}$$

Phase Any physically and chemically distinct part of a system.

Triple point The set of conditions of temperature and pressure under which three phases can exist in equilibrium.

Critical point The conditions of temperature and pressure under which a gas will just liquify.

Henry's law The mass of gas dissolved by a given volume of solvent is directly proportional to the pressure.

Raoult's law The vapour pressure of a constituent in an ideal solution is equal to the vapour pressure exerted by the pure constituent at that temperature, multiplied by the mole fraction by which it is present.

$$P_A = X_a P_A^0 \qquad X = \text{mole fraction}$$

Eutectic mixture The mixture which freezes with constant composition.

Distribution law (Nernst's law) The ratio of the concentrations of a solute distributed between two immiscible solvents is a constant provided the temperature remains constant and the molecular state of the solute is the same in both solvents.

$$\frac{\text{Concentration of solute in solvent } A}{\text{Concentration of solute in solvent } B} = K$$

Chemical equilibrium

$$aA + bB \rightleftharpoons cC + dD$$

$$K_c, \text{ equilibrium constant} = \frac{[C]^c[D]^d}{[A]^a[B]^b}$$

$$[\ ] = \text{concentration (mol dm}^{-3})$$

for gases:

$$K_p = \frac{(p_C)^c \times (p_D)^d}{(p_A)^a \times (p_B)^b} \qquad p = \text{partial pressure}$$

Le Chatelier's principle If a constraint is applied to a system in equilibrium, the equilibrium position changes so as to nullify the constraint.

Factors affecting chemical reactions in equilibrium

Pressure change only affects reactions involving gases. When the pressure is increased the equilibrium is driven to the side having the smaller volume. Pressure does not alter K_p.

Concentration change Increasing the concentration of a species drives the equilibrium away from the side containing that species. It does not alter K_c.

Temperature change does alter K. For an exothermic reaction K decreases with increase in temperature and the concentration of the products decreases. For endothermic reactions K increases with temperature rise and the concentration of products also increases.

Catalysts do not alter K or the position of equilibrium.

Chapter 3
Thermochemistry and Reaction Kinetics

Thermodynamics

Thermodynamics deals with the flow of energy under equilibrium or near equilibrium conditions. Energy can be defined as the capacity to do work and is measured in **joules**, J, or in **kilojoules,** kJ, (1 kJ = 1000 J). The most fundamental form of energy is heat and thermochemistry is concerned with the measurement of heat changes in chemical reactions.

First law of thermodynamics This law is often stated as the principle of conservation of energy: **energy can neither be created nor destroyed**. Consider the application of this principle to a closed system (any system whose mass cannot be transferred to or from the surroundings). If an amount of heat, q, is supplied to the system then some of this heat will be used in changing the **internal energy** of the system, U, while the rest may be used up as work done on the surroundings, w.

$$q = \Delta U + w \tag{3.1}$$

Equation 3.1 is the mathematical statement of the 1st law. Δ is the Greek letter delta and means 'change in'. Thus,

$$\Delta U = \text{final internal energy} - \text{initial internal energy}$$

Only changes in internal energy can be measured as absolute internal energy cannot be determined. Internal energy, not to be confused with heat, is the energy stored in a substance due to thermal agitation of the atoms and molecules. It is therefore generally kinetic energy of rotation, vibration and translation.

Chemical reactions may be carried out under conditions of constant volume or constant pressure. At constant volume no work is done on the atmosphere, but at constant pressure the system is allowed to expand (particularly if a gas is produced) and the atmosphere is 'pushed back' external work being done.

It is far more common in chemistry to carry out reactions under constant pressure. It can be shown that the work done due to expansion is the product of the external pressure and the volume change.

$$w = P\Delta V$$

Therefore, $$q_p = \Delta U + P\Delta V$$

(if no other external work is done, e.g. electrical).
q_p, heat change of a chemical reaction at constant pressure, is called **enthalpy change** and is given the symbol ΔH. It has units of Joules.

$$\Delta H = \Delta U + P\Delta V$$

Thermochemistry: Heats of reaction

Thermochemistry is the study of the heat changes which accompany chemical reactions, formation of solutions, changes of state etc. The heat change is written alongside the equation for the given physico-chemical change, e.g.

$$H_{2(g)} + \tfrac{1}{2}O_{2(g)} \rightarrow H_2O_{(g)} \quad \Delta H = -242\ \text{kJ} \qquad (3.2)$$

A negative value indicates that heat is evolved in the reaction. This is the aquisitive convention which considers what happens to the system itself. The system above (eq. 3.2) loses heat to the surroundings (ΔH negative) and the reaction is therefore **exothermic**. When ΔH is positive heat is absorbed and the reaction is **endothermic** e.g.

$$H_2O_{(g)} \rightarrow H_{2(g)} + \tfrac{1}{2}O_{2(g)} \quad \Delta H = +242\ \text{kJ} \qquad (3.3)$$

The value of ΔH given is for the number of moles indicated by the equation. It will also depend on the state of the reactants and products and on the conditions under which the reaction is carried out, e.g.

$$H_{2(g)} + \tfrac{1}{2}O_{2(g)} \rightarrow H_2O_{(l)} \quad \Delta H = -286\ \text{kJ} \qquad (3.4)$$

The difference in equations 3.2 and 3.4 is the latent heat of vaporization of water. The values of enthalpies quoted are normally **standard enthalpies**, ΔH^θ_{298}, which are for reactants and products in their normal states at 298 K and 1 atmosphere pressure. Subscripts s, l, and g, refer to the solid, liquid and gaseous states respectively.

Heat of formation is the enthalpy change when one mole of a compound is formed from its elements under standard conditions and is given the symbol ΔH^θ_f, e.g.

$$C_{(s)graphite} + 2H_{2(g)} \rightarrow CH_{4(g)} \quad \Delta H^\theta_f = -74{\cdot}9\ \text{kJ mol}^{-1}$$

Elements in their normal state under standard conditions are assigned a heat of formation of zero.

Thus $\quad C_{(s)graphite} \quad \Delta H^\theta_f = 0\ \text{kJ mol}^{-1}$

$\quad C_{(s)diamond} \quad \Delta H^\theta_f = 1{\cdot}9\ \text{kJ mol}^{-1}$

indicating that diamond is the metastable form of carbon. Often heats of formation cannot be measured directly and have to be calculated from other data.

Heat of combustion is the enthalpy change when one mole of a substance is completely burnt in oxygen, corrected to standard conditions, symbol ΔH^θ_c, e.g.

$$C_{(s)graphite} + O_{2(g)} \rightarrow CO_{2(g)} \quad \Delta H^\theta_c = -394\ \text{kJ mol}^{-1}$$

Note that the heat of combustion of a substance may be the same as the heat of formation of the oxide.

Measurement of heat of combustion by bomb calorimeter

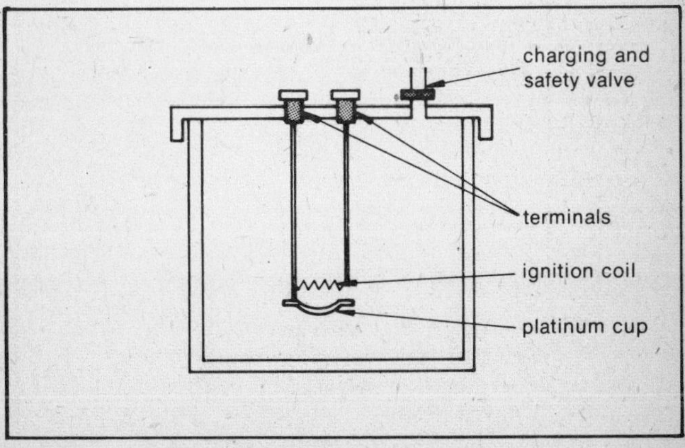

Figure 18. A bomb calorimeter

About 0·5 g of the sample is placed inside the platinum cup and the calorimeter filled with oxygen to a pressure of 25 atmospheres. The bomb is then placed in a water calorimeter of known heat capacity and the whole apparatus thermally insulated. A current is passed through the heating coil to ignite the sample and the rise in temperature noted. After allowing for heat losses the heat evolved during combustion can be calculated. This heat change can then be converted to an enthalpy change by allowing for external work, $P\Delta V$ (fig. 18).

Heat of neutralization is the enthalpy change when one mole of hydrogen ion (from an acid) is just neutralized by a base in dilute solution, e.g.

$$HCl_{(aq)} + NaOH_{(aq)} \rightarrow NaCl_{(aq)} + H_2O_{(l)} \qquad \Delta H = -57{\cdot}1\ \mathrm{kJ\ mol^{-1}}$$

Note that this value is almost constant for strong acids and bases in dilute solution.

Heat of solution is the heat change when one mole of substance is dissolved in a specified volume of solvent. The value depends on the volume of solvent used but tends towards a fixed value at high dilution.

These latter two enthalpy changes can be measured using a vacuum flask.

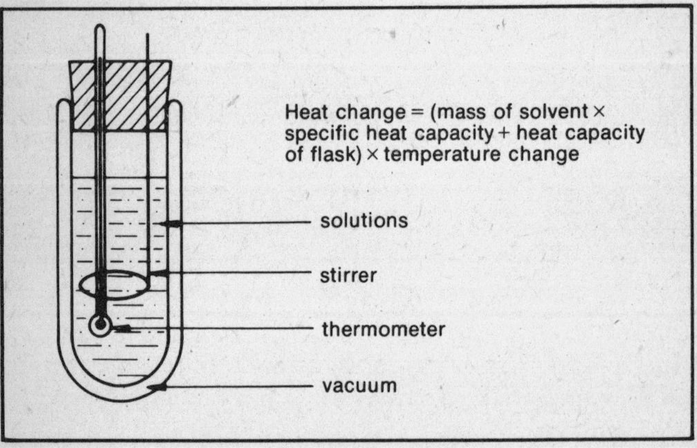

Figure 19. Vacuum flask calorimeter

A vacuum flask reduces heat loss. Known amounts of substance are placed in the flask and the temperature change is noted after addition of solvent or base. The heat evolved on mixing can then be calculated, allowing for the heat capacity of the flask.

Hess's law

Heats of formation and other enthalpy changes which cannot be measured directly may be calculated by using **Hess's law of constant heat summation.** This states that the total heat change in a chemical reaction is independent of the path taken. This is a particular form of the 1st law of thermodynamics. For example, if a compound A can react to give a compound C either directly or via an intermediate B then the total heat change for the reaction $A \rightarrow B \rightarrow C$ will be the same as that for $A \rightarrow C$ directly (fig. 20).

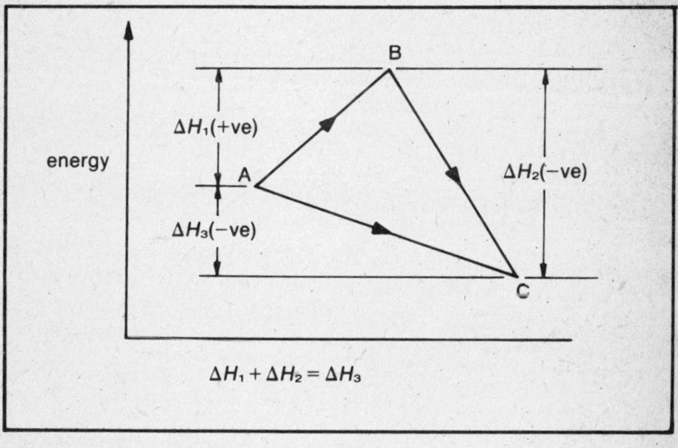

Figure 20. Hess's law

Examples

1. Find the heat of formation of methane given that its heat of combustion = −891 kJ mol^{-1} and the heats of formation of carbon dioxide and water are −394 kJ mol^{-1} and −286 kJ mol^{-1} respectively.

The equation for the combustion of methane is

i. $CH_{4(g)} + 2O_{2(g)} \rightarrow CO_{2(g)} + 2H_2O_{(g)}$ $\quad \Delta H_c^\theta = -891$ kJ mol^{-1}

The equations for the formation of CO_2 and H_2O are

ii. $C_{(s)} + O_{2(g)} \rightarrow CO_{2(g)}$ $\Delta H_f^\theta = -394$ kJ mol^{-1}

iii. $H_{2(g)} + \frac{1}{2}O_{2(g)} \rightarrow H_2O_{(g)}$ $\Delta H_f^\theta = -286$ kJ mol^{-1}

rearranging equations and adding gives the equation for the formation of methane (reversing i. reverses the heat change)

$$CO_{2(g)} + 2H_2O_{(g)} \rightarrow CH_{4(g)} + 2O_{2(g)} \quad \Delta H = -(-891)\text{ kJ}$$

$$C_{(s)} + O_{2(g)} \rightarrow CO_{2(g)} \quad \Delta H_f^\theta = -394\text{ kJ}$$

$$2H_{2(g)} + O_{2(g)} \rightarrow 2H_2O_{(g)} \quad \Delta H = 2 \times (-286)\text{ kJ}$$

$$C_{(s)graphite} + 2H_{2(g)} \rightarrow CH_{4(g)} \quad \Delta H_f^\theta = -75{\cdot}0\text{ kJ (see fig. 21)}$$

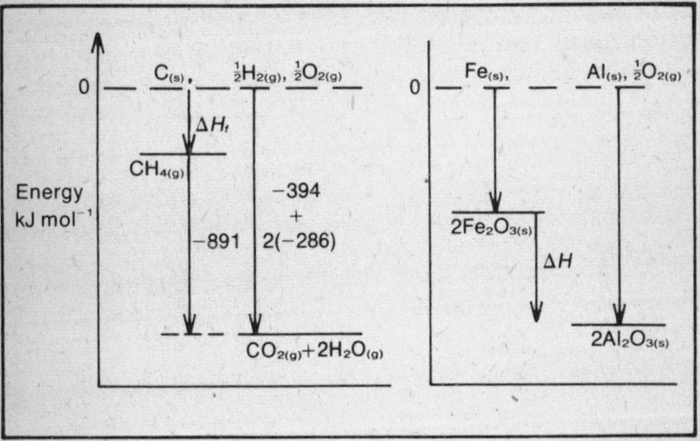

Figure 21

2. Find the enthalpy change for the reaction between aluminium and iron(III) oxide given that the heats of formation of aluminium oxide and iron(III) oxide are respectively:

	ΔH_f^θ
$2Al_{(s)} + \frac{3}{2}O_2 \rightarrow Al_2O_{3(s)}$	-1669
$2Fe_{(s)} + \frac{3}{2}O_{2(g)} \rightarrow Fe_2O_{3(s)}$	-822
$2Al_{(s)} + Fe_2O_{3(s)} \rightarrow Al_2O_{3(s)} + 2Fe_{(s)}$	-847 kJ mol^{-1}

The heat of reaction is the difference in the heats of formation of product and reactant (see fig. 21).

Bond energy

The energy changes in chemical reactions are due to bonds being formed and broken. A bond is a link between two atoms and represents a lowering of energy. Work must be done if the atoms are to be separated. If in the course of a reaction the bonds being formed are stronger than those being broken then energy will be liberated (exothermic reaction). In an endothermic reaction the bonds formed are weaker than those broken. Information on bond energy can help in the understanding of chemical reactivity.

Covalent bonds An ideal covalent bond is formed when two atoms share a pair of electrons equally between them. To find the bond energy it is not sufficient to consider just the standard heat of formation of a compound. Bond energy is the energy change in forming a bond from the free atoms (not from the elements in their standard states). For example, benzene has a heat of formation of $+82{\cdot}9\,\text{kJ mol}^{-1}$ and is therefore endothermic but is still stable with respect to the free atoms which make it up. The energy of a bond between a given pair of atoms depends on the exact situation in which it occurs.

For example, if the hydrogen atoms of methane are removed one at a time four possible values of the C–H bond energy can be found.

$$CH_{4(g)} \rightarrow CH_{3(g)} + H_{(g)} \qquad \Delta H^{\theta} = +423\,\text{kJ mol}^{-1}$$

$$CH_{3(g)} \rightarrow CH_{2(g)} + H_{(g)} \qquad \Delta H^{\theta} = +368\,\text{kJ mol}^{-1}$$

$$CH_{2(g)} \rightarrow CH_{(g)} + H_{(g)} \qquad \Delta H^{\theta} = +519\,\text{kJ mol}^{-1}$$

$$CH_{(g)} \rightarrow C_{(g)} + H_{(g)} \qquad \Delta H^{\theta} = +335\,\text{kJ mol}^{-1}$$

These figures are difficult to obtain (by mass spectroscopy) and are very approximate. The C–H bonds in methane are clearly identical and the average bond dissociation energy will be

$$\frac{423 + 368 + 519 + 335}{4} = 411\,\text{kJ mol}^{-1}.$$

Average bond energies can be calculated to a reasonable degree of accuracy from thermochemical data. If the heat of formation of a compound is known then all that is needed is the **atomization energy** of the elements: the energy required to convert one mole of an element into the free atoms at 298 K and one atmosphere. In most cases it is not too difficult to obtain these atomization energies. For metals it will be the sublimation energy, e.g.

$$Na_{(s)} \rightarrow Na_{(g)} \qquad \Delta H^{\theta}_{atom} = +109 \text{ kJ mol}^{-1}$$

For diatomic gases it will be the dissociation energy, e.g.

$$H_{2(g)} \rightarrow 2H_{(g)} \qquad 2 \times \Delta H^{\theta}_{atom} = +436 \text{ kJ mol}^{-1}$$

However for other elements it must be calculated from spectroscopic data. Unfortunately one of the hardest to find is carbon on which many measurements depend.

C–H bond energy can be determined from the following thermochemical data:

1. Heat of atomization of graphite (sublimation energy)

	ΔH kJ mol^{-1}
$C_{(s)graphite} \rightarrow C_{(g)}$	+715

2. Heat of atomization of hydrogen

$H_{2(g)} \rightarrow 2H_{(g)}$	+436

3. Heat of formation of methane

	$C_{(s)} + 2H_{2(g)} \rightarrow CH_{4(g)}$	−75
By Hess's law:	$C_{(s)} \rightarrow C_{(g)}$	+715
	$2H_{2(g)} \rightarrow 4H_{(g)}$	2 × (+436)
	$CH_{4(g)} \rightarrow C_{(g)} + 2H_{2(g)}$	−(−75)
	$CH_{4(g)} \rightarrow C_{(g)} + 4H_{(g)}$	+1662
Therefore average C–H bond energy = 1662/4 =		+415.5

C–C bond energy can be determined in a similar manner:

$$C_2H_{6(g)} \rightarrow 2C_{(g)} + 6H_{(g)} \qquad +2822.7$$

Hence if C–H bond energy is 415.5 kJ mol^{-1} and ethane is made up of one C–C and six C–H bonds then the C–C bond energy is $2822.7 - 6 \times 415.5 = 329.7$ kJ mol^{-1}.

It is necessary to distinguish between the energies of single bonds and those of double and triple bonds. Average bond energies determined in the manner above are approximately additive and can be used to estimate heats of reaction and stabilities of compounds. However, as will be seen in chapter 5 few bonds are purely covalent, many being polarized which alters the bond energy.

Ionic bonding, when ideal, involves the complete transfer of one or more electrons. The resulting ions form a lattice held together by electrostatic attraction. Lattice enthalpy is the energy required to separate the gaseous ions of a crystal an infinite distance apart. It relates to many properties of ionic crystals such as melting point, solubility, stability etc.

Born-Haber cycle

Values of lattice energy can be calculated from thermochemical data. For example, consider the stages in the formation of sodium chloride from the elements in their normal states under standard conditions. First, energy must be supplied to produce the atoms in their free state (atomization energy).

1. $Na_{(s)} \rightarrow Na_{(g)}$ $\qquad \Delta H_1^\ominus = +109\ \text{kJ mol}^{-1}$

2. $\frac{1}{2}Cl_{2(g)} \rightarrow Cl_{(g)}$ $\qquad \Delta H_2^\ominus = +121\ \text{kJ mol}^{-1}$

Next, each atom must form an ion. The energy required to remove the outer electron from one mole of the free atoms is termed 1st ionization energy, *I*.

3. $Na_{(g)} \rightarrow Na^+_{(g)} + e^-$ $\qquad I_1 = +494\ \text{kJ mol}^{-1}$

The energy change in producing one mole of an anion from the free atoms is termed electron affinity, *E.A.*

4. $Cl_{(g)} + e^- \rightarrow Cl^-$ $\qquad E.A. = -364\ \text{kJ mol}^{-1}$

(note that energy is liberated in the above process).

Finally, the **lattice energy, *U***, is released when one mole of Na^+ ions and one mole of Cl^- ions combine to form crystalline sodium chloride.

5. $Na^+_{(g)} + Cl^-_{(g)} \rightarrow NaCl_{(s)}$ $\qquad U$

By the application of **Hess's law** the sum of these heat changes must equal the heat of formation of sodium chloride (see fig. 22). Therefore if ΔH_f for NaCl is known the lattice energy may be calculated. ΔH_f for NaCl is found experimentally to be -411 kJ mol^{-1}.

$$\Delta H_1 + \Delta H_2 + I + E.A. + U = \Delta H_f$$

$$109 + 121 + 494 + (-364) + U = -411$$

$$\therefore \quad U = -771 \text{ kJ mol}^{-1}$$

The most important energy change in the cycle is the lattice energy and it is often the factor controlling whether a bond is ionic or covalent. Lattice energy increases with increasing charge on the cation or anion and decreasing distance between anion and cation (which is governed by the size of the ions and the packing). A high lattice energy generally means that a salt will have a high melting point. On dissolving, the lattice is broken down and the ions are closely surrounded by solvent molecules (solvation). If the solvation energy is larger than the lattice energy then heat is evolved and if the lattice energy is larger than the solvation energy heat is absorbed on dissolving.

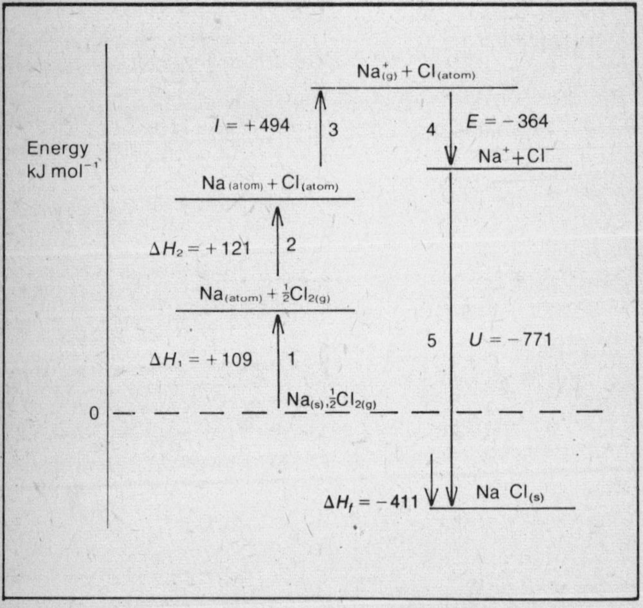

Figure 22. Born-Haber cycle

If the lattice energy can be estimated then it enables values of the electron affinity to be found (these are not easy to obtain). Estimates can be obtained from the Born equation which is developed from the law of force governing the attraction of oppositely charged ions. Differences between lattice energies obtained in this way and those obtained from the Born-Haber cycle indicate a divergence from pure ionic bonding.

Entropy and free energy

Enthalpy changes are not the only factor governing the feasibility of a chemical reaction. Many reactions occur spontaneously with absorption of energy. Two factors govern physico-chemical changes, one is a tendency towards minimum energy and the other is a **tendency towards maximum entropy**. The latter condition is the **second law of thermodynamics**.

Entropy is the degree of randomness or disorder of a system and is a measure of the unavailable energy of a system (energy lost for the purpose of doing work). Any spontaneous change in an isolated system (one having constant volume and energy) must be accompanied by an increase in entropy.

Entropy change, ΔS, is defined as the ratio of the heat put into a system, q, divided by the absolute temperature of the system, T, (for a reversible process). It is measured in Joules kelvin^{-1}.

$$\Delta S = \frac{q_{\text{reversible}}}{T}$$

Standard entropy, S^θ, at 298 K and 101325 Pa					
substance	*S^θ J-K^{-1} mol^{-1}*	*substance*	*S^θ J-K^{-1} mol^{-1}*	*substance*	*S^θ J-K^{-1} mol^{-1}*
graphite	5·7	H_2O	69·9	H_2O	189
diamond	2·4	Br_2	152	Br_2	245
iron	27·2	Hg	77·4	Hg	175
sulphur (α)	31·9	$CHCl_3$	203	S	168
NaCl	72·4	CCl_4	214	S_8	430
quartz	41·8	C_2H_5OH	161	C_2H_5OH	282
solids		liquids		gases	

Table 1. Standard entropies

Systems having perfect order, i.e. pure crystalline compounds and elements at 0 K have zero entropy. Entropy increases in going from solid → liquid → gas. A table of standard entropies S^θ at 1 atmosphere pressure and 298 K is given on p. 59.

Free energy, *G*, (sometimes called Gibb's free energy) is a measure of the useful work that a system is capable of doing (apart from volume changes). Only if ΔG, change in free energy, is negative (i.e. work is done by the system) will a reaction proceed. The two factors influencing a reaction, enthalpy change and entropy change are related to free energy by the following expression.

$$\Delta G = \Delta H - T\Delta S \qquad (3.5)$$

Since reactions are feasible only if ΔG is negative, if the enthalpy change is positive (endothermic reaction) then for a reaction to proceed the entropy change must be large enough for the product $T\Delta S$ to exceed ΔH. If ΔG is positive then no useful work can be obtained from the system and the reaction is not feasible. If ΔG is zero or close to zero for a reaction then it will come to equilibrium. It can be shown that free energy is related to the equilibrium constant (k) by the expression

$$\Delta G = -RT \log_e K$$

R = gas constant, T = temperature in kelvin

Estimation of free energy change Equation 3.5 can be used to estimate values of ΔG and to predict how systems will behave.

At low temperatures the factor $T\Delta S$ becomes small and so ΔH controls the sign of ΔG. Therefore only exothermic reactions are feasible at low temperatures. Similarly gases tend to condense to liquids and liquids tend to solidify as these changes are accompanied by a decrease in entropy (also an evolution of latent heat making ΔH negative).

At high temperatures the factor $T\Delta S$ becomes large and more important, hence endothermic reactions, accompanied by an increase in disorder, become feasible as long as $T\Delta S$ exceeds ΔH. Exothermic reactions become explosive, e.g.

$$H_{2(g)} + \tfrac{1}{2}O_{2(g)} \rightleftharpoons H_2O_{(g)} \qquad \Delta H \text{ negative}$$
$$N_{2(g)} + 3H_{2(g)} \rightleftharpoons 2NH_{3(g)} \qquad \Delta H \text{ negative}$$

These reactions are accompanied by a decrease in entropy in going from left to right as the gas volume on the left hand side is bigger than that on the right and so although exothermic, become less favourable as the temperature increases ($T\Delta S$ becomes large and negative making ΔG small).

$$(NH_4)_2Cr_2O_{7(s)} \rightarrow N_2 + Cr_2O_{3(s)} + 4H_2O_{(l)} \qquad \Delta H \text{ negative}$$

The decomposition of ammonium dichromate (above) is exothermic and accompanied by an increase in gas volume (0 volume to 5 volumes). Hence this reaction is extremely favourable and explosive at high temperatures.

$$CaCO_{3(s)} \rightleftharpoons CaO_{(s)} + CO_{2(g)} \qquad \Delta H \text{ positive}$$

The decomposition of calcium carbonate (above) is accompanied by an increase in entropy and is endothermic. The equilibrium moves increasingly to the right at higher temperatures.

Chemical kinetics

It has been seen that the feasibility of a reaction depends on the value of the free energy change. For practical purposes however it is necessary to know not only whether a reaction is feasible but also whether it takes place fast enough to be of any use. Chemical kinetics is the study of the velocity or rate of reaction.

Reaction rate theory

1. Collision theory This theory is particularly applicable to reactions in the gas phase but can also be applied to those in solution. The basis of the theory is that reactions occur due to favourable collisions between the reacting molecules. Kinetic theory shows that collisions between gas molecules occur very frequently and so it may be expected that all reactions would occur almost instantaneously. However this is not the case and Arrhenius suggested that only a very small fraction of collisions (between molecules with sufficient energy) could lead to a reaction. This critical minimum energy is termed **activation energy, E_A.**

It can be shown both experimentally and by the kinetic theory of gases that the spread of kinetic energies of gas molecules at a particular temperature follows a Maxwell-Boltzmann distribution (see fig. 23).

A few molecules possess a very small kinetic energy, others a great deal of energy and many possess near average kinetic energy. Raising the temperature raises the average kinetic energy and also increases the spread of energies (the peak of the curve falls at the higher temperature). If E_A represents activation energy then the diagram shows the fraction of molecules with energy greater than E_A (those molecules able to react on collision).

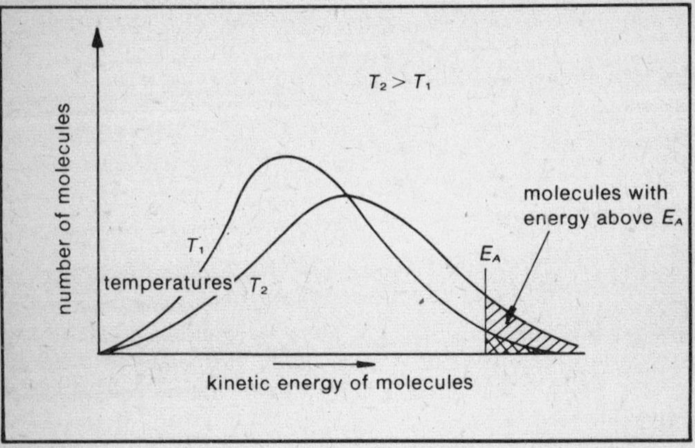

Figure 23. Distribution of energies in gas molecules

The number of molecules, n, possessing this energy is given by

$$n = n_0 e^{-E_A/RT}$$

where n_0 = total number of molecules, R = gas constant, T = temperature in Kelvin.

As T increases the number of molecules with E_A or above increases rapidly.

The rate of reaction is proportional to the number of molecules with energy $\geqslant E_A$. Hence if k is the **rate constant**

$$k \propto ne^{-E_A/RT}$$
$$k = Ae^{-E_A/RT} \quad (3.6)$$

where A is a constant termed the Arrhenius constant.

Taking logs of equation 3.6 it becomes

$$\log k = \text{const.} - E_A/RT$$

and this is called the **Arrhenius equation**. This equation applied to simple one step reactions can show how the rate varies with temperature and can give values for the activation energy.

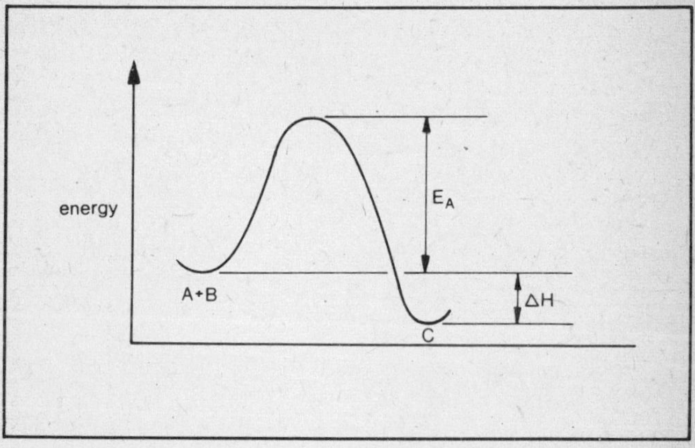

Figure 24. Energy diagram of a reaction

An energy profile of the reaction $A + B \rightarrow C$, fig. 24, shows that the forward reaction is exothermic. Hence when molecules with energy above E_A react, energy (ΔH) will be released into the system raising the energy of the remaining molecules and thus allowing more to react. The reverse reaction, the decomposition of C, is endothermic and has a greater activation energy, $E_A + \Delta H$. The constant A in equation 3.6 which depends on, among other things, collision geometry and whether the molecules collide in a favourable aspect, can be found for simple reactions.

The collision theory agrees fairly well with experiment for one step bimolecular reactions. The **molecularity** of a reaction is the number of molecules participating in the **rate determining step** (r.d.s.), the slowest stage in a reaction pathway. Bimolecular reactions, where only two molecules participate, are fairly common. Even more common are unimolecular reactions in which only one molecule participates in the r.d.s.; termolecular reactions in which three molecules participate are extremely rare. When the collision theory deviates markedly from experiment a more complex reaction pathway is suspected. Collision theory is particularly good at predicting the effects of temperature on reaction rate.

2. Transition state theory is more widely applicable than the collision theory. The theory presumes that when molecules react they do so via some intermediate complex termed an **activated complex.** The activated complex is unstable with respect to both reactants and products and contains bonds which are in the process of shortening to form the product molecule and stretching to break up the reactant molecule. The activated complex is generally very short lived but there is evidence for their formation. Applying this theory to the hydrogen and iodine reaction the mechanism shown schematically in fig. 25 is proposed.

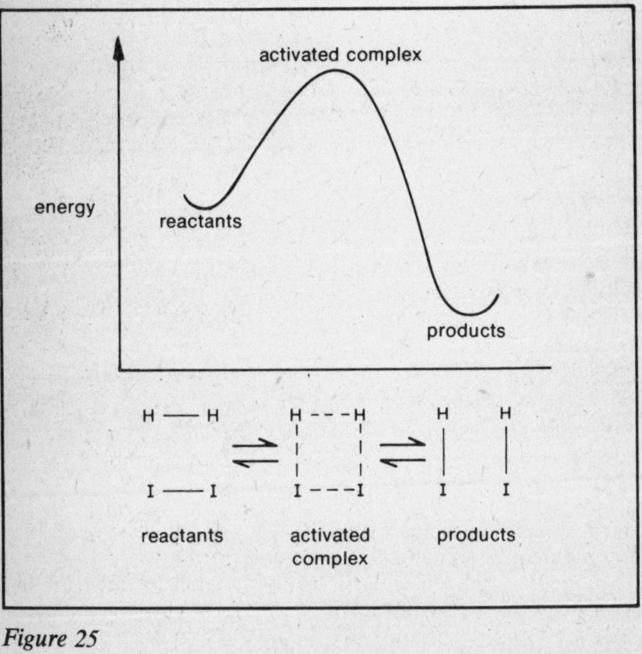

Figure 25

The bonds in the activated complex are shown dotted indicating that they are slightly longer than ordinary covalent bonds. The activated complex is able to break down into either reactants or products which are therefore in equilibrium with each other. Activation energy in this theory becomes the enthalpy change in forming the activated complex. The theory leads to the equation

$$k = \text{constant} \times e^{-\Delta G/RT}$$

where k = rate constant, G = free energy change in forming the activated complex

but $$\Delta G = \Delta H - T\Delta S$$

$$\therefore \quad k = \text{constant} \times e^{\Delta S/R} \, . \, e^{-\Delta H/RT}$$

but $$\Delta H = E_A, \text{ activation energy}$$

$$\therefore \quad k = \text{constant} \times e^{\Delta S/R} \, . \, e^{-E_A/RT}$$

This compares with the Arrhenius equation (eq. 3.6) with the constant A replaced by the term – constant × $e^{\Delta S/R}$. This theory does have some advantages over the collision theory in that it allows at least a qualitative treatment of slightly more complex reactions. Modern reaction rate theories consider features of both collision and transition state theories.

Factors affecting rate of reaction

1. State of reactants Reaction rates are increased by allowing thorough mixing of the reactants. This is achieved by increasing the surface area of solids, i.e. finely divided solids react faster than solid blocks, or by carrying out reactions in solvents thus allowing individual molecules to mix and approach closely enough to react.

2. Temperature Temperature has a marked effect on reaction rate. It can be shown experimentally and by application of the Arrhenius equation that a temperature rise of 10 K will approximately double the rate of reaction (between 20 K and 60 K). In terms of the collision theory this is explained by the increase in the frequency of collisions and more importantly by the fact that a higher fraction of colliding molecules possesses the necessary energy of activation. The transition state theory explanation is that the bonds in the reacting molecules will be more stretched due to higher vibrational energy, hence slightly weaker, and the enthalpy change in forming the activated complex will be lowered. Exothermic reactions can quickly go out of control in a confined space as the energy liberated is retained by the system causing an increase in rate.

3. Concentration Nearly all reactions occur at faster rates if the concentration of the reactants is increased. The exact relationship between rate and concentration can only be determined experimentally. Few reactions take place as indicated by the equation, normally they proceed by a number of stages which are known overall as the reaction mechanism. The rate equation which relates rate of reaction with concentration may give information about the rate determining step but it is unwise to try and connect the stoichiometric equation, the rate equation and the mechanism.

Order of reaction For the reaction $A + B \rightarrow$ products experiment may show that the rate of reaction is proportional to the concentration of A to the power x, i.e.

$$\text{Rate} \propto [A]^x$$

Similarly it may also be proportional to the concentration of B to the power y. Hence overall

$$\text{Rate} \propto [A]^x[B]^y$$

$$\text{Rate} = k[A]^x[B]^y$$

where k is the rate constant. This equation is termed the rate equation. The reaction is said to have an order of x with respect to reactant A and y with respect to reactant B and to have an overall order of $x + y$. x and y **may have** integral values, i.e. 1, 2 or 3 for simple reactions but they can take any value, **not necessarily integral**. The order can only be determined experimentally. For example, the elementary reaction between hydrogen and iodine is shown to follow the rate expression

$$\text{rate} = k[H_2][I_2]$$

i.e. 1st order with respect to H_2 and I_2, and 2nd order overall. However the corresponding reactions between hydrogen and bromine or chlorine are much more complex although they have the same stoichiometric equation. For H_2 and Br_2,

$$\text{Rate} = k[H_2][Br_2]^{1/2}$$

with an overall order of 1·5.

Experimental determination of rate equation The concentration of the various reactants and products is followed while the reaction is in progress. In some cases this may be achieved in situ by a physical process. These include: 1. spectroscopy. Individual bonds or groups in molecules give specific peaks in a spectrum and hence their destruction or formation can be followed, 2. optical properties, changes in colour, refractive index, rotation of polarized light, 3. conductivity changes, 4. pH changes, 5. chromatography, 6. volume of gas evolved. To follow a reaction by chemical means requires the extraction of aliquots from the reaction mixture at regular intervals. The reaction in each aliquot must then be quenched either by freezing or addition of a chemical. These aliquots are then analyzed at will by titration or any of the above physical methods. Rate of reaction can be expressed as rate of disappearance of a reactant with time or rate of appearance of a product with time.

For example, in the reaction $A + B \rightarrow C$

$$\text{rate} = -\frac{\mathrm{d}[A]}{\mathrm{d}t} = -\frac{\mathrm{d}[B]}{\mathrm{d}t} = +\frac{\mathrm{d}[C]}{\mathrm{d}t} = k[A]^x[B]^y \qquad (3.7)$$

The negative sign indicates a decrease in concentration. Figure 26 is a graph showing how the concentration of A might vary with time. The gradient, $\frac{\mathrm{d}[A]}{\mathrm{d}t}$, becomes smaller with time.

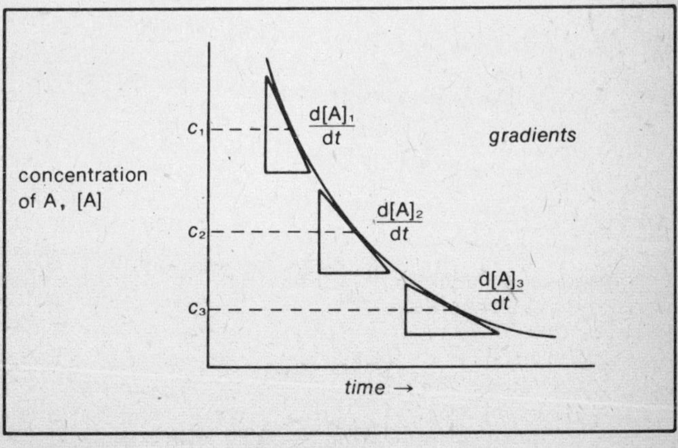

Figure 26

Hence the rate of reaction decreases as the concentration decreases.

To evaluate the rate constant and to determine the order, gradients are taken from the graph of concentration against time at various concentrations. These gradients give the rate of reaction and may be plotted against the concentrations of A (i.e. c_1, c_2, c_3 in the figure) raised to various powers until a straight line is achieved. The power which yields the straight line gives the order with respect to A. Alternatively taking logs of equation 3.7 gives

$$\log\left(\frac{-\mathrm{d}[A]}{\mathrm{d}t}\right) = x \log [A] + \log k$$

and plotting $\log\left(\frac{-\mathrm{d}[A]}{\mathrm{d}t}\right)$ against $\log [A]$ will give a straight line of gradient x and intercept $\log k$ (fig. 27).

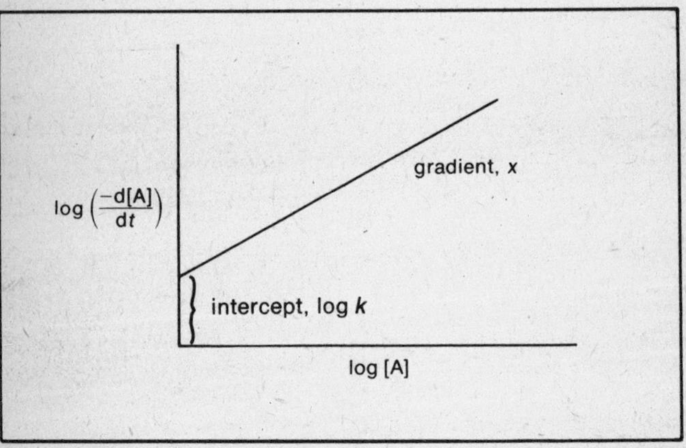

Figure 27

Mathematics of a first order reaction The rate of a first order reaction: $A \rightarrow$ products

is given by
$$\frac{-\mathrm{d}[A]}{\mathrm{d}t} = k[A] \qquad (3.8)$$

Initially, at time $t = 0$, let a moles of A be present and suppose at time t after the start of the reaction x moles of A have reacted, then $a-x$ moles remain. If the volume is 1 dm^3 then at time t

$$\frac{-d[A]}{dt}=\frac{-d(a-x)}{dt}=\frac{dx}{dt}$$

$$\therefore\quad \frac{dx}{dt}=k(a-x) \qquad \text{(from eq. 3.8)}$$

Integration of this expression leads to the equation

$$k=\frac{1}{t}\log_e\frac{(a)}{(a-x)}$$

$$t=\frac{2\cdot303}{k}\log_{10}\frac{(a)}{(a-x)}$$

For a given reaction a graph of t against $\log_{10}(a/a-x)$ will be a straight line if the reaction is first order. The gradient will be $\frac{2\cdot303}{k}$. Unit of the rate constant is sec^{-1}.

Half-life time is the time taken for half the initial moles of substance to react or when $x=a/2$ in the above expression. Hence,

$$\text{half-life, } t_{1/2}=\frac{2\cdot303}{k}\log_{10}\frac{(a)}{(a-\frac{1}{2}a)}$$

$$t_{1/2}=\frac{2\cdot303}{k}\log_{10}2=\frac{0\cdot693}{k}$$

Half-life time is independent of the initial concentration. Radioactive decay is an example of first order kinetics.

Equation for a second-order reaction If both reactants have the same initial concentration, a, or only one reacting species is involved the integrated rate law is

$$t=\frac{1}{k}\cdot\frac{x}{a(a-x)}$$

Here k has units $dm^3\ mol^{-1}\ s^{-1}$.

4. Pressure Pressure can only influence a reaction involving gases and has the effect of altering concentration. Raising the pressure increases the rate.

5. Catalysis A catalyst is a substance which alters the rate of a chemical reaction without itself undergoing chemical change. Catalysts have a profound effect on rate. A **positive** catalyst speeds up a reaction, a **negative** one slows down a reaction. They cannot affect the yield of a reaction. **Homogeneous** catalysis is the term applied to reactions in which the catalyst is in the same phase as the reactants and **heterogeneous** catalysis refers to reactions in which the catalyst is in a different phase from the reactants.

Catalysis

Properties of catalysts Autocatalysis is the process whereby one of the products in a reaction catalyzes the reaction. It results in an increase in rate as the reaction proceeds. Normally only a trace of catalyst is sufficient to affect a reaction, although occasionally as in Friedel-Crafts reactions, greater amounts are required. A few catalysts, particularly platinum, palladium and other transition metals, catalyze a range of reactions. Others are more specific and sometimes different catalysts can affect the products formed by the same set of reactants. This appears to contradict the laws of thermodynamics but a reaction may be proceeding so slowly that it is not noticed beside a much faster reaction unless a catalyst is present (e.g. the catalytic oxidation of ammonia, see p. 148). Catalysts may be inhibited (poisoned) or improved (promoted) by other substances.

Observations on catalysis offer a clue to the mechanism. Many gas reactions are catalyzed by glass. Coating the surface of the glass reaction vessel with wax can stop some gas reactions. Filling the vessel with glass wool increases the rate. Metals which catalyze gas reactions, e.g. iron in the Haber process or platinum in the contact process work a great deal better if finely divided. Therefore it appears that for heterogeneous catalysis it is important for the catalyst to have a large surface area. Transition metals make excellent catalysts. Two general properties of transition metals are that they can form many oxidation states and form coordination compounds or complex ions. This suggests that transition metals can form intermediate compounds with the reactants on route to the products. Vacant *d* orbitals in transition metals may also be used by reactant molecules forming dative links with a heterogeneous catalyst surface.

Theories of catalysis

Intermediate compound formation In all homogeneous and some heterogeneous catalysis it is considered that the reaction proceeds via the formation of an intermediate compound between catalyst and reactant. This has the effect of lowering the activation energy barrier for the overall reaction. The lowering of activation energy is the same for both the forward and reverse reactions. Hence both forward and backward rates are affected by the same amount.

Surface action theory This theory was put forward to explain heterogeneous catalysis. It seems probable that these catalysts succeed by adsorption of one or both reactants onto their surface.

A surface reaction may be broken down into stages.

1. Diffusion of reactants to surface
2. Adsorption of reactants at surface
3. Chemical reaction
4. Desorption of products
5. Diffusion of products away from surface

An example of surface action catalysis is the platinum catalyzed hydrogen iodide reaction (fig. 28).

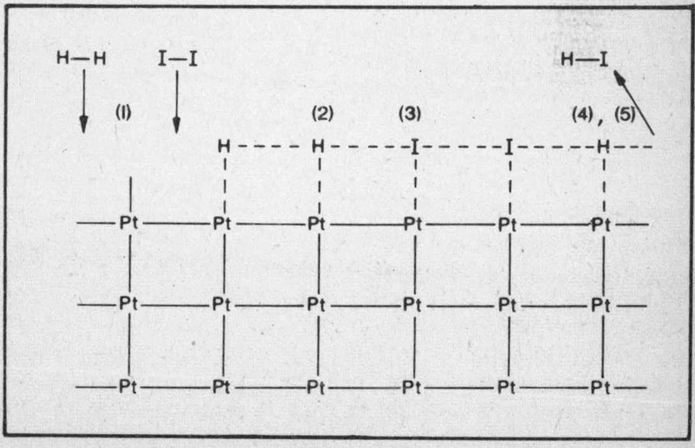

Figure 28

In this type of catalysis reaction rates are increased because the adsorption increases the concentration of reactants. It may also be that the chances of collision are increased by pinning one reactant to a site and that the orientation of the adsorped molecules makes the collision geometry more favourable. Furthermore, if the reactant molecules are chemisorped, bonded to the surface, (as shown in fig. 28) then bonds are weakened in the reactant molecules and the reaction rate is increased by intermediate compound formation.

Enzymes Biological systems are able to perform extremely specific chemical reactions in high yield. This is achieved by catalysts known as enzymes. These are complex proteins of fairly large size and are considered midway between hetero- and homogeneous catalysts. The proposed mechanism of the enzyme surface involves a complex three dimensional array containing atoms which are able to form weak Van der Waals' bonds with incoming molecules. Only a specific molecule can fit into a particular enzyme surface (enzymes can easily distinguish optical isomers) and does so in the exact conformation for subsequent reaction.

6. Light Many chemical reactions are influenced by light. Ether is stored in dark coloured bottles to help prevent the formation of poisonous phosgene. Hydrogen and chlorine react only very slowly in the dark but explode when exposed to bright light. These reactions are termed photochemical and proceed by the formation of free radicals. Free radicals are atoms which form by homolytic dissociation of bonds, each atom taking a bonding electron

$$X \div X \rightarrow X\cdot \quad \cdot X$$

free radicals

Free radical reactions help to explain the complicated rate expression governing hydrogen chloride and hydrogen bromide formation. The proposed mechanism of the hydrogen and bromine reaction is:

chain initiation	1. $Br_2 \rightarrow 2Br\cdot$
chain propagation	2. $Br\cdot + H_2 \rightarrow HBr + H\cdot$
	3. $H\cdot + Br_2 \rightarrow HBr + Br\cdot$
chain inhibition	4. $H\cdot + HBr \rightarrow H_2 + Br\cdot$
chain termination	5. $2Br\cdot \rightarrow Br_2$

Key terms

Enthalpy change, ΔH, is the heat change accompanying a chemical reaction carried out at constant pressure. A negative enthalpy change indicates that heat is evolved and the reaction is exothermic. A positive change indicates absorption of heat and an endothermic reaction.

Standard enthalpy of formation, ΔH_f^θ, is the enthalpy change when one mole of a compound is formed from its elements under standard conditions (1 atmosphere and 298 K).

Standard enthalpy of combustion, ΔH_c^θ, is the enthalpy change when one mole of a compound is burnt completely in oxygen corrected to standard conditions.

Hess's law The enthalpy change accompanying a chemical reaction is independent of the path taken. It depends only on the initial and final states.

Bond energy The energy evolved when a covalent bond is formed from the free atoms in the gaseous state.

Born-Haber cycle This connects the energy changes in forming an ionic crystal lattice. **Atomization energy** is the energy required to convert solids, liquids or gaseous elements into the free atoms. **Ionization energy** is the energy required to remove electrons to form the cation. **Electron affinity** is the energy change in forming the anion. **Lattice energy** is the energy given out when the ions combine to form a mole of solid compound.

Entropy, S, is the degree of randomness and is defined as the ratio of the heat put into a system divided by the Kelvin temperature

$$S = q/T \qquad \mathrm{J\,K^{-1}\,mol^{-1}}$$

Free energy change ΔG. The energy of a system which is available for doing work at constant pressure

$$\Delta G = \Delta H - T\Delta S$$

Reactions only occur if ΔG is negative.

Activation energy Energy barrier to a reaction. It is the minimum energy which reacting molecules must have before they can react.

Factors affecting reaction rate 1. State of reactants
2. Temperature Increased temperature increases the rate.
3. Concentration The rate of a reaction is proportional to the concentration of the reactants raised to a certain power.
4. Pressure only affects gas reactions. **5. Catalysts** alter the rate of a reaction without undergoing permanent chemical change. **6. Light** greatly affects free-radical reactions.

Chapter 4
Electrochemistry and Ionic Equilibria

Electrolysis

An **electrolyte** is a compound which when molten, or dissolved in a suitable solvent, will conduct electricity. The conduction of electricity is always accompanied by decomposition of the electrolyte. Figure 29 shows an electrolytic cell. Conventional current is taken as flowing in the direction of positive charge. Electron flow is in the opposite direction to current flow. The current flows into and out of the solution via **electrodes**. The positive electrode is termed the **anode** and the negative electrode is the **cathode**. When an electrolyte is in solution the ionic lattice is broken down and the ions are free to move under the influence of the electric field. Positive ions (**cations**) are attracted towards the negative cathode where they accept electrons and undergo reduction. The cathode is a reducing agent (electron donor). Negative ions (**anions**) are attracted towards the positive anode where they give up electrons undergoing oxidation. The anode is an oxi-

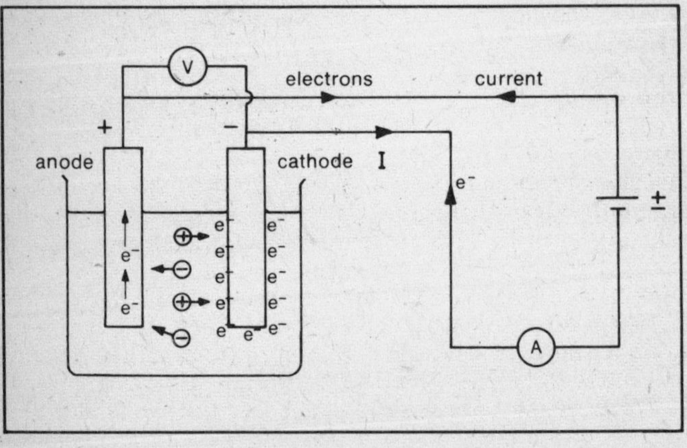

Figure 29

dizing agent (electron acceptor). Conduction of electricity is movement of charge, which in the connecting wire is achieved by electron movement and in solution by movement of the (charged) ions.

Faraday's laws These were discovered after quantitative work on electrolysis.

1. The mass of a product of electrolysis is proportional to the quantity of electricity passed.

Quantity of electricity Q = current in amps × time in seconds ($I \times t$) and is measured in coulombs.

$$\text{mass liberated} \propto I \times t$$

2. If the same quantity of electricity is passed through a series of electrolytes in separate cells then the masses of the different products are proportional to their chemical equivalents.

$$\text{mass liberated} \propto E \text{ where } E = \text{chemical equivalent}$$

$$E = \frac{\text{weight of 1 mole of ion}}{\text{unit of charge of ion}}$$

Combining the laws,

$$\textbf{mass liberated} \propto \boldsymbol{EIt}$$

It is found by experiment that the quantity of electricity required to liberate one mole of a univalent ion or half a mole of a divalent ion etc. is 96 500 coulombs. This is called a Faraday. It is in fact the charge carried by one mole of electrons.

One Faraday = charge on one electron × Avogadro's number

$$\text{One Faraday} = 1{\cdot}61 \times 10^{-19} \times 6{\cdot}03 \times 10^{23} = 96\,480\ \text{C}$$

$$\text{Therefore mass liberated} = \frac{EIt}{96\,500}\ \text{grams}$$

$$\boldsymbol{M = ZIt}$$

where Z is the electrochemical equivalent and is $E/96\,500$.

Example When a solution of a salt of a metal of relative atomic mass 112 was electrolyzed for 15 minutes with a current of 1·5 amp, 0·783 g of the metal was deposited. Calculate the valency of the metal in this salt.

$$Z = \frac{\text{equivalent weight}}{96\,500}$$

$$Z = \frac{112}{n \times 96\,500} \quad \text{where } n = \text{valency}$$

$$M = ZIt$$

$$0{\cdot}783 = 1{\cdot}5 \times \frac{112 \times 15 \times 60}{n \times 96\,500}$$

$$n = 2$$

Discharge of ions Before electrolysis can take place a minimum voltage must be applied. This voltage is the decomposition voltage and is equal to the sum of the redox potentials (see p. 96) for the two electrode processes. In practice the voltage required for electrolysis will often exceed this minimum. This excess is termed **over voltage** and may be due to the activation energy required for the combination of the atoms formed on the electrodes. Hydrogen often has high over voltages at metal cathodes. If a mixture of ions is electrolyzed then the least active ions are generally discharged first. Thus the least electropositive cations and the least electronegative anions discharge first. Factors such as concentration, high current density and nature of the electrodes may alter the order.

Conductivity This is the reciprocal of resistance

$$\text{Conductivity} = \frac{1}{\text{resistance}}$$

It is measured in Siemens (formerly ohm^{-1}). In electrochemistry **specific conductivity (*K*)** or conductance is used instead of resistivity. Specific conductivity is the current flowing through a solution placed between electrodes 1 cm apart and of 1 cm^2 cross-sectional area when a potential difference of 1 volt is applied. In other words it is the reciprocal of the resistance of a solution placed between such electrodes. The units are $\text{ohm}^{-1}\,\text{cm}^{-1}$.

To measure specific conductivity the test solution is placed in a conductivity cell and the resistance found by connecting to a Wheatstone bridge circuit (see fig. 30). The conductivity cell does not have accurately known dimensions (area and distance between electrodes) but has a cell constant which is a constant to convert the cell to the proper dimensions. The cell constant is determined by measuring the resistance of a solution of potassium chloride of known specific conductivity. In measuring the resistance alternating current is used, which prevents polarization or any other change in the solution occurring.

$$\text{Specific conductivity, } K = \frac{1}{\text{measured resistance}} \times \text{cell constant}$$

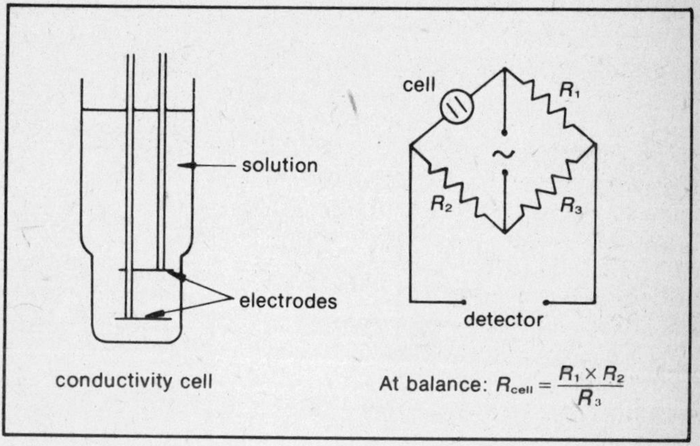

Figure 30

Molar (or equivalent) conductivity Specific conductivity increases as the concentration of the solution increases, reaching a maximum value and then eventually declining (provided the solution does not become saturated). The terms molar and equivalent conductivity were introduced so that different electrolytes could be compared directly, eliminating variations in conductance due to varying amounts of electrolyte. Molar (or equivalent) conductivity is the conductivity of a volume of solution containing one mole (or one equivalent) of the electrolyte when placed between electrodes 1 cm apart.

Molar conductivity, Λ is related to specific conductivity, K, by the expression:

$$\Lambda = KV \text{ ohm}^{-1} \text{ cm}^2$$

where V is the dilution, the volume in cm^3 which contains one mole (or one equivalent) and is the reciprocal of concentration $\times$ 1000.

Example The resistance of 0·02 molar potassium chloride contained in a cell with electrodes of area $1{\cdot}8\,\text{cm}^2$ placed 0·5 cm apart is 111 ohms. Find (i) the conductivity, (ii) the specific conductivity and (iii) the molar conductivity.

(i)
$$\text{conductivity} = \frac{1}{\text{resistance}}$$

$$\text{conductivity} = \frac{1}{111}$$

$$= 9{\cdot}009 \times 10^{-3}\,\Omega^{-1}$$

(ii) reducing the area of the electrodes to $1\,\text{cm}^2$ or increasing the distance between them to 1 cm would reduce the conductivity.

Hence specific conductivity

$$= \frac{\text{conductivity} \times \text{distance apart}}{\text{area}}$$

$$K = \frac{9{\cdot}009 \times 10^{-3} \times 0{\cdot}5}{1{\cdot}8}$$

$$K = 2{\cdot}5 \times 10^{-3}\,\Omega^{-1}\,\text{cm}^{-1}$$

(iii) concentration of solution $= 0{\cdot}02\,\text{mol dm}^{-3}$

$$\text{dilution} = \frac{1}{0{\cdot}02} = 50\,\text{dm}^3\,\text{mol}^{-1}$$

$$V\ \text{(volume containing one mol.)} = 50 \times 1000\,\text{cm}^3$$

$$\Lambda = KV$$

$$\Lambda = 2{\cdot}5 \times 10^{-3} \times 50 \times 1000\,\Omega^{-1}\,\text{cm}^2$$

$$= 125\,\Omega^{-1}\,\text{cm}^2$$

Note that for binary electrolytes (A^+B^-) molar and equivalent conductivity are the same.

Variation of molar conductivity with dilutions Molar conductivities measure the conductance of the same amount of compound (one mole) but in different volumes of solvent. Figure 31 shows how molar conductivities vary with dilution. Most electrolytes either follow the shape of the curve for potassium chloride or that for ethanoic acid.

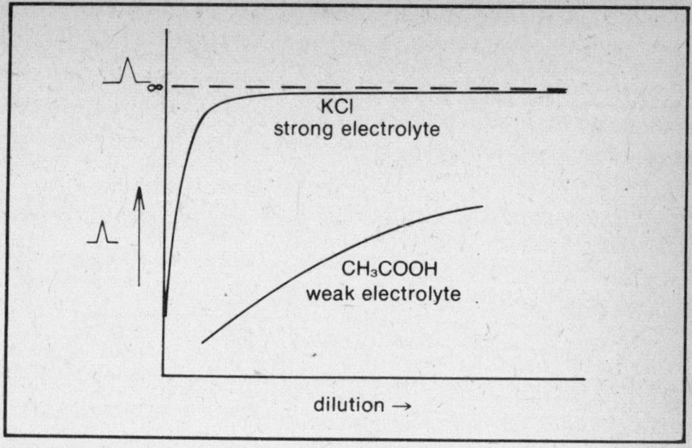

Figure 31. Graph of molar conductivities.

Both curves show an increase in molar conductivity with increasing dilution. The curve for potassium chloride quickly reaches a limiting value. This is termed the molar conductivity at infinite dilution, Λ_∞. The curve for ethanoic acid tends to a maximum only slowly. This behaviour is consistent with the degree of ionization increasing on dilution. Thus, strong electrolytes such as KCl rapidly become fully ionized whereas weak electrolytes like CH_3COOH are fully ionized only at infinite dilution (zero concentration). Strong electrolytes include the strong acids, alkalis and most salts; weak electrolytes include the organic acids and aqueous ammonia.

Degree of ionization, α, is the fraction of one mole which is ionized.

For complete ionization $\alpha = 1$. For an electrolyte AB:

$$AB \rightleftharpoons A^+ + B^- \tag{4.1}$$

amounts at equilibrium	$1-\alpha$	α	α	per mole of AB

Only the ionic species on the right hand side of equation 4.1 conduct so molar conductivity is proportional to α.
At infinite dilution ionization is complete, $\alpha = 1$.

$$\therefore \quad \frac{\Lambda}{\Lambda_\infty} = \alpha \tag{4.2}$$

The degree of ionization at any dilution can be found therefore by measuring the molar conductivity and determining Λ_∞ which for strong electrolytes can be found from graphs as in fig. 31. For weak electrolytes Λ_∞ cannot be obtained graphically, and is calculated using **Kohlrausch's law of independent ionic mobilities** which states that **the molar conductivity of an electrolyte at infinite dilution is the sum of the ionic conductivities of the ions produced by that electrolyte.**

Therefore $$_{AB}\Lambda_\infty = {}_{A^+}\Lambda_\infty + {}_{B^-}\Lambda_\infty$$

An example will illustrate the principle.
Find the molar conductivity of ethanoic acid at infinite dilution given that the molar conductivities at infinite dilution of sodium chloride, hydrochloric acid and sodium ethanoate (all strong electrolytes) are 113, 398, and 97 $\Omega^{-1}\,cm^2$ respectively.

1. $$_{NaCl}\Lambda_\infty = {}_{Na^+}\Lambda_\infty + {}_{Cl^-}\Lambda_\infty = 113\ \Omega^{-1}\,cm^2$$

2. $$_{HCl}\Lambda_\infty = {}_{H^+}\Lambda_\infty + {}_{Cl^-}\Lambda_\infty = 398\ \Omega^{-1}\,cm^2$$

3. $$_{CH_3COONa}\Lambda_\infty = {}_{Na^+}\Lambda_\infty + {}_{CH_3COO^-}\Lambda_\infty = 97\ \Omega^{-1}\,cm^2$$

$2+3-1$ gives:

$$_{CH_3COOH}\Lambda_\infty = {}_{H^+}\Lambda_\infty + {}_{CH_3COO^-}\Lambda_\infty = 382\ \Omega^{-1}\,cm^2$$

By selecting suitable strong electrolytes and measuring their molar conductivity at infinite dilution the value for all weak electrolytes can be found.

Values of the degree of ionization, α, found by the above method agree very closely with values of α found by measurements of colligative properties and the Van't Hoff factor (see p. 21). Another factor in support of the complete ionization of strong electrolytes is the constancy of the heat of neutralization of a strong acid and a strong base (see p. 52).

Ostwald's dilution law Ostwald applied the equilibrium law (law of mass action, see p. 43) to ionic dissociation.

For a 1:1 electrolyte AB, if α is the degree of ionization

$$AB \rightleftharpoons A^+ + B^-$$

amounts at equilibrium	$1-\alpha$	α	α per mole

concentrations at equilibrium $\frac{1-\alpha}{V}$ $\frac{\alpha}{V}$ $\frac{\alpha}{V}$ moles dm^{-3}

where V is the volume in dm^3 containing one mole.

Hence $$K = \frac{[A^+][B^-]}{[A]} \quad ([\ ] = \text{concentration of})$$

$$\therefore \quad K = \frac{\alpha^2}{(1-\alpha)V}$$

if α is very small $1-\alpha \rightarrow 1$

$$\therefore \quad K = \frac{\alpha^2}{V} \qquad (4.3)$$

$$\text{or} \quad \alpha = \sqrt{KV}$$

Equation 4.3 is known as Ostwald's dilution law, K being the dissociation constant.

Example Find the percentage dissociation and hydrogen ion concentration of 0·1 M ethanoic acid if the dissociation constant is $1{\cdot}8 \times 10^{-5}$ mol dm^{-3}.

$$\alpha = \sqrt{KV}$$

$$\alpha = \sqrt{1{\cdot}8 \times 10^{-5} \times 10}$$

$$\alpha = 1{\cdot}34 \times 10^{-2}$$

Therefore the acid is 1·34% dissociated.

$$[H^+] = \frac{\alpha}{V} = \frac{1{\cdot}34 \times 10^{-2}}{10}$$

$$= 1{\cdot}34 \times 10^{-3} \text{ mol dm}^{-3}$$

Bronsted-Lowry theory of acids and bases Much evidence points to the fact that the presence of hydrogen ions is responsible for acid characteristics. Acid character is only displayed when the acid is dissolved in a suitable solvent such as water. Hydrogen chloride when dissolved in benzene shows no acid character.

Bronsted and Lowry defined an acid as any substance which could act as a proton (H^+) donor, and a base as a species which could accept a proton.

A proton cannot exist on its own and is considered to accept a lone pair and become bonded coordinately to other species, for example water or ammonia. Such solvents are called protophilic, and must contain a lone pair. The strength of an acid will therefore depend on the base strength of the solvent.

$$\underset{\text{acid (1)}}{HA} + \underset{\text{base (2)}}{:S} \rightleftharpoons \underset{\text{acid (2)}}{H^+ \leftarrow :S} + \underset{\text{base (1)}}{A^-}$$

HA is the proton donor or acid version of species 1 and A^- its conjugate base. :S is the solvent, proton acceptor, species 2 and HS^+ the conjugate acid. Ethanoic acid is a strong acid in liquid ammonia, a weak acid in water and has no acidic properties in benzene. The ionizations of water and ammonia are equivalent

$$H_2O + H_2O \rightleftharpoons H_3O^+ + OH^-$$

$$NH_3 + NH_3 \rightleftharpoons NH_4^+ + NH_2^-$$

acid (1) base (2) acid (2) base (1)

Strength of acids and bases The relative strengths of weak acids and bases can be determined by comparing their dissociation constants.

$$HA \rightleftharpoons H^+ + A^-$$

Provided the acid is weak the concentration of water will be constant and need not be considered. Thus the acid dissociation constant, K_a, is given by the expression

$$K_a = \frac{[H^+][A^-]}{[HA]}$$

from Ostwald's dilution law

$$K_a = \frac{\alpha^2}{V}$$

where α is the degree of dissociation and V the dilution. Hence α is proportional to $\sqrt{K_a}$. Similarly base strength depends on K_b, the base dissociation constant.

Ionic product of water Water, when absolutely pure, is a very poor conductor of electricity. To obtain pure water it must be distilled many times in a vacuum. This so-called 'conductivity water' is used in making solutions for conductivity experiments. Neglecting the hydration of the protons the equilibrium may be represented as

$$H_2O \rightleftharpoons H^+ + OH^-$$

hence
$$K_c = \frac{[H^+][OH^-]}{[H_2O]}$$

The concentration of water may be taken as being constant since very few molecules ionize (about 1 in ten million)

$$\therefore \quad K_c[H_2O] = [H^+][OH^-] = K_w$$

K_w is termed the ionic product of water. It has a value of 10^{-14} mol^2 dm^{-6} at 25°C. Since there are equal numbers of hydrogen and hydroxide ions in pure water

$$[H^+] = [OH^-] = 10^{-7} \text{ mol dm}^{-3}$$

In acid solutions the concentration of hydrogen ions is increased at the expense of hydroxide ions and in basic solutions the reverse happens. To avoid using negative powers of ten pH value was introduced.

The pH value is defined as the negative logarithm to base ten of the hydrogen ion concentration

$$\text{pH} = -\log_{10}[H^+] = \log_{10}\frac{1}{[H^+]}$$

Neutral solutions have a pH value of 7 ($-\log_{10}(10^{-7})$).
Acid solutions have a pH value below 7 and basic solutions a pH value above 7.

Calculation of pH of strong acids and bases These are considered to be fully ionized (for concentrations below 1 M) and for acids and bases producing one hydrogen ion or one hydroxide ion per molecule the concentration of these ions is equal to that of the acid or base.

Example Find the pH of 0·1 M hydrochloric acid.

$$[H^+] = 0{\cdot}1 \text{ mol dm}^{-3}$$

$$\text{pH} = -\log_{10} 0{\cdot}1 = -(\bar{1}) = 1$$

Example Find the pH of 0·2 M sodium hydroxide.
For bases it is simpler to find pOH and subtract from 14.

$$[OH^-] = 0{\cdot}2 \text{ mol dm}^{-3}$$

$$\text{pOH} = -\log_{10} 0{\cdot}2 = -(\bar{1}{\cdot}3010) = -(-1 + 0{\cdot}3010) = 0{\cdot}7$$

$$\text{pH} = 14 - \text{pOH} = 13{\cdot}3$$

For dibasic acids, e.g. sulphuric acid, two hydrogen ions are produced per molecule of acid. Bases may also furnish more than one hydroxide ion, e.g. barium hydroxide.

Example Find the pH of 0·01 M sulphuric acid.

$$[H^+] = 2 \times 0{\cdot}01 \text{ mol dm}^{-3}$$

$$pH = -\log_{10}(2 \times 0{\cdot}01) = -(\bar{2}{\cdot}3010) = 1{\cdot}7$$

Bar numbers are negatives.

Calculation of pH for weak acids and bases For these Ostwald's dilution law is used. They are not fully ionized and the dissociation constant must be known.

For a weak monobasic acid:

$$HA \rightleftharpoons H^+ + A^-$$

equilibrium concentration $\quad \frac{1-\alpha}{V} \quad \frac{\alpha}{V} \quad \frac{\alpha}{V}$ mol dm^{-3}

But $\quad K_a = \frac{\alpha^2}{V}$

$$\therefore \quad \frac{K_a}{V} = \frac{\alpha^2}{V^2} \quad \text{but} \quad [H^+] = \frac{\alpha}{V}$$

$$\therefore \quad [H^+] = \sqrt{\frac{K_a}{V}} \quad \text{or} \quad \sqrt{K_a C} \quad \text{where } C \text{ is concentration}$$

$$pH = -\tfrac{1}{2}\log_{10} K_a - \tfrac{1}{2}\log_{10} C$$

$-\log_{10} K_a$ is written pK_a.

$$\therefore \quad pH = \tfrac{1}{2}pK_a - \tfrac{1}{2}\log_{10} C$$

similarly for a weak base (with one hydroxide group)

$$pH = 14 - pK_b + \tfrac{1}{2}\log_{10} C$$

Example Find the pH of a solution of 0·5 M ethanoic acid if $K_a = 1{\cdot}8 \times 10^{-5}$ mol dm^{-3}.

$$[H^+] = \sqrt{K_a C} = \sqrt{1{\cdot}8 \times 10^{-5} \times 0{\cdot}5}$$

$$[H^+] = \sqrt{9 \times 10^{-6}} = 3 \times 10^{-3} \text{ mol dm}^{-3}$$

$$pH = -\log_{10}(3 \times 10^{-3})$$

$$pH = 3 - 0{\cdot}477 = 2{\cdot}523$$

Example Find the pH of a solution of 0·01 M aqueous ammonia if $K_b = 1{\cdot}7 \times 10^{-5}$ mol dm^{-3}.

$$[OH^-] = \sqrt{K_b C}$$

$$= \sqrt{1{\cdot}7 \times 10^{-5} \times 10^{-2}}$$

$$[OH^-] = \sqrt{17} \times 10^{-4} = 4{\cdot}12 \times 10^{-4} \text{ mol dm}^{-3}$$

$$pOH = -\log_{10}(4{\cdot}12 \times 10^{-4})$$

$$pOH = 4 - 0{\cdot}62 = 3{\cdot}38$$

But $$pH = 14 - pOH$$

$$\therefore \quad pH = 14 - 3{\cdot}38 = 10{\cdot}62$$

Example Find the degree of dissociation of a 0·1 M solution of a weak acid if the pH is 4.

$$-\log_{10}[H^+] = 4 \qquad \therefore \quad [H^+] = 10^{-4} \text{ mol dm}^{-3}$$

$$[H^+] = \frac{\alpha}{V}$$

$$\therefore \quad \frac{\alpha}{V} = 10^{-4} \text{ mol dm}^{-3}$$

$$\therefore \quad \alpha = 10^{-4} \times 10 = 10^{-3} \quad \text{or} \quad 0{\cdot}1\%$$

Hydrolysis of salts Salts which are derived from a weak acid, or a weak base or both can be hydrolyzed in aqueous solution to give a solution which may not be neutral. Salts of a strong acid with a strong base are always neutral in aqueous solution.

Salt of strong base and weak acid, e.g. sodium ethanoate. The following equilibria are set up in water.

$$CH_3COONa \rightleftharpoons CH_3COO^- + Na^+$$

$$H_2O \rightleftharpoons H^+ + OH^-$$

$$\updownarrow \qquad \updownarrow$$

$$CH_3COOH \quad NaOH$$

Sodium ethanoate is fully ionized and the ethanoate ions produced compete with hydroxide ions for the hydrogen ions. This results in an excess of hydroxide ions, the hydrogen ions are removed as ethanoic acid (undissociated) and the solution will be alkaline.

Salt of strong acid and weak base, e.g. ammonium chloride

$$\begin{array}{lcl}
NH_4Cl \rightleftharpoons & NH_4^+ & + & Cl^- \\
 & + & & + \\
H_2O \rightleftharpoons & OH^- & + & H^+ \\
 & \updownarrow & & \updownarrow \\
 & NH_3\ (\text{aqueous}) & & HCl
\end{array}$$

The hydroxide ions are removed as aqueous ammonia leaving an excess of hydrogen ions. Hydrochloric acid is a strong acid and remains fully dissociated. The solution is acidic.

Salt of weak acid and weak base, e.g. ammonium ethanoate

$$\begin{array}{lcl}
CH_3COONH_4 \rightleftharpoons & CH_3COO^- & + & NH_4^+ \\
 & + & & + \\
H_2O \qquad \rightleftharpoons & H^+ & + & OH^- \\
 & \updownarrow & & \updownarrow \\
 & CH_3COOH & & NH_3\ (\text{aqueous})
\end{array}$$

For these salts the resulting pH depends on the relative strengths of the acid and base. If the acid is stronger the solution is acidic and if the base is stronger it is alkaline. Ammonium ethanoate is neutral.

Buffer solutions These are solutions containing a weak acid and the sodium or potassium salt of the weak acid (pH less than 7) or a weak base and a salt of the weak base (pH greater than 7). The purpose of buffers is to provide a solution of accurate pH which will not change even on the addition of small quantities of acid or base or on dilution. If a buffer is made up of a weak acid and its salt the following equilibria are set up.

$$HA \rightleftharpoons A^- + H^+$$

$$NaA \rightleftharpoons Na^+ + A^-$$

The presence of the large quantity of anions from the salt suppresses the ionization of the weak acid and controls the pH.

If hydrogen ions (acid) are added they can be removed by the large quantity of acid anions (A^-) to form the weak acid HA leaving the concentrations relatively unaffected. If hydroxide ions are added they will react with the hydrogen ions present to form water. More weak acid will then ionize to replace these hydrogen ions. Therefore the pH is controlled. The pH of a buffer may be calculated as follows:

$$\text{for the weak acid, } K_a = \frac{[H^+][A^-]}{[HA]}$$

$$\therefore \quad [H^+] = K_a \frac{[HA]}{[A^-]} = K_a \frac{[\text{acid}]}{[\text{salt}]}$$

since the concentration of unionized acid, HA, may be considered to be the total acid concentration as so little ionizes and the acid radical ion concentration, $[A^-]$ comes almost entirely from the added salt.

$$\text{pH} = -\log_{10}[H^+] = \log_{10} K_a - \log_{10}\frac{[\text{acid}]}{[\text{salt}]}$$

$$\text{pH} = \text{p}K_a + \log_{10}\frac{[\text{salt}]}{[\text{acid}]}$$

A buffer made up of a weak base controls pH in a similar manner, e.g. ammonium chloride dissolved in aqueous ammonia

$$NH_3(aq) \rightleftharpoons NH_4^+ + OH^-$$

$$NH_4Cl \rightleftharpoons NH_4^+ + Cl^-$$

In this case addition of hydroxide ions is balanced by reaction with ammonium ions and hydrogen ions are removed as water.

To calculate pH:

$$K_b = \frac{[B^+][OH^-]}{[BOH]}$$

$$[OH^-] = K_b \frac{[\text{base}]}{[\text{salt}]}$$

$$\text{pH} = 14 - \text{p}K_b + \log_{10}\frac{[\text{base}]}{[\text{salt}]}$$

Example What mass of sodium propanoate must be added to 1·00 dm^3 of propanoic acid of concentration 0·100 mol dm^{-3} to give a solution of pH 5·00.
The pK_a of propanoic acid is 4·87 at 25°C ($pK_a = -\log_{10} K_a$)

$$pH = pK_a + \log_{10}\frac{[\text{salt}]}{[\text{acid}]}$$

$$5 = 4.87 + \log_{10}\frac{[\text{salt}]}{(0.1)}$$

$$0{\cdot}13 = \log_{10}[\text{salt}] - \log_{10} 0{\cdot}1$$

$$0{\cdot}13 = \log_{10}[\text{salt}] + 1$$

$$[\text{salt}] = \text{antilog}\,(-0{\cdot}87)$$

$$\text{salt} = 0{\cdot}135 \text{ mol dm}^{-3}$$

M_r sodium propanoate (C_2H_5COONa)

$$= 3 \times 12 + 2 \times 16 + 5 \times 1 + 23 = 96$$

$$\text{mass of salt in 1 dm}^3 = 0{\cdot}135 \times 96 = 12{\cdot}96 \text{ g}$$

Indicators These are weak acids or weak bases which are highly coloured and lose or change their colour when they become ionized. Taking a weak acid as an example:

$$\underset{\text{colour A}}{HIn} \rightleftharpoons \underset{\text{colour B}}{H^+ + In^-}$$

When the indicator is placed in acid solution the high concentration of hydrogen ions forces the equilibrium to the left and colour A predominates. In base the hydrogen ions are removed as water and the equilibrium is forced to the right and colour B predominates. The intermediate colour occurs when [HIn] = $[In^-]$, applying the dilution law:

$$K_a = \frac{[H^+][In^-]}{[HIn]}$$

hence

$$[H^+] = K_a \frac{[HIn]}{[In^-]}$$

Therefore at the colour change $[H^+] = K_a$. Different indicators will therefore change colour at different pHs, e.g. phenolphthalein changes between pH 8·3 and 10, and methyl orange between pH 3·1 and 4·4.

Acid-base titrations The equivalence or end point in an acid-base titration is when equal amounts of acid and base are present. The pH at the end point, which will not necessarily be 7·0, depends on the nature of the salt formed, and determines the choice of indicator. Figure 32 shows the four possible titration curves for strong and weak acid and base systems. The curves can be obtained either by calculating the pH at various points or by taking readings with a pH meter whilst titrating. The graphs show pH change against cm^3 of added acid. It can be seen in fig. 32(i) that for strong acids and bases the pH changes from about 10 to 3 at the end point with the addition of about one drop of acid (0·05 cm^3), and both indicators will change colour. For the titration of a strong base against a weak acid fig. 32(ii) the rapid change at the end point is from pH 10 to pH 7 and only phenolphthalein will change colour. For a weak base with a strong acid fig. 32(iii) the pH change is from 7 to 3 and only methyl orange will change colour. The titration between a weak acid and a weak base fig. 32(iv), will not give rise to a rapid pH change at the end point, no indicator is suitable, and these titrations cannot be carried out.

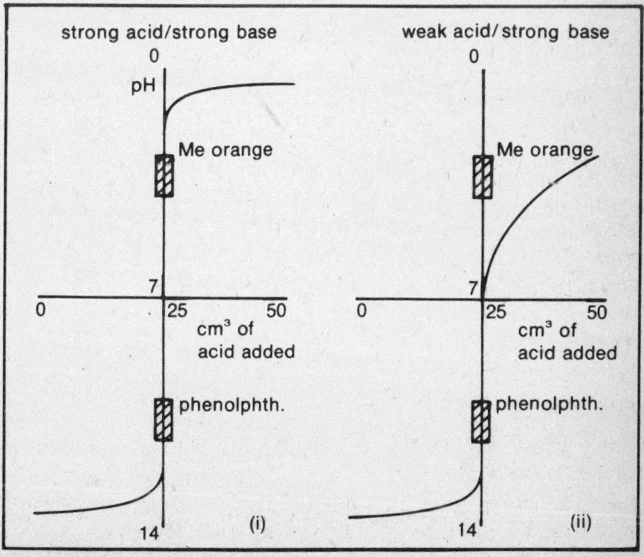

Figure 32a

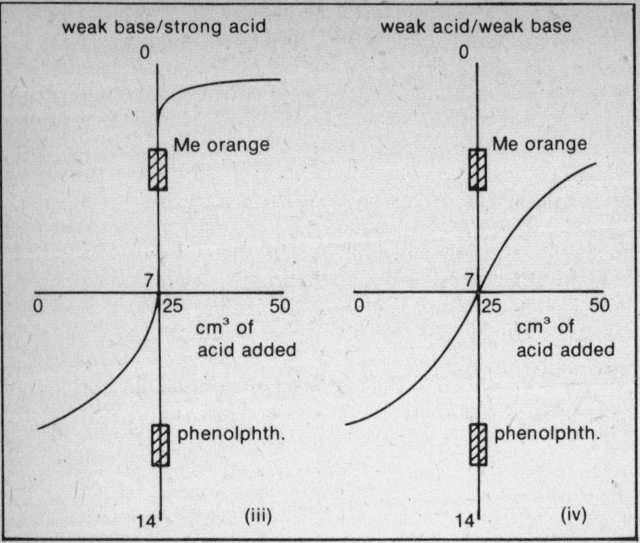

Figure 32b

Solubility product The equilibrium law can be applied to sparingly soluble electrolytes, e.g. AgCl is only very slightly soluble in water and the following equilibrium exists:

$$AgCl_{(s)} \rightleftharpoons Ag^+_{(aq)} + Cl^-_{(aq)}$$

undissolved dissolved

$$K_c = \frac{[Ag^+][Cl^-]}{[AgCl_{(s)}]}$$

Since the concentration of a solid is constant

$$K_c[AgCl_{(s)}] = K_{sp} = [Ag^+][Cl^-]$$

K_{sp} is termed the solubility product. It is the ionic product of the dissolved ions and will vary with temperature, similarly for calcium fluoride:

$$K_{sp} = [Ca^{2+}][F^-]^2$$

since two fluoride ions are produced on ionization. The principle may only be applied to sparingly soluble salts.

The conversion of solubility to solubility product
Solubilities are normally given in grams per dm^3. The solubility of silver chloride at 18°C is $1{\cdot}58 \times 10\ g\ dm^{-3}$.
For each mole of solid dissolved one mole of silver ions and one mole of chloride ions are produced.

Molecular mass of AgCl = 143·5

$$\text{Molarity} = \frac{1{\cdot}58 \times 10^{-3}}{143{\cdot}5} = [Ag^+] = [Cl^-] \text{ in mol dm}^{-3}$$

$$K_{sp}\,AgCl = [Ag^+][Cl^-] = \left(\frac{1{\cdot}58}{143{\cdot}5} \times 10^{-3}\right)^2 = 1{\cdot}2 \times 10^{-10}\ \text{mol}^2\ \text{dm}^{-6}$$

The conversion of solubility product to solubility
The solubility product of lead iodide (PbI_2) at 298 K is $1{\cdot}00 \times 10^{-9}\ mol^3\ dm^{-9}$.

$$\underset{\text{undissolved solid}}{PbI_2} \rightleftharpoons \underset{\text{dissolved ions}}{Pb^{2+} + 2I^-}$$

$$K_{sp} = [Pb^{2+}][I^-]^2 = 1{\cdot}000 \times 10^{-9}\ \text{mol}^3\ \text{dm}^{-9}$$

if x moles dissolve (i.e. ionize) $[Pb^{2+}] = x$ and $[I^-] = 2x$

$$x \times (2x)^2 = 1{\cdot}00 \times 10^{-9}$$

$$4x^3 = 1{\cdot}00 \times 10^{-9}$$

$$x = 0{\cdot}63 \times 10^{-3}\ \text{mol dm}^{-3}$$

$$\text{solubility} = 0{\cdot}63 \times 10^{-3} \times M_r PbI_2 = 0{\cdot}63 \times 10^{-3} \times 461$$
$$= 0{\cdot}29\ \text{g dm}^{-3}$$

Common ion effect Precipitation of an electrolyte will occur when the solubility product is exceeded. It can be exceeded by increasing the concentration of just one of the ions. For example adding chloride ion, as sodium chloride, to a saturated solution of silver chloride will induce precipitation because the increase in concentration of the chloride ion will cause the solubility product to be exceeded. This is referred to as the common ion effect. Adding silver ion in the form of silver nitrate will also cause precipitation.

Electrode potential If a metal is placed in a liquid, such as water, there is a tendency for ions to leave the metal and become hydrated in solution. The metal becomes negatively charged and eventually the ions are unable to move away from the metal and a **Helmholtz double layer** results. There will now be a potential difference between the negatively charged metal and the positive ions in solution. The amounts of ions leaving the metal is immeasurably small for most metals.

If two different metals are placed in a conducting solution an electric current will flow if the metals are connected by a wire. This current flows as a result of the difference in the potentials of the two metals in solution and the system is a **simple cell**. The Daniell cell is made from the two metals copper and zinc.

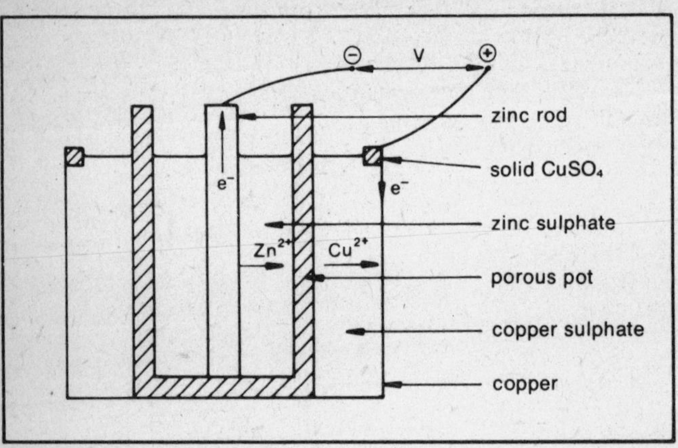

Figure 33. Daniell cell

The potential difference between the zinc and copper is found to be 1·1 volts and is independent of the manner in which the cell is made up. The porous pot allows charge to flow but prevents the solutions mixing.

At the zinc cathode:

Zn	$\rightarrow Zn^{2+}$	$+2e^-$
from zinc rid	into solution	flow in external circuit to copper

At the copper anode:

Cu^{2+}	$+2e^-$	$\rightarrow Cu$
in soln	from external circuit	deposited on copper container

These two equations represent the two half-cell reactions. The electrical energy is produced from chemical energy liberated during the oxidation of zinc and reduction of copper,

$$\text{overall } Cu^{2+} + Zn \rightarrow Cu + Zn^{2+}$$

It is not possible to measure the potential difference between a metal and its ions in solution without placing another electrode in the solution. This other metal would interfere with the system and affect the potential difference. As absolute potentials cannot be measured the metals are compared with the potential of a **standard hydrogen electrode**. This electrode, fig. 34, is made by passing hydrogen gas at one atmosphere pressure over the surface of platinum which is covered with platinum black and placed in a molar solution of hydrogen ions at 25°C. The platinum catalyzes the equilibrium between hydrogen gas and hydrogen ions. The potential of the hydrogen electrode is defined as 0·00 V.

Standard electrode potential The potential between metals

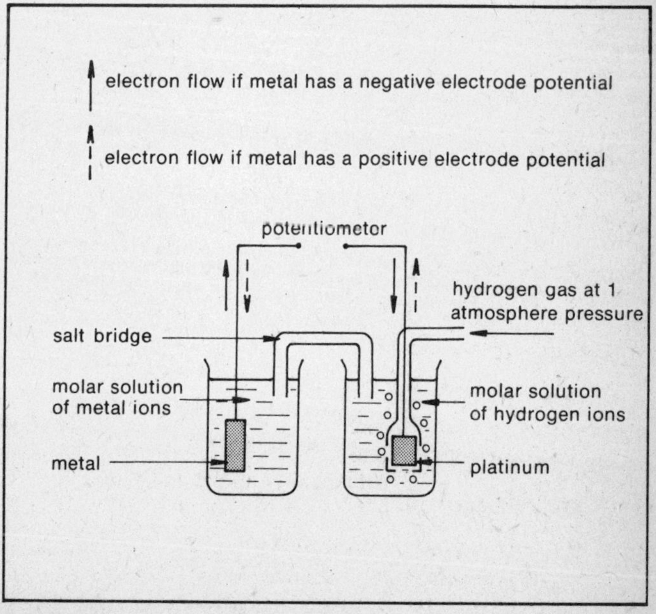

Figure 34

and their ions can now be compared by measuring their potentials with respect to hydrogen.

The standard electrode potential is defined as the potential difference between the half-cell made by placing a metal in a molar solution of its ions at 25°C and the standard hydrogen electrode.

The apparatus is shown in fig. 34. The salt bridge is made up of potassium chloride jelly and completes the circuit between the half-cells whilst preventing mixing of the solutions.

A list of standard electrode potentials, E^θ, often referred to as the **electrochemical series**, is given in the Data Book. This list places the metals in order of reactivity and shows the displacement order. Metals displace metals lying below them in the table from solutions of their salts.

Electrode potential and sign convention The negative pole of the cell formed between a metal/metal-ion half-cell and the hydrogen electrode is given a negative electrode potential. When the tendency of metal ions to leave the metal lattice and go into solution exceeds the tendency of metal ions from solution to deposit on the metal a negative charge is left on the metal. All metals above hydrogen in the electrochemical series have negative potentials. The systems are written down with the metal ion on the left hand side, e.g.

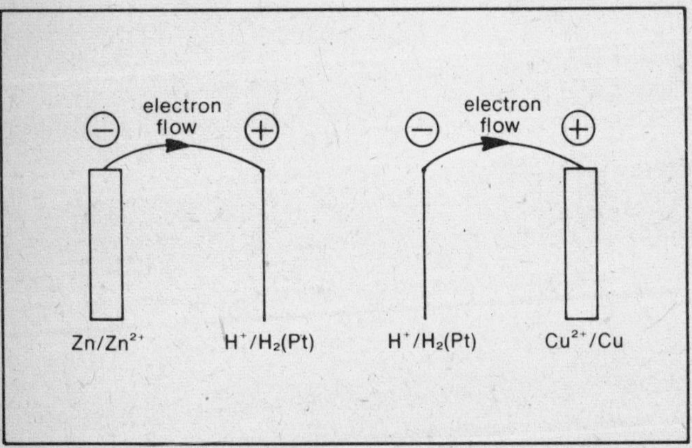

Figure 35

$$Zn^{2+} + 2e^- \rightarrow Zn \qquad E^\theta = -0{\cdot}76\ V$$
$$Cu^{2+} + 2e^- \rightarrow Cu \qquad E^\theta = +0{\cdot}34\ V$$

Copper ions show less tendency to enter solution than hydrogen ions and will not displace hydrogen from an acid. Figure 35 shows the electron flow for zinc and copper connected to a hydrogen half-cell.

The e.m.f. of a cell formed by joining two metal half-cells is found by subtracting the two electrode potentials. For the Daniell cell (zinc/copper);

Electron flow →

Zn/Zn^{2+} (molar) ‖ Cu^{2+}(molar)/Cu

-ve   salt bridge   + ve

The e.m.f. of the cell is the standard electrode potential of the right hand cell minus that of the left.

$$E = 0{\cdot}34 - (-0{\cdot}76) = 1{\cdot}1\ V$$

Enthalpy changes and electrode potential Electrode potentials are a measure of the energy changes which take place when a solid metal is converted to an ion in aqueous solution.

$$M_{(S)} \rightarrow M^{n+} + ne^-$$

This change must take place via three stages:

1. $M_{(S)} \rightarrow M_{(g)}$ sublimation energy

Energy is required to generate free metal atoms from the solid lattice.

2. $M_{(g)} \rightarrow M^{n+}_{(g)} + ne$ ionization potential

Energy is required to remove electrons from the gaseous atom.

3. $M^{n+}_{(g)} \xrightarrow{\text{water}} M^{n+}_{(aq)}$ hydration energy

Energy is liberated as the ions combine with water molecules.

In comparing the degree of metallic character, i.e. the tendency for an element to lose electrons (electropositivity), only

2 above need be considered. Since electrode potential is a measure of all three some anomalies arise. Lithium has an exceedingly small radius and has an extremely high hydration energy, consequently it has a more negative electrode potential than sodium and potassium. Since electropositivity should increase with atomic radius it would be expected that the larger potassium would have the largest electrode potential.

Redox potentials The process of metals losing electrons to form ions is one of oxidation. The electrode potential measures the relative willingness of metals to be oxidized or reduced. The table can be extended to include non-metals and any system involving oxidation and reduction. **Standard redox potentials** of non-metals may be measured in a similar manner to that used for metals. Non-metals are placed in solutions of their ions, and gases passed over platinum at one atmosphere pressure in a solution of their ions, and connected

Table 2

Standard redox potentials at 25°C

Half-cell reaction	*E^θ Volts*
$Li^+ + e^- \rightarrow Li$	−3·04
$Na^+ + e^- \rightarrow Na$	−2·71
$Al^{3+} + 3e^- \rightarrow Al$	−1·66
$Zn^{2+} + 2e^- \rightarrow Zn$	−0·76
$Fe^{2+} + 2e^- \rightarrow Fe$	−0·44
$H^+ + e^- \rightarrow \frac{1}{2}H_2$	0·00
$Cu^{2+} + e^- \rightarrow Cu^+$	+0·17
$Cu^{2+} + 2e^- \rightarrow Cu$	+0·34
$\frac{1}{2}I_2 + e^- \rightarrow I^-$	+0·54
$MnO_4^- + e^- \rightarrow MnO_4^{2-}$	+0·56
$Fe^{3+} + e^- \rightarrow Fe^{2+}$	+0·76
$Ag^+ + e^- \rightarrow Ag$	+0·80
$Cr_2O_7^{2-} + 14H^+ + 6e^- \rightarrow 2Cr^{3+} + 7H_2O$	+1·33
$\frac{1}{2}Cl_2 + e^- \rightarrow Cl^-$	+1·36
$MnO_4^- + 8H^+ + 5e^- \rightarrow Mn^{2+} + 4H_2O$	+1·52
$\frac{1}{2}S_2O_8^{4-} + 2e^- \rightarrow SO_4^{2-}$	+2·01
$\frac{1}{2}F_2 + e^- \rightarrow F^-$	+2·85

$$\text{oxidant} + ne^- \rightarrow \text{reductant}$$

to the hydrogen half-cell. For other redox systems a platinum electrode is placed in a solution containing both the oxidized and reduced form of a system, both molar at 25°C, and this half-cell is coupled to the standard hydrogen electrode. The platinum acts as a catalyst. The table above shows some standard redox potentials. The oxidized form is on the left and the reduced form on the right. The acidity of the solution may influence the redox potential, e.g. potassium manganate(VII) is a stronger oxidizing agent in acid than in base.

A substance on the right of the table is capable of reducing any substance on the left of the table that lies below it. For example, iodide ions will reduce iron(III) to iron(II).

$$2Fe^{3+} + 2I^- \rightarrow 2Fe^{2+} + I_2$$

A substance on the left of the table oxidizes any substance to the right and above it in the table. Fluorine oxidizes bromide.

$$F_2 + 2Br^- \rightarrow 2F^- + Br_2$$

Thus substances can be both oxidizing and reducing agents depending on the relative strengths of other species present. It can be shown that

$$\Delta G^\theta = -nFE^\theta$$

where ΔG^θ is the standard free energy change for the reaction, n is the number of electrons transferred, F is the faraday constant and E^θ is the standard redox potential for the reaction. For a reaction to be feasible ΔG^θ must be negative. Hence for a redox reaction to proceed E^θ must be positive.

Example given that

$$Cr^{3+} + e^- \rightarrow Cr^{2+} \qquad E_1^\theta = -0{\cdot}41\ \text{V} \qquad (1)$$

$$H_3PO_4 + 2H^+ + 2e^- \rightarrow H_3PO_3 + H_2O \qquad E_2^\theta = -0{\cdot}28\ \text{V} \qquad (2)$$

deduce whether Cr^{3+} can be reduced by phosphorous acid under standard conditions.

The electron gain and loss must be balanced so equation (1) must be multiplied by two. This does not effect the E^θ value as it is independent of amount. Hence

$$2Cr^{3+} + 2e^- \rightarrow 2Cr^{2+} \qquad E^\theta = -0{\cdot}41\ \text{V}$$

$$H_3PO_4 + 2H^+ + 2e^- \rightarrow H_3PO_3 + H_2O \qquad E^\theta = -0{\cdot}28\ \text{V}$$

Subtracting

$$2Cr^{3+} + H_3PO_3 + H_2O = 2Cr^{2+} + H_3PO_4 + 2H^+$$

$$E^\theta = E_1^\theta - E_2^\theta$$
$$= -0{\cdot}41 - (-0{\cdot}28) = -0{\cdot}13 \text{ V}$$

If E^θ is negative ΔG^θ for the reaction is positive and the reaction will not proceed from left to right.

Nernst equation Redox potentials vary with concentration and temperature. The relationship between E, redox potential, and E^θ, redox potential under standard conditions is given by the Nernst equation.

$$E = E^\theta + \frac{RT}{nF}\log_e \frac{[\text{oxidized form}]}{[\text{reduced form}]}$$

R is the gas constant, n is the number of electrons transferred, T is absolute temperature, and the square brackets refer to concentrations.

Key terms

Faraday's laws 1. Mass of a product of electrolysis is proportional to the quantity of electricity passed.
2. Mass of a product of electrolysis is proportional to its chemical equivalent.

$$\boldsymbol{M = IZt} \quad Z = \frac{\text{relative atomic mass}}{\text{valency} \times 96\,500}$$

Specific conductivity, K, is the reciprocal of the resistance of a solution placed between electrodes of 1 cm^2 area placed 1 cm apart.

Molar conductivity, Λ, is specific conductivity × dilution, V.

$$\Lambda = KV \quad V = \text{volume in cm}^3 \text{ containing one mole}$$

Molar conductivity increases with increasing dilution, rapidly reaching a maximum value, molar conductivity at infinite dilution, Λ_∞, for strong electrolytes. Λ_∞ for weak electrolytes may be found from Kohlrausch's law of independent ionic mobilities.

$$_{AB}\Lambda_\infty = {}_{A^+}\Lambda_\infty + {}_{B^-}\Lambda_\infty$$

Ostwald's dilution law

$$K = \frac{\alpha^2}{(1-\alpha)V} \sim \frac{\alpha^2}{V} \quad \text{or} \quad \alpha = \sqrt{KV}$$

where α = degree of ionization, V = dilution and K = dissociation constant.

Bronsted-Lowry An acid is a proton donor. A base is a proton acceptor.

Ionic product of water $K_w = [H^+][OH^-] = 10^{-14}$ at 25°C

pH is minus log to base 10 of the hydrogen ion concentration

$$pH = -\log_{10}[H^+]$$

Hydrolysis of salts The salt of a strong acid with a weak base is acidic in aqueous solution. The salt of a weak acid with a strong base is basic in aqueous solution.

Buffer solutions are made from weak acids and the sodium salt of the weak acid or from weak bases and a salt of the weak base. They control pH.

For acid salts: $pH = pK_a + \log_{10}\frac{[salt]}{[acid]}$

For basic salts: $pH = 14 - pK_b + \log_{10}\frac{[base]}{[salt]}$

where pK_a and pK_b are $-\log_{10} K_a$ and $-\log_{10} K_b$ respectively. K_a = acid dissociation constant, K_b = base dissociation constant.

Indicators are weak acids or bases which have a different colour ionized from unionized. The pH of the solution will affect their colour.

Solubility product, K_{sp}. For sparingly soluble electrolytes

e.g. $\underset{\text{undissolved}}{AB} \rightleftharpoons \underset{\text{dissolved}}{A^+ + B^-}$ $\quad K_{sp} = [A^+][B^-]$

Standard electrode potential, E^θ, is the potential difference between the half-cell made by placing a metal in a molar solution of its ions at 25°C and the standard hydrogen electrode. The standard hydrogen electrode is made by passing hydrogen gas at 1 atmosphere pressure over platinum metal placed in a molar solution of hydrogen ions at 25°C.

Standard redox potential, E^θ. For other redox systems a platinum electrode is placed in a solution containing an equimolar mixture of both the oxidized and reduced form of the system and is coupled to the hydrogen electrode.

Redox potential varies with concentration and temperature.

Nernst equation

$$E = E^\theta + \frac{RT}{nF}\log_e\frac{[\text{oxidized form}]}{[\text{reduced form}]}$$

E = redox potential, E^θ = standard redox potential, R = gas constant, n = number of electrons transferred, F = the faraday constant, and [oxidized form] and [reduced form] refer to the molar conc. of the oxidized and reduced forms of the species.

Chapter 5
Electronic Structure and Bonding; Radioactivity

Almost since the discovery of electricity it was realized that this phenomenon was related to chemical behaviour. Faraday, as early as 1833 had established the electrical nature of matter, and using Faraday's experimental laws of electrolysis, Stoney in 1871, suggested the existence of a unit of electricity which he termed the 'electron'. Crookes, in 1879, experimented on the effects of high potentials on gases under low pressure (0·01 to 0·001 mm of mercury) in discharge tubes and showed that streams of rays were produced at the cathode which caused the walls of the tube to fluoresce. He and others carried out further work on these rays and showed that they consisted of negatively charged particles. J. J. Thompson in 1897 determined the charge/mass ratio for the cathode rays obtained using a number of different gases. He discovered that this ratio was the same for all gases, thus indicating that electrons were fundamental particles of all matter. Millikan, in 1911, determined the absolute charge of the electron and from values of charge/mass ratio calculated the mass of the electron as 1/1837 of the mass of the hydrogen atom.

Goldstein (1886), in further experiments with cathode ray discharge tubes had shown that positive rays were also produced. Unlike electrons, determination of the charge/mass ratio and hence of the mass of the particles showed that for different gases the mass varied, the lightest being obtained from hydrogen. The masses of particles from other gases were multiples of that of hydrogen. Rutherford called the positive particles obtained from hydrogen protons. Helium produced particles which are now known to be α-particles. The mass of a proton is 1.0081 relative to $^{12}_{6}C$.

Radioactivity

Investigations by scientists in the early 1900s, particularly by the Curies, led to the discovery that elements, including uranium, radium and polonium, disintegrated spontaneously emitting radiation. Elements of this type are said to be radioactive. It was found that their rate of disintegration was dependent on the number and nature of the atoms but independent of external conditions (temperature, pressure, etc).

Rutherford investigated the penetrating power of the radiations from these radioactive substances by subjecting them to electric and magnetic fields, and as a result, deduced that there were 3 different types of radiation. These are now known as:

1. α-rays, which have proved to be fast moving helium nuclei (the deflection by a magnetic field indicated they were positively charged). They can ionize air, produce flashes on a fluorescent screen, but have limited penetrating power (1 to 2 cm in air, but will not pass through a thin metal foil).
2. β-rays, which have proved to be fast moving electrons (deflection by a magnetic field indicated these were negatively charged) with a range of 1 to 2 m in air and 1 to 2 mm in lead.
3. γ-rays, which are not deflected by a magnetic field, have proved to be short wave electromagnetic radiations, similar to X-rays. They are extremely penetrating, with a range of 15 to 20 cm in lead. They have the ability to eject high speed electrons from matter.

The diagram below indicates the effect of a magnetic field on the radiation from a radium source.

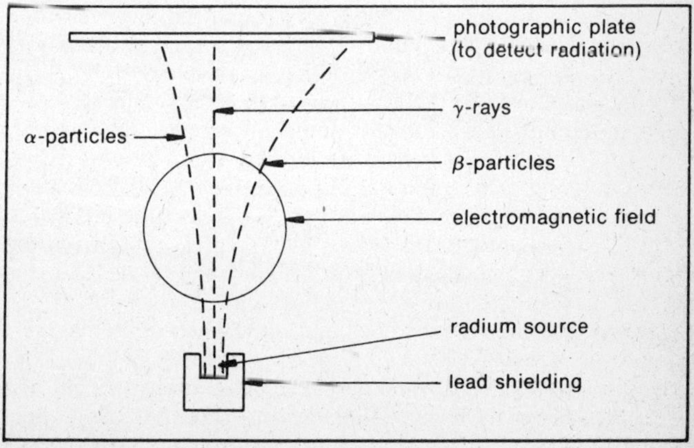

Figure 36

Rutherford and other workers made use of α-particles in their investigation of the structure of the atom. By bombarding a very thin sheet of gold foil (4×10^{-7} m thick) they found that about one in every 20 000 α-particles was deflected through large angles (90° or more), the rest either passing straight through, or being only slightly deflected. This suggested that there were particles in the gold which were of similar charge, and of at least the same size as the α-particles, but which were largely surrounded by space. Rutherford pictured the atom to be a small, dense, positively charged nucleus, surrounded by 'planetary' electrons. The diameter of the nucleus was estimated to be 10^{-15} m approx., about 10^{-5} of the diameter of the atom (diameter of an atom had been estimated as 10^{-10} m).

The mass of the α-particle had by now been established as four times that of the proton. At first it was thought that the nucleus of this particle contained 4 protons and 2 electrons, which would explain why the net charge was only double that of the proton. However, Chadwick in 1932, by bombarding beryllium with α-particles, established the existence of another fundamental particle with no charge (the penetrating radiation obtained was not deflected by electric or magnetic fields). These neutrons as they were called, were found to have a mass of 1·0090 relative to $^{12}_{6}C$.

Atomic number

Earlier, in 1895, Röntgen bombarded metal targets with fast moving electrons (cathode rays), and found that a penetrating radiation, X-rays, was emitted. These are electromagnetic waves, similar to γ-rays but with longer wavelength. Analysis of the spectra of these X-rays showed that they consisted of a series of sets of lines. The sets of lines were termed K, L, M, etc., and the individual lines were termed α, β, γ, etc. (the first of the K lines is K_α and so on). Moseley, in 1913, used a number of different metals as targets, and when he compared the wavelengths of corresponding lines (e.g. K_α etc.) from the spectra of different elements, he noted that the wavelengths decreased with increasing atomic weight. The graph of the square root of the frequency of the lines, when plotted against relative atomic mass gave an approximate straight line, but when plotted against atomic number, an accurate straight line was obtained. Moseley concluded from this that the atomic number Z was a fundamental property of the atom and was of more significance than relative atomic mass. He suggested that the atomic number, Z, was equal to the number of protons in the nucleus (and as the atom was neutral, to the number of electrons in the atom). He supposed that the difference between the atomic number, Z, and atomic weight, W, was due to there being $(W - Z)$ protons in the nucleus, associated with an equal number of electrons. Rutherford suggested that the difference in weight was due to an as yet undiscovered particle, with approximately the same mass as the proton, but with no charge. He called this the neutron, a particle which was later discovered by Chadwick.

We now have a picture of the atom, which can be summarized:
(a) the atom consists of a small, dense, positively charged nucleus, containing protons and neutrons;
(b) this nucleus is surrounded by a number of electrons equal to the number of protons in the nucleus;
(c) the atomic number, Z, of an atom is equal to the number of protons in the nucleus, and therefore also equal to the number of electrons surrounding the nucleus;
(d) the relative atomic mass of an atom = (number of protons × mass of one proton) + (number of neutrons × mass of one neutron) + (number of electrons × mass of one electron)

The masses of these particles, on the $^{12}_{6}C$ scale are

proton, 1·008 1; neutron, 1·009 0; electron, 0·000 55

This would suggest that, even for heavy atoms which contain large numbers of protons and neutrons, the relative atomic masses might be expected to be close to whole numbers, as the mass of the electrons is negligible. This is the case for most elements, but there are exceptions, notably chlorine (35·453) and copper (63·54). This presented a problem to scientists, until development of the mass spectrograph gave a more detailed knowledge of atomic mass. (Other particles have since been discovered, e.g. the positron (a positive electron), neutrino etc. It is thought that these particles may play a part in the stabilization of the nucleus. The proton, neutron and electron are however the particles of major importance in explaining chemical phenomena.)

Mass spectrograph

This has played a significant role in the determination of relative atomic masses. In the mass spectrograph, positive gaseous ions of elements to be investigated are produced in a discharge tube, and then passed through magnetic and electric fields, so that rays of one velocity emerge. These are then subjected to a magnetic field, which deflects them, the amount of deflection depending on the mass of the particles. The particles are then focused onto a photographic plate, or in some instruments onto an electrical recorder, which not only detects the different components, but also measures their abundance in the mixture. The apparatus is first calibrated with a compound containing $^{12}_{6}C$, within the expected range. Then, either the element or a compound containing the element is investigated, and by determining the masses of the atoms present, and their relative abundance, the relative atomic mass of the element may be determined. Thus oxygen gives three lines, indicating the existence of three types of oxygen atom, the masses being 15·995, 16·999 and 17·999, with relative abundance 99·76, 0·04 and 0·20 respectively. The relative atomic mass of oxygen is determined from this as follows:

$$\text{Relative Atomic Mass} = \frac{15{\cdot}995 \times 99{\cdot}76}{100} + \frac{16{\cdot}999 \times 0{\cdot}04}{100} + \frac{17{\cdot}999 \times 0{\cdot}20}{100}$$

$$= 15{\cdot}9566 + 0{\cdot}0068 + 0{\cdot}0360 = 15{\cdot}9994$$

The majority of elements contain more than one type of atom. As they are atoms of the same element, they have the same atomic number, and therefore the same number of protons and electrons, so the different masses are due to the nuclei of the different atoms containing different numbers of neutrons. Atoms of the same element which have the same atomic number, but different mass number are called isotopes. For the three isotopes of oxygen, which can be represented as $^{16}_{8}O$, $^{17}_{8}O$ and $^{18}_{8}O$, the constitution of the nuclei are:

	Atomic Number (Z)	Mass Number (A)	Number of Protons ($= Z$)	Number of Neutrons ($= A - Z$)
$^{16}_{8}O$	8	16	8	8
$^{17}_{8}O$	8	17	8	9
$^{18}_{8}O$	8	18	8	10

As the isotopes have the same number of electrons, they have the same chemical properties, and their separation can generally only be achieved by physical means.

In this example, the mass number has been quoted as the nearest whole number to the isotopic mass. If it is considered that the masses of the neutron and proton relative to $^{12}_{6}C$ are 1·0089 and 1·0076 respectively, it might be thought that the non integral nature of the isotopic masses could be explained in these terms. However, this is not the complete answer. Manganese has only one stable isotope, $^{55}_{25}Mn$, thus its nucleus contains 30 neutrons and 25 protons, and the atomic mass might therefore be expected to be $(30 \times 1{\cdot}0089) + (25 \times 1{\cdot}0076) = 55{\cdot}457$. The actual figure is less than this, 54·9380, and it is characteristic of this element. There are similar discrepancies for all atoms except that of $^{1}_{1}H$, in which the nucleus contains a single proton. The actual mass defect as it is termed cannot be predicted, but it can be related to the stability of the nucleus. Einstein's equation $E = mc^2$ can be used to convert the mass defect to a corresponding energy (E = energy derived from mass m, c represents the speed of light). This energy is considered as the binding energy of the

Table 3. Relative binding energies

Symbol	*Mass No.*	*Relative binding energy (MeV)*	*Symbol*	*Mass No.*	*Relative binding energy (MeV)*
H	1	0	Ca	40	8·5
He	4	7·0	Se	45	8·6
Li	7	5·6	Cr	52	8·7
Be	9	6·4	Mn	55	8·7
B	10	6·4	Fe	56	8·7
C	12	7 6	Ni	58	8·6
N	14	7·4	Cu	63	8·6
O	16	7·9	Zn	64	8·6
F	19	7·7	Br	79	8·6
Ne	20	8·0	Mo	98	8·5
Na	23	8·1	Sn	120	8·5
Mg	24	8·2	Xe	132	8·4
Al	27	8·3	Nd	146	8·2
Si	28	8·4	Pt	195	7·8
P	31	8·4	Au	197	7·8
S	32	8·5	Hg	200	7·9
Cl	35	8·5	Pb	208	7·8
Ar	40	8·5	Th	232	7·5
K	39	8·5	U	238	7·5

nucleus and it can be shown that the total binding energy of isotopes increases with increasing atomic number. A more important value for each isotope however is the relative binding energy, i.e. the total binding energy divided by the mass number. The value of this for some isotopes is given in the table below. MeV is the abbreviation for megaelectron volt.

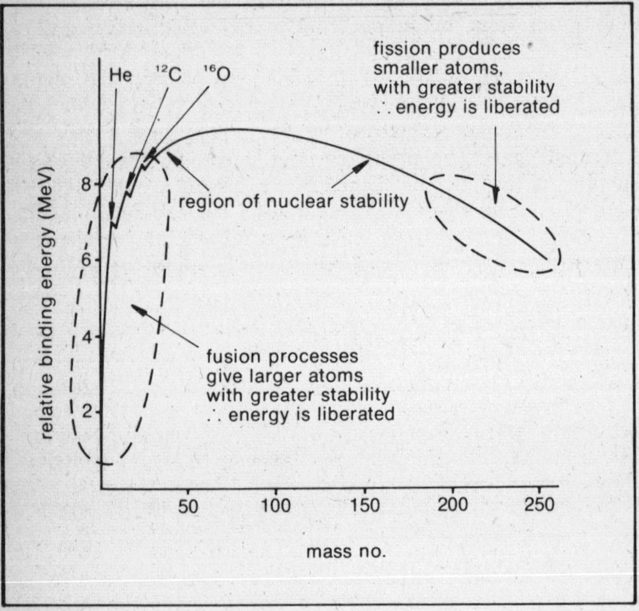

Figure 37

Radioactive disintegration

Many elements with atomic number 82 or more are spontaneously unstable, undergoing radioactive decay but all elements with atomic number over 34 have at least one isotope which also disintegrates, emitting radiation, until a stable isotope is formed (this may involve the formation of several other unstable intermediate elements). Part of the $^{238}_{92}U$ disintegration series may be represented as in figure 38.

Note

(i) the loss of an α-particle by a nucleus results in the decrease of mass number by 4 units and of atomic number by 2 units;

(ii) the loss of a β-particle results in no change of mass number, but an increase by 1 unit in the atomic number;

(iii) the half life ($t_{1/2}$) is the time during which half of the atoms of a particular isotope originally present disintegrate. This is independent of the original mass and is exponential in nature.

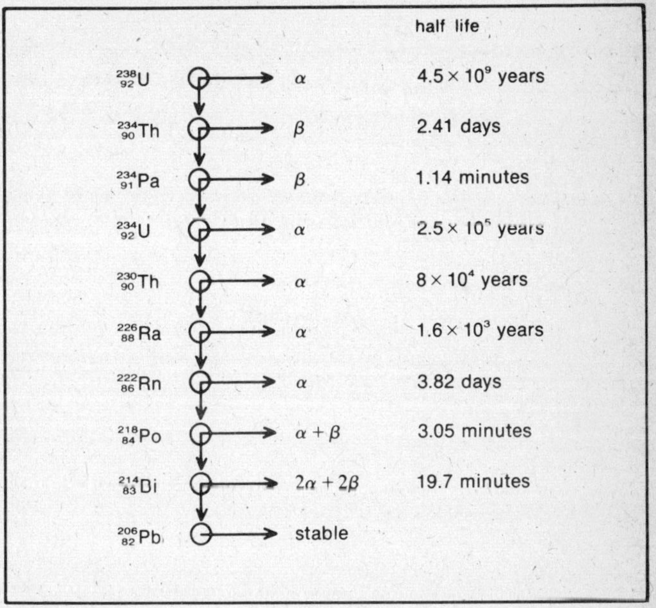

Figure 38

The half lives of various radioactive isotopes of the same element differ greatly. The half life of an isotope can be considered as a measure of the stability (or instability) of its nucleus. Knowledge of the half lives of some isotopes (e.g. $^{14}_{6}C$) may be used to determine the age of specimens.

Artificial nuclear reactions

Rutherford, in 1919, carried out the first experiments involving 'artificial' nuclear reactions (transmutations), in which he bombarded nitrogen atoms with α-particles from a radioactive source. He established that the reaction involved could be represented:

$$^{14}_{7}N + ^{4}_{2}He \rightarrow ^{17}_{8}O + ^{1}_{1}H$$

Note that in this, and in other similar processes:
(i) the sum of the mass numbers of the 'reactants' = the sum of the mass numbers of the 'products';
(ii) the sum of the atomic numbers of the 'reactants' = the sum of the atomic numbers of the 'products'.

Other transmutations can be brought about by using different particles such as the proton $^{1}_{1}H$, deuteron $^{2}_{1}H$ (or $^{2}_{1}D$), γ-rays and neutrons $^{1}_{0}n$, e.g.

α-particles:

$^{9}_{4}Be + ^{4}_{2}He \rightarrow ^{12}_{6}C + ^{1}_{0}n$ (this can be called an α : n reaction as an α-particle is used and a neutron is produced)

$^{27}_{13}Al + ^{4}_{2}He \rightarrow ^{1}_{0}n + ^{30}_{15}P \rightarrow ^{31}_{14}Si + {}_{+1}^{0}e$
(positron)

$^{30}_{15}P$ which is radioactive, is the first example of a radioactive substance being produced by an artificial method.

deuterons:

$$^{12}_{6}C + ^{2}_{1}D \rightarrow ^{13}_{7}N + ^{1}_{0}n \quad \text{(D:n reaction)}$$

$$^{16}_{8}O + ^{2}_{1}D \rightarrow ^{14}_{7}N + ^{4}_{2}He \quad (\text{D}:\alpha \text{ reaction})$$

protons:

$$^{14}_{7}N + ^{1}_{1}H \rightarrow ^{15}_{8}O + \gamma \quad (\text{p}:\gamma \text{ reaction})$$

$$^{9}_{4}Be + ^{1}_{1}H \rightarrow ^{6}_{3}Li + ^{4}_{2}He \quad (\text{p}:\alpha)$$

$$^{8}_{4}Be + ^{2}_{1}D \quad (\text{p}:\text{D})$$

$$^{10}_{5}B + \gamma \quad (\text{p}:\gamma)$$

γ-rays:

$$^{9}_{4}Be + \gamma \rightarrow ^{8}_{4}Be + ^{1}_{0}n \quad (\gamma:\text{n})$$

neutrons:
these reactions are used to produce radioactive isotopes of importance in various fields, as indicated below:

(i) $^{23}_{11}Na + ^{1}_{0}n \rightarrow ^{24}_{11}Na + \gamma$

$^{24}_{11}Na$ is used as a 'tracer' element to follow blood flow, e.g. in the diagnosis of thrombosis.

(ii) $$^{31}_{15}P + ^{1}_{0}n \rightarrow ^{32}_{15}P + \gamma$$

$^{32}_{15}P$ may be used in the relief of some forms of leukaemia, as it destroys excess white corpuscles, and in biology to follow phosphorus assimilation by plants.

(iii) $$^{131}_{52}Te + ^{1}_{0}n \rightarrow ^{132}_{53}I + ^{0}_{-1}e$$

$^{132}_{53}I$ is used in the treatment of thyroid conditions, e.g. goitre, cancer.

(iv) $$^{59}_{27}Co + ^{1}_{0}n \rightarrow ^{60}_{27}Co + \gamma$$

the radioactive cobalt produced is used in the treatment of cancers, being of greater penetrating power than radium.

(v) $$^{14}_{7}N + ^{1}_{0}n \rightarrow ^{14}_{6}C + ^{1}_{1}H$$

$^{14}_{6}C$ produced by this method is widely used in establishing metabolic pathways, e.g. in tissue respiration and in photosynthesis. The $^{14}_{6}C$ present in all carbonaceous material has arisen as a result of bombardment of the atmospheric carbon dioxide by cosmic rays (neutrons).

Synthesis of new elements

Until relatively recently the heaviest element known was uranium, ($Z = 92$). However, methods involving bombardment of heavy atoms with suitable 'ammunition' has led to the synthesis of atoms with higher atomic numbers, e.g.

$$^{238}_{92}U + ^{1}_{0}n \rightarrow ^{239}_{92}U \rightarrow ^{0}_{-1}e + ^{239}_{93}Np \rightarrow ^{239}_{94}Pu + 2\,^{0}_{-1}e$$

$$^{239}_{94}Pu + ^{4}_{2}He \rightarrow ^{242}_{96}Cm + ^{1}_{0}n$$

$$^{242}_{96}Cm + ^{4}_{2}He \rightarrow ^{244}_{98}Cf + 2^{1}_{0}n$$

although even heavier bombarding particles may be used:

$$^{246}_{96}Cm + ^{12}_{6}C \rightarrow ^{254}_{102}No + 4^{1}_{0}n$$

$$^{250}_{98}Cf + ^{11}_{5}B \rightarrow ^{257}_{103}Lw + 4^{1}_{0}n$$

Mass defect

If the mass of a helium atom is compared to the sum of the masses of its constituent particles the results show a small but significant difference:

Helium nucleus = 2 protons + 2 neutrons

Mass of 2 protons + 2 neutrons $= 2 \times 1{\cdot}0081 + 2 \times 1{\cdot}009$ a.m.u.
$= 4{\cdot}0342$ a.m.u. (atomic mass units)

Mass of helium atom $= 4{\cdot}0026$ a.m.u.

Helium atom = helium nucleus + 2 electrons

Mass of helium nucleus = mass of helium atom
− 2e (mass of electron)
$= 4{\cdot}0026 - 2 \times 0{\cdot}00055$ a.m.u.
$= 4{\cdot}0015$ a.m.u.

The difference between these values is the mass defect – in the case of the helium nucleus the mass defect $= 4{\cdot}0342 - 4{\cdot}0015$
$= 0{\cdot}0327$ a.m.u.

This mass can be related to an amount of energy by using Einstein's relationship

$$E = mc^2$$

where E = energy in ergs
m = mass in grams
c = velocity of light in cm s^{-1}

$$1 \text{ a.m.u.} = \frac{1}{N} = \frac{1}{6{\cdot}023 \times 10^{23}} \text{ g} = 1{\cdot}66 \times 10^{-24} \text{ g}$$

for loss of 1 a.m.u.

$$E = 1{\cdot}66 \times 10^{-24} \times (3 \times 10^{10})^2$$
$$= 1{\cdot}49 \times 10^{-3} \text{ ergs}$$

The energy is conventionally quoted in terms of the unit of electron volts ($1 \text{ eV} \simeq 1{\cdot}6 \times 10^{-19}$ J).

In electron volts, for 1 a.m.u. loss

$E = 931$ MeV (megaelectron volt, i.e. 1000000 eV)

In the formation of the helium nucleus, the energy produced is

$$0{\cdot}0327 \times 931 \text{ MeV} = 30{\cdot}44 \text{ MeV}$$

Binding energy per nucleon (no. of particles in the nucleus, i.e. no. of protons + no. of neutrons)

$$= \frac{30{\cdot}44}{4} = 7{\cdot}61 \text{ MeV}$$

By reference to the curve in fig. 37 the possibility exists of using differences in binding energy as a means of producing large amounts of energy. This may be achieved either by splitting large, unstable atoms with low relative binding energy into two or more smaller, more stable atoms with higher relative binding energy or by fusing small atoms to give large atoms. Both of these processes have indeed been used, the first by fission of $^{235}_{92}U$, and the second by fusion of $^{1}_{1}H$ and $^{2}_{1}H$. The energy released by the former has been harnessed for peaceful uses, but the latter still has not been controlled for use on a commercial scale.

Fission of uranium

The basic process which can initiate the fission of uranium involves the use of one only of the three natural uranium isotopes, namely $^{235}_{92}U$, which only occurs to the extent of about 0·72%. This isotope has to be concentrated (e.g. by a large scale fractional diffusion process of the hexafluorides $^{235}_{92}UF$ and $^{238}_{92}UF$). The enriched uranium may then be used in the fission process which may be represented

$$^{235}_{92}U + ^{1}_{0}n \rightarrow ^{140}_{56}Ba + ^{93}_{36}Kr + 2{\cdot}5\,^{1}_{0}n$$

Thus, bombardment of $^{235}_{92}U$ by 1 neutron produces approximately $2\frac{1}{2}$ neutrons per fission, and the loss in mass corresponds to the release of approximately 200 MeV mol^{-1}. With small amounts of $^{235}_{92}U$, the neutrons emitted mostly escape, but once the 'critical mass' of a few kilograms is exceeded the process becomes self propagating, and the chain reaction, involving the neutrons released initiating further fission reactions, releases a large amount of energy very rapidly. The basis of the atomic bomb is to fire one sub-critical mass of the isotope at another, the total mass formed being critical. The peaceful use of this, and other fission processes, e.g. of $^{239}_{94}Pu$ (which can be obtained from $^{238}_{92}U$) is to moderate the reaction (i.e. slow it down) in an atomic reactor by use of carbon rods and/or 'heavy water' to absorb excess neutrons and so prevent the reaction becoming too rapid. The heat produced is removed from the reactor by use of suitable coolants which is then used in a heat exchange system to produce steam, and hence electricity using turbo-alternators.

Fusion of hydrogen

The basic processes involve, e.g.

(i) $4\,^{1}_{1}H \rightarrow ^{4}_{2}He + 2\,^{0}_{+1}e$

(ii) $2\,^{2}_{1}D \rightarrow ^{4}_{2}He + \gamma$

(iii) $^{2}_{1}D + ^{3}_{1}H \rightarrow ^{4}_{2}He + ^{1}_{0}n$

By means of a calculation similar to that for the calculation of the mass defect for helium, it can be shown that for the production of 1 mole of helium by reaction (ii) above 26·9 MeV are produced and, mass for mass, the relative amounts of energy produced by fission of uranium:fusion of deuterium are 0·85 MeV:6·72 MeV, i.e. the latter process releases considerably more energy for equal masses used.

Electronic structure of the atom

The negative electrons occupying the space around the positively charged nucleus might be expected to lose energy and collapse into the nucleus. They do not, however, do this which can be explained by the electrons having sufficient energy to counteract this effect. Planck, in 1900, suggested that energy is quantized (energy changes only occur in small, definite amounts or quanta). Bohr in 1913 used this quantum theory to construct a model of the atom consisting of a positively charged nucleus with the electrons in specific orbits associated with a particular energy level. If an electron was transferred from one orbit to a higher one, a particular number of quanta was absorbed and when the electron returned to its original orbit the energy was released, giving rise to the spectral lines observed in the emission spectra of elements. In Bohr's theory successive orbits were capable of accomodating 2, 8, 18 and 32 electrons. In view of the further examination of spectra the modern theory of atomic structure has been developed, particularly as electrons show some properties not characteristic of particulate substances. One result is that, at a particular instant, the position of an electron cannot be precisely located but only the region (volume) where it is most likely to be determined. These regions are referred to as orbitals (fig. 39).

Each electron in an atom has its energy defined by four quantum numbers. The principal quantum number defines the main energy level the electron occupies. This is given the symbol, n. The azimuthal (angular) quantum number, symbol l, governs the shape of the orbital. This can have values $l = 0, 1$ up to $(n - l)$. When $l = 0$ the electrons are called s electrons, when $l = 1$ they are p electrons, when $l = 2$ d electrons and when $l = 3$ they are f electrons. The third quantum number is the magnetic quantum number, symbol m, and for each value of l, m has values $l, (l-1), \ldots, 0, -1, \ldots, -l$. Finally, the spin quantum number, symbol s, can have values of either $+\frac{1}{2}$ or $-\frac{1}{2}$

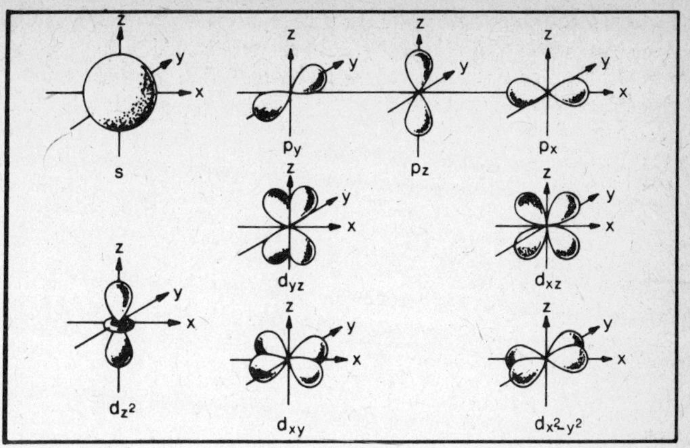

Figure 39

for each value of *m*. Using these quantum numbers it is possible to determine the number of electrons each main energy level can accomodate (see below).

n	*l*	*Electron type*	*m*	*s*	*No. of electrons*
1	0	*s*	0	$\pm\frac{1}{2}$	2
2	0	*s*	0	$\pm\frac{1}{2}$	2 } 8
	1	*p*	1, 0, -1	$\pm\frac{1}{2}$	6
3	0	*s*	0	$\pm\frac{1}{2}$	2
	1	*p*	1, 0, -1	$\pm\frac{1}{2}$	6 } 18
	2	*d*	2, 1, 0, -1, -2	$\pm\frac{1}{2}$	10
4	0	*s*	0	$\pm\frac{1}{2}$	2
	1	*p*	1, 0, -1	$\pm\frac{1}{2}$	6 } 32
	2	*d*	2, 1, 0, -1, -2	$\pm\frac{1}{2}$	10
	3	*f*	3, 2, 1, 0, -1, -2, -3	$\pm\frac{1}{2}$	14

In filling the available orbitals, electrons will enter the orbital with the lowest total energy content (*f* electrons have more quanta (energy) than *d*, *d* more than *p* and *p* more than *s* electrons for the same value of *n*). The order of filling is:

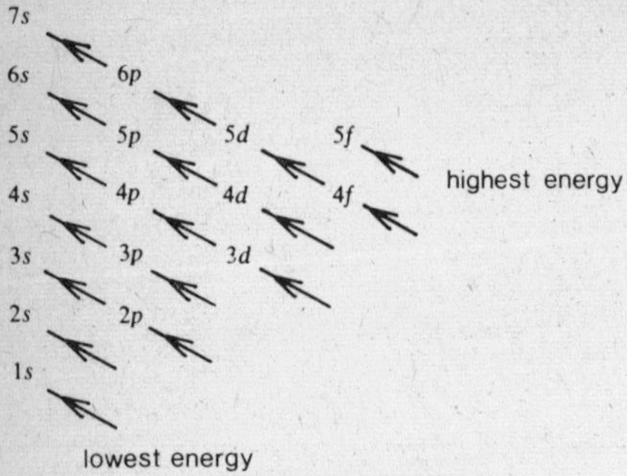

This selective filling of orbitals explains the framework of the Periodic Table. Besides filling the lowest possible energy level, electrons will fill all available orbitals with the same value of *l* before electron spins are paired (**Hund's rule**). The electron configurations of some elements are given below.

Li	$1s^2 2s^1$
Be	$1s^2 2s^2$
B	$1s^2 2s^2 2p^1$
C	$1s^2 2s^2 2p^2$
N	$1s^2 2s^2 2p^3$
O	$1s^2 2s^2 2p^4$

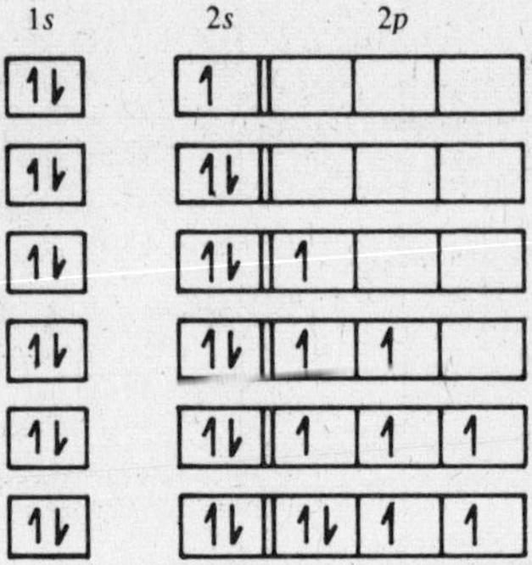

Ca	$Ne3s^2 3p^6 4s^2$
Sc	$Ne3s^2 3p^6 3d^1 4s^2$
Cr	$Ne3s^2 3p^6 3d^5 4s^1$
Mn	$Ne3s^2 3p^6 3d^5 4s^2$

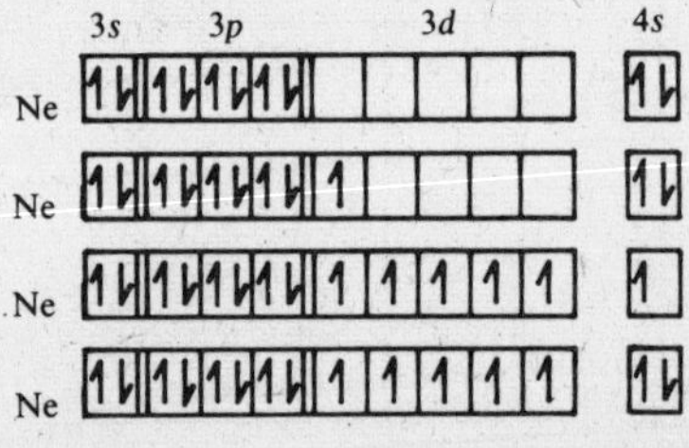

Other evidence for the electronic structures of elements and the relative stabilities of the sub energy levels are first ionization energies, (fig. 40) and successive ionization energies of elements (fig. 41). The former shows peaks at the noble gases and also minor peaks at beryllium and nitrogen indicating the increased stability of a filled sub shell and a half-filled sub shell. The latter gives evidence of the electron configuration of the element, there being significant increases when the next electron is lost from an orbital with a lower value of *n*.

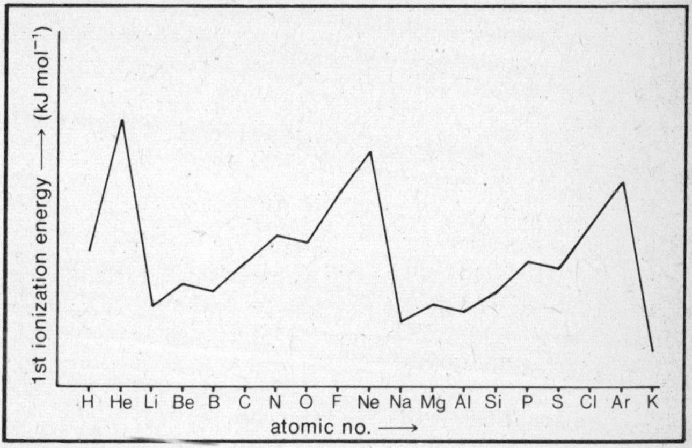

Figure 40

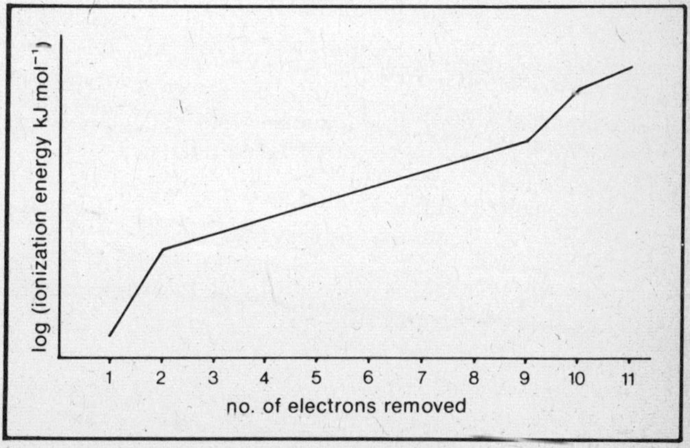

Figure 41

Bonding

The chemical behaviour of an atom is determined to a large extent by the number and arrangement of the electrons in the outer orbitals of that atom. These electrons in the outer orbital, which are involved in chemical combination, may be termed valency electrons. The electronic theory of valency recognizes the stability of the noble (or inert) gases, indicated by their chemical inertness (they are not completely inert but, compared to other elements they are exceedingly unreactive). If the outer electron shells of all of these elements are examined, it will be seen that they all have the arrangement ns^2np^6.

He	$\underline{1s^2}$
Ne	$\underline{1s^22s^22p^6}$
Ar	$1s^22s^22p^6\underline{3s^23p^6}$
Kr	$1s^22s^22p^63s^23p^63d^{10}\underline{4s^24p^6}$
Xe	$1s^22s^22p^63s^23p^63d^{10}4s^24p^64d^{10}\underline{5s^25p^6}$

Only helium has two electrons in its outer shell, as there is no $1p$ energy level. The theory of valency supposes that, in the formation of compounds, atoms attempt to achieve the nearest noble gas configuration (they do not always manage to do this).

Atoms can attain this noble 'gas configuration' by
1. loss of electrons, if the atom has only a few electrons more than the nearest inert gas (maximum of 3 electrons) or gain of electrons (again a maximum of 3) to increase the number to the ns^2np^6 configuration;
2. sharing of electrons with other atoms.

First, a simplified treatment of the main types of bond is given, which is then followed by a more detailed treatment.

Ionic (electrovalent) bond

The formation of a compound by loss of electrons (by a metal atom or atoms) with a corresponding gain of electrons (by an atom or atoms of a non-metal) results in the formation of charged particles, known as ions, e.g.

Atom/ion	$Na \rightarrow$	$Na^+ + e^-$
Electronic structure	$1s^22s^22p^63s^1$	$1s^22s^22p^6$
No. of protons	11	11
No. of protons in excess	0	1
Relative charge	0	+1

This only takes place, in chemical combination, when a suitable acceptor atom is available to accept the electron(s) lost by the sodium atom(s), e.g.

Atom/ion	$Cl + e^- \rightarrow Cl^-$	
Electronic structure	$1s^2 2s^2 2p^6 3s^2 3p^5$	$1s^2 2s^2 2p^6 3s^2 3p^6$
No. of protons	17	17
No. of electrons in excess	0	1
Relative charge	0	−1

In the example given, for every sodium atom losing one electron, one chlorine atom gains an electron and the compound formed, sodium chloride, can be represented as Na^+Cl^-. Other examples are:

Magnesium oxide, $Mg^{2+}O^{2-}$

$$\begin{array}{cccc} Mg & \rightarrow \quad Mg^{2+} & + & 2c^- \\ 1s^2 2s^2 2p^6 3s^2 & 1s^2 2s^2 2p^6 & & \end{array}$$

$$\begin{array}{cc} O + 2e^- \rightarrow O^{2-} & \\ 1s^2 2s^2 2p^4 & 1s^2 2s^2 2p^6 \end{array}$$

Calcium chloride, $Ca^{2+}(Cl^-)_2$

$$\begin{array}{cccc} Ca & \rightarrow \quad Ca^{2+} & + & 2e^- \\ 1s^2 2s^2 2p^6 3s^2 3p^6 4s^2 & 1s^2 2s^2 2p^6 3s^2 3p^6 & & \end{array}$$

Cl as for Na^+Cl^- except that as one chlorine atom only gains one electron, two chlorine atoms are needed to accept the two electrons lost by each calcium atom, i.e.

$$\begin{array}{cc} 2Cl \quad + 2e^- \rightarrow & 2Cl^- \\ 2(1s^2 2s^2 2p^6 3s^2 3p^5) & 2(1s^2 2s^2 2p^6 3s^2 3p^6) \end{array}$$

It should be remembered that formation of ionic compounds is favoured by
(i) low ionization potential for the metal
(ii) high electron affinity of the non-metal
(iii) high lattice energy of the resultant compound.

With regard to (i) the ionization potential for elements with a single electron is less than for elements with two electrons, and the further removed the electron is from the nucleus the more readily it is lost.

With regard to (ii), the electron affinities of elements with 7 electrons (i.e. the ns^2np^5 configuration) are negative, i.e. heat is given out when the gaseous ions are formed from the gaseous atoms of the element, but for elements with fewer electrons in the valency shell, the formation of gaseous ions from gaseous atoms of the element is an endothermic process, e.g.

$$O_{(g)} + e^- \rightarrow O^- \qquad \Delta H_{ea} = -142 \text{ kJ mol}^{-1}$$

Although the process as indicated is exothermic, the formation of the O^{2-} ion requires considerable absorption of energy to overcome the repulsion between the negatively charged O^- ion and the similarly charged electron, so that the overall energy change for the process is given below:

$$O_{(g)} + 2e^- \rightarrow O^{2-} \qquad \Delta H_{ea} = +844 \text{ kJ mol}^{-1}$$

It is factor (iii), i.e. the lattice energy, which explains why ions with multiple charges can form ionic compounds readily (lattice energy of magnesium oxide is -3918 kJ mol^{-1}).

General properties of ionic compounds

As single ions of metals are never associated with single ions of a non metal, separate units of ionic compounds do not exist and it is therefore wrong to talk about a molecule of an ionic compound. The formula only indicates the combining ratio of the elements concerned, the solid crystal being made up of large numbers of oppositely charged ions, arranged in set positions relative to each other (fig. 42). Each ion is surrounded by a fixed number of oppositely charged ions, so that

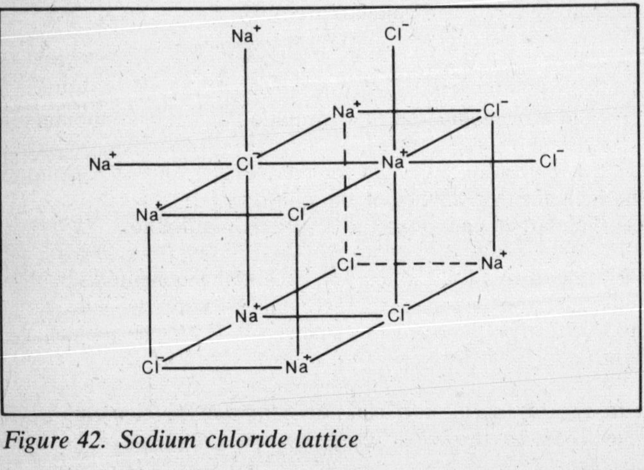

Figure 42. Sodium chloride lattice

the strong electrostatic forces between the ions act in all directions through the crystal. As energy is required to counteract these electrostatic forces, ionic compounds have high melting and boiling points. When molten (fused) or when dissolved in water they can conduct electricity and, unlike metals which also conduct electricity, ionic compounds are decomposed by the passage of a current (i.e. they are electrolytes). This behaviour on the passage of a current can be explained in terms of the free movement of ions which is only possible when the crystal lattice structure is broken down by melting or by dissolving in water.

Ionic substances are soluble in water and other similar polar liquids because of the electrostatic attraction between the ions and the polar molecules of the solvent. This results in an energy release (solvation energy) which generally counters, wholly or in part, the high lattice energy of the ionic compounds. Insoluble ionic compounds (e.g. the sulphates, phosphates and fluorides of Ca, Sr and Ba) have very high lattice energies, and insufficient energy is available from the solvation of ions to counteract these high lattice energies for such substances to be soluble. Because there is no attraction between the ions of ionic compounds and the molecules of non-polar liquids such as benzene, carbon tetrachloride etc. ionic compounds are generally insoluble in such solvents.

The chemical properties of ionic compounds are the properties of its constituent ions. Thus all chlorides will give characteristic reactions of the chloride ion (e.g. reactions with conc. sulphuric acid, $AgNO_3$ solution etc.), the recognition of this fact being the basis of qualitative analysis of inorganic salts.

Covalent bond

This type of bond involves the sharing of electrons between the two atoms joined by the bond, each atom generally contributing one electron to the formation of the bond. Sufficient numbers of bonds are also generally formed to complete the ns^2np^6 configuration of an inert gas. The formation of these bonds may be represented using a 'dot and cross' diagram, where the valency electrons only are illustrated, e.g. the hydrogen molecule, H_2 is represented as:

$H\overset{\times}{\circ}H$ (this can be represented as H–H where the line between atoms indicates the sharing of two electrons, one from each atom) and the chlorine molecule, Cl_2 is represented as:

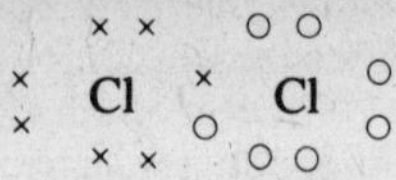

(or Cl—Cl)

Molecules of compounds can be similarly represented:

Hydrogen chloride

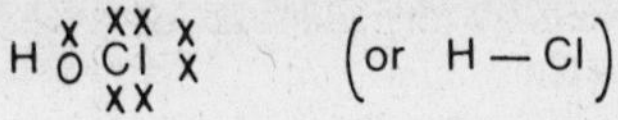

Water

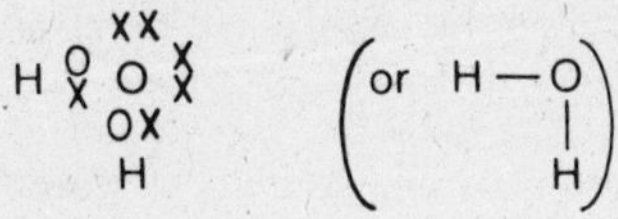

Ammonia

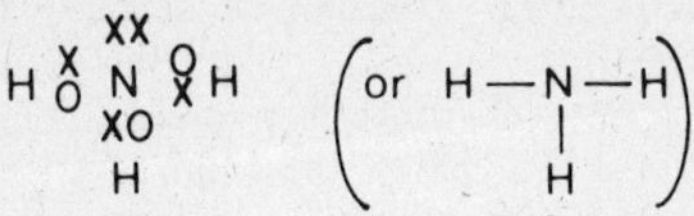

Methane

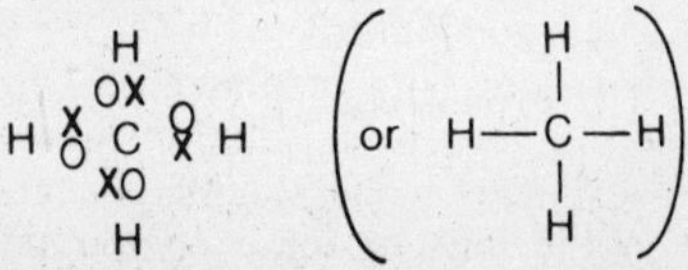

In the above each atom has attained the ns^2np^6 configuration of the inert gas nearest to it. However, it should be emphasized again that this configuration is not essential to covalent bond formation. Thus boron forms compounds such as boron trifluoride

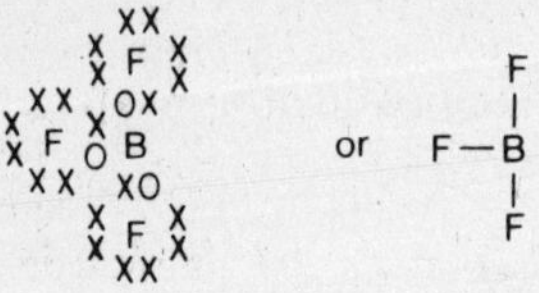

and sulphur can form SF_6

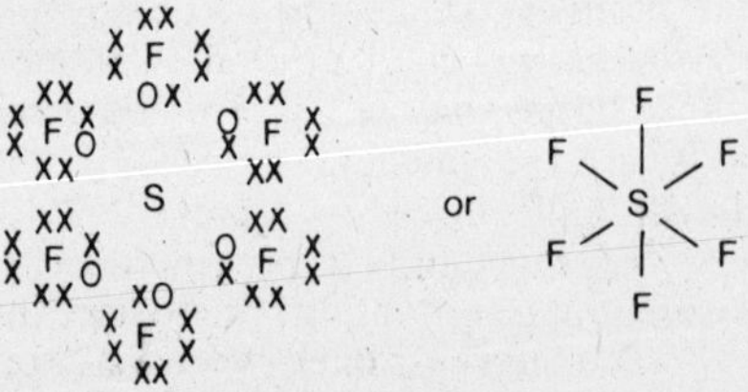

General properties of covalent compounds

As, ideally, the electrons in the bond are shared equally between the atoms linked by the bond, the resultant particles formed are not electrically charged. As a result, separate molecules of covalent compounds exist, and there is no attraction between these. Covalent compounds may therefore be expected to be volatile liquids or gases or low melting solids (held together by weak forces, known as Van der Waals forces). They are non-electrolytes, insoluble in water and other polar liquids, soluble in benzene and other non-polar liquids.

Special cases, where covalent bonds are formed by one of the atoms donating both electrons are also met. This special case may be called a **coordinate or dative covalent bond**. Examples include:

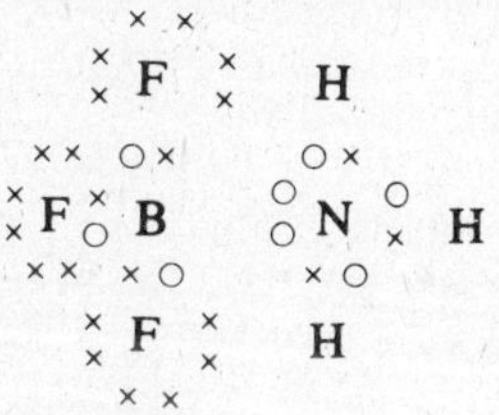

which may be represented as

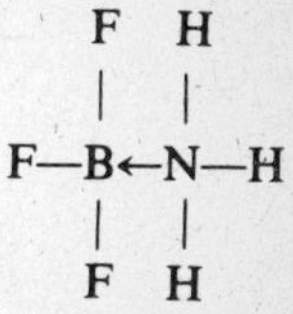

or as

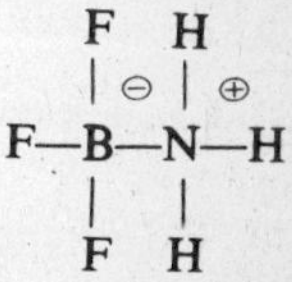

The dative covalent bond is represented either by use of an arrow, from the donor atom to the acceptor, or by means of a line, conventionally used to represent a covalent bond but with inclusion of charges, ⊕ for the donor atom, ⊖ for the acceptor atom. The formation of the ammonium and the hydroxonium ions are also explained by this type of bonding.

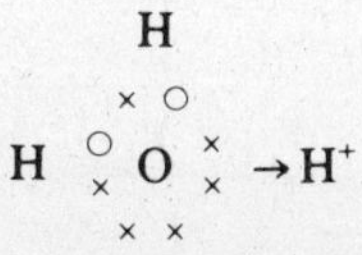

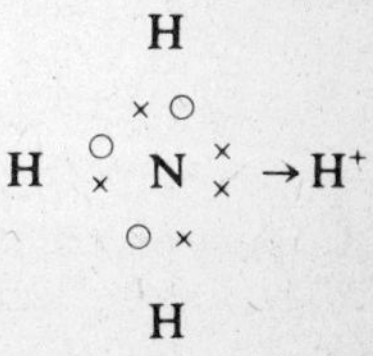

More detailed treatment

The treatment above does not give any indication as to the expected shape of molecules, nor does it explain how, for instance, carbon has a valency of 4, or why the measured heat of formation of benzene is not the theoretical value but is considerably different from this value, or why some compounds which would appear to be ionic, exhibit some characteristics of covalent compounds and vice versa. The achievement of the stable outer octet (i.e. the ns^2np^6 configuration) has been mentioned as a guide to the expected valencies of elements, but the unreliability of this is indicated by the existence of such compounds as BF_3, PCl_5 etc. The formation of bonds involves the pairing of electrons and the modern theory of valency accepts that this involves pairing of electron spins. This theory also supposes that the relevant number of unpaired electrons are present in the atom concerned. Refering to the electronic structure of carbon, it will be seen that, as represented there are only two unpaired electrons

C (ground state) $1s^2 2s^2 2p^2$

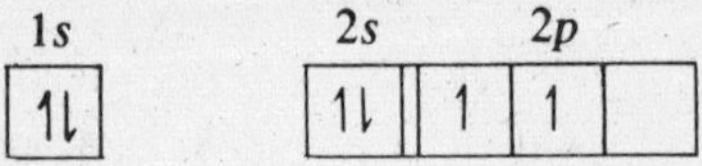

However, if the electrons in the $2s$ orbital are unpaired, one being promoted to the vacant $2p$ orbital, the resultant structure has four unpaired electrons

C (e.g. in CH_4)

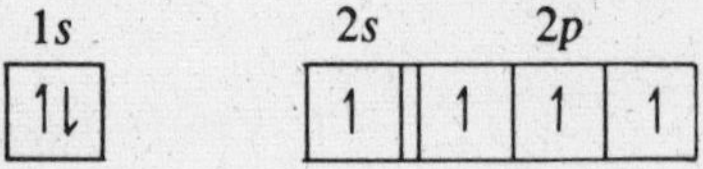

Similar promotion of electrons is only possible between orbitals with the same principal quantum number (i.e. promotion is not possible between, e.g. the 2nd and 3rd main energy levels, as the energy required is too great, and cannot be supplied by the bond energy for the extra bond so formed).

Nitrogen, the next element to carbon can only have a valency of three, as in the ground state the structure is

N $1s^2 2s^2 2p^3$

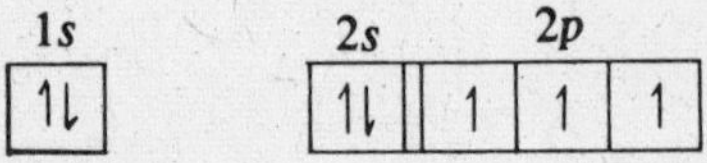

An electron cannot therefore be promoted from the $2s$ orbital as in carbon, because there is no orbital available to which it can be promoted. Phosphorus, $1s^2 2s^2 2p^6 3s^2 3p^3$, has a similar number of electrons to nitrogen in its outer orbital, but unlike nitrogen, there is a $3d$ orbital available to which one of the paired s electrons can be promoted

P (ground state)

1s	2s	2p			3s	3p			3d				
↑↓	↑↓	↑↓	↑↓	↑↓	↑↓	↑	↑	↑					

P (e.g. in PCl_5)

1s	2s	2p			3s	3p			3d				
↑↓	↑↓	↑↓	↑↓	↑↓	↑	↑	↑	↑	↑				

This, therefore, suggests that the valency of an element depends on the number of unpaired electrons in the outer orbital and also on the number of vacant orbitals to which paired electrons with the same principal quantum number may be promoted. A final example is iodine, $1s^2 2s^2 2p^6 3s^2 3p^6 3d^{10} 4s^2 4p^6 4d^{10} 5s^2 5p^5$

	5s	5p			5d				
I (ground state)	↑↓	↑↓	↑↓	↑					
I (+3)	↑↓	↑↓	↑	↑	↑				
I (+5)	↑↓	↑	↑	↑	↑	↑			
I (+7)	↑	↑	↑	↑	↑	↑	↑		

Thus, iodine can have valencies (oxidation states) of −1, +1, +3, +5 and +7, e.g. in KI, ICl, IF_3, KIO_3 and IF_7 respectively.

Further evidence for the fact that a stable ns^2np^6 configuration is attained, is the existence of a compound H_2^+, in which two protons are held together by a single electron, so that pairing of electron spins is not possible either. A simplified quantum mechanical approach (an advanced study of the structure of atoms and the motion of electrons round the nucleus) helps to provide the answer. These studies establish that a number of molecular orbitals is available to the single electron, just as various atomic orbitals are available to electrons around the nucleus of an uncombined atom. The various molecular orbitals each have distinct energy levels, the one with the lowest energy level being such that the electron is most likely to be found between the two nuclei (the electron is attracted by both nuclei and its potential energy is thus less than it would be when in the 1*s* orbital around a single uncombined nucleus). This system, of two protons and one electron (i.e. H_2^+) is more stable than when the protons are separated (i.e. as H + H) by 2·78 eV. The energetically favourable molecular orbital is termed a **bonding orbital**.

A second electron added to this system can also occupy this bonding orbital (the spins of the electrons are paired), and although the electrons repel each other, they render the hydrogen molecule, H_2, more stable than two uncombined hydrogen atoms by 4·72 eV, indicating the greater stability of the hydrogen molecule (with paired electrons) compared to H_2^+. This helps to establish that electron pair bonds are usually to be expected, one electron bonds being rare exceptions.

As the electron spins are paired in the hydrogen molecule, any additional electrons (e.g. in forming H_2^-) cannot occupy the thermodynamically favourable bonding orbital, but, according to **Pauli's exclusion principle**, must occupy the next available orbital, in which it is most likely to be found outside the two nuclei, and not between them. For this to happen, the electron needs to possess more energy than if it were in a 1*s* orbital around a single uncombined nucleus. This is thermodynamically unfavourable, and this unfavourable molecular orbital is known as an **antibonding orbital**.

All covalent bonds are rigid and directional, and the observed shapes of covalent molecules can be explained by an extension of this molecular orbital theory. A complete explanation is beyond the scope of this course, but the simple idea, that bonds are formed by overlapping of the atomic orbitals of the valency electrons is not the complete answer, as otherwise the bond angle of the H–N bonds in ammonia might be expected to be 90°, rather than the observed 106° 45′, and the bonds in carbon compounds, e.g. methane, CH_4, might also be expected to differ in direction to the observed 109° 28′. This is explained by the hybridization of the bonds. In both of the examples given above, instead of there being electron pairs in the 2*s*, $2p_x$, $2p_y$, $2p_z$ orbitals, with different energy levels, four hybrid sp^3 orbitals are formed, all being of equal energy content, and being distributed symmetrically around the central nucleus. This structure involves a tetrahedral arrangement (fig. 43).

In ammonia, NH_3, one of the sp^3 hybrid orbitals is occupied by an unshared pair of electrons. The repulsion between this lone pair of electrons and the other sp^3 hybrid orbitals (each containing an electron from a hydrogen atom) results in a slight closing of the theoretical tetrahedral bond angle to the observed 106° 45′.

The repulsion by lone pair electrons is seen even more in the water molecule, in which the bond angle is reduced to 104° 27′.

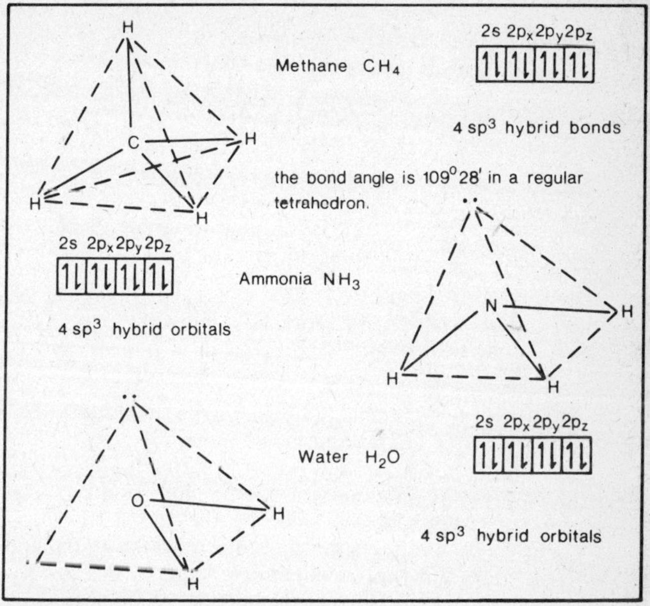

Figure 43

Non-ideal character of bonds

The discussion so far on the formation of covalent bonds between two atoms implies equal sharing of the bonding electron pair between the atoms concerned. However, this is only the case when both atoms have a similar attraction for the electrons (i.e. they are of equal electronegativity). Similarly, the discussion on ionic valency implies complete transfer of the electron(s) concerned from the metal atom(s) to the non-metal atom(s), but this ideal situation is only likely to occur if the electronegativity difference is sufficiently large. In practice, neither extreme is found in bonding between atoms of different elements, so that all such covalent bonds have some degree (no matter how slight) of ionic character, and all ionic bonds have some degree of covalent character. There are scales quoting electronegativity available, but the values quoted are only relative and a simple measure of the electronegativity can be obtained from the relative positions of the elements in the periodic classification.

increasing electronegativity →

	Li	Be		B	C	N	O	F	
increasing	Na	Mg		Al	Si	P	S	Cl	increasing
electro-	K	Ca	Transition	Sc	Ge	As	Se	Br	electro-
positivity	Rb	Sr	Metals	Y	Sn	Sb	Te	I	negativity
	Cs ↓	Ba		Tl	Pb	Bi	Po	At	

← increasing electropositivity

Fajan summarized the factors favouring formation of ionic or covalent bonds in the following rules.

Ionic bonds are favoured by
(i) large cations with small charge, bonding with
(ii) small anions with small charge.

Covalent bonds are favoured by
(iii) atoms with small cations and high charge, bonding with
(iv) atoms with large anions and high charge.

The non-ideal nature of bonds in compounds results in distortion, or polarization of the anion by the cation (the positively charged cation attracts the electrons from the anion) and the bond thus has a partial covalent character. In this distorting effect, cations with *d* electrons in the outer shell (e.g. having the $s^2p^6d^{10}$ configuration) are more strongly polarizing than cations with 8 electrons (the s^2p^6 configuration), as the *d* electrons are less efficient at screening the nuclear charge than the *s* and *p* electrons in the 8 electron shell. The result is that cations with 18 electrons in the outer orbital behave as if they have greater charge. The cations thus exert a greater polarizing effect, and the compounds have a resultant greater covalent character. This effect is illustrated by the halides of copper(I) and silver(I), which are generally insoluble, and with low ionic character compared to the predominantly ionic character of sodium and potassium halides. Silver fluoride is an exception, being water soluble, due to the small ionic radius and high electronegativity of fluorine, which results in the compound being mainly ionic in character. A change in colour, as well as lower melting point and differences between calculated and observed lattice energies (see table below) are an indication of increased polarization of the anion by the cation.

Table 4

Compound	*Lattice energy* (kJ mol^{-1})		Difference
	Experimental	*Calculated*	
AgF	−966	−870	96
AgCl	−916	−769	147
AgBr	−908	−759	149
AgI	−865	−736	129

The metallic bond

On detailed examination, metal atoms can be shown to be arranged in a lattice structure, generally one of three types – face centred cubic, body centred cubic or close packed hexagonal. The theories of bonding discussed previously do not explain the strong bonds generally found between metal atoms. The close packing of atoms in metal structures, and the general physical properties of metals, such as ductility, malleability and conductivity of heat and of electricity, are explained by the suggestion that the metal is present in the lattice as positive ions, formed from the metal atoms by loss of the valency electrons. The valency electrons are present in the spaces between the metal ions, and bind them together. These electrons are not bound to one particular ion, but are free to move from one atom to the next, hence the observed conductivity. The malleability and ductility can be explained by the movement of layers of the lattice when the metal is subjected to stresses.

The strength of metal bonds depends on the size of the metal cation, and the number of electrons available for binding. Thus the bonding is weak in alkali metals, as these elements have large cations, and only one electron per atom, resulting in soft, low melting solids. On the other hand, transition metals generally have small cations, with a number of electrons available for bonding, and these are high melting, hard solids, most of them with melting points in excess of 1000°C.

Hydrogen bonding

When hydrogen is bonded to small electronegative atoms such as nitrogen, oxygen and fluorine the molecule will be polarized. The slightly positive hydrogen atom is attracted by the slightly negatively charged electronegative atom. The small size of the latter allows the particles to come sufficiently close for the resultant attraction to have a significant effect on properties such as m.p. and b.p. As a result, the first hydride in Groups 5, 6 and 7 of the Periodic Table have significantly higher b.p.s and m.p.s than the other hydrides of these Groups.

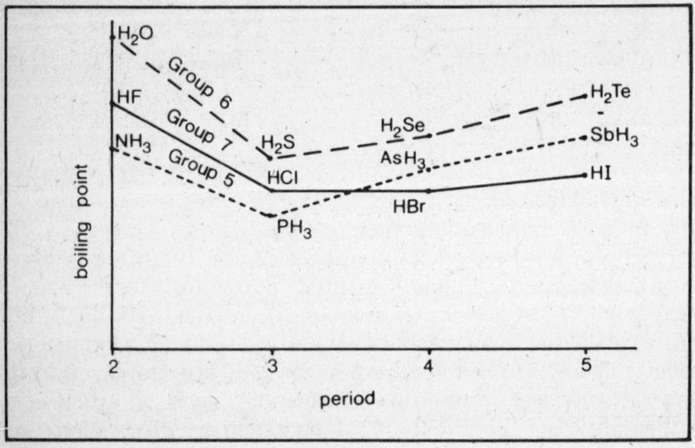

Figure 44

Note that although fluorine is more electronegative than oxygen, water has a higher boiling point than hydrogen fluoride. This is because the oxygen atom has two unshared electron pairs and there are two polar hydrogen atoms present enabling three dimensional bonding, whereas in hydrogen fluoride there is only one polar hydrogen atom and it is therefore only possible for chains of limited length to form.

Van der Waals forces These are weak forces acting between the molecules of a covalent compound and are produced when two adjacent molecules distort the electron clouds of each other and induce a weak electrostatic attraction between them. The bond strength increases with increasing number of electrons so, provided no other stronger forces operate (such as hydrogen bonds), increased b.p. and m.p. are observed with increasing molecular mass (fig. 44). Hydrogen bond strength in hydrogen fluoride, water and ammonia (that is for H . . . F, H . . . O, H . . . N) is 41·8, 29·4 and 8·4 kJ mol^{-1} respectively whereas Van der Waals forces rarely exceed 8 kJ mol^{-1}.

Key terms

Radioactivity Spontaneous emission by certain substances of penetrating radiation.
α-rays Fast moving helium nuclei emitted by certain radioactive nuclei.
β-rays Fast moving electrons emitted by some radioactive nuclei.
γ-rays Electromagnetic radiation emitted during radioactive decay.
Mass number The number of nucleons (protons + neutrons) in an atom of an element.
Atomic number The number of protons in an atom of an element. It also equals the number of electrons and gives the position of the element in the Periodic Table.
Neutron A fundamental atomic particle with approximate relative mass of 1 and no charge.
Proton A fundamental atomic particle with approximate relative mass of 1 and relative charge of +1.
Electron A fundamental atomic particle with negligible mass and relative charge of −1.
Relative atomic mass The average mass of one atom of the naturally occurring isotopic mixture of an element on the scale on which $^{12}_{6}C = 12$ exactly.
Isotope Atoms of a particular element (therefore with the same atomic number) but with a different mass number.
Half-life The time for half of the atoms of a particular radioactive isotope originally present to disintegrate.
Ionization energy The energy required to remove an electron from a gaseous atom.
Ionic (electrovalent) bonding Bonding arising by metal atoms losing electrons to non metal atoms forming positive ions (cations) and negative ions (anions) respectively.
Covalent bonding Bonding between atoms involving sharing of electrons.
Hydrogen bonding Bonding between polar hydrogen atoms and polar small electronegative atoms, usually nitrogen, oxygen or fluorine.
Van der Waals forces Weak bonding between molecules arising from temporary electron movement in the molecules.

Chapter 6
s and *p* Block Elements

Hydrogen

electron configuration		ionization energy	electron affinity	electro-negativity
H	$1s^1$	$1310\ kJ\ mol^{-1}$	$-72\ kJ$	2·1

Hydrogen is not placed in any specific group in the periodic table. Its chemistry resembles both group 1a metals and group 7, the halogens. In forming compounds hydrogen acquires the electronic structure of helium. It can do this in three ways; by sharing its 1*s* electron in a covalent bond, by gaining an electron to form the H^- ion or by losing the electron and subsequently accepting a lone pair of electrons.

Preparation. Industrial 1. by electrolysis of dilute sodium hydroxide solution

At cathode $$2H^+ + 2e^- \rightarrow H_2$$

2. as a by-product from the Castner-Kellner cell.
3. by reduction of steam with carbon (water gas process),

$$C + H_2O_{(g)} \rightarrow \underbrace{H_2 + CO}_{\text{water gas}}$$

followed by further reduction of steam with carbon monoxide (shift reaction)

$$CO + H_2O_{(g)} \rightarrow H_2 + CO_2$$

Laboratory 1. by the action of dilute acid on zinc or other metals above hydrogen in the electrochemical series.

$$2H^+ + Zn \rightarrow Zn^{2+} + H_2$$

2. by the action of concentrated alkali on certain metals (zinc or aluminium).

$$2Al + 2OH^- + 6H_2O \rightarrow 2[Al(OH)_4]^- + 3H_2$$

Properties
It will react with most non-metals under the appropriate conditions. It reacts with most group 1a and 2a elements to form ionic hydrides and with transition metals to form interstitial hydrides. It will reduce many metal oxides to the metal at high temperatures. This is used in the extraction of tungsten

$$WO_3 + 3H_2 \rightarrow W + 3H_2O$$

In the presence of a platinum catalyst it adds to carbon–carbon double and triple bonds.

Hydrides
The classification of hydrides is in three groups according to the type of bonding.

1. **Ionic** Heating a group 1a or 2a metal in hydrogen up to 700°C produces ionic hydrides. Only the most electropositive elements are capable of reducing hydrogen, e.g. sodium and potassium. Electrolysis of an ionic hydride causes hydrogen to be produced at the anode, indicating the presence of H^- ions. Group 1a hydrides have a rock salt structure.

2. **Covalent** These form the greatest number of hydrides. They are formed by the more electronegative elements boron and groups 4a to 7a. Their stability decreases down a group. They are all discrete molecules and commonly gases.

3. **Interstitial** These are formed by heating *d* block elements in a hydrogen atmosphere. They are non-stoichiometric (formulae are not clearly defined and can be altered by pressure), e.g. $TiH_{1\cdot73}$, $ZrH_{1\cdot92}$. The hydrogen atoms occupy spaces in the metal lattice.

Isotopes of hydrogen
Three isotopes are known of mass numbers 1 (hydrogen), 2 (deuterium) and 3 (tritium). Deuterium occurs in one part in six thousand in the gas. Tritium is radioactive and very rare. Deuterium is very slightly less reactive than hydrogen and has different physical properties, e.g. D_2O has a boiling point of 101·4°C, a melting point of 3·8°C and specific gravity 1·1. Deuterium is extracted as D_2O (heavy water) by prolonged electrolysis. It is used as a tracer to study reaction mechanisms.

Group 1a: Alkali metals

	electronic configuration (outer 2 orbitals)	ionic radius (nm)	1st ionization energy kJ mol^{-1}	electro-negativity	redox potential V
Li	$1s^2 2s^1$	0·060	519	1·0	−3·04
Na	$..2s^2 2p^6 3s^1$	0·095	494	0·9	−2·71
K	$..3s^2 3p^6 4s^1$	0·133	418	0·8	−2·92
Rb	$..4s^2 4p^6 5s^1$	0·148	402	0·8	−2·92
Cs	$..5s^2 5p^6 6s^1$	0·169	376	0·7	−2·92

The alkali metals are the most reactive of all metals. They have the lowest first ionization energies, large negative redox potentials and are the most electropositive elements (prone to lose electrons). They possess one electron in the outer shell and all show a single oxidation state of +1 (they form an M^+ ion). The ionization energies and redox potentials indicate that reactivity increases from sodium, Na, to caesium, Cs, which is in accordance with the increase in radius. On descending the group each successive element has one more complete quantum shell. Although the positive charge of the nucleus increases the outer electrons become less strongly held due to the increased screening of the nuclear charge by inner electron shells. In aqueous solution lithium, Li, is the most reactive because of its exceptionally small size and therefore large hydration energy. The metals are all powerful reducing agents, particularly in liquid ammonia. The compounds are predominantly ionic and highly soluble in water. The oxides are strongly basic and dissolve in water to form alkalis (soluble hydroxides). The metals give characteristic flame colours Li – red, Na – yellow, K – lilac, Rb – red and Cs – blue.

Occurrence and extraction Sodium occurs as the chloride in sea water and salt deposits and as sodium nitrate, $NaNO_3$, Chile saltpetre. All the metals have to be extracted by electrolytic processes because of the large negative redox potentials. The metal ions are reduced at the cathode. For sodium the Down's cell is used, (fig. 45).

Sodium chloride is mixed with caesium chloride, CsCl, to lower the melting point and the fused melt is electrolyzed with a graphite anode and iron cathode.

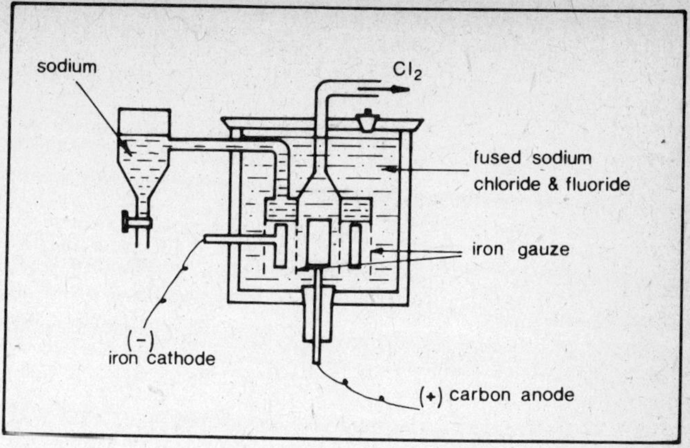

Figure 45. Down's cell

At anode	$2Cl^- \rightarrow Cl_2 + 2e^-$	oxidation
At cathode	$Na^+ + e^- \rightarrow Na$	reduction

Compounds

Oxides Li only forms the normal oxide.

$$4Li + O_2 \rightarrow 2Li_2O$$

Na forms a normal oxide and with excess air a peroxide.

$$2Na + O_2 \rightarrow Na_2O_2$$

The others form a superoxide as well as a normal oxide and peroxide.

$$K + O_2 \rightarrow KO_2$$

The increasing stability of higher oxides down the group is due to the increasing size of cation.

Chlorides The metals quickly form a chloride when placed in a chlorine atmosphere.

Amides Hot sodium reacts in dry ammonia gas to form sodamide, with the liberation of hydrogen.

$$2Na + 2NH_3 \rightarrow \underset{\text{sodamide}}{2NaNH_2} + H_2$$

In water sodamide gives off ammonia and forms sodium hydroxide.

$$NaNH_2 + H_2O \rightarrow NaOH + NH_3$$

Hydrides When heated in a stream of hydrogen the metals form an ionic hydride.

$$2Na + H_2 \rightarrow 2Na^+H^-$$
sodium hydride

On electrolysis of the solid hydride hydrogen is given off at the anode indicating the presence of H^- ions. Addition of water produces hydrogen

$$NaH + H_2O \rightarrow NaOH + H_2$$

Sodium hydroxide can be made by dissolving the oxide or the metal in water, e.g.

$$2Na + 2H_2O \rightarrow 2NaOH + H_2$$

This reaction becomes increasingly violent on descending the group.

Manufacture of sodium hydroxide by the Castner-Kellner cell

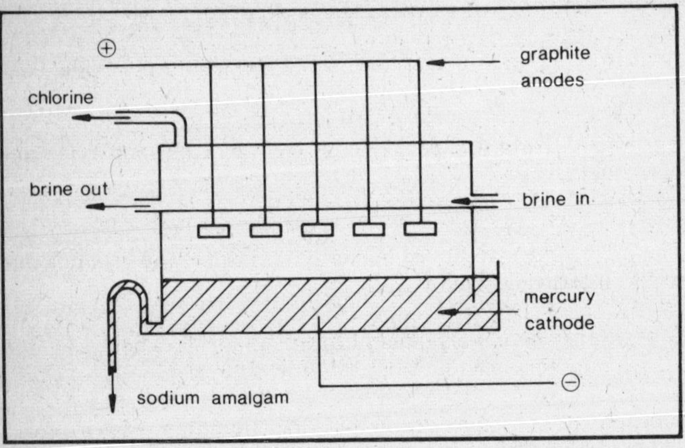

Figure 46. Castner-Kellner cell

A saturated solution of brine is electrolyzed using a flowing mercury cathode and graphite anodes.

At anode: $2Cl^- \rightarrow Cl_2 + 2e^-$

The chlorine is a useful by-product.

At cathode: $Na^+ + e^- + Hg \rightarrow Na/Hg$ (sodium amalgam)

Hydrogen, although having a lower redox potential than sodium is not discharged due to its high 'over potential' at a mercury cathode (see p. 76). The sodium amalgam now flows out of the cell and through iron grids where it meets a counter-current of water and forms sodium hydroxide and hydrogen (also a useful by-product). The mercury is then returned to the cell.

$$2Na/Hg + 2H_2O \rightarrow 2NaOH + H_2 + 2Hg$$

Reactions of hydroxides Because of the small ionic radii of Na^+ and K^+ both have large hydration energies and the hydroxides are deliquescent. In dilute aqueous solution (up to 2M) they are fully ionized and therefore act as strong bases. With acids they form a salt and water

$$NaOH + HCl \rightarrow NaCl + H_2O$$

With solutions of other metal salts (not group 1a or 2a) the corresponding metal hydroxides precipitate

$$CuSO_4 + 2NaOH \rightarrow \underset{\text{insoluble}}{Cu(OH)_2\downarrow} + Na_2SO_4$$

For some metals (e.g. zinc and aluminium) with amphoteric oxides the precipitate redissolves in excess alkali

$$Al(OH)_3 + OH^- \rightarrow [Al(OH)_4]^- \text{ (also written } [AlO_2]^-\text{)}$$

The metals give off hydrogen in conc. sodium hydroxide.

$$Zn + 2NaOH + 2H_2O \rightarrow \underset{\text{sodium zincate}}{Na_2[Zn(OH)_4]} + H_2$$

Sodium hydroxide reacts with a variety of non-metals forming sodium salts with the anion of the non-metal, e.g. with chlorine.

$$Cl_2 + \underset{\text{cold dilute}}{2NaOH} \rightarrow NaCl + H_2O + \underset{\text{sodium chlorate(I)}}{NaOCl}$$

$$3Cl_2 + \underset{\text{hot conc.}}{6NaOH} \rightarrow 5NaCl + 3H_2O + \underset{\text{sodium chlorate(V)}}{NaClO_3}$$

Dilute sodium hydroxide is used extensively to hydrolyze organic esters, amides etc. and to saponify fats.

Sodium carbonate Manufacture by the Solvay Process The direct reaction between calcium carbonate and salt does not take place

$$CaCO_3 + 2NaCl \not\rightarrow Na_2CO_3 + CaCl_2$$

Calcium carbonate is roasted to give the oxide and CO_2.

$$CaCO_3 \rightarrow CaO + CO_2$$

The carbon dioxide is passed up a tower which has ammoniated brine streaming down it

$$NaCl + NH_3 + H_2O + CO_2 \rightarrow NaHCO_3 + NH_4Cl$$

Sodium hydrogencarbonate is not very soluble in water particularly with excess Na^+ ions present and a slurry forms at the foot of the tower. The precipitate is filtered off and heated

$$2NaHCO_3 \rightarrow Na_2CO_3 + H_2O + CO_2$$

The sodium carbonate is purified by recrystallization from water. The calcium oxide and ammonium chloride are heated together to produce ammonia which is reintroduced to the tower along with the carbon dioxide produced on heating the hydrogencarbonate. There is very little waste in the process.

Sodium carbonate is used in paper and glass manufacture. When crystallized from aqueous solution it forms the decahydrate $Na_2CO_3.10H_2O$ (washing soda) which is used to precipitate calcium from hard water. Of the group 1a **carbonates** only lithium decomposes before melting

$$Li_2CO_3 \xrightarrow{\text{heat}} Li_2O + CO_2$$

The reactions of chlorine with sodium carbonate are the same as for the hydroxide.

Nitrates All the group 1a metal nitrates decompose on heating to give the nitrite (nitrate(III)) and oxygen.

$$2NaNO_3 \xrightarrow{\text{heat}} 2NaNO_2 + O_2$$

Sulphates These are stable to heat and are used as drying agents. **A diagonal relationship** exists between lithium and magnesium, lithium resembling magnesium more than its fellow group members. The extremely small ionic radius of Li^+ causes a high degree of polarization of anions which results in strong covalent character in the compounds. They also have similar electronegativities.

Similarities between Li and Mg

1. both form normal oxides on heating in air.
2. nitrates decompose on heating.
3. many salts are insoluble in water, but both the chlorides are soluble in some organic solvents (indicating covalent character).
4. many salts are deliquescent.

Group 2a: Alkali earths

	electronic configuration (outer 2 orbitals)	1st and 2nd ionization energies kJ mol^{-1}		ionic radius M^{2+} nm	electro-negativity	redox potential V
Be	$1s^2 2s^2$	900	1760	0·031	1·5	−1·85
Mg	$..2s^2 2p^6 3s^2$	736	1450	0·065	1·2	−2·38
Ca	$..3s^2 3p^6 4s^2$	590	1150	0·099	1·0	−2·87
Sr	$..4s^2 4p^6 5s^2$	548	1060	0·113	1·0	−2·89
Ba	$..5s^2 5p^6 6s^2$	502	966	0·135	0·9	−2·90

The metals are all very reactive as indicated by their large negative redox potentials. They possess two electrons in the outer shell and generally form an M^{2+} ion. The ease of formation of this ion and the similarity in reactivity to group 1a metals is surprising in view of the large ionization energy required to form the M^{2+} ion. The reason is that the ion once formed is very small and highly charged exerting a strong electrostatic force on neighbouring anions which results in very high lattice energies (see Born-Haber cycle p. 57). The high charge density of the ion also leads to a large hydration energy which can explain the redox potentials. The two valence electrons make the metallic bond very strong and the metals are harder and denser than group 1a. The higher charge on the metal ions results in more complexes being formed by group 2a. The atomic radius increases down the group and consequently the ionization energies decrease. This increases reactivity in passing down the group. This increase in radius also lowers the hydration energy and causes a decrease in solubility of salts in passing down the group. The metals are all readily oxidized. Calcium, Ca, strontium, Sr, and barium, Ba, can only form ionic compounds but the small size of Mg^{2+} and Be^{2+} causes polarization of the anion and a high degree of covalency in their compounds.

Occurrence and extraction The metals occur as carbonates and sulphates and are widespread. The presence of the ions, Ca^{2+} and Mg^{2+}, causes hardness in water. In accordance with their high position in the electrochemical series the metals are extracted by electrolysis of the fused halide with other halides added to lower the melting point. Magnesium and calcium are used as reducing agents to extract other metals such as titanium and uranium.

Compounds Like group 1a the metals quickly oxidize in air and are attacked by cold water and acids. They combine directly with a variety of non-metals.

Oxides All form a normal oxide, $M^{2+}O^{2-}$, on heating in oxygen. Strontium and barium also form a peroxide, $M^{2+}O_2^{2-}$, on prolonged heating. The formation of the higher oxide is favoured by increased size of cation. The oxides are generally prepared by decomposition of the carbonate.

$$CaCO_3 \xrightleftharpoons{\text{heat}} CaO + CO_2$$

The oxides combine readily with water with evolution of heat to form the hydroxide.

$$\underset{\text{lime}}{CaO} + H_2O \rightleftharpoons \underset{\text{slaked lime}}{Ca(OH)_2}$$

The oxides are all strongly basic (metallic character).

Hydroxides The hydroxides of Ca, Sr and Ba are all strong bases. They react with acids and liberate ammonia from its salts.

$$Sr(OH)_2 + 2HCl \rightarrow SrCl_2 + 2H_2O$$

$$Ca(OH)_2 + 2NH_4Cl \rightarrow CaCl_2 + 2NH_3 + 2H_2O$$

Halides The fluorides are only slightly soluble in water (MgF_2 is insoluble) due to their high lattice energy. The other halides are soluble. The chlorides are deliquescent and $CaCl_2$ is used as a drying agent. It complexes with ammonia and ethanol and therefore cannot be used to dry them:

$$Ca(NH_3)_8Cl_2 \qquad Ca(C_2H_5OH)_4Cl_2$$

When heated, hydrated $MgCl_{2(g)}$ hydrolyzes

$$MgCl_2 + H_2O \rightleftharpoons MgO + 2HCl$$

Anhydrous $MgCl_2$ is prepared by heating the hydrated chloride in a stream of HCl gas which suppresses the above reaction.

Carbides The carbides are really ethynides (acetylides) because they contain the $(C{\equiv}C)^{2-}$ ion. The commercially important calcium carbide is prepared by heating quicklime and carbon at 2000°C

$$CaO + 3C \rightleftharpoons \underset{\text{calcium carbide}}{CaC_2} + CO$$

Addition of water produces ethyne (C_2H_2)

$$CaC_2 + 2H_2O \rightleftharpoons C_2H_2 + Ca(OH)_2$$

Calcium carbide combines with nitrogen at red heat to form cyanamide

$$CaC_2 + N_2 \rightleftharpoons CaCN_2 + C$$

It is used as a fertilizer or to make ammonia

$$CaCN_2 + 3H_2O \rightleftharpoons CaCO_3 + 2NH_3$$

Nitrides At high temperatures group 2a metals combine with nitrogen to form nitrides, e.g. Mg_3N_2. In water they liberate ammonia.

Hydrides These are formed by direct combination on heating and contain the H^- ion.

Carbonates These occur naturally and are also obtained as a precipitate when sodium carbonate is added to a solution of the metal ion. Magnesium salts give a basic carbonate $3MgCO_3.Mg(OH)_2.4H_2O$ but the normal carbonate can be made by adding sodium hydrogencarbonate. The high charge density of the metal ion makes them strongly polarizing and they distort the carbonate anion. Consequently they are all thermally unstable. The hydrogencarbonates are only known in solution.

$$CaCO_3 + H_2O + CO_2 \rightarrow Ca(HCO_3)_2$$

Nitrates are obtained by reacting the metal, oxide, hydroxide or carbonate with nitric acid. They decompose on heating to give the oxide and nitrogen(IV) oxide.

$$2Ca(NO_3)_2 \rightarrow 2CaO + 4NO_2 + O_2$$

They are all water soluble and deliquescent.

Sulphates These occur naturally and can be reduced to the sulphide on heating with carbon.

$$\underset{\text{anhydrite}}{CaSO_4} + 2C \rightarrow CaS + 2CO_2$$

Group 3: Aluminium

	electron configuration	ionization energy Al^{3+}	ionic radii Al^{3+}	electro-negativity	redox potential
Al	$1s^2 2s^2 2p^6 3s^2 3p^1$	5137 kJ mol^{-1}	0·050 nm	1·5	−1·66 V

Diagonal relationships Beryllium and aluminium.

increase in electropositivity ←				
increase in electropositivity ↓	Li ↘	Be ↘	B ↘	C
	Na	Mg	Al	Si
	K	Ca		

Atomic radius increases in going down a group because each successive element has one more quantum shell of electrons. This leads to elements becoming more electropositive down a group. Across a period electrons are being added to the same quantum shell and the nuclear charge is increasing resulting in a decrease in atomic radius. Thus along a row elements become less electropositive. From the diagram above it can be seen that aluminium and beryllium will be more electropositive than boron by about the same degree. The similarity of the electronegativities of Al and Be leads to a similarity in their properties. Other pairs which exhibit diagonal relationships are lithium and magnesium, and boron and silicon.

Similarities between Al and Be

1. both are made passive by nitric acid.
2. both evolve hydrogen with caustic alkali (NaOH, KOH).
3. both have amphoteric oxides.

4. the chlorides are covalent and give off HCl when hydrolyzed.
5. the carbides give methane on hydrolysis (unlike group 2a).
6. the compounds have similar stabilities.

Occurrence and extraction Aluminium occurs as bauxite, $Al_2O_3.2H_2O$, and is extracted from the ore by electrolysis of the fused salt with cryolite, Na_3AlF_6, added to lower the melting point. The container has a graphite lining which is made the cathode

At graphite cathode $Al^{3+} + 3e^- \rightarrow Al$
At graphite anode $4AlO_3^{2-} \rightarrow 2Al_2O_3 + 3O_2 + 8e^-$

Aluminium shows an oxidation number of +3 and the compounds are practically covalent. It shows metallic character, combining directly with many non-metals. The oxide is amphoteric.

Chloride $AlCl_3$. Made by passing Cl_2 over heated aluminium.

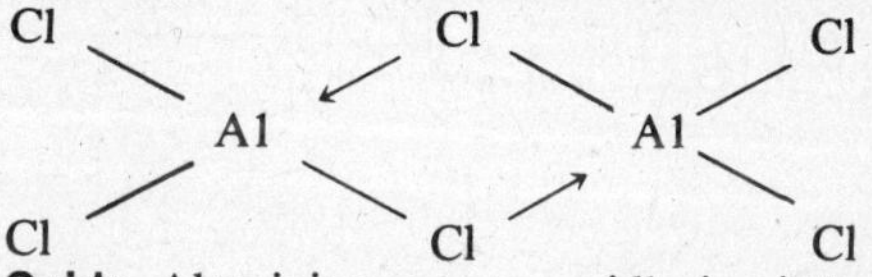

in vapour state

Oxide Aluminium reacts rapidly in air to form a strong oxide layer.

Thermit process The high heat of formation of aluminium oxide makes Al a powerful reducing agent. With iron oxide:

$$Fe_2O_3 + 2Al \rightarrow 2Fe + Al_2O_3 + heat$$

The powdered oxide and aluminium powder are intimately mixed and fired with burning magnesium ribbon.

Group 4

	electron configuration	electro-negativity	atomic radius nm	ionic radius nm
C	$1s^2 2s^2 2p^2$	1·5	0·077	–
Si	$..2s^2 2p^6 3s^2 3p^2$	1·8	0·117	–
Ge	$..3p^6 3d^{10} 4s^2 4p^2$	1·8	0·122	0·093 (2+)
Sn	$..4p^6 4d^{10} 5s^2 5p^2$	1·8	0·140	0·112 (2+)
Pb	$..5p^6 5d^{10} 6s^2 6p^2$	1·8	0·154	0·120 (2+)

All have an outer shell of four electrons and since the energy required to add or remove four electrons would be enormous they all show a covalency of 4. In addition, tin and lead can form the M^{2+} ion, a property known as the **inert pair effect**. On descending the group there is a smooth trend from non-metal through metalloid and finally to metal. This is accounted for by the change in electronegativity due to increasing atomic radius.

Carbon

It occurs as two allotropes, graphite and diamond. Graphite is stable under normal conditions and is an example of monotropy.

Electron structure

ground state excited state sp^3 hybrid

A $2s$ electron can be promoted to the vacant $2p$ orbital forming four unpaired electrons. The energy gained in forming four covalent bonds overcomes the energy required to promote the electron. The four bonds are evenly displaced about the atom resulting in tetrahedral compounds. Carbon is relatively inert but combines directly with oxygen, sulphur, fluorine and some metals. It can reduce steam at 1000°C.

Hydrides Carbon forms a limitless range of covalent hydrides due to its unique property of **catenation** (the formation of chains). The reason for the stability of hydrides is the strength of the carbon-carbon and the carbon-hydrogen bonds, the latter due to the similarity in electronegativities of carbon and hydrogen.

Oxides Carbon burns in excess air to form a dioxide

$$C + O_2 \rightarrow CO_2$$

It can also be formed by the action of acids on carbonates, e.g. marble

$$CaCO_3 + 2HCl \rightarrow CaCl_2 + H_2O + CO_2$$

CO_2 is an acidic gas and reacts with bases,

$$\underset{\text{limewater}}{Ca(OH)_2} + CO_2 \rightarrow CaCO_3 \downarrow + H_2O$$

e.g. limewater gives a white precipitate and is a test for the gas. Excess CO_2 redissolves the precipitate

$$CaCO_3 + H_2O + CO_2 \rightarrow Ca(HCO_3)_2$$

Structure of CO_2 O=C=O linear
CO_2 is very stable due to the existence of resonance hybrids

$$\overset{-}{O}-C\equiv O^+ \leftrightarrow \overset{+}{O}\equiv C-O^-$$

CO_2 dissolves in water to form carbonic acid, a weak acid.

$$CO_2 + H_2O \rightleftharpoons H_2CO_3 \rightleftharpoons H^+ + HCO_3^- \rightleftharpoons 2H^+ + CO_3^{2-}$$

It forms two ranges of salts, carbonates and hydrogencarbonates. The addition of a soluble carbonate to a solution of a metal salt usually results in the precipitation of a basic carbonate, e.g.

$$CuCO_3.Cu(OH)_2$$

This is because CO_3^{2-}, in solution, abstracts protons from water

$$CO_3^{2-} + H_2O \rightleftharpoons HCO_3^- + OH^-$$

Addition of a hydrogencarbonate suppresses the above ionization. Al^{3+}, Cr^{3+} and Fe^{3+} carbonates do not exist because the ions are strongly hydrated and CO_3^{2-} abstracts protons and precipitates the hydroxide.

$$Al(H_2O)_6^{3+} + 3CO_3^{2-} \rightarrow Al(OH)_3 \downarrow + 3H_2O + 3HCO_3^-$$

Burning carbon in a limited amount of air produces carbon monoxide, CO.

$$2C + O_2 \rightarrow 2CO$$

or

$$C + CO_2 \rightleftharpoons 2CO$$

It is a powerful reducing agent and reduces iron(III) oxide to iron

$$Fe_2O_3 + 3CO \rightarrow 2Fe + 3CO_2$$

Carbon monoxide can form volatile carbonyl complexes with

transition elements. It is used in the Mond process to purify nickel.

$$Ni + 4CO \xrightarrow{90°C} Ni(CO)_4 \xrightarrow{180°C} Ni + 4CO$$

It also reacts with non-metals:

$$CO + S \rightarrow COS; \; CO + Cl_2 \rightarrow \underset{\text{phosgene}}{COCl_2}$$

It is a neutral oxide but under pressure it will react with sodium hydroxide to form **sodium formate**

$$NaOH + CO \rightarrow HCOONa$$

Methanol is synthesized by reacting CO with hydrogen under pressure in the presence of a catalyst.

$$CO + 2H_2 \xrightarrow{Cr_2O_3/ZnO} CH_3OH$$

Structure of CO It is a resonance hybrid of the following forms:

$$\overset{+}{C}{\equiv}\overset{-}{O} \leftrightarrow \overset{+}{C}{-}\overset{-}{O} \leftrightarrow C{=}O$$

Carbon disulphide is made by reacting methane with sulphur under pressure with a catalyst

$$CH_4 + 4S \rightleftharpoons CS_2 + 2H_2S$$

Tetrachloromethane is made by the reaction of CS_2 with chlorine

$$CS_2 + 3Cl_2 \xrightarrow{FeCl_3} CCl_4 + S_2Cl_2$$

$$CS_2 + 2S_2Cl_2 \longrightarrow CCl_4 + 6S$$

Silicon

Occurs widely as silica, SiO_2, e.g. sand, quartz or as silicates, SiO_3^{2-}. The element is non-metallic but is quite different from carbon because as a third row element it has vacant *d* orbitals. It reacts directly with chlorine to form silicon tetrachloride, $SiCl_4$, which is readily hydrolyzed by water, unlike CCl_4. The incoming water molecules can utilize the vacant *d* orbitals in hydrolysis. Silicon is also slowly attacked by alkali

$$Si + 2OH^- + H_2O \rightarrow SiO_3^{2-} + 2H_2$$

Hydrides It does not form such a wide range of hydrides as carbon. The Si–Si bond is much weaker than the C–C bond and so it cannot catenate to the same degree.

Silica, SiO_2 It is a hard crystalline solid (as opposed to CO_2, a gas) because it is a macromolecule containing silicon bonded tetrahedrally to four oxygen atoms.

Germanium, tin and lead

The +2 oxidation state first shows with germanium in which the outer *s* electrons constitute an 'inert pair' which is not involved in bonding. The reason the *s* electrons are strongly held by the nucleus is that the *f* orbitals have a weak screening effect.

Compounds of Ge, Sn and Pb

oxidation state	+2	+4
Ge	strongly reducing	stable
Sn	reducing	stable
Pb	stable	strongly oxidizing
oxides	basic amphoteric	amphoteric
bonding	ionic	covalent

Oxides of Sn and Pb Burning tin in air gives tin(IV) oxide

$$Sn + O_2 \rightarrow SnO_2$$

whereas lead forms lead(II) oxide

$$2Pb + O_2 \rightarrow 2PbO$$

and at high temperatures lead(II)(IV) oxide

$$6PbO + O_2 \rightarrow 2Pb_3O_4$$

Lead(II) oxide can also be obtained by heating the nitrate and is a basic oxide forming lead(II) salts when reacted with acid

$$PbO + H_2SO_4 \rightarrow PbSO_4 + H_2O$$

Pb_3O_4 on warming with dilute nitric acid produces **lead(IV) oxide**, PbO_2.

$$Pb_3O_4 + 4HNO_3 \rightarrow 2Pb(NO_3)_2 + PbO_2 + 2H_2O$$

PbO_2 is strongly oxidizing and amphoteric, forming salts with acids

$$PbO_2 + 4HCl \rightarrow PbCl_2 + 2H_2O + Cl_2$$

and with alkalis a plumbate

$$PbO_2 + 2OH^- + 2H_2O \rightarrow [Pb(OH)_6]^{2-}$$

SnO_2 is also amphoteric forming stanates

$$SnO_2 + 2OH^- + 2H_2O \rightarrow [Sn(OH)_6]^{2-}$$

and tin(IV) salts with dilute acids. Tin(II) oxide, SnO, is formed by heating tin(II) oxalate

$$Sn(COO)_2 \rightarrow SnO + CO + CO_2$$

The carbon monoxide forms a reducing atmosphere.

Halides Germanium and tin form the **tetrahalide** on heating, e.g. in chlorine and they are readily hydrolyzed in water. Lead forms a tetrachloride but bromine and iodine are not sufficiently oxidizing. All form an ionic dichloride, e.g.

$$Pb^{2+} + 2Cl^- \rightarrow PbCl_2$$

Lead(II) chloride is sparingly soluble and serves as a test for Pb^{2+} ions. In hot excess conc. hydrochloric acid it redissolves as a complex ion, tetrachloro lead(II).

$$PbCl_2 \rightleftharpoons Pb^{2+} + 2Cl^- \xrightarrow{2Cl^-} [PbCl_4]^{2-}$$

Both lead and tin can react with water.

Reaction with acids Tin reacts slowly with dilute acids to form Sn(II) compounds and Sn(IV) in concentrated oxidizing acids. Lead is rendered passive by conc. hydrochloric acid but reacts with dilute nitric acid to form NO or NO_2 and lead(II) nitrate.

Group 5

	electron configuration	atomic radius nm	electro-negativity
N	$1s^2 2s^2 2p^3$	0·074	3·0
P	$..2s^2 2p^6 3s^2 3p^3$	0·110	2·1
As	$..3p^6 3d^{10} 4s^2 4p^3$	0·121	2·0
Sb	$..4p^6 4d^{10} 5s^2 5p^3$	0·141	1·9
Bi	$..5p^6 5d^{10} 6s^2 6p^3$	0·170	1·9

All the elements have an outer shell of five electrons and can theoretically gain three electrons to form an anion, or share with three electrons to form three covalent bonds. It is energetically impossible to lose five electrons. In practice only nitrogen can form the N^{3-} ion and the group chemistry is predominantly that of non-metals forming covalent compounds. The trend towards metallic character down a group is shown by the formation of Sb^{3+} and Bi^{3+} due to the 'inert pair' effect. Phosphorus and subsequent members have *d* orbitals available and can expand the octet to form compounds with a covalency of five.

Nitrogen

It exists as a diatomic gas with a triple bond. The extremely high bond energy accounts for its inertness. It only reacts directly with magnesium, and lithium to form nitrides. When sparked with oxygen it can form oxides.

Hydrides

Ammonia, NH_3. Laboratory preparation is by heating an ammonium salt with a base. It is dried by passing over calcium oxide as calcium chloride and acid drying agents combine with it. Industrial preparation is by the **Haber process** in which nitrogen and hydrogen are reacted together at high temperatures and pressure in the presence of an iron catalyst (see p. 46).

Structure It is tetrahedral having three bond pairs and one lone pair.

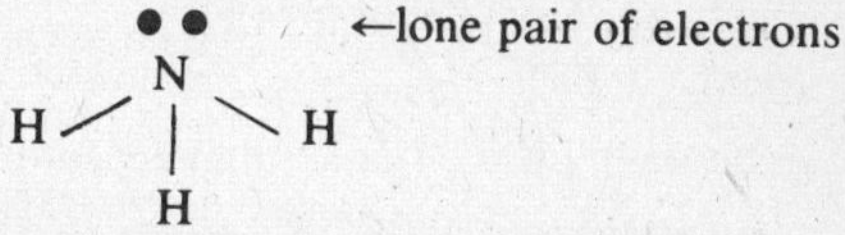

Reactions 1. Ammonia, because of the lone pair of electrons, can coordinate with positive or electron deficient sites. In water it combines with a proton to form the ammonium ion.

$$NH_3 + H_2O \rightleftharpoons NH_4^+ + OH^- \qquad K_b = 1{\cdot}81 \times 10^{-5}\ \mathrm{mol\ dm^{-3}}$$

It serves as a weak base in water therefore and reacts with acids to form salts. These are similar to group 1a salts since the ammonium ion has a radius between that of K^+ and Rb^+.

They are often thermally unstable:

$$NH_4Cl \rightleftharpoons NH_3 + HCl$$

It also complexes with transition metals, e.g.

$$Cu^{2+} + 4NH_3 \rightleftharpoons [Cu(NH_3)_4]^{2+}$$

tetraamine copper(II)

2. Ammonia can act as a reducing agent. Chlorine and sodium hypochlorite oxidize ammonia at room temperature

$$2NH_3 + 3Cl_2 \rightarrow N_2 + 6HCl$$
$$2NH_3 + 3OCl^- \rightarrow N_2 + 3Cl^- + 3H_2O$$

It also reduces copper oxide. In air it burns to form nitrogen.

$$4NH_3 + 3O_2 \rightarrow 2N_2 + 6H_2O$$

With a catalyst the less stable nitrogen oxide is formed

$$4NH_3 + 5O_2 \xrightarrow{Pt} 4NO + 6H_2O$$

This is the start of the Ostwald process to make nitric acid.

3. Ammonia can form the amide ion, NH_2^-, by heating a group 1a element in the gas

$$2Na + 2NH_3 \rightarrow 2NaNH_2 + H_2$$

The amide ion is an exceedingly strong base and is quickly hydrolyzed by water

$$NH_2^- + H_2O \rightarrow OH^- + NH_3$$

and reacts with ammonium chloride:

$$\underset{\text{acid}}{NH_4Cl} + \underset{\text{base}}{NaNH_2} \rightarrow \underset{\text{salt}}{NaCl} + \underset{\text{ammonia}}{2NH_3}$$

Ammonia can be both a proton donor and acceptor.

Hydrazine, $NH_2.NH_2$. A covalent liquid (the nitrogen in hydrazine has an oxidation number of -2) which is made by oxidizing ammonia with sodium hypochlorite in the presence of glue (which complexes metal ions):

$$NH_3 + OCl^- \rightarrow OH^- + NH_2Cl$$

$$NH_2Cl + NH_3 + OH^- \rightarrow N_2H_4 + Cl^- + H_2O$$

It is a weaker base than ammonia.

Oxides

Nitrous oxide, N_2O. Oxidation state of nitrogen is +1. This oxide is prepared by heating ammonium nitrate or a mixture of ammonium sulphate and potassium nitrate which is safer.

$$NH_4NO_3 \rightarrow N_2O + 2H_2O$$

Structure $\overset{-}{N}=\overset{+}{N}=O \leftrightarrow N\equiv\overset{+}{N}-\overset{-}{O}$ (linear)

It can support combustion, rekindling a glowing splint

$$2N_2O \xrightarrow{\text{heat}} 2N_2 + O_2$$

Nitric oxide, NO. Oxidation state of nitrogen is +2. This is prepared by the action of medium concentrated nitric acid on copper.

$$3Cu + 8HNO_3 \rightarrow 3Cu^{2+} + 6NO_3^- + 4H_2O + 2NO$$

Other oxides are also formed during the reaction. It can be purified by absorbing it in iron(II) sulphate solution with which it forms a dark brown complex

$$FeSO_4 + NO \rightleftharpoons FeSO_4.NO$$

This is the basis of the 'brown-ring' test for nitrates. Nitric oxide is recovered by heating the solution. It is insoluble in water and reacts quickly with oxygen to form the dioxide. It can reduce manganate(VII) ions

$$3MnO_4^- + 4H^+ + 5NO \rightarrow 3Mn^{2+} + 5NO_3^- + 2H_2O$$

and halogens:

$$2NO + Cl_2 \rightarrow \underset{\text{nitrosyl chloride}}{2NOCl}$$

Structure

$$:\overset{\cdots}{N}=O: \longleftrightarrow :N=\overset{\cdot\ \cdot\cdot}{O}: \longleftrightarrow :N=\overset{\cdot\cdot\ \cdot}{O}:$$

It has eleven bonding electrons and is therefore paramagnetic but is not particularly reactive and does not dimerize.

Nitrogen dioxide–dinitrogen tetroxide, NO_2, N_2O_4. Oxidation state of nitrogen is +4. These oxides may be prepared by heating a metal nitrate (not group 1a or 2a). Lead nitrate is normally used because it has no water of crystallization

$$2Pb(NO_3)_2 \rightarrow 2PbO + 4NO_2 + O_2$$

The dimer N_2O_4 boils at 22°C and may be frozen out as a liquid and separated from oxygen. The following equilibria exist:

$$\underset{\text{colourless}}{N_2O_4} \underset{\text{cool}}{\overset{\text{heat}}{\rightleftharpoons}} \underset{\text{dark brown}}{2NO_2} \underset{\text{cool}}{\overset{\text{heat}}{\rightleftharpoons}} 2NO + O_2$$

At low temperatures the gas exists as the dimer and is colourless. As the temperature is raised it becomes a darker and darker brown as the percentage of NO_2 increases. It eventually decomposes. NO_2 dissolves in water to form a mixture of nitric(III) and (V) acids.

$$2NO_2 + H_2O \rightarrow HNO_3 + HNO_2$$

It is an oxidizing agent and at room temperature oxidizes hydrogen sulphide to sulphur, sulphur dioxide to sulphuric acid and iodide to iodine.

$$H_2S + NO_2 \rightarrow NO + H_2O + S$$

$$SO_2 + H_2O + NO_2 \rightarrow H_2SO_4 + NO$$

$$2I^- + H_2O + NO_2 \rightarrow I_2 + 2OH^- + NO$$

Structures, NO_2

NO_2 is a planar triangular molecule with an unpaired electron.

N_2O_4

Oxyacids of nitrogen

Nitric(III) acid Nitrous acid (HNO_2). This acid is unstable and decomposes when concentrated. It can only be prepared in cold dilute solution by adding dilute HCl to a solution of sodium nitrate(III), (nitrite).

$$NaNO_2 + HCl \rightarrow HNO_2 + NaCl$$

The group 1a nitrites are stable and are prepared by heating a nitrate. The acid and acidified solutions of the salts are oxidizing agents, oxidizing iodide to iodine and iron(II) to iron(III)

$$2I^- \rightarrow I_2 + 2e^-$$

$$Fe^{2+} \rightarrow Fe^{3+} + e^-$$

$$NO_2^- + 2H^+ + e^- \rightarrow NO + H_2O \qquad E^\theta = +0.99\ V$$

The nitrite ion is planar and a resonance hybrid of:

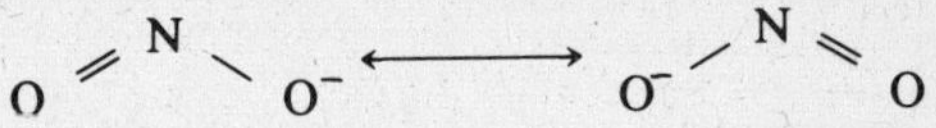

Nitric(V) acid In the laboratory it is prepared by heating a nitrate with conc. sulphuric acid, then distilling the acid. Industrially it is made by the catalytic oxidation of ammonia to nitrogen(II) oxide, NO, (see p. 148). The gases from this reaction are cooled and NO reacts with excess air to form NO_2. Adding NO_2 and more air to water makes nitric acid:

$$4NO_2 + 2H_2O + O_2 \rightarrow 4HNO_3$$

Nitric acid, when pure, is a colourless covalent liquid which is slightly ionized. It is a powerful oxidizing agent.

Structure

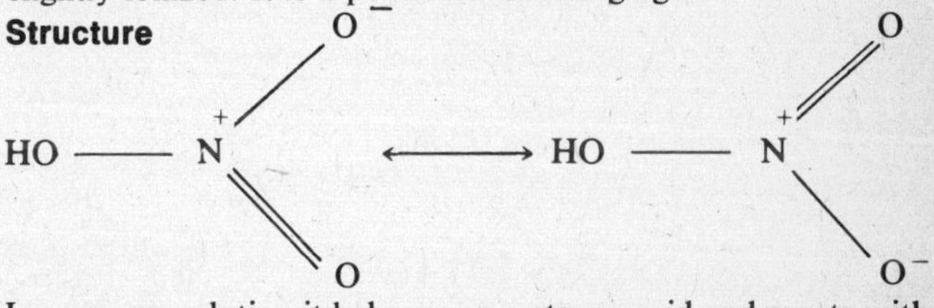

In aqueous solution it behaves as a strong acid and reacts with metals, metal oxides, hydroxides and carbonates to produce nitrates. The action of the acid on metals depends on both the concentration of the acid and the metal used. Magnesium with dilute nitric acid is the only occasion when hydrogen is produced.

$$Mg + 2HNO_3 \rightarrow Mg(NO_3)_2 + H_2$$

This is considered to be the primary reaction of all metals with the acid but the hydrogen produced is normally oxidized. The extent of the reduction depends on the strength of the acid. Thus with copper and conc. acid, NO_2 is produced.

$$Cu \rightarrow Cu^{2+} + 2e^- \qquad E^\theta = -0{\cdot}34\ V$$

$$2H^+ + 2HNO_3 + 2e^- \rightarrow 2H_2O + 2NO_2 \qquad E^\theta = +0{\cdot}81\ V$$

$$Cu + 4H^+ + 2NO_3^- \rightarrow Cu^{2+} + 2H_2O + 2NO_2 \qquad E^\theta = +0{\cdot}47\ V$$

$$N(V) \rightarrow N(IV)$$

With copper and 50% nitric acid NO is produced.

$$3Cu \rightarrow 3Cu^{2+} + 6e^- \qquad E^\theta = -0{\cdot}34\ V$$

$$6H^+ + 2HNO_3 + 6e^- \rightarrow 2NO + 4H_2O \qquad E^\theta = +0{\cdot}96\ V$$

$$\underset{N(V)\rightarrow}{3Cu + 8H^+ + 2NO_3^-} \rightarrow 3Cu^{2+} + 4H_2O + \underset{N(II)}{2NO} \qquad E^\theta = +0{\cdot}62\ V$$

With more electropositive metals and hot dilute acid ammonia may be produced (as ammonium nitrate).

$$4Zn + 10HNO_3 \rightarrow 4Zn(NO_3)_2 + NH_4NO_3 + 3H_2O \qquad E^\theta = +0{\cdot}11\ V$$

$$N(V) \quad \rightarrow \quad N(\text{-}III)$$

The acid has no effect on gold, platinum, aluminium, iron or chromium (passivity).

Oxidation of non-metals Sulphur and phosphorus give their highest oxide with conc. nitric acid, the oxide then reacting with water to form the acid:

$$P + 5HNO_3 \rightarrow H_3PO_4 + 5NO_2 + H_2O$$

$$S + 6HNO_3 \rightarrow H_2SO_4 + 6NO_2 + 2H_2O$$

Oxidation of weak metals Tin gives tin(IV) oxide

$$Sn + 4HNO_3 \rightarrow SnO_2 + 4NO_2 + 2H_2O$$

Certain compounds will also be oxidized, e.g. iron(II) salts to iron(III) salts. In the presence of a stronger acid (sulphuric) nitric acid can be forced to accept a proton and act as a base:

$$HNO_3 + H_2SO_4 \rightarrow NO_2^+ + H_2O + HSO_4^-$$

The nitronium ion, NO_2^+, is involved in nitration of organic compounds.

Nitrates They contain the planar NO_3^- ion.

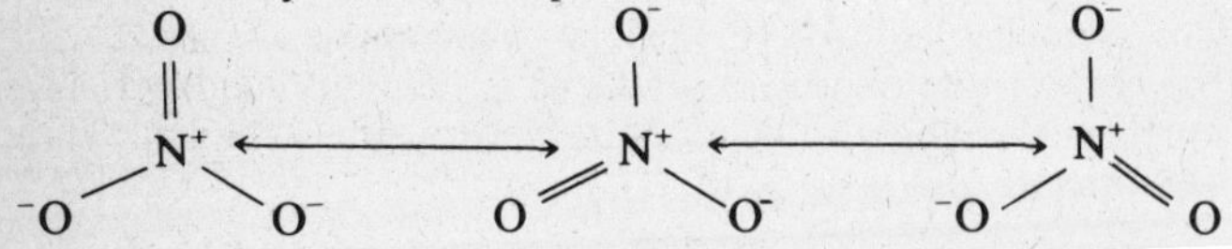

All are soluble in water. Their **thermal stability** depends on the redox potential of the metal. Group 1a nitrates decompose to nitrite and oxygen, the rest decompose to the oxide and NO_2. Some oxides are also unstable and break down to the metal and oxygen as well (e.g. mercury).

Nitrates are detected by the **brown ring test**. The suspected nitrate is dissolved in iron(II) sulphate and cold conc. sulphuric acid is carefully poured down the side of the test tube. A brown ring develops between the two layers. This is the complex $FeSO_4.NO$.

Phosphorus

It has two major allotropes: red and white (or yellow) phosphorus. Only the red form is stable under normal conditions and so it is an example of monotropy. The two forms are quite different. White P is very reactive and poisonous, red P is less reactive and non-poisonous.

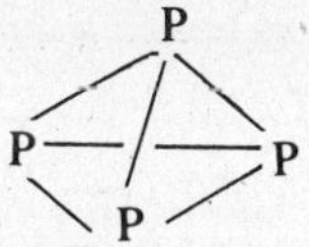

White phosphorus, P.
Tetrahedral discrete molecules.
Bond angle 60°.

Red phosphorus is macromolecular. The reactivity of white phosphorus is probably due to the high strain imposed by the 60° bond angle.

Unlike nitrogen, phosphorus can show valencies of 3 and 5. This is done by promoting an *s* electron into a vacant *d* orbital (expanding the octet).

Electronic structure

	$3s^2$	$3p^3$	$3d^0$
ground state 3 valent	1 l	1 | 1 | 1	| | | |
	lone pair	3 electrons to share	

	$3s^1$	$3p^3$	$3d^1$
excited state 5 valent	1	1 | 1 | 1	1 | | | |
		5 electrons to share	

The 5 valence state is more stable.

Hydride Phosphine, PH_3, is a colourless poisonous gas with an unpleasant smell. It is formed by the reaction of sodium hydroxide on white phosphorus.

$$3NaOH + 3H_2O + P_4 \rightarrow PH_3 + 3NaH_2PO_2$$

This is a disproportionation reaction

$$4P(0) \rightarrow P(\text{-III}) + 3P(+\text{I})$$

Air must be excluded since phosphine is a strong reducing agent and burns in air

$$4PH_3 + 8O_2 \rightarrow P_4O_{10} + 6H_2O$$

It is more powerfully reducing than ammonia. It can convert Ag^+ to Ag

$$6Ag^+ + PH_3 + 3H_2O \rightarrow 6Ag + H_3PO_3 + 6H^+$$

Phosphorus is not as electronegative as nitrogen and phosphine is a weaker base than ammonia. It does not complex with transition metals but can react with hydrogen iodide

$$PH_3 + HI \rightarrow PH_4I$$

Halides Passing dry chlorine over red or white phosphorus in excess produces the **trichloride**, PCl_3. It is tetrahedral

$$P_4 + 6Cl_2 \rightarrow 4PCl_3$$

It is readily hydrolyzed by water to phosphoric(III) acid.

$$PCl_3 + 3H_2O \rightarrow H_3PO_3 + 3HCl$$

Phosphorus pentachloride, PCl_5, is formed by passing excess chlorine over heated phosphorus.

$$PCl_3 + Cl_2 \rightleftharpoons PCl_5$$

Dissociation to PCl_3 occurs at 150°C. PCl_5 is a trigonal bypyramid in the vapour state,

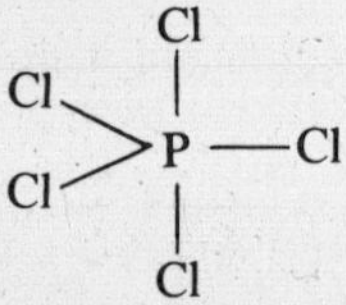

When solid it is ionic, $[PCl_4]^+[PCl_6]^-$. It readily hydrolyzes to phosphoric(V) acid.

$$PCl_5 + 5H_2O \rightarrow H_3PO_4 + 5HCl + H_2O$$

It also reacts with organic –OH groups replacing them with chlorine.

Oxides Burning phosphorus in a limited amount of air

produces the **trioxide**, P_4O_6, and in excess air the **pentoxide**, P_4O_{10}.

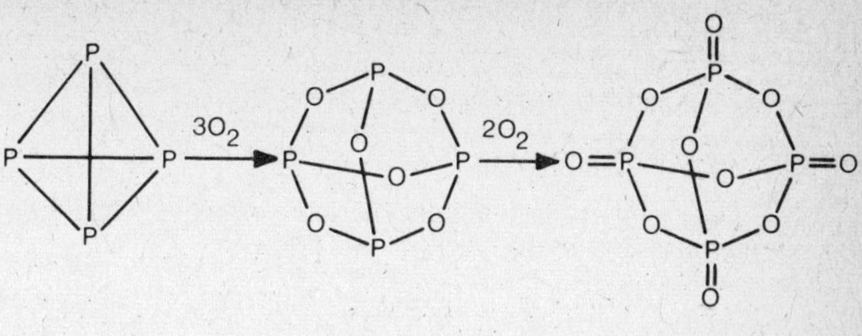

P_4 P_4O_6 P_4O_{10}

The pentoxide is used as a drying agent. On hydrolysis the P–O–P bonds are broken.

Oxyacids Hydrolysis of the oxides produces oxyacids

$$P_4O_6 + 6H_2O \rightarrow 4H_3PO_3$$

phosphoric(IV) acid

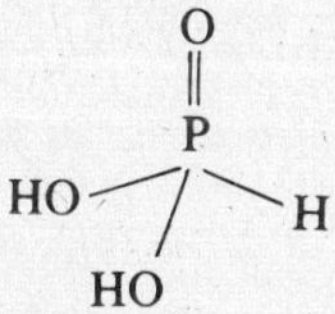

tetrahedral

Phosphoric(IV) acid is dibasic. Only hydrogens attached to oxygens are acidic. It is a moderately strong acid and forms two sets of salts. Both acids and salts are strong reducing agents. Hydrolysis of phosphorus pentoxide produces **phosphoric(V) acid.**

$$P_4O_{10} + 6H_2O \rightarrow 4H_3PO_4$$

It is a crystalline solid but is deliquescent and normally is a viscous solution due to extensive hydrogen bonding. The acid is tribasic and therefore forms three sets of salts.

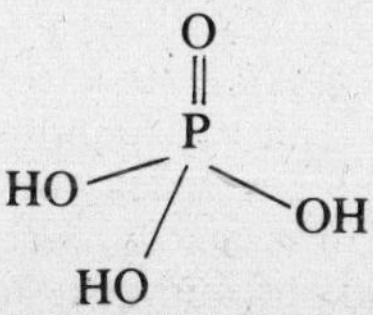

phosphoric(V) acid

Three end-points should be found when titrating with NaOH:

$$NaOH + H_3PO_4 \rightarrow NaH_2PO_4 + H_2O$$

detected with methyl orange.

$$NaOH + NaH_2PO_4 \rightarrow Na_2HPO_4 + H_2O$$

detected by phenolphthalein.

The last end-point cannot usually be detected as the PO_4^{3-} ion is a strong base and hydrolyzes in solution.

$$Na_3PO_4 + H_2O \rightarrow NaOH + Na_2HPO_4$$

Most phosphates are insoluble in water. They are used as fertilizers.

Arsenic, antimony and bismuth

The chemistry of these elements is somewhat similar to phosphorus but the five valent state becomes less stable from P through to Bi. They follow the normal trend of becoming more metallic with increasing atomic number. Bismuth is able to form a Bi^{3+} ion (inert pair effect) and is metallic. The hydrides, arsine AsH_3, stibine, SbH_3 and bismuthine, BiH_3, become increasingly unstable and more difficult to form. They are made by hydrolysis of the binary compound of magnesium with the group 5 element using water or dilute acid, e.g.

$$Mg_3As_2 + 6H_2O \rightarrow 2AsH_3 + 3Mg(OH)_2$$

They are much less basic than phosphine as the donation of the lone pair becomes more difficult as the atomic number increases.

Group 6: Oxygen and sulphur

	electron configuration	ionic radius (2−)	electro-negativity
O	$1s^2 2s^2 2p^4$	0·140 nm	3·5
S	$..2s^2 2p^6 3s^2 3p^4$	0·184 nm	2·5

The elements all have an outer shell of six electrons and therefore show a valency of two which can be both covalent or ionic. In addition sulphur shows a covalency of 4 and 6 by promoting electrons. The elements form acidic oxides and are all non-metals but the lower members of the group have slight metallic character. The elements are highly electronegative and reactive.

Oxygen

Laboratory preparation 1. Catalytic decomposition of hydrogen peroxide. 2. Oxidation of hydrogen peroxide with acidified potassium manganate(VII). 3. Thermal decomposition of an anion rich in oxygen, e.g. manganate(VII), chlorate(VII). 4. Electrolysis of dilute aqueous solutions. 5. The action of a peroxide on water.

Compounds: Ozone This gas occurs to a slight extent in the upper atmosphere. In the laboratory it is prepared by passing a stream of dry oxygen through a silent electric discharge. About 10% conversion to ozone occurs.

$$3O_2 \rightleftharpoons \underset{\text{ozone}}{2O_3}$$

There is a loss of entropy and the free energy change greatly favours oxygen in the equilibrium. Ozone is highly unstable and sparks decompose it.

Structure

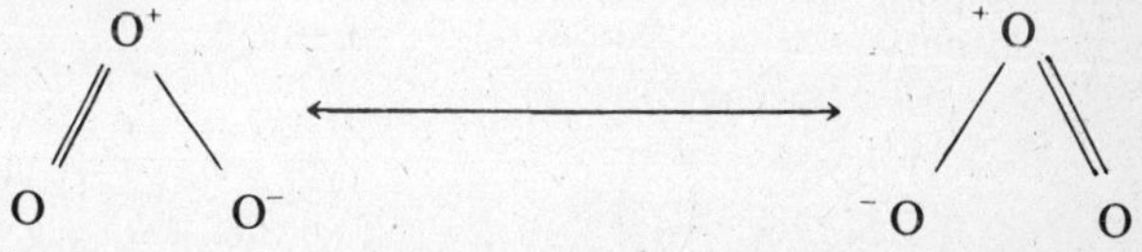

It is an extremely powerful oxidizing agent in acid solution.

$$O_3 + 2H^+ + 2e^- \rightarrow O_2 + H_2O \qquad E^\theta = +2{\cdot}07\ \text{V}$$

It will oxidize sulphides to sulphates:

$$S^{2-} + 4O_3 \rightarrow SO_4^{2-} + 4O_2$$

and tin(II) to tin(IV):

$$3Sn^{2+} + 6H^+ + O_3 \rightarrow 3Sn^{4+} + 3H_2O$$

It adds across carbon–carbon double bonds; (see p. 232).

Water, H_2O. It has unusually high melting and boiling points, and ice has a lower density than water. These properties are explained by the existence of extensive hydrogen bonding. This is due to the high electronegativity of oxygen which also gives the molecule a large dipole moment. It is a good solvent for ionic compounds. Hydration of ions is due to electrostatic attractions of water molecules, the energy released on hydration overcomes the lattice energy and many ionic solids dissolve.

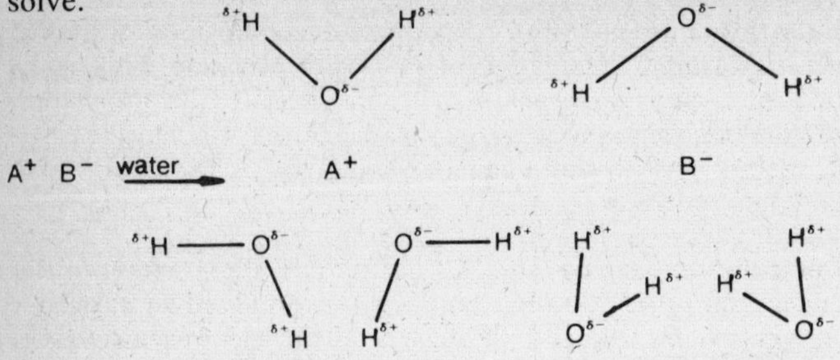

The electrostatic attraction leads to water being retained in a lattice when salts are recrystallized from water. This is termed water of crystallization. Water molecules form many complexes with metal cations.

It can act as a proton donor (acid) when a base is present or as a proton acceptor (base) when an acid is present.

Hydrogen peroxide, H_2O_2. It is prepared in the laboratory by adding a group 1 or 2 peroxide to cold dilute acid.

$$BaO_2 + H_2SO_4 \rightarrow BaSO_4 + H_2O_2$$

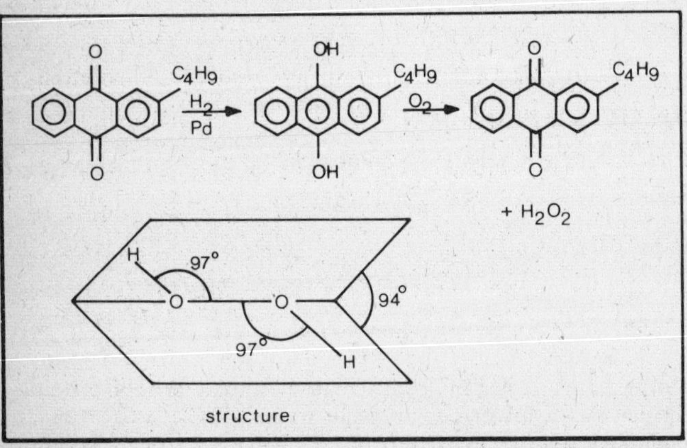

Figure 47

Industrially 2-butyl anthraquinone is catalytically reduced to 2-butyl anthraquinol which is then oxidized by oxygen enriched air giving hydrogen peroxide.

All true peroxides contain an O—O linkage, which is a fairly weak bond and accounts for their instability. Hydrogen peroxide is a strong oxidizing agent in acid solution,

$$H_2O_2 + 2H^+ + 2e^- \rightarrow 2H_2O \qquad E^\theta = +1{\cdot}77\ V$$

It will convert iodide to iodine and iron(II) to iron(III). It may also behave as a reducing agent in acid solution in the presence of strong oxidizing agents such as $KMnO_4$,

$$H_2O_2 \rightarrow O_2 + 2H^+ + 2e^- \qquad E^\theta = -0{\cdot}69$$

$$2MnO_4 + 5H_2O_2 + 6H^+ \rightarrow 2Mn^{2+} + 8H_2O + 5O_2$$

Oxides 1. **Basic oxides** These are oxides of metals of low oxidation state and contain the O^{2-} ion. All basic oxides react with acids to form salts. If the oxide is soluble it will form a hydroxide.

in acid: $O^{2-} + 2H_3O^+ \rightarrow 3H_2O$

in water: $O^{2-} + H_2O \rightarrow 2OH^-$

The ionic and basic character of metal oxides decreases with (a) decreasing size and (b) increasing charge of metal ion:

$$Na_2O > MgO > Al_2O_3$$

most basic — least basic

2. **Acidic oxides** These are oxides of non-metals and transition metals in high oxidation states. They are predominantly covalent and usually simple molecules which dissolve in water to form acids, e.g. SO_3, P_4O_{10}, CO_2. Insoluble acidic oxides combine with basic oxides on heating to form salts.

3. **Amphoteric oxides** These can form salts with both strong acids or strong bases. They are oxides of the less electropositive metals, e.g. Zn and Al.

$$ZnO + 2HCl \rightarrow ZnCl_2 + H_2O$$

$$ZnO + 2NaOH \rightarrow Na_2ZnO_2 + H_2O$$

4. **Neutral oxides** These show no acid or base character, e.g. CO, H_2O, N_2O.

The classifications are not rigid with many oxides able to be in more than one group.

Sulphur

Allotropy Solid sulphur generally adopts S_8 rings which can stack in two ways. This gives rise to two allotropes: rhombic or α-sulphur, stable below 95·6°C, and monoclinic or β-sulphur which is stable above 95·6°C. Because the forms are readily inter-convertible it is known as **enantiotropy**.

Compounds Sulphur combines directly with most metals to form **sulphides**, S^{2-}. These are much less ionic than the corresponding oxides

$$Mg + S \rightarrow Mg^{2+}S^{2-}$$

Sulphur also combines directly with some non-metals, e.g. fluorine, chlorine, oxygen and carbon. It has no reaction with water or dilute acids but is oxidized by conc. sulphuric and nitric acids.

Sulphur can show a valency of 4 and 6 in addition to the normal valency of 2 by promoting electrons into the vacant $3d$ orbital.

ground state, valency 2

1st excited state, valency 4

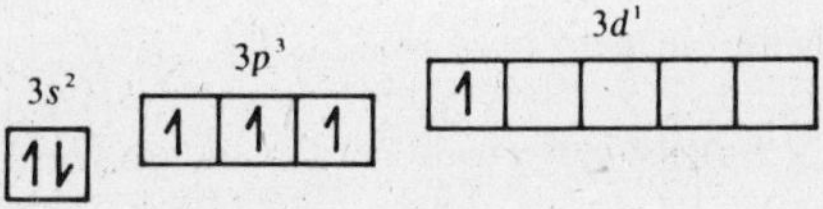

2nd excited state, valency 6

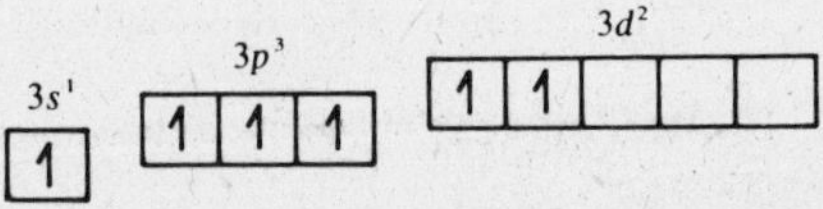

Only fluorine and oxygen can give sulphur a valency of six.

Hydrogen sulphide, H_2S. The gas is prepared by the action of dilute acid on a sulphide. It dissolves slightly in water forming an acid solution:

$$H_2S \xrightleftharpoons{\text{weak}} H^+ + HS^- \xrightleftharpoons{\text{very weak}} 2H^+ + S^{2-}$$

It is a weak acid and can form two sets of salts. It acts as a reducing agent depositing sulphur:

$$S^{2-} \rightarrow S + 2e^- \qquad E^\theta = +0{\cdot}51\ V$$

e.g.

$$SO_2 + 2H_2S \rightarrow 2H_2O + 3S$$

$$Cl_2 + H_2S \rightarrow 2HCl + S$$

$$2MnO_4^- + 6H^+ + 5H_2S \rightarrow 2Mn^{2+} + 8H_2O + 5S$$

Sulphur(IV) oxide The gas is prepared by (1) burning sulphur in air, (2) acidification of a sulphate(IV) (sulphite) or hydrogen sulphate(IV), (3) reduction of concentrated sulphuric(VI) acid by a metal such as copper

$$Cu + 2H_2SO_4 \rightarrow CuSO_4 + 2H_2O + SO_2$$

Structure

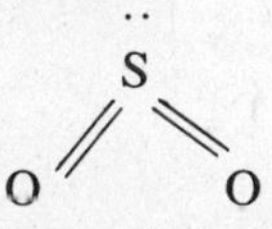

oxidation state of sulphur, +4.

The gas is soluble in water forming a weak acid solution. The acid decomposes when concentrated.

$$SO_2 + H_2O \rightleftharpoons \underset{\text{sulphuric(IV) acid.}}{H_2SO_3} \xrightleftharpoons{\text{weak}} H^+ + HSO_3^- \xrightleftharpoons{\text{very weak}} 2H^+ + SO_3^{2-}$$

The gas and the acid react with bases to form salts. Moist sulphur(IV) oxide and sulphate(IV) compounds behave as reducing agents. Sulphur(IV) is converted to sulphur(VI)

$$SO_3^{2-} + H_2O \rightarrow SO_4^{2-} + 2H^+ + 2e^- \qquad E^\theta = -0{\cdot}17\ V$$

e.g. Mn(VII) goes to Mn(II)

$$2MnO_4^- + 5SO_2 + 2H_2O \rightarrow 2Mn^{2+} + 4H^+ + 5SO_4^{2-}$$

and chlorine to chloride:

$$Cl_2 + SO_3^{2-} + H_2O \rightarrow 2Cl^- + SO_4^{2-} + 2H^+$$

Sulphur(VI) oxide Industrial preparation is by the **Contact process**. Sulphur(IV) oxide and oxygen at one atmosphere pressure are heated to 400°C and passed over a vanadium(V) oxide catalyst (see p. 46).

Structure

in the gaseous state

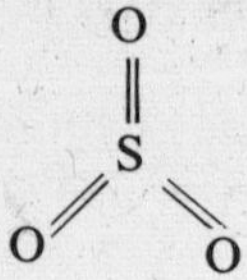

oxidation state of sulphur +6.

planar

In the laboratory SO_3 is prepared by strongly heating a sulphate

$$Fe_2(SO_4)_3 \rightarrow Fe_2O_3 + 3SO_3$$

or by dehydrating conc. H_2SO_4 with phosphorus(V) oxide

$$H_2SO_4 \rightarrow H_2O + SO_3$$

The gas is an extremely acidic oxide reacting explosively with water to form sulphuric(VI) acid. It is an oxidizing agent

$$SO_3 + 2H^+ + 2e^- \rightarrow SO_2 + H_2O \qquad E^\theta = +0{\cdot}17\ V$$

Sulphuric(VI) acid It is prepared industrially via the contact process. The sulphur(VI) oxide produced is cooled and absorbed in 98% sulphuric(VI) acid to produce oleum ($H_2S_2O_7$). Direct absorption by water is too dangerous. Dilution of oleum gives sulphuric acid.

Reactions of sulphuric(VI) acid 1. **Acidic properties**. In aqueous solution the acid has two ionizations:

$$\underset{\text{complete}}{H_2SO_4 \rightleftharpoons H^+ + HSO_4^-} \underset{\text{about 10\%}}{\rightleftharpoons 2H^+ + SO_4^{2-}}$$

It can form both normal and acid salts.

2. **Dehydrating properties** The acid has a strong affinity for water and is used extensively as a drying agent, particularly for gases. It is capable of removing elements of water from compounds such as carbohydrates and oxalates.

$$\underset{\text{glucose}}{C_6H_{12}O_6} \xrightarrow{-6H_2O} 6C$$

$$H_2C_2O_4 \xrightarrow{-H_2O} CO + CO_2$$
oxalic acid

3. **Oxidizing properties** The hot concentrated acid is a strong oxidizing agent but not as strong as nitric(V) acid. Generally sulphur(IV) oxide is produced.

metals:

$$2H_2SO_4 + 2e^- \rightarrow SO_4^{2-} 2H_2O + SO_2 \qquad E^\ominus = +0{\cdot}17\ V$$
$$S(VI) \rightarrow S(IV)$$
$$Cu \rightarrow Cu^{2+} + 2e^-$$

$$Cu + 2H_2SO_4 \rightarrow CuSO_4 + 2H_2O + SO_2$$

non-metals:

$$C + 2H_2SO_4 \rightarrow 2H_2O + CO_2 + SO_2$$
$$S + 2H_2SO_4 \rightarrow 2H_2O + 3SO_2$$
$$(S(0) + 2S(VI) \rightarrow 3S(IV))$$

compounds: $2HBr + H_2SO_4 \rightarrow Br_2 + 2H_2O + SO_2$

but with iodide, a stronger oxidizing agent:

$$H_2SO_4 + 8H^+ + 8e^- \rightarrow H_2S + 4H_2O$$
$$8I^- \rightarrow 4I_2 + 8e^-$$

$$8HI + H_2SO_4 \rightarrow H_2S + 4I_2 + 4H_2O$$

4. **Sulphonation** The acid is used extensively to sulphonate organic compounds (addition of $-OSO_3H$).

Sulphates These are prepared by reacting metal, metal oxide, hydroxide or carbonate with sulphuric acid. Most are soluble (except Ba, Pb, Sr and Ca) and they are more thermally stable than nitrates.

Structure

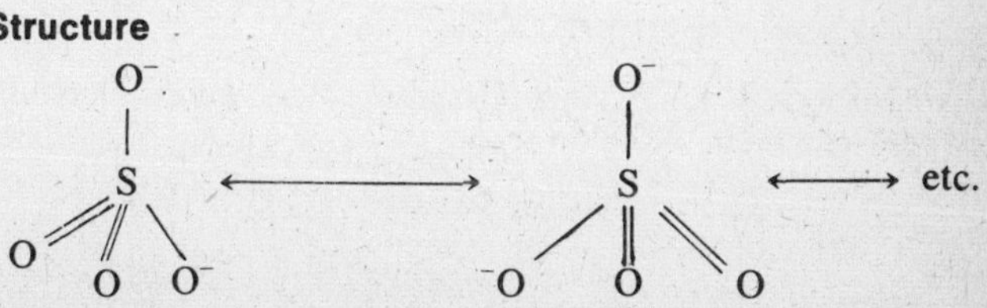

tetrahedral

Thiosulphate, $S_2O_3^{2-}$. The acid has never been isolated but the salts are well known. It is regarded as being derived from the sulphate ion, with an oxygen being replaced by a sulphur.

Structure

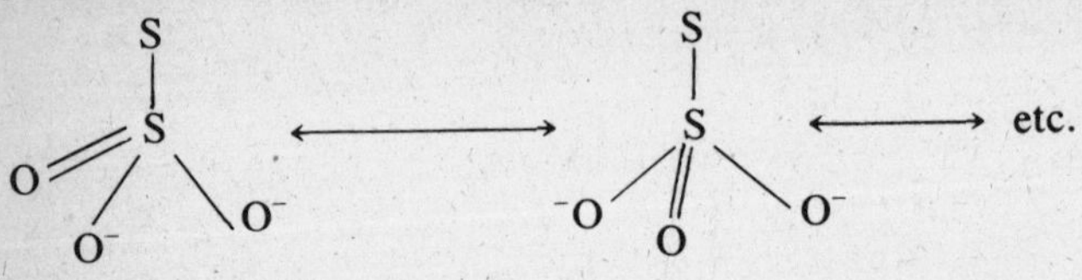

Sodium thiosulphate, $Na_2S_2O_3$, the most important salt, is obtained by boiling sodium sulphate(IV) with sulphur; in acid the reverse reaction occurs

$$S + SO_3^{2-} \rightarrow S_2O_3^{2-}$$

It is a reducing agent

$$2S_2O_3^{2-} \rightarrow \underset{\text{tetrathionate}}{S_4O_6^{2-}} + 2e^-$$

Iodine is reduced to iodide (this is used in volumetric analysis).

$$I_2 + 2S_2O_3^{2-} \rightarrow 2I^- + S_4O_6^{2-}$$

Halides and oxyhalides Sulphur combines directly with chlorine.

$$\underset{\text{molten}}{2S} + Cl_2 \rightarrow \underset{\text{disulphur dichloride}}{S_2Cl_2}$$

S_2Cl_2 is an evil smelling red liquid. When reacted with chlorine at 0°C sulphur dichloride is formed,

$$S_2Cl_2 + Cl_2 \rightarrow 2SCl_2$$

With fluorine, **sulphur hexafluouride** SF_6, is formed.
Thionyl chloride, $SOCl_2$, is made by reacting sulphur(IV) oxide with phosphorus (V) chloride:

$$SO_2 + PCl_5 \rightarrow SOCl_2 + POCl_3$$

It is hydrolyzed rapidly by –OH groups, e.g. water, alcohols, and replaces them by chlorine, e.g.

$$\underset{\text{ethanoic acid}}{CH_3COOH} + SOCl_2 \rightarrow \underset{\text{ethanoyl chloride}}{CH_3COCl} + SO_2 + HCl$$

Group 7. The halogens

	electronic structure	atomic radius(nm)	ionic, X^- radius(nm)	electro-negativity	redox potential
F	$1s^2 2s^2 2p^5$	0·072	0·136	4·0	+2·87 V
Cl	$\ldots 3s^2 3p^5$	0·099	0·181	3·0	+1·36
Br	$\ldots 4s^2 4p^5$	0·114	0·195	2·8	+1·07
I	$\ldots 5s^2 5p^5$	0·133	0·216	2·5	+0·54

The halogens are all non-metallic electronegative (electron attracting) elements. There is a steady increase in radius with increasing atomic number. This accounts for the trend to lower electronegativity and redox potential down the group due to the increased shielding of the nucleus. The elements are oxidizing agents, fluorine being an extremely powerful one and combine readily with metals and hydrogen.

There is still a slight trend to metallic character with increasing atomic number and iodine shows one or two metallic properties. They have seven outer electrons and can gain an electron to form the X^- ion or share an electron to form a covalent bond. Fluorine is restricted to an oxidation state of −1 but the remaining elements have vacant *d* orbitals available and can promote electrons to give oxidation states of +1, +3, +5 and +7 as well. They are all diatomic molecules.

Fluorine

Its extreme reactivity (it is the most electronegative element) is due to (1) the low fluorine–fluorine bond strength, (2) the high bond strength between fluorine and other elements, (3) the small size of atom and anion.

Preparation Because of its reactivity fluorine can only be extracted by electrolysis of fused potassium fluoride. Water must be absent as fluorine would immediately react with it.

Properties Fluorine combines with almost all other elements, even some 'inert' gases. In combination with other elements it will often bring out their highest oxidation state. It oxidizes all other halides and will displace them from their salts.

Hydrogen fluoride It is prepared by the action of conc. sulphuric acid on calcium fluoride:

$$CaF_2 + H_2SO_4 \rightarrow CaSO_4 + 2HF$$

The direct reaction between hydrogen and fluorine is explosive. The boiling point of HF is high compared with the other hydrogen halides due to hydrogen bonding.

—H - - - F—H - - - F—H - - - F—H - - - F—H - - -

In water it behaves as a **weak acid** (unlike other hydrogen halides) due to the high H–F bond strength.

$$HF + H_2O \rightleftharpoons H_3O^+ + F^- \qquad K_a = 7 \times 10^{-4}\ \text{mol dm}^{-3}$$

The solution attacks most metals to form fluorides. These are extremely ionic and consequently in general more soluble than other halides, e.g. AgF is more soluble than other silver halides. The small size of the fluoride ion however may result in a high lattice energy which occasionally reduces solubility, e.g. CaF_2.

Chlorine, bromine and iodine

Industrial preparation of chlorine is by the electrolysis of brine, chlorine being a by-product of many industrial processes. Bromine is obtained by displacement from sea water with chlorine.

Laboratory preparation of chlorine is by oxidation of hydrochloric acid with potassium manganate(VII) or manganese(IV) oxide, e.g.

$$MnO_2 + 4HCl \rightarrow MnCl_2 + Cl_2 + 2H_2O$$

Similar methods are used for bromine and iodine.

Chemical properties All three combine directly with many metals and non-metals (not N, C and O). Chlorine is the most and iodine the least reactive. They show oxidation states of −1, 1, 3, 5 and 7. This is due to the vacant *d* orbitals, e.g. for bromine see below.

ground state, valency one

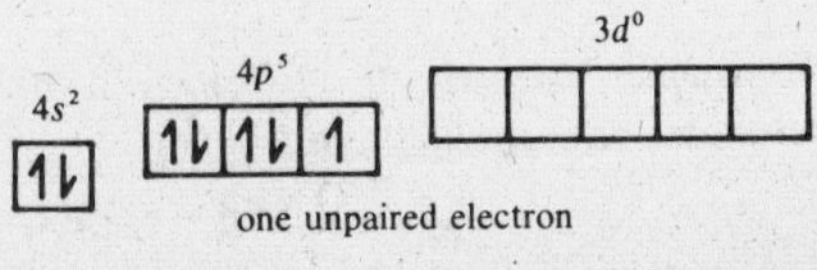

1st excited state, valency 3

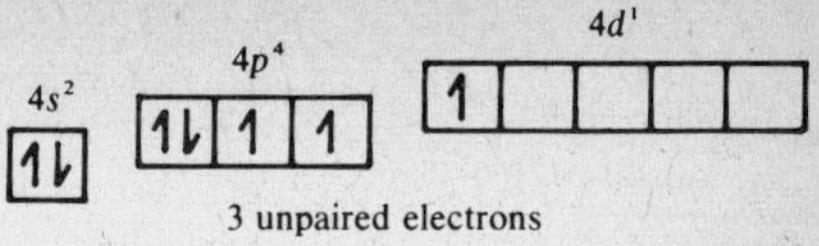

2nd excited state, valency 5

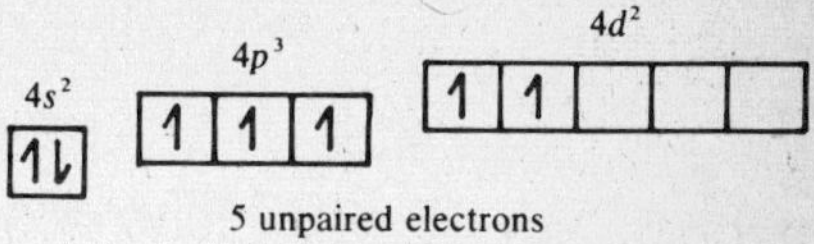

3rd excited state, valency 7

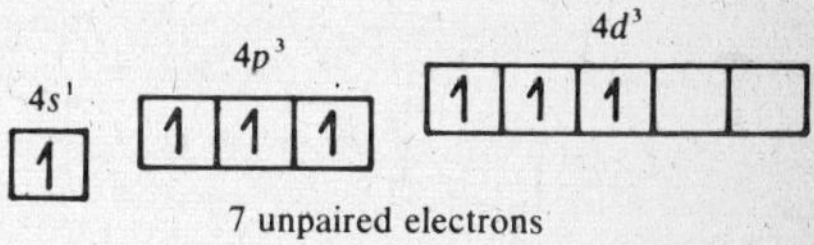

Reaction with water Chlorine and bromine are moderately soluble and iodine sparingly soluble in water. Only chlorine is extensively hydrolyzed.

$$Cl_{2(aq)} + 2H_2O \rightarrow \underset{\text{chloric(I) acid}}{HOCl} + Cl^- + H_3O^+$$

The corresponding bromic(I) acid forms to a limited extent.

Reaction with alkali In the presence of alkali the above equilibrium is shifted to the right and chlorate(I) (hypochlorite) ions are produced

$$HOCl + OH^- \rightarrow H_2O + ClO^-$$

Bromate(I) and iodate(I) ions are also formed but they disproportionate to halate(V) and halide ion, e.g.

$$\underset{\text{bromate(I)}}{3BrO^-} \rightarrow \underset{\text{bromide}}{2Br^-} + \underset{\text{bromate(V)}}{BrO_3^-}$$

The chlorate(I) ion only disproportionates above 75°C (see reaction of chlorine with sodium hydroxide p. 135).

Oxidizing reactions There is a decrease in oxidizing power with increase in atomic number. This trend can be shown by a series of displacement

$$Cl_2 > Br_2 > I_2$$
$$\leftarrow \text{oxidizing power}$$

reactions. Chlorine displaces bromide and iodide from their salts and bromine displaces iodide. Carrying out these reactions in aqueous solution above a layer of tetrachloromethane the organic layer will turn red if bromine and violet if iodine is displaced.

$$Cl_2 + 2e^- \rightarrow 2Cl^- \quad \text{reduction}$$
$$2Br^- \rightarrow Br_2 + 2e^- \quad \text{oxidation}$$

$$Cl_2 + 2Br^- \rightarrow 2Cl^- + Br_2$$

and $$Br_2 + 2I^- \rightarrow 2Br^- + I_2$$

All three halogens oxidize sulphide to sulphur, e.g.

$$H_2S + Cl_2 \rightarrow 2HCl + S$$

and sulphite to sulphate

$$SO_3^{2-} + H_2O + Br_2 \rightarrow 2H^+ + 2Br^- + SO_4^{2-}$$

Chlorine and bromine oxidize thiosulphate to sulphate,

$$S_2O_3^{2-} + 4Cl_2 + 5H_2O \rightarrow 2SO_4^{2-} + 10H^+ + 8Cl^-$$

while iodine only oxidizes it to tetrathionate, $S_4O_6^{2-}$ (see p. 164).

Complex ion Iodine dissolved in KI solution forms the complex $[I_3]^-$.

Hydrogen halides. Preparation 1. Direct synthesis from halogen and hydrogen. Reaction proceeds faster in sunlight and is catalyzed by water vapour.

$$H_2 + X_2 \rightarrow 2HX$$

2. Hydrolysis of phosphorus halide, e.g. HBr is obtained by dropping bromine onto a paste of red phosphorus and water.

$$6H_2O + 2P + 3Br_2 \rightarrow 2H_3PO_3 + 6HBr$$

3. Hydrogen chloride may be obtained by dropping conc. sulphuric acid onto an ionic halide.

$$Cl^- + H_2SO_4 \rightarrow HCl + HSO_4^-$$

This method is not suitable for HBr or HI because they can be oxidized by sulphuric acid

$$2HBr + H_2SO_4 \rightarrow Br_2 + SO_2 + 2H_2O$$

$$8HI + H_2SO_4 \rightarrow 4I_2 + H_2S + 4H_2O$$

Chemical properties Hydrogen chloride is stable to heat, hydrogen bromide shows slight decomposition and hydrogen iodide produces violet fumes of iodine when a red hot iron needle is plunged in the gas. This indicates the change in H–X bond strength.

$$H\text{—}Cl > H\text{—}Br > H\text{—}I$$

increasing stability and bond strength ←

increasing acid strength and reducing power. →

The change in bond strength means that in aqueous solution HI is the strongest and HCl the weakest acid. All three are completely ionized in aqueous solution.

$$HX + H_2O \rightarrow H_3O^+ + X^-$$

The reducing power also increases down the group. This is seen from the reaction with sulphuric acid.

Oxides and oxyacids **Oxyacids of chlorine**

		E^θ		
+7	ClO_4^-	+1·2 V	chlorate(VII)	(perchlorate)
+5	ClO_3^-	+1·2 V	chlorate(VI)	(chlorate)
+3	ClO_2^-	+1·6 V	chlorate(III)	(chlorite)
+1	ClO^-	+1·6 V	chlorate(I)	(hypochlorite)
0	Cl_2	+1·4 V	chlorine	
−1	Cl^-		chloride	

All the positive oxidation states are oxidizing agents. An increase in oxygen content leads to 1. an increase in acid strength, 2. decrease in oxidizing power.

Key terms

Variation in atomic radii Two factors contribute to the size of an atom: 1. the number of protons in the nucleus, 2. the 'screening effect' of the electrons. The protons exert a pull on all the outer electrons which would lead to a contraction in radius with increasing atomic number. This is the overriding factor when adding electrons to the same quantum shell and it is found that **atomic radius decreases in going across a period**. The 'screening effect' is the mutual repulsion between electrons which causes an increase in atomic radius with increasing numbers of electrons (hence atomic number). This latter factor is more important in progressing down a group and hence **atomic radius increases down a group**.

Ionization energy The energy required to remove one electron completely from the neutral atom. **Ionization energy increases across a period** due to the decrease in atomic radius. **It decreases down a group** due to increase in radius.

Electronegativity This expresses the relative attraction of an atom for the electrons in a covalent bond formed with another element. It varies in a similar manner to ionization energy. There is a decrease in electronegativity, and therefore an increase in metallic character, in going down a group and an increase in electronegativity, or decrease in metallic character in going across a period.

Table of electronegativities

H 2·1						
Li 1·0	Be 1·5	B 2·0	C 2·5	N 3·0	O 3·5	F 4·0
Na 0·9	Mg 1·2	Al 1·5	Si 1·8	P 2·1	S 2·5	Cl 3·0
K 0·8	Ca 1·0					Br 2·8
Rb 0·8	Sr 1·0					I 2·5
Cs 0·7	Ba 0·9					

Variation in properties of compounds of the third period elements Na to Ar

Hydrides Hydrogen is more electronegative than the earlier members of the period but is less electronegative than the later members. The polarity of the bond between hydrogen and a third row element therefore varies across the row. With sodium the hydride is ionic with the electrons residing completely with hydrogen, MgH_2 is ionic but with a degree of covalent character and AlH_3, which only exists in ethereal solution, is partially covalent. All these three produce hydrogen on addition of water. PH_3 is a non-polar covalent molecule and with sulphur and chlorine there is a degree of ionic character but the hydrogen is now the positive end of the dipole. In water these latter two hydrides are acidic.

NaH	MgH_2	(AlH_3)	SiH_4	PH_3	H_2S	HCl
ionic	ionic		covalent	covalent	partially ionic	
← give off H_2 in → water			gives off H_2 if OH^- present	no reaction	← acidic →	

Chlorides Chlorine is more electronegative than all the other elements in the third row and all the element–chlorine bonds are polarized with chlorine the more negative. NaCl is wholly ionic, $AlCl_3$ is essentially covalent, it will not conduct electricity when molten and is soluble in some organic solvents. $SiCl_4$ is covalent and is hydrolyzed by water, PCl_5 is slightly anomalous since it exists as $[PCl_4]^+[PCl_6]^-$ in the solid state but the vapour is covalent. Sulphur chlorides are covalent but rather unstable. The chlorides become more covalent and more readily hydrolyzed across the period.

NaCl	$MgCl_2$	$AlCl_3$	$SiCl_4$	PCL_5	S_2Cl_2
← ionic →		← covalent →			
hydrolyzes on heating		partial hydrol.	complete hydrolysis		

Oxides Oxygen is the secondmost electronegative element and the oxides have a higher degree of ionic character than the chlorides. Sodium, magnesium and aluminium oxides are all ionic, silica $(SiO_2)_n$ is a macromolecule with ionic character and the remaining oxides are essentially covalent. Across the period the oxides begin by being strongly basic and progress via the amphoteric aluminium oxide to the strongly acidic SO_3 and Cl_2O_7.

Na_2O	MgO	Al_2O_3	$(SiO_2)_n$	P_2O_5	SO_3	Cl_2O_7
ionic	ionic	ionic	macromolecule	← covalent →		
basic	basic	amphoteric	← acidic →			

Hydroxides The hydroxides can be basic if they ionize to produce hydroxide ions or acidic if they ionize to produce hydrogen ions. The ionization depends on the electronegativity of the third row element. The less electronegative sodium and magnesium produce hydroxide ions and are basic, aluminium hydroxide is amphoteric and the rest are acidic.

$NaOH$ $Mg(OH)_2$ $Al(OH)_3$ H_2SiO_3 H_3PO_4 H_2SO_4 $HClO_4$
⟵ basic ⟶ amphoteric ⟵ acidic ⟶

Variation of properties in groups

Groups 1 and 2 All the elements in these groups are metallic, they tend to lose their outer electrons to form positive ions and the oxides are basic. Atomic radius increases down a group and so the ease with which an outer electron is lost also increases. Hence there is an increase in metallic character (electropositivity) down the group. The compounds of the elements are generally ionic with the exception of Li, Be and some Mg compounds. The thermal stability of the nitrates, carbonates and sulphates increases down the group. Lithium has an anomalously high reactivity in aqueous solution due to its extremely small size.

Groups 4 and 5 Again the atomic radius increases down the group and there is a subsequent trend from non-metals at the top of the groups, through metalloid and finally to metallic elements at the bottom. This trend can be seen in the change in acidity of the oxides in group 4:

CO_2 SiO_2 GeO_2 SnO PbO
←acidic→ ←amphoteric⟶ basic

Carbon and nitrogen show differences from the remaining members of each group, due to the much higher electronegativity of these elements and to the lack of available *d* orbitals which restricts them to valencies of 4 and 3 respectively.

Groups 6 and 7 These contain the most electronegative elements (prone to accept electrons). Electronegativity decreases down the group but all the elements are principally non-metals although iodine does show slight metallic character.

Halogens With electropositive elements these form ionic compounds. They become less powerful oxidizing agents in going down the group, i.e. the $\frac{1}{2}X_2/X^-$ redox potential becomes smaller. Thus fluorine displaces chloride ions, Cl_2 displaces Br^- ions etc. With the more electronegative elements the halogens form covalent bonds. The hydrogen halides gain more ionic character from iodine to fluorine and this is reflected in the decrease in bond strength from HF down to HI. Hydrogen iodide is the strongest acid in aqueous solution.

Chapter 7
d Block and First Row Transition Elements

	outer electronic configuration	atomic radius (nm)	ionic (M^{3+}) radius (nm)	redox potentials $M^{3+}_{(aq)} + 3e^- \rightarrow M_{(s)}$
Sc	$...3s^23p^63d^14s^2$	0·144	0·081	−2·10 V
Ti	$...3s^23p^63d^24s^2$	0·132	0·076	−1·21
V	$...3s^23p^63d^34s^2$	0·122	0·074	−0·85
Cr	$...3s^23p^63d^54s^1$	0·117	0·069	−0·74
Mn	$...3s^23p^63d^54s^2$	0·117	0·066	−0·28
Fe	$...3s^23p^63d^64s^2$	0·116	0·064	−0·04
Co	$...3s^23p^63d^74s^2$	0·116	0·063	+0·40
Ni	$...3s^23p^63d^84s^2$	0·115	0·062	
Cu	$...3s^23p^63d^{10}4s^1$	0·117	0·069(+2)	
Zn	$...3s^23p^63d^{10}4s^2$	0·125	0·074(+2)	

Transition elements

These are elements whose ions have partially filled inner sub-shells, the 3*d* sub-shell in the case of the first row transitions. Copper is included since it forms $Cu^{2+}(...3d^94s^0)$ but scandium, which can only form $Sc^{3+}(...3d^04s^0)$ and is similar to aluminium, and zinc, which only forms $Zn^{2+}(...3d^{10}4s^0)$ and is similar to group 2a elements, are not. The 3*d* and 4*s* sub-shells have very similar energies and a fully or half-filled sub-shell, where each orbital contains two or one electron respectively, is very stable. Hence, the ground state of chromium is $3d^54s^1$ and of copper is $3d^{10}4s^1$. Transition elements have small atomic radii and the large number of valence electrons, 3*d* and 4*s*, cause them to be hard, dense and very metallic. Because they possess similar atomic and ionic radii they have similar electronegativities and ionization potentials and show a remarkable horizontal similarity.

Special properties of transition metals

1. Coloured ions Transition metal ions are coloured both as solid salts and in solution.

Colours of some *d* block hydrated metal ions

No. of unpaired *d* electrons	Ions and colour
0	Sc^{3+},$3d^0$; Zn^{2+},$3d^{10}$, both colourless
1	Ti^{3+},$3d^1$, purple; V^{4+},$3d^1$, blue
2	V^{3+},$3d^2$, green; Ni^{2+},$3d^8$, green
3	Cr^{3+},$3d^3$, violet; Co^{2+},$3d^7$, pink
4	Cr^{2+},$3d^4$, blue; Fe^{2+},$3d^6$, green
5	Mn^{2+},$3d^5$, pink; Fe^{3+},$3d^5$, yellow

The colour of the ions is due to absorption of the complementary colour of light by promotion of unpaired *d* electrons to higher energy states. Sc^{3+} and Zn^{2+} are colourless because they have 0 and 10 *d* electrons respectively. Colour is due to the incomplete *d* shell and also to the nature of the ligand (see next section) surrounding the ion. The ligand can alter the *d* orbital energy and change the wavelength of light absorbed. Thus Cu^{2+} anhydrous is white, Cu^{2+} hydrated is light blue, Cu^{2+} ammoniated is a deep blue and Cu^{2+} in the presence of chloride ions is green.

$$\underset{\text{green}}{[CuCl_4]^{2-}} \xleftarrow{Cl^-} Cu^{2+} \xrightarrow{H_2O} \underset{\text{blue}}{[Cu(H_2O)_6]^{2+}}$$

$$Cu^{2+} \xrightarrow{NH_3} \underset{\text{deep blue}}{[Cu(NH_3)_4]^{2+}}$$

2. Complex ions, also called **coordination compounds**, consist of a central atom or ion linked to other atoms, ions or molecules which are called ligands. Ligands must have a lone pair and are either neutral or negative. Common ligands are Cl^-, CN^-, H_2O, NH_3, O^{2-}, OH^-. The bond between ligand and central atom or ion may in some cases be electrostatic but it is normally considered to be a coordinate bond with the ligand donating a lone pair to a vacant orbital on the central atom or ion. Complex formation is favoured by having small highly charged central ions which can exert a strong attraction over the negative or polar ligands. Transition metal ions, often small and highly charged and having vacant *d* orbitals, form many complex ions. The number of ligands in a complex ion is commonly four or six; the ligands mutually repel each other and the shapes adopted are either square or tetrahedral (four coordinate) or octahedral (six coordinate).

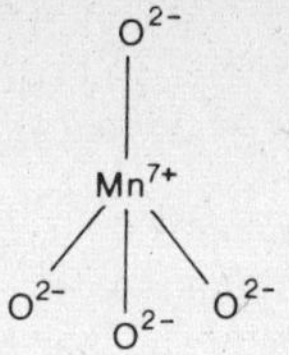

$[MnO_4]^-$, manganate(VII)

tetrahedral

$[Ni(CN)_4]^{2-}$, tetracyanonickel(II)

square planar

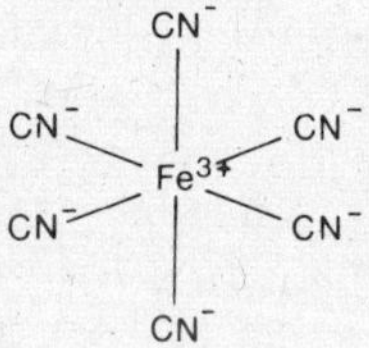

$[Fe(CN)_6]^{3-}$ hexacyanoferrate(III)

octahedral

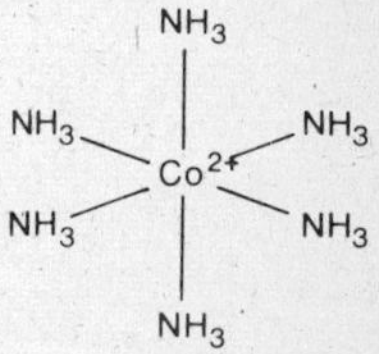

$[Co(NH_3)_6]^{2+}$ hexaaminocobalt(II)

octahedral

Some ligands (O^{2-}, CN^-) are hard to remove or non-labile and form stable complexes. Others (H_2O, NH_3, Cl^-) are easy to remove, labile, and form unstable complexes. These ligands can be changed merely by altering their concentration in the solution. If cobalt(II) chloride solution is treated with excess ammonia and then oxidized different compounds of formula $CoCl_3.xNH_3$ are formed, e.g.

$[Co(NH_3)_6]^{3+}Cl_3$ $\quad$ $[Co(NH_3)_5Cl]^{2+}Cl_2$ $\quad$ $[Co(NH_3)_4Cl_2]^+Cl$

Chloride present in the complex does not precipitate as silver chloride. Treatment of the three complexes results in 3, 2, and 1 mole of silver chloride per mole of complex precipitating respectively.

Nomenclature of complex ions

1. Cation named before anion
2. Negative ligands named before neutral ones, otherwise alphabetical

3. Number of a group is indicated by prefix di-, tetra- etc.
4. Negative ligands end in -o, e.g. chloro-, cyano-, neutral ligands are named variously, e.g. NH_3 amine, CO carbonyl.

Examples $K_4Fe(CN)_6$ potassium hexacyanoferrate(II); $KMnO_4$ potassium manganate(VII); $Cu(NH_3)_4SO_4$ tetraamine copper(II) sulphate; $Ni(CO)_4$ tetracarbonyl nickel(0).

3. Variable oxidation state Transition metals show a wide range of oxidation states, up to a maximum of seven. In practice however some will be very unstable.

Oxidation states shown by first transition series

Sc	Ti	V	Cr	Mn	Fe	Co	Ni	Cu	(Zn)
								1	
–	2	2	2	$\underline{2}$	2	$\underline{2}$	$\underline{2}$	$\underline{2}$	$\underline{2}$
$\underline{3}$	3	3	$\underline{3}$	3	$\underline{3}$	3	–	–	
–	$\underline{4}$	$\underline{4}$	–	4	–	4	4		
–	–	5	–	–	–	–	–		
–	–	–	6	6	6	–	–		
–	–	–	–	7	–	–	–		

The most stable oxidation states are underlined. All the transition elements, except scandium, show a +2 oxidation state where both 4*s* electrons are used in bonding. Most also show a +3 state. Compounds of both these oxidation states are predominantly covalent. The large number of different oxidation states is due to the very gradual increase in successive ionization energies for the *d*-block elements. The stability of the various hydrated ions can be found from the standard redox potentials for the M^{n+}/M systems and depends on the electronic structure. An empty, half-filled or fully filled *d* shell is stable, hence Sc^{3+}, Ti^{4+} (both $3d^0$), Mn^{2+} ($3d^5$) and Zn^{2+} ($3d^{10}$) are particularly stable. In general, the oxides of lower oxidation states tend to be basic, the middle oxides amphoteric and the higher oxides acidic in character. Lower oxidation states are often reducing and the higher states oxidizing.

4. Paramagnetic character All substances either weakly repel magnetic fields (diamagnetism) or weakly attract them (paramagnetism). Paramagnetism is due to the magnetic field produced by an **unpaired electron** and transition elements often have unpaired *d* electrons. By Hund's rule electrons tend to fill orbitals of the same energy singly before pairing in the same orbital, e.g. Fe^{3+} has an outer electronic structure $3d^5 4s^0$

	$3d^5$						$4s^0$
Fe^{3+}	1	1	1	1	1		

and has five unpaired electrons. The paramagnetic effect for iron, cobalt and manganese is so strong that they can be permanently magnetized and are known as **ferromagnetic** materials.

5. Catalytic activity Transition metals are used extensively as catalysts, iron in the Haber process, vanadium(V) oxide in the contact process, nickel for hydrogenations etc. There are two theories of catalysis – the intermediate compound theory and the surface action theory (see page 70) and transition elements have properties which can aid both mechanisms. In the formation of intermediate compounds catalysts offer alternative pathways of lower activation energy by forming compounds with reactants which then decompose to the eventual products. The variable oxidation states of transition elements make them particularly suitable to forming reaction intermediates. The solid metals make good surface catalysts because of the large number of valence electrons capable of bonding gases to the surface. This helps to concentrate the reacting gases and weaken their bonds prior to reaction.

6. Isomorphism This means 'same shape' and refers to crystal structures. There are some compounds of transition elements where the transition element can be exchanged for another without altering the crystal structure. For example, the alums, $K_2^+M_2^{3+}(SO_4)_4.24H_2O$ where M^{3+} is a transition ion or aluminium. Isomorphism is due to the similarity in size of the ions.

7. Interstitial compound formation These compounds, sometimes called non-stoichiometric, are not true 'bonded' compounds. They do not have a definite chemical formula. Hydrides, carbides and nitrides of the transitions are interstitial compounds with the hydrogen, carbon and nitrogen atoms occupying spaces within the metal lattice. The relative proportion of the atoms can be varied by altering the conditions of temperature and pressure under which they are made.

Chromium

The metal is stable in air at ordinary temperatures. At elevated temperatures it reacts with air, steam and chlorine to produce the relevant Cr(III) compounds. In dilute acids chromium forms Cr^{2+} salts which rapidly oxidize in air to Cr^{3+} salts. Nitric acid renders the metal passive.

Compounds The common oxidation states are +2, +3 and +6.

oxidation state	+6	+3	+2
ion	$Cr_2O_7^{2-}$ dichromate	Cr^{3+} chromate(III)	Cr^{2+} chromate(II)
colour	orange	green	blue
	oxidizing	stable	reducing
nature of oxide	acidic	amphoteric	basic

Electronic structures

	$3d^5$					$4s^1$
Cr^0	1	1	1	1	1	1

	$3d^3$					$4s^0$	$4p^0$		
Cr^{3+}	1	1	1	×	×	×	×	×	×

X = lone pair donated by ligand

The +3 oxidation state is principly ionic having lost an *s* and two *d* electrons. It can accept six pairs of electrons by forming six d^2sp^3 hybrid orbitals from the vacant 3*d*, 4*s* and 4*p* orbitals. It therefore forms octahedral complexes.

Standard redox potentials

$$Cr^{2+} + 2e^- \rightarrow Cr \qquad E^\ominus = -0{\cdot}91\ V$$
$$Cr^{3+} + 3e^- \rightarrow Cr \qquad E^\ominus = -0{\cdot}74\ V$$
$$Cr^{3+} + e^- \rightarrow Cr^{2+} \qquad E^\ominus = -0{\cdot}41\ V$$

The Cr^{2+}/Cr electrode potential is more negative than the Cr^{3+}/Cr electrode potential and so in acid the Cr^{2+} salts are formed first. The negative value for the Cr^{3+}/Cr^{2+} electrode indicates that chromium(II) salts are unstable with respect to chromium(III) salts.

+2 oxidation state This is the least stable state and is powerfully reducing. A solution of Cr^{2+} salt can be prepared by reducing a solution of Cr(III) or Cr(VI) salt with zinc amalgam and acid. **Chromium(II) chloride** is prepared by passing hydrogen chloride gas over heated chromium. In aqueous solution Cr^{2+} salts are blue and only stable in the absence of air. Addition of ethanoic acid to a solution of $CrCl_2$ precipitates the more stable, red coloured **chromium(II) ethanoate** $[Cr(CH_3COO)_2]_2.2H_2O$.

+3 oxidation state This is the most stable state. **Chromium(III) oxide** may be prepared by heating ammonium dichromate

$$(NH_4)_2Cr_2O_7 \rightarrow Cr_2O_3 + 4H_2O + N_2$$

or by heating the metal in air. It is amphoteric; in acid solution it produces Cr^{3+} salts and in concentrated alkali it reacts to give chromate(III) (chromite).

$$Cr_2O_3 + 6H^+ \rightarrow 2Cr^{3+} + 3H_2O$$

$$Cr_2O_3 + 6OH^- + 3H_2O \rightarrow 2Cr(OH)_6^{3-}$$

In aqueous solution the Cr^{3+} ion forms a complex with water:

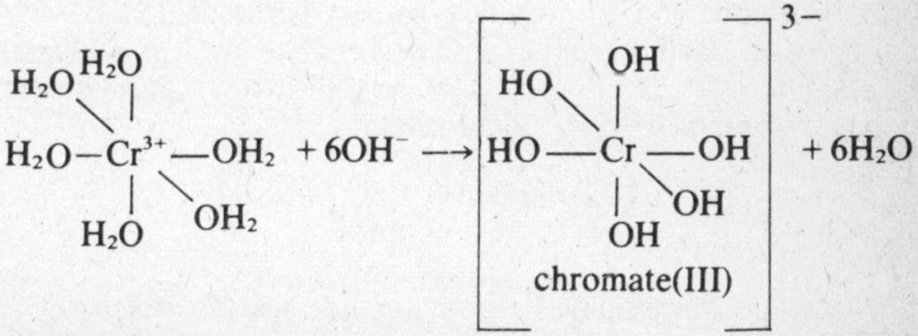

This complex is a Bronsted-Lowry acid, the water molecules are strongly held and the O–H bond is weakened. The base OH^- can abstract protons to form the chromate(III) ion. **Chromium(III) chloride** is prepared by passing dry chlorine over the heated metal. When prepared in aqueous solution three different hydrated chlorides may precipitate. Chromium(III) sulphate, $Cr_2(SO_4)_3.xH_2O$, when prepared in aqueous solution forms a range of hydrates. **Chrome alum,**

$K_2Cr_2(SO_4)_4.24H_2O$, crystallizes from equimolar solutions of the sulphate and potassium sulphate. Alternatively it may be prepared by reducing potassium dichromate with sulphur dioxide

$$K_2Cr_2O_7 + H_2SO_4 + 3SO_2 \rightarrow K_2SO_4 + Cr_2(SO_4)_3 + H_2O$$

Chromium(III) forms a large number of octahedral (six coordinate) complexes with both neutral and charged ligands.

+6 oxidation state This is powerfully oxidizing. **Chromium(VI) oxide**, CrO_3, is precipitated when concentrated sulphuric acid is added to cold saturated potassium dichromate solution. This oxide is a powerful oxidizing agent. On heating it gives the chromium(III) oxide

$$4CrO_3 \rightarrow 2Cr_2O_3 + 3O_2$$

The oxide dissolves in water to give a solution of chromic acid, H_2CrO_4, and dichromic acid, $H_2Cr_2O_7$. Many salts of these acids are known but the acids cannot be obtained in the pure state.

Chromates and dichromates To prepare sodium chromate a chromium salt is oxidized by sodium peroxide in aqueous solution.

$$2Cr^{3+} + 4OH^- + 3O_2^{2-} \rightarrow 2CrO_4^{2-} + 2H_2O$$

The hydroxide ion is provided by the peroxide ion (a very strong base). Both chromate and dichromate are less oxidizing in alkaline solution. Addition of an acid to a chromate eliminates water to give the dichromate, $Cr_2O_7^{2-}$

$$\underset{\text{yellow}}{2CrO_4^{2-}} + 2H^+ \rightarrow \underset{\text{orange}}{Cr_2O_7^{2-}} + H_2O$$

Sodium and potassium dichromates are used extensively as oxidizing agents, e.g. conversion of primary alcohol→ aldehyde→acid. Thev are also used in volumetric analysis to estimate reducing ag nts, e.g. Fe^{2+} in acid solution (see chapter 8). The sodium salt absorbs water and cannot be used as a primary standard. Potassium dichromate is a primary standard. The half equation for the reduction of dichromate in acid is

$$Cr_2O_7^{2-} + 14H^+ + 6e^- \rightarrow 2Cr^{3+} + 7H_2O \quad E^\theta = +1{\cdot}33\ \text{V}$$

and in base

$$CrO_4^{2-} + 4H_2O + 3e^- \rightarrow Cr(OH)_3 + 5OH^- \quad E^\theta = -0{\cdot}13\ V$$

Thus, in base it is a weaker oxidizing agent.

Manganese

The pure metal is not attacked appreciably by air or water but when heated strongly it will combine with non-metals such as oxygen, nitrogen, sulphur and chlorine. It dissolves in dilute acids to form Mn^{2+} salts liberating hydrogen. It is used extensively in alloys with iron.

Compounds The common oxidation states are +2, +3, +4, +6 and +7.

oxidation state	+7	+6	+4	+3	+2
ion	MnO_4^-	MnO_4^{2-}	Mn^{4+}	Mn^{3+}	Mn^{2+}
colour	purple	green	insol.	brown	pink
	← all oxidizing →				stable
nature of oxide	acidic	acidic	amphot.	basic	basic

Electronic structures

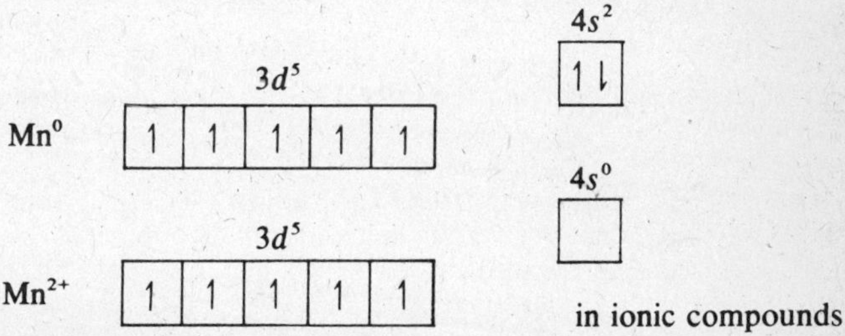

In octahedral complexes four d electrons pair up and the vacant d, $4s$ and $4p$ orbitals combine to form six d^2sp^3 hybrids.

Standard redox potentials

$$MnO_4^- + 8H^+ + 5e^- \rightarrow Mn^{2+} + 4H_2O \qquad E^\theta = +1{\cdot}52\ V$$
$$MnO_4^- + e^- \rightarrow MnO_4^{2-} \qquad E^\theta = +0{\cdot}56\ V$$
$$MnO_4^- + 4H^+ + 3e^- \rightarrow MnO_2 + 2H_2O \qquad E^\theta = +1{\cdot}67\ V$$

$$MnO_2 + 4H^+ + 2e^- \rightarrow Mn^{2+} + 2H_2O \qquad E^\theta = +1{\cdot}23\ V$$
$$Mn^{3+} + e^- \rightarrow Mn^{2+} \qquad E^\theta = +1{\cdot}5\ V$$
$$Mn^{2+} + 2e^- \rightarrow Mn \qquad E^\theta = -1{\cdot}18\ V$$

A consideration of the E^θ values indicates that Mn(VI) will disproportionate to Mn(VII) and Mn(IV) in acid solution

$$3Mn(VI) \rightarrow 2Mn(VII) + Mn(IV)$$

Also Mn(II) and Mn(VII) will convert to Mn(III) under acid conditions

$$4Mn(II) + Mn(VII) \rightarrow 5Mn(III)$$

Raising the pH causes further disproportionation

$$2Mn(III) \rightarrow Mn(IV) + Mn(II)$$

+2 oxidation state This is the most stable oxidation state. **Manganese(II) oxide**, MnO, is prepared by heating manganese(II) oxalate

$$MnC_2O_4 \rightarrow MnO + CO + CO_2$$

The carbon monoxide prevents aerial oxidation to MnO_2. Soluble Mn^{2+} salts may be formed by reacting the metal or oxide with acids, e.g.

$$Mn + H_2SO_4 \rightarrow \underset{\text{manganese(II) sulphate}}{MnSO_4} + H_2$$

The hydrated salts contain the $[Mn(H_2O)_6]^{2+}$ ion which is pale pink. There is no reaction with base.

+4 oxidation state Oxidizing. **The oxide, MnO_2,** occurs naturally (it is the ore pyrolusite) and can be prepared by heating manganese(II) nitrate

$$Mn(NO_3)_2 \rightarrow MnO_2 + 2NO_2$$

It is an insoluble black ionic solid and is a powerful oxidizing agent. It can oxidize hydrochloric acid to give chlorine

$$MnO_2 + 4HCl \rightarrow MnCl_2 + 2H_2O + Cl_2$$

It is feebly amphoteric, and may react with concentrated acids to form Mn^{4+} salts and possibly reacts with fused alkalis.

+6 oxidation state Neither the oxide nor the acid have been prepared. Only the sodium and potassium salts of the acid are known. They are dark green solids and contain the MnO_4^{2-} ion. **Potassium manganate(VI)** is prepared by oxidizing manganese(IV) oxide. MnO_2, potassium hydroxide and an oxidizing agent, e.g. potassium chlorate, are fused together. A green solid is obtained which is soluble in water. It is only stable in alkaline solution

$$3MnO_2 + 6OH^- + ClO_3^- \rightarrow \underset{\text{manganate(VI)}}{3MnO_4^{2-}} + 3H_2O + Cl^-$$

+7 oxidation state Strongly oxidizing. The oxide, Mn_2O_7, is extremely unstable and the acid is unknown. The potassium salt, **potassium manganate(VII)**, $KMnO_4$, is the only important compound. It is prepared by passing CO_2 through a solution of potassium manganate(VI). The weak acid carbonic acid is sufficient to cause disproportionation

$$\underset{\text{manganate(VI)}}{3MnO_4^{2-}} + 2H_2O \rightleftharpoons \underset{\text{manganate(VII)}}{2MnO_4^-} + \underset{\text{manganate(IV)}}{MnO_2} + 4OH^-$$

MnO_2 is filtered off and the solution evaporated until $KMnO_4$, potassium permanganate, begins to crystallize. It is a powerful oxidizing agent, oxidizing hydrochloric acid to chlorine and hydrogen peroxide to oxygen. It is a stronger oxidizing agent in acid solution than in alkali as can be seen from the redox potentials:

alkaline $\quad MnO_4^- + 2H_2O + 3e^- \rightarrow MnO_2 + 4OH^- \quad E^\theta = +1{\cdot}23\ V$

acid $\quad MnO_4^- + 8H^+ + 5e^- \rightarrow Mn^{2+} + 4H_2O \quad E^\theta = +1{\cdot}52\ V$

Under alkaline conditions it is used to convert alkenes to diols. In acid solution it is used as a volumetric reagent but is not a primary standard because it slowly reduces to MnO_2.

Iron

It is the second most abundant element in the earth's crust, due to a high nuclear stability, and shows similarities to cobalt and nickel. It occurs as oxides, haematite (Fe_2O_3) and magnetite (Fe_3O_4). It reacts with non metals at high temperatures.

Extraction Iron is manufactured by reduction of the oxide with coke in a blast furnace (fig. 48).

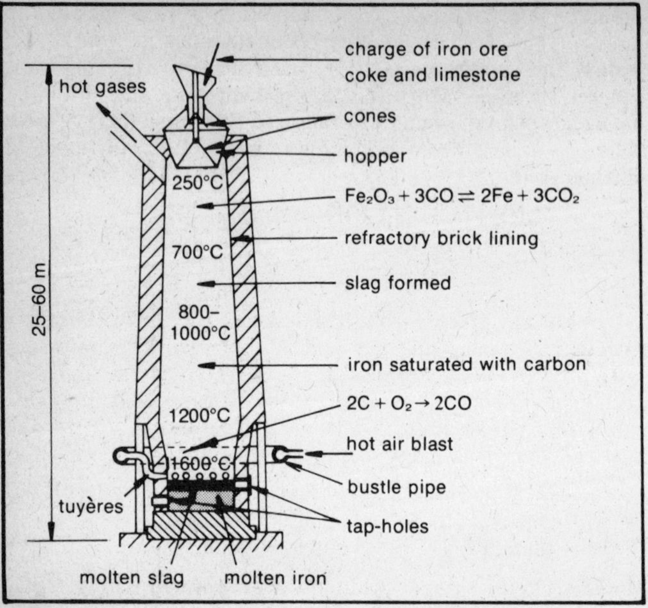

Figure 48. A blast furnace

Iron ore, coke and limestone are fed into the top of the blast furnace and air preheated to 600°C is blown into the base. The reduced iron sinks to the bottom and a layer of slag separates out on top of the liquid iron. They are then tapped from separate holes. The coke burns to give CO which raises the temperature of the furnace. In the cooler, upper part of the furnace the carbon monoxide reduces the iron oxide to spongy iron

$$Fe_2O_3 + 3CO \rightarrow 2Fe + 3CO_2$$

At 800° C the limestone decomposes to calcium oxide and carbon dioxide. The calcium oxide reacts with clay and sand impurity to form slag, calcium silicate

$$CaO + SiO_2 \rightarrow CaSiO_3$$

Reduction of any unchanged iron oxide is completed by carbon at about 1000°C and some carbon combines with the iron to form cementite, Fe_3C.

The iron produced contains impurities of carbon (up to 4·5%), phosphorus, silicon, sulphur and manganese. It is called cast iron and is hard but brittle.

Steel The manufacture of steel involves the removal of the impurities followed by addition of controlled amounts of carbon and metals to vary the properties of the metal. There are two processes:

1. Siemens-Martin Open Hearth process The impure iron, scrap steel and haematite are heated in a furnace with a lining of CaO and MgO. The haematite, Fe_2O_3, oxidizes the non metal impurities which either combine with the basic lining to form slag (SiO_2, P_2O_5) or leave as gases (CO).

2. Bessemer process The impure molten iron is introduced to a 'converter' and oxygen, diluted with steam or carbon dioxide, is blown through the charge. The impurities rapidly burn off or form a slag. The advantage of this process is that nitrogen, which can combine with iron and make it brittle, is not present (fig. 49).

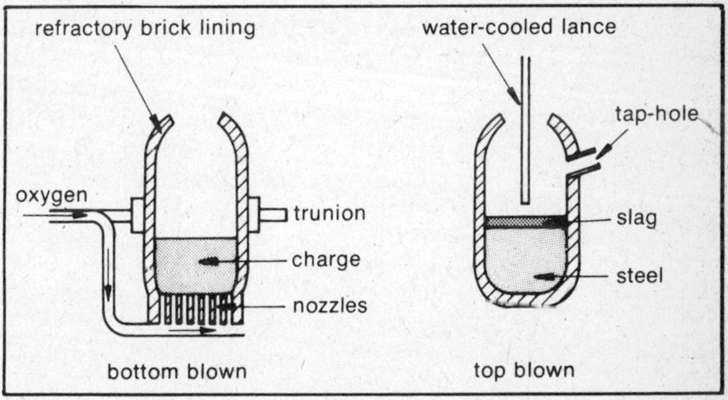

Figure 49. Bessemer converters

Compounds It forms compounds of oxidation state +2, +3, +6.

oxidation state	+6	+3	+2
ion	$[FeO_4]^{2-}$ ferrate	Fe^{3+} iron(III)	Fe^{2+} iron(II)
colour	red	brown	green
	strongly oxidizing	oxidizing	reducing
nature of oxide	acidic	amphoteric	basic

Electronic structures

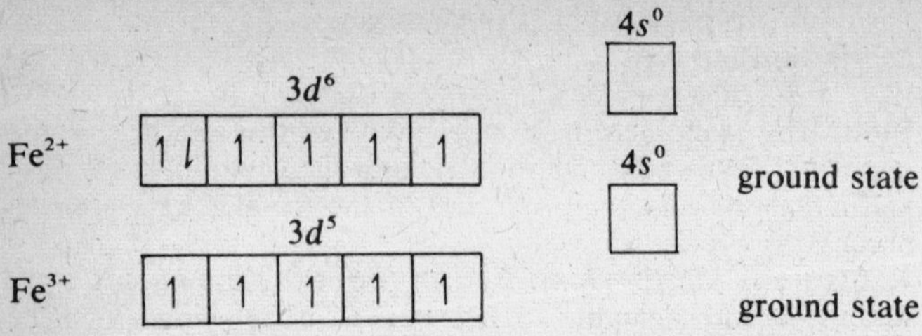

In forming complex ions the d electrons pair up to leave two vacant d orbitals which form d^2sp^3 hybrids (octahedral).

Standard redox potentials

$$Fe^{2+} + 2e^- \rightarrow Fe \qquad E^\theta = -0{\cdot}44\ V$$

$$Fe^{3+} + 3e^- \rightarrow Fe \qquad E^\theta = -0{\cdot}04\ V$$

$$Fe^{3+} + e^- \rightarrow Fe^{2+} \qquad E^\theta = +0{\cdot}77\ V$$

In acid solution it will first form Fe^{2+} salts which slowly oxidize to Fe^{3+} salts.

Rusting The process is very complicated and is principally electrolytic. For rusting to occur both water and oxygen must be present. Areas of the iron surface are considered to become anodic (where there is a low oxygen concentration) and donate electrons to areas where the oxygen content is high (cathodic).

At anode	*At cathode*
$2Fe \rightarrow 2Fe^{2+} + 4e^-$	$O_2 + 2H_2O + 4e^- \rightarrow 4OH^-$

An electrolytic cell is set up and iron(II) hydroxide forms between the two electrodes. This slowly becomes oxidized by air to form rust which is hydrated iron(III) oxide. The process is accelerated by having a more conducting electrolyte, e.g. salt. It can be prevented by having a sacrificial metal such as zinc or magnesium present which have more negative electrode potentials than iron and dissolve away, producing electrons which protect the iron.

+2 oxidation state. Iron(II) oxide, FeO, is prepared by heating iron(II) oxalate

$$FeC_2O_4 \rightarrow FeO + CO + CO_2$$

The carbon monoxide prevents aerial oxidation to Fe_2O_3. Like other transition metals the oxide is never exactly Fe_1O_1 but is non-stoichiometric having slightly less iron than oxygen. **Iron(II) hydroxide** is formed as a green gelatinous precipitate when sodium hydroxide is added to a solution of an iron(II) salt. **Anhydrous iron(II) chloride**, $FeCl_2$, is made by passing dry hydrogen chloride over heated iron. It is predominantly ionic. **Iron(II) sulphate**, $FeSO_4$, is prepared by the action of dilute sulphuric acid on the metal. It crystallizes out as the heptahydrate and careful drying produces the anhydrous salt. Strong heating produces iron(III) oxide.

$$2FeSO_4 \rightarrow Fe_2O_3 + SO_2 + SO_3$$

In solution the Fe^{2+} ion becomes hydrated forming the green $[Fe(H_2O)_6]^{2+}$ ion. In the presence of nitric oxide (NO) the brown complex $[Fe(H_2O)_5NO]^{2+}$ is formed which is used in purifying the gas. It is also the basis of the brown ring test for nitrates. **Iron(II) ammonium sulphate**, $FeSO_4.(NH_4)_2SO_4$, is a double salt and is prepared by crystallizing equimolar solutions of the two sulphates. It is stable in air and is used as a primary volumetric standard. Other iron(II) salts may be prepared by direct synthesis (e.g. the sulphide) or by double decomposition (e.g. carbonate, oxalate).

The complex **potassium hexacyanoferrate(II)**, $K_4[Fe(CN)_6]$ is obtained by adding potassium cyanide, KCN, to a solution of an iron(II) salt. It is a very stable complex.

+3 oxidation state. Iron (III) oxide, Fe_2O_3, is prepared by heating iron(II) sulphate (see above); it is ionic. **Iron(III) hydroxide** is believed to be a hydrate of the oxide, $Fe_2O_3.xH_2O$, and precipitates as a brown gelatinous solid when hydroxide ions are added to a solution of an Fe^{3+} salt. It is amphoteric since with acids it forms Fe^{3+} salts and in strong alkali it forms ferrate(III), e.g. sodium ferrate(III), $NaFeO_2$. The Fe^{3+} ion forms a hexa aquo complex, $Fe(H_2O)_6^{3+}$, which is acidic, and a base can abstract protons to form the ferrate ion. **Iron(III) chloride** is produced by passing chlorine over heated iron. It is covalent. **Iron(III) sulphate** is made by oxidizing iron(II) sulphate with peroxide.

$$2FeSO_4 + H_2SO_4 + H_2O_2 \rightarrow Fe_2(SO_4)_3 + 2H_2O$$

It forms alums. To test for the presence of iron(III) ions potassium hexacyanoferrate(II) is added to the solution and a dark blue precipitate (prussian blue) is formed.

$$K^+ + Fe(Cn)_6^{4-} + Fe^{3+} \rightarrow KFe[Fe(CN)_6]$$

potassium iron(III) hexacyanoferrate(II)

The complex, **potassium hexacyanoferrate(III)**, $K_3[Fe(CN)_6]$, is made by the oxidation of $K_4Fe(CN)_6$ with chlorine. It is a mild oxidizing agent and produces the prussian blue colour when added to a solution of iron(II) ions by oxidizing them to iron(III) ions.

$$Fe^{2+} + Fe(CN)_6^{3-} \rightarrow Fe^{3+} + Fe(CN)_6^{4-}$$
$$K^+ + Fe^{3+} + Fe(CN)_6^{4-} \rightarrow KFe[Fe(CN)_6]$$

+6 oxidation state The oxide and acid are unknown and only a few salts have been prepared. **Potassium ferrate(VI)** is made by fusing together iron filings and potassium nitrate (an oxidizing agent). In solution the ferrate(VI) ion, FeO_4^{2-}, is a deep red colour. It is tetrahedral and powerfully oxidizing.

Copper

The metal is in group 1b which includes silver and gold and is referred to as the coinage group. It has an outer shell containing only one *s* electron like group 1a elements but is chemically quite unlike them. This is because copper has a penultimate shell containing 18 electrons, the weak screening effect of the *d* orbitals causing a contraction in radius, and the outer electron is fairly strongly held. Consequently it has a high ionization potential and a positive electrode potential which means that it is very resistant to chemical attack. It is a noble metal (below hydrogen in the electrochemical series) and will not produce hydrogen with acids. Copper exhibits oxidation states of +1 and +2. The +2 state is more stable because the higher charge leads to stronger bonding which compensates for the energy required to remove a 3*d* as well as the 4*s* electron.

Standard redox potentials

$$Cu^+ + e^- \rightarrow Cu \qquad E^\theta = +0{\cdot}52\ V$$
$$Cu^{2+} + 2e^- \rightarrow Cu \qquad E^\theta = +0{\cdot}36\ V$$

+1 oxidation state Copper(I) salts are unstable in aqueous solution, they convert to copper(II) and copper as can be seen from the redox potentials

$$Cu^+ + e^- \rightarrow Cu \qquad E^\theta = +0{\cdot}52\ V$$

$$Cu^{2+} + e^- \rightarrow Cu^+ \qquad E^\theta = +0{\cdot}16\ V$$

overall: $$2Cu^+ \rightarrow Cu + Cu^{2+} \qquad E^\theta = +0{\cdot}36\ V$$

As the redox potential for the overall reaction is positive it means that ΔG for the reaction is negative and that Cu will disproportionate in solution.

Copper(I) oxide, Cu_2O, is obtained by reduction of alkaline copper(II) sulphate with glucose. $CuSO_4$ is first complexed with tartrate ions to prevent precipitation of copper(II) hydroxide. Therefore, $CuSO_4$ and sodium potassium tartrate are mixed and on warming with glucose red copper(I) oxide, Cu_2O, is precipitated. This is the basis of the **Fehling test** for sugars. **Copper(I) chloride**, CuCl, is obtained by boiling concentrated hydrochloric acid with copper turnings and copper(II) chloride. The complex $[CuCl_2]^-$ is formed and on pouring the solution into water precipitates as a white solid. It must be dried quickly as it slowly converts to $CuCl_2$. **Copper(I) sulphate**, Cu_2SO_4, is formed by heating copper(I) oxide with anhydrous dimethyl sulphate

$$Cu_2O + (CH_3)_2SO_4 \rightarrow Cu_2SO_4 + (CH_3)_2O$$

It also disproportionates to Cu^{2+} and Cu in aqueous solution.

+2 oxidation state This is the more stable state. Salts are blue in aqueous solution due to the formation of the $Cu(H_2O)_6^{2+}$ ion. Dilute non-oxidizing acids do not attack the metal but in hot concentrated sulphuric acid, dilute and concentrated nitric acid Cu(II) salts are formed:

$$\underset{\text{conc.}}{Cu + 2H_2SO_4} \rightarrow \underset{\substack{\text{copper(II)}\\ \text{sulphate}}}{CuSO_4} + 2H_2O + SO_2$$

$$\underset{\text{dilute}}{3Cu + 8HNO_3} \rightarrow \underset{\substack{\text{copper(II)}\\ \text{nitrate}}}{3Cu(NO_3)_2} + 4H_2O + 2NO$$

$$\underset{\text{conc.}}{Cu + 4HNO_3} \rightarrow Cu(NO_3)_2 + 2H_2O + 2NO_2$$

Copper(II) oxide, CuO, is made by heating copper(II) carbonate or nitrate, e.g.

$$CuCO_3 \rightarrow CuO + CO_2$$

At high temperatures it decomposes to Cu_2O and oxygen. It forms Cu(II) salts with dilute acids and is reduced to copper in a stream of hydrogen. **Copper(II) hydroxide**, $Cu(OH)_2$, is precipitated as a green gelatinous solid when hydroxide is added to a solution of a copper(II) salt. In excess aqueous ammonia the precipitate redissolves to form a deep blue solution due to the formation of the complex **tetraamine copper(II)**,

$$Cu(OH)_2 + 4NH_3 \rightleftharpoons \underset{\text{tetraamine copper(II)}}{Cu(NH_3)_4^{2+}} + 2OH^-$$

Copper(II) chloride, $CuCl_2$, is made by passing chlorine over heated copper. It is predominantly covalent. **Copper(II) sulphate**, $CuSO_4.5H_2O$, is made by reacting copper(II) carbonate or oxide with dilute sulphuric acid. Four of the waters of crystallization are coordinated to the copper and are lost fairly easily, the remaining molecule is hydrogen bonded between the sulphates.

Zinc

The metal is in group 2b which includes cadmium and mercury. It has an outer shell containing two *s* electrons like the elements of group 2a but apart from showing some resemblance to magnesium it is chemically different from elements of that group. Once again, like copper, this difference is due to the penultimate shell of 18 electrons rather than 8. Zinc has a completed *d* shell and these electrons are not available for bonding.

Standard redox potential

$$Zn^{2+} + 2e^- \rightarrow Zn \qquad E^\theta = -0{\cdot}76\ V$$

The negative electrode potential is surprising as it would be expected to be about as reactive as copper. The value is due to the low sublimation (atomization) energy of zinc which is in turn due to the weak metallic bond (caused by lack of available *d* electrons). Zinc is non-transitional and only forms compounds in the +2 oxidation state. It is fairly reactive, forming an oxide in air at room temperature and displacing hydrogen from dilute acids. It will also react with caustic alkalis.

+2 oxidation state. Zinc oxide, ZnO, is prepared by heating the carbonate or nitrate, e.g.

$$ZnCO_3 \rightarrow ZnO + CO_2$$

It is a white covalent solid which turns yellow on heating reverting back to white on cooling. The oxide dissolves in acids to give salts and in sodium hydroxide to give a zincate i.e. it is **amphoteric**

In acid $\quad ZnO + 2H^+ \rightarrow Zn^{2+} + H_2O$

In alkali $\quad ZnO + 2OH^- + H_2O \rightarrow [Zn(OH)_4]^{2-}$

Zinc hydroxide, $Zn(OH)_2$, precipitates on addition of sodium hydroxide to an aqueous Zn^{2+} salt. It is also amphoteric. Ammonia redissolves the precipitate forming tetraamine zinc hydroxide.

$$Zn(OH)_2 + 4NH_3 \rightarrow [Zn(NH_3)_4]^{2+}(OH^-)_2$$

Zinc chloride, $ZnCl_2$, is made by passing chlorine over the heated metal. Zinc complexes generally have a coordination number of four, e.g. the acidic hydrated zinc ion

$$[Zn(H_2O)_4]^{2+} + H_2O \rightarrow [Zn(H_2O)_3(OH)]^+ + H_3O^+$$

In alkali the remaining three protons are removed

$$[Zn(H_2O)_3(OH)]^+ + 3OH^- \rightarrow \underset{\text{zincate}}{[Zn(OH)_4]^{2-}} + 3H_2O$$

Key terms

Transition elements These are elements with an incomplete inner *d* sub-shell.

Special properties 1. **Coloured ions** Electrons in *d* orbitals can absorb visible photons. 2. **Complex ion formation** This is favoured by the high charges and vacant *d* orbitals of transition ions. 3. **Variable oxidation state** This is due to the *s* and *d* electrons being available for bonding. 4. **Paramagnetism** This effect is due to unpaired electrons. 5. **Catalytic activity** Variable oxidation states and vacant *d* orbitals make transition elements good catalysts. 6. **Isomorphism** Transition elements can replace each other in some compounds because of their similar size. 7. **Interstitial compounds** Hydrogen, nitrogen and carbon can occupy lattice spaces in the metals.

Chromium

oxidation states	+6	+3	+2
ion	$Cr_2O_7^{2-}$	Cr^{3+}	Cr^{2+}
	oxidizing	stable	reducing
nature of oxide	acidic	amphoteric	basic

Manganese

oxidation states	+7	+6	+4	+3	+2
ion	MnO_4^-	MnO_4^{2-}	Mn^{4+}	Mn^{3+}	Mn^{2+}
	← oxidizing →				stable
nature of oxide	← acidic →		amphoteric		basic

Mn(VI) disproportionates to Mn(VII) and Mn(IV). Mn(II) and Mn(VII) convert to Mn(III) in acid. Mn(III) then disproportionates to Mn(IV) and Mn(II).

Iron

oxidation states	+6	+3	+2
ion	FeO_4^{2-}	Fe^{3+}	Fe^{2+}
	strongly oxidizing	oxidizing	reducing
nature of oxide	acidic	amphoteric	basic

In acid solution iron first forms iron(II) salts which then slowly oxidize to iron(III) salts.

Copper

Copper(I) salts are unstable in aqueous solution. They quickly oxidize to copper(II) salts.

Zinc

The metal only forms zinc(II) salts. Although having only two outer electrons it is unlike group 2a metals. It is amphoteric and forms tetrahedral complexes.

Chapter 8
Quantitative and Qualitative Analysis

Quantitative analysis

Quantitative analysis is concerned with determining the amounts of known substances present in a sample of material. A number of methods are available to the chemist including volumetric analysis, gravimetric analysis and a variety of physical methods requiring complex equipment such as ultra violet, infra red and colorimetric analysis. At this level detailed knowledge is generally only required of volumetric analysis.

In **volumetric analysis** the volumes of solutions of reacting substances are measured using burettes and pipettes. Dilute solutions are used for a number of reasons, particularly expense of materials, the need to reduce the violence of reaction and to avoid changes in concentration of solutions (as occurs to many pure substances due to their hygroscopic nature, or to their reacting with constituents of the air). The concentration of the solutions used may be expressed in grams of solute per unit volume (dm^3 is the volume generally used) or in moles per unit volume. The relationship between these is

$$\text{mol dm}^{-3} = \frac{\text{g dm}^{-3}}{\text{mass of 1 mol}}$$

The concentration term mol dm^{-3} is commonly referred to as molarity but is more correctly termed the molar concentration.

In practical examinations knowledge of titrations of acids with bases, of oxidizing and reducing agents and of silver nitrate with halides is expected.

Acid–base titrations are based on the reaction

$$H^+_{(aq)} + OH^-_{(aq)} \rightarrow H_2O_{(l)}$$

A suitable indicator is required, the choice depending on the strength of the acid and base used (see chapter 4). For titrations involving strong acids methyl orange is generally used, for those involving strong bases phenolphthalein may be used.

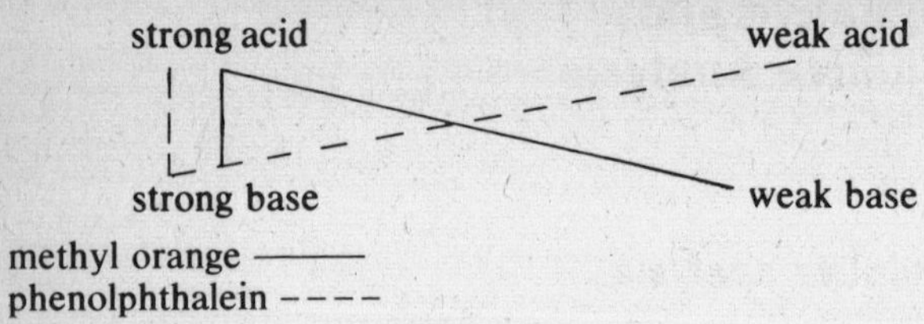

The mineral acids, sulphuric(VI), nitric(V) and hydrochloric acids are strong acids; other acids including organic acids are weak acids. Strong bases include sodium, potassium and calcium hydroxides. Weak bases include sodium carbonate and hydrogencarbonate, sodium borate and ammonia solution.

Redox titrations are of two types. In the first, potassium manganate(VII) is used in the burette and added to the reducing agent. The reducing agents used are iron(II) salts, particularly the double salt, ammonium iron(II) sulphate-6-water, ethandioic (oxalic) acid and its salts and hydrogen peroxide. The reaction is self indicating as the potassium manganate(VII) is pink whereas the reduction product is colourless. Whilst reducing agent is present the manganate will lose its colour but when all the reducing agent has reacted the next drop of manganate solution added will colour the solution pink.

The second type of redox titration involves the reaction of iodine with sodium thiosulphate. Iodine dissolves in excess potassium iodide to give a brown solution (due to formation of a complex, $I_2 + KI \rightleftharpoons KI_3$) and reacts with sodium thiosulphate to give a colourless solution. As a result the titration can be self indicating, the end point being when the solution turns colourless, although a more definite end point can be obtained using starch as the indicator. Starch gives a characteristic blue black coloration with iodine so that when it is used as an indicator the end point is from blue black to colourless.

The iodine estimated in the titration is generally obtained by oxidation of potassium iodide by one of the oxidizing agents: potassium manganate(VII); potassium chromate(VI) or dichromate(VI); iodate(V) or bromate(V); copper(II) sulphate(VI); hydrogen peroxide.

Silver nitrate titrations are best carried out using potassium chromate as indicator. This depends on the greater solubility of silver chromate relative to silver halides (see Chapter 4) so that silver chromate (which is red) is only given when all halide ions have reacted. The end point is therefore when a permanent red colour is given. If an acid solution is being titrated the acid should first be neutralized by addition of precipitated calcium carbonate (this is used because it is insoluble and does not therefore provide ions likely to react with silver ions as do most bases) as the presence of hydrogen ions will cause the chromate(VI) ions to convert to dichromate(VI) ions. As silver dichromate(VI) is more soluble than silver chromate(VI) it does not form immediately when all halide ions have reacted.

Calculations from the results of a titration generally require a knowledge of the equation for the reaction. For acid–base titrations the reacting ratios depend on the basicity of the acid (the number of moles of protons donated by 1 mol of the acid) and the acidity of the base (the number of moles of protons accepted by 1 mol of the base). Thus for hydrochloric acid, HCl, and sodium hydroxide, NaOH, 1 mol of the acid is neutralized by 1 mol of the base, whereas for sulphuric acid, H_2SO_4, and the same base, 1 mol of the acid reacts with 2 mols of the base. In a few cases, the reacting ratio can depend on the indicator used. For the titration of Na_2CO_3 with hydrochloric acid, phenolphthalein gives an end point for the reaction:

$$CO_3^{2-} + H^+ \rightarrow HCO_3^-$$

whereas methyl orange gives an end point for the reaction:

$$CO_3^{2-} + 2H^+ \rightarrow H_2O + CO_2$$

For redox titrations the reacting ratios may be determined either from the half equations for the oxidation and reduction reactions or from the change of oxidation state.

The half equation method relates to the definition of oxidation as a process of electron loss by a substance and reduction as a process of electron gain. Oxidizing agents are electron acceptors and reducing agents electron donors. Half equations for oxidizing agents may be constructed by (i) writing the formulae for the oxidized form on the L.H.S and the reduced form on the R.H.S.; (ii) if extra oxygen is present on the L.H.S. it is represented as being present in water on the

R.H.S.; (iii) the necessary hydrogen for this water can be considered as being present as hydrogen ions on the L.H.S.; (iv) any imbalance of charge is then rectified by indicating the relevant number of electrons on the L.H.S. Half equations for reducing agents may be determined by the reverse to the above, (i) the reduced form being written on the L.H.S, oxidized form on R.H.S; (ii) water added to the L.H.S. if extra oxygen is on the R.H.S; (iii) hydrogen ions on the R.H.S. if water is on the L.H.S; (iv) electrons on the R.H.S. to balance the charge.

The half equations for oxidizing agents mentioned above are (the stages in the balancing process are only given for the first two oxidizing and reducing agents):

Oxidizing agents

potassium manganate(VII) (reduced to manganese(II), Mn^{2+})

$$MnO_4^- \rightarrow Mn^{2+} \quad \text{(i)}$$
$$MnO_4^- \rightarrow Mn^{2+} + 4H_2O \quad \text{(ii)}$$
$$MnO_4^- + 8H^+ \rightarrow Mn^{2+} + 4H_2O \quad \text{(iii)}$$
$$MnO_4^- + 8H^+ + 5e^- \rightarrow Mn^{2+} + 4H_2O \quad \text{(iv)}$$

potassium dichromate(VI) (reduced to chromium(III), Cr^{3+})

$$Cr_2O_7^{2-} \rightarrow 2Cr^{3+} \quad \text{(i)}$$
$$Cr_2O_7^{2-} \rightarrow 2Cr^{3+} + 7H_2O \quad \text{(ii)}$$
$$Cr_2O_7^{2-} + 14H^+ \rightarrow 2Cr^{3+} + 7H_2O \quad \text{(iii)}$$
$$Cr_2O_7^{2-} + 14H^+ + 6e^- \rightarrow 2Cr^{3+} + 7H_2O \quad \text{(iv)}$$

iodate(V) (reduced to iodide, I^-)

$$IO_3^- + 6H^+ + 6e^- \rightarrow I^- + 3H_2O$$

bromate(V) (reduced to bromide, Br^-)

$$BrO_3^- + 6H^+ + 6e^- \rightarrow Br^- + 3H_2O$$

chromate(VI) (reduced to chromium(III), Cr^{3+})

$$CrO_4^{2-} + 8H^+ + 3e^- \rightarrow Cr^{3+} + 4H_2O$$

copper(II) (reduced to copper(I), Cu^+)

$$Cu^{2+} + e^- \rightarrow Cu^+$$

iodine (reduced to iodide, I^-)

$$I_2 + 2e^- \rightarrow 2I^-$$

Reducing agents

iron(II) (oxidized to iron(III), Fe^{3+})

$$Fe^{2+} \rightarrow Fe^{3+} + e^-$$

ethandioic acid (or its salts), (oxidized to carbon dioxide, CO_2)

$$(COO^-)_2 \rightarrow 2CO_2 + 2e^-$$

hydrogen peroxide (oxidized to oxygen, O_2)

$$H_2O_2 \rightarrow 2H^+ + O_2 + 2e^-$$

sodium thiosulphate (oxidized to tetrathionate, $S_4O_6^{2-}$)

$$2S_2O_3^{2-} \rightarrow S_4O_6^{2-} + 2e^-$$

iodide (oxidized to iodine, I_2)

$$2I^- \rightarrow I_2 + 2e^-$$

Reacting ratios may then be determined so that (i) the number of mols of oxidizing agent required equals the number of electrons lost by the reducing agent; (ii) the number of mols of reducing agent required equals the number of electrons gained by the oxidizing agent. Thus for the reactions:

manganate(VII) with iron(II)
one manganate(VII) is equivalent to five iron(II) or

$$1MnO_4^- \equiv 5Fe^{2+}$$

manganate(VII) with ethandioic acid

$$2MnO_4^- \equiv 5(COO^-)_2$$

manganate(VII) with hydrogen peroxide

$$2MnO_4^- \equiv 5H_2O_2$$

iodine with thiosulphate

$$2S_2O_3^{2-} \equiv I_2$$

iodide with iodate(V)

$$6I^-(3I_2) \equiv IO_3^- \quad (\therefore \quad IO_3^- \equiv 6S_2O_3^{2-})$$

and similarly for bromate(V)

iodide with manganate(VII)

$$5I^- \equiv 1MnO_4^- \quad (\therefore \quad 1MnO_4^- \equiv 5S_2O_3^{2-})$$

iodide with dichromate(VI)

$$6I^- \equiv 1Cr_2O_7^{2-} \quad (\therefore \quad 1Cr_2O_7^{2-} \equiv 6S_2O_3^{2-})$$

iodide with copper(II)

$$1I^- \equiv 1Cu^{2+} \quad (\therefore \quad 1Cu^{2+} \equiv 1S_2O_3^{2-})$$

iodide with hydrogen peroxide

$$2I^- \equiv 1H_2O_2 \quad (\therefore \quad 1H_2O_2 \equiv 2S_2O_3^{2-})$$

Oxidation state refers to the valency of an element in a compound but it also takes into account the electronegativity of the element relative to other constituent elements. In assigning an oxidation state to an element in a compound, (i) the most electronegative element present is given a negative oxidation state numerically equal to its valency; (ii) the least electronegative (most electropositive element) is given a positive oxidation state equal to its valency; (iii) the oxidation states of other elements present have sign and number such that the total oxidation state of the compound is zero. Thus in potassium manganate(VII), $KMnO_4$, (i) oxygen is the most electronegative element and therefore has an oxidation state of −2; (ii) potassium is the least electronegative element and therefore has an oxidation state of +1; (iii) as four oxygen atoms have total oxidation state −8 and one potassium atom is +1 manganese must therefore be +7 as

$$(+1) + \text{Mn} + (-8) = 0 \quad \therefore \quad \text{Mn} = +8 - 1 = +7$$

(Note that systematic names quote the oxidation states of elements with variable valency.) In potassium dichromate(VI), $K_2Cr_2O_7$, (i) oxygen is −2; (ii) potassium is +1; (iii) chromium is therefore $(7(+2) - 2)/2 = +6$. The changes in oxidation state observed when the oxidizing agents quoted above are reduced are:

Oxidized form	*Reduced form*	*Change (for 1 mol)*
manganate(VII)	manganese(II)	$2 - 7 = -5$
chromate(VI)	chromium(III)	$3 - 6 = -3$
dichromate(VI)	chromium(III)	$2(3) - 2(6) = -6$
iodate(V)	iodide	$-1 - 5 = -6$
hydrogen peroxide	water	$2(-2) - 2(-1) = -2$
copper(II)	copper(I)	$1 - 2 = -1$
iodine	iodide	$2(-1) - 2(0) = -2$

Note that change of oxidation state is final minus initial and that oxidation state of uncombined elements is zero. For the reducing agents above:

Reduced form	*Oxidized form*	*Change (for 1 mol)*
iron(II)	iron(III)	$3 - 2 = +1$
carbon in ethandioate	carbon in CO_2	$2(+4) - 2(+3) = +2$
oxygen in hydrogen peroxide	oxygen	$2(0) - 2(-1) = +2$
sulphur in thiosulphate	sulphur in tetrathionate	$2(2\frac{1}{2}) - 2(2) = +1$
iodide	iodine	$2(0) - 2(-1) = +2$

As the oxidation state of whole compounds and of uncombined elements is zero, the overall change of oxidation state in a redox reaction is zero. This means there must be sufficient reducing agent present to balance the change observed in the oxidizing agent. Thus for manganate(VII) and iron(II), $5Fe^{2+}$ reacts with $1MnO_4^-$; for manganate(VII) and ethandioate, $5(COO^-)_2 \equiv 2MnO_4^-$ etc., giving the same reacting ratios as with the other method.

For silver nitrate titrations as the reaction of silver nitrate with halides is

$$Ag^+ + Hal^- \rightarrow Ag^+Hal^-$$

the factor determining reacting ratios will be the number of moles of halide ions in one mole of the halide. For Group I metal halides (NaCl, KCl etc.) the reacting ratio will be $1AgNO_3 \equiv 1NaCl$ etc. For bivalent metal halides such as Group II metals ($CaCl_2$, $BaCl_2$ etc.) $2AgNO_3 \equiv 1CaCl_2$ etc.

The calculation then rests on the recognition that the reacting ratio of substance *A* with substance *B* is equal to the ratio

$$\frac{\text{number of moles of } A \text{ used in titration}}{\text{number of moles of } B \text{ used in titration}}$$

If the solution of *A* used has molar concentration M_A and V_A cm^3 are used in the titration then

$$1 \text{ dm}^3 \text{ of the solution contains } M_A \text{ mols } A$$
$$V_A \text{ cm}^3 \text{ of the solution contains } \frac{V_A M_A}{1000} \text{ mols } A$$

Similarly if the solution of *B* used has molar concentration M_B and V_B cm^3 are used in the titration then

$$V_B \text{ cm}^3 \text{ of the solution contains } \frac{V_B M_B}{1000} \text{ mols } B$$

If the equation shows that *a* mols *A* react with *b* mols $B \rightarrow$ products then

$$\text{reacting ratio} = \frac{a}{b} = \frac{V_A M_A}{1000} \div \frac{V_B M_B}{1000}$$

that is

$$\frac{a}{b} = \frac{V_A M_A}{1000} \times \frac{1000}{V_B M_B} \quad \text{or} \quad \frac{a}{b} = \frac{V_A M_A}{V_B M_B}$$

Most calculations require the calculation of either the molar concentrations (and hence the mass of 1 mol) using

$$\text{molar concentration} = \frac{\text{concentration (g dm}^{-3})}{\text{mass of 1 mol}}$$

$$\text{or the ratio } \frac{a}{b}$$

Recording of results in a practical notebook or in an examination should always be neat. Some examining boards have prepared answer papers which leave spaces for entering a students own results, but should these not be provided the following layout is recommended (in this example x, y, z and w are to be calculated, given the solution is 0·05 M and that 1 mol of the compound A, an ethandioate, is 254 g).

Results

Titration 1 25 cm³ of 0·10 M sodium hydroxide in flask, 0·05 M solution of $K_xH_y(COO^-)_z.\ wH_2O$ in burette.

Indicator: phenolphthalein; End Point: colourless to pink.

	Rough	1	2
Burette reading (final) cm³	17·25	33·95	17·95
Burette reading (initial) cm³	0·25	17·25	1·30
Volume used, cm³	17·00	16·70	16·65

$$\text{Average titre} = (16{\cdot}70 + 16{\cdot}65)/2 = 16{\cdot}675\ \text{cm}^3$$

Calculation 1

25 cm³ 0.10 M sodium hydroxide contains

$$\frac{25}{1000} \times 0{\cdot}1 \text{ mol NaOH}$$

16·675 cm³ 0·05 M $K_xH_y(COO^-)_z.wH_2O$ contains

$$\frac{16{\cdot}675}{1000} \times 0{\cdot}05 \text{ mol}$$

$$\text{reacting ratio} = \frac{25 \times 0{\cdot}1}{1000} \times \frac{1000}{16{\cdot}675 \times 0{\cdot}05} = \frac{50}{16{\cdot}675}$$

$$= \frac{3}{1} \text{ (to nearest whole number)}$$

Titration 2 25 cm^3 of 0·05 M $K_xH_y(COO^-)_z.wH_2O$ in flask, 2 M H_2SO_4 added and heated to 60–70°C, 0·04 M MnO_4^- in burette.

No indicator   End point: colourless to pink.

	Rough	1	2
Burette reading (final) cm^3	27·20	26·50	27·05
Burette reading (initial) cm^3	1·65	1·50	2·05
Volume used, cm^3	25·55	25·00	25·00

Average titre = 25·00 cm^3

Calculation 2

25 cm^3 0·05 M $K_xH_y(COO^-)_z.wH_2O$ contains

$$\frac{25}{1000} \times 0{\cdot}05 \text{ mol } (COO^-)_2$$

25 cm^3 0·04 M MnO_4^- contains $\frac{25}{1000} \times 0{\cdot}04$ mol

$$\text{reacting ratio} = \frac{25}{1000} \times 0{\cdot}05 \times \frac{1000}{25 \times 0{\cdot}04}$$

$$= \frac{5}{4} = \frac{1{\cdot}25}{1}$$

Conclusions

From the first calculation, as sodium hydroxide is a monoacidic base, 1 mol of the compound must donate 3 protons, hence $y = 3$.

From the second calculation, as the half equations for reduction of manganate(VII) and oxidation of ethandioate are

$$MnO_4^- + 8H^+ + 5e^- \rightarrow Mn^{2+} + 4H_2O$$

and

$$(COO^-)_2 \rightarrow 2CO_2 + 2e^-$$

the reacting ratio of ethandioate and manganate(VII) = 5 : 2 = 2·5 : 1

The equation indicates 1 mol MnO_4^- reacts with 2·5 mols $(COO^-)_2$.

The titration indicates 1 mol MnO_4^- reacts with 1·25 mols of *A*

1·25 mols *A* contains 2·5 mols ethandioate

Therefore 1 mol *A* contains 2 mols ethandioate

$$\text{Hence } z = 2$$

As the ethandioate ion is bivalent, the valency of two of these ions is four. Three of these valencies are satisfied by the three protons leaving one valency for potassium hence $x = 1$.

Formula mass of $KH_3(COO^-)_2.wH_2O$

$$= 39 + 3 + 4(12 + 32) + w(2 + 16) = 254 \text{ (given)}$$
$$42 + 4{\cdot}44 + 18w = 254$$
$$18w = 254 - 218$$
$$18w = 36$$
$$\therefore \quad w = 2$$

Formula is $KH_3(COO^-)_2.2H_2O$

Qualitative analysis

Qualitative analysis is concerned with determining which elements or ions are present. This can involve a systematic investigation or in many practical exams may involve carrying out a series of tests as indicated in the question. The following gives a summary of the properties of common inorganic ions.

(A) General tests

1. Colour of solid or solution

Colour	*Indication*
blue	hydrated copper(II); anhydrous cobalt(II)
green	copper(II) salts; nickel(II); chromium(III)(dark green); iron(II) (pale green)
purple	chromium(III) salts
brown	some manganese compounds; iron(III) compounds
yellow	some iron(III) compounds
pink	hydrated cobalt(II) salts (reddish pink); manganese(II) salts (pale pink)
white	absence of ions listed above

2. Action of heat on solid

Heat the dry solid in a dry ignition tube, gently at first then more strongly.

Observation		*Indication*
(a) sublimate	(i) white	ammonium or mercury compound
	(ii) grey, sometimes with metallic globules	mercury compound
	(iii) black, violet vapour	some iodides
(b) gas evolved	(i) colourless, clouds lime water	CO_2 from CO_3^{2-} or HCO_3^-
	(ii) brown gas	NO_2 from NO_3^- (nitrate(V)); Br_2 from Br^- (bromide)
	(iii) colourless, acid gas turns $Cr_2O_7^{2-}$ paper green	SO_2 from some SO_4^{2-} (sulphate(VI))
	(iv) colourless gas	O_2 from oxidizing anion (NO_3^- or ClO_3^-) or oxide (PbO_2 etc.) or N_2O from NH_4NO_3
(c) decrepitation	(i) with brown gas	$Pb(NO_3)_2$, lead(II) nitrate
	(ii) with no gas	alkali metal halide
(d) residue changes colour	(i) white cold, yellow hot	Zn^{2+} (zinc)
	(ii) yellow cold, red hot	lead compound
	(iii) red, brown or black	heavy metal salt
	(iv) colour change, evolution of water	hydrated salt, e.g. Cu^{2+}, Co^{2+} etc.

(B) Tests for anions

Tests on solid

1. Add **dil. HCl.** If necessary warm gently.

Observation		*Indication*
(a) colourless gas, pungent odour	(i) turns brown on contact with air, turns $Cr_2O_7^{2-}$ paper green	NO (and NO_2) from a nitrate(III) (nitrite)
	(ii) turns $Cr_2O_7^{2-}$ paper green, no action on lead ethanoate paper	SO_2 from SO_3^{2-}(sulphate(IV))
(b) colourless gas, 'bad egg' smell	(i) turns $Cr_2O_7^{2-}$ paper green and lead ethanoate paper black	H_2S from S^{2-} (sulphide)
(c) colourless gas, precipitate of sulphur	(i) turns $Cr_2O_7^{2-}$ paper green, no action on lead ethanoate paper	SO_2 and sulphur from a thiosulphate, $S_2O_3^{2-}$
(d) colourless gas, no smell	(i) considerable effervescence, no action on $Cr_2O_7^{2-}$ nor on lead ethanoate paper, turns lime water milky	CO_2 from carbonate, CO_3^{2-}, or hydrogencarbonate, HCO_3^-

2. Add a few drops of **conc. H_2SO_4** to the solid. Warm if necessary.

Observation		*Indication*
(a) Anions as in 1(b), (c) and (d) react as already indicated but SO_2 may be given by reducing agents (e.g. Fe^{2+}, Br^-)		
(b) colourless gas	(i) white fumes in moist air, intensified by ammonia	HCl from chloride, Cl^-
	(ii) cily drops condense on tube walls. Brown fumes on stronger heating or on adding copper turnings	HNO_3, NO_2 } from nitrate(V)
(c) colourless gas, brown fumes on strong heating	(i) white fumes in moist air, intensified by ammonia	HBr and some Br_2 from bromide, Br^-
(d) violet vapour, black sublimate	brown colour may also be noted in solution	I_2 from iodide, I^-
(e) colourless gas, burns with blue flame	(i) charring of solid	CO from methanoate, $HCOO^-$
	(ii) no charring	CO and CO_2 from ethandioate $(COO^-)_2$
(f) colourless vapour, vinegar smell		ethanoic acid from ethanoate, (CH_3COO^-)
(g) sulphate(VI) and phosphate do not react.		

3. Specific tests on solution or solid for ions mentioned above. (It is best to prepare a sodium carbonate extract to remove interfering cations by heating 20 mg of solid with 0·2 g Na_2CO_3 and 3 cm^3 water. Boil gently for 15 minutes, replacing water lost by evaporation. Centrifuge and discard precipitate. Divide solution, using separate portions for the solution tests below.)

(a) *for chloride, bromide and iodide*
(i) Add dil. HNO_3 till soln is acid. Warm to expel CO_2. Cool. Add silver nitrate soln.

Cl^- white ppt, soluble in dil. NH_3(aq)
Br^- cream ppt, soluble in conc. NH_3(aq)
I^- pale yellow ppt, insoluble in conc. NH_3(aq)

(ii) to solution add tetrachloromethane (CCl_4), then sodium chlorate(I) and dil. HCl. Mix well.

Cl^- no colour in CCl_4 layer
Br^- yellow to brown colour in CCl_4 layer
I^- violet colouration in CCl_4 layer

(iii) to solid add solid MnO_2 then conc. H_2SO_4. Warm.

Cl^- greenish yellow gas, bleaches moist litmus
Br^- brown/red vapour
I^- violet vapour, black sublimate

(iv) for chloride only: mix solid with solid potassium dichromate(VI) and conc. H_2SO_4. Heat gently. A red vapour of chromium(VI) dichloride dioxide is evolved.

(b) *for sulphate(VI)*
(i) to the solution add dil. HCl. Warm to expel CO_2 (if using sodium carbonate extract) then add barium chloride solution. White ppt of barium sulphate.
(ii) to the solution add dil. nitric acid. Warm to expel CO_2. Add lead nitrate (or ethanoate) solution. White ppt of lead sulphate.

(c) *for nitrate (V)*, NO_3^-
(i) to solution add dil. H_2SO_4 (if using sodium carbonate extract) and freshly prepared iron(II) sulphate solution. Mix well and carefully add conc. H_2SO_4 down the side of the tube. Brown ring at junction of two layers.
(ii) to solid add aluminium powder (or Devarda's alloy) then dil. NaOH. Warm. Ammonia gas (alkaline, pungent).
(If ammonium ion is present decompose it before testing for nitrate.)

(d) *for nitrate(III)*, NO_2^-
(i) to cold aqueous solution (acidify if necessary with dil. H_2SO_4) add freshly prepared iron(II) sulphate then further dil. H_2SO_4. Brown solutions, whose colour disappears on warming.

(e) *for sulphate(IV)*, SO_3^{2-}
(i) to solution add barium chloride solution then hydrogen peroxide followed by dil. HCl. White precipitate.
(ii) to solution add 4 drops potassium manganate(VII) immediately followed by dil. H_2SO_4. Solution decolourized.

(f) *for phosphate*, PO_4^{3-}
(i) add 5 drops conc. HNO_3 then 2 drops ammonium molybdate. Warm. Bright yellow precipitate.
(ii) acidify with dil. HCl. Add solid magnesium chloride and then ammonium chloride. Shake to dissolve. Slowly add aqueous ammonia down the side of the tube. White ring at the junction of the two layers.

Tests for cations

1. Summary of insoluble compounds of cations

(a) hydroxides — all but Na^+, K^+, NH_4^+ are insoluble or only slightly soluble

Colours of ppts with dil. alkalis (NaOH or aqueous ammonia)

white, sol. in excess NaOH	Bi^{3+}, Zn^{2+}, Al^{3+}, $Sn^{2+/4+}$, Pb^{2+}
white, sol. in excess $NH_3(aq)$	Zn^{2+}
white, insol. in excess alkali	Ba^{2+}, Ca^{2+}, Sr^{2+} (only ppted by NaOH not $NH_3(aq)$) Mg^{2+}
pale blue	Cu^{2+} (sol. in excess $NH_3(aq)$)
green	Fe^{2+}, Ni^{2+}
brown	Fe^{3+}
grey blue	Cr^{3+}
blue (turns green on heating)	Co^{2+}

(b) chlorides — Pb^{2+}, Hg_2^{2+}, Ag^+

(c) sulphates	Pb^{2+}, Ba^{2+}, Sr^{2+}, Ca^{2+} (slightly sol.)	
(d) bromides	as for chlorides	
(e) iodides	as for chlorides and also Cu^+, Hg^{2+}	
(f) chromates	Pb^{2+}, Ba^{2+} (both yellow), Ag^+ (red)	
(g) sulphides	black/brown, insol. in dil. HCl	Cu^{2+}, Hg^{2+}, Pb^{2+}, Sn^{2+}
	black/brown, sol. in dil. HCl	$Fe^{2+/3+}$, Co^{2+}, Ni^{2+}
	yellow, insol. in dil. HCl	Cd^{2+}, Sn^{4+}
	buff, sol. in dil. HCl	Mn^{2+}
	white, sol. in dil. HCl	Zn^{2+}

2. Flame tests Use a cleaned platinum or nichrome wire or silica rod. Dip in clean conc. HCl on a watch glass then put into flame until no colouration is noted. Then dip into the acid and a separate sample of the solid. Heat in a non-luminous bunsen flame.

golden yellow	Na^+ (red)	Ca^{2+} (brick red)
lilac	K^+	Sr^{2+} (carmine)
green	Ba^{2+} (apple green)	Li^+ (crimson)
	Cu^{2+} (blue/green)	

blue flashes may be given by $Sn^{2+/4+}$, Pb^{2+}, Zn^{2+}
sparkler effect may be given by $Fe^{2+/3+}$

3. Systematic analysis for non interfering cations

(a) To solution of solid add dil. HCl (a few drops only – add more only if a precipitate is given, then add sufficient to precipitate all of the ion present). Centrifuge to separate ppt from solution (used for test (b)).
White precipitate given by Pb^{2+}, Ag^+, Hg_2^{2+}. (These are referred to as Group I of the separation table – this does not refer to a group of the Periodic Table.)

(b) To solution (or filtrate) from (a), pass hydrogen sulphide. Sulphides with a low solubility product are precipitated (Group II – Cu^{2+}, Cd^{2+}, Sn^{2+}, Sn^{4+}, Hg^{2+}). Centrifuge, retain ppt. for further tests to identify the cation, use centrifugate (filtrate) for (c).

(c) Boil to expel hydrogen sulphide. Add 1 drop conc. HNO_3, warm. Add 0·1 g solid NH_4Cl then aqueous ammonia till soln is alkaline. Hydroxides with low solubility products are given. (Group III – $Fe^{2+/3+}$, Al^{3+}, Cr^{3+}). Centrifuge.

(d) Pass hydrogen sulphide through filtrate from (c). Sulphides with higher solubility products are precipitated (Group IV – Ni^{2+}, Co^{2+}, Zn^{2+}, Mn^{2+}). Centrifuge.

(e) Evaporate centrifugate from (d) to reduce volume to 1 cm^3. Add 1 drop aqueous ammonia then conc. ammonium carbonate. Carbonates of remaining cations are given (Group V – Ba^{2+}, Ca^{2+}, Sr^{2+}) as white precipitates.

(f) Evaporate solution from (e) to dryness, continuing heating till no further fuming is noted. White residue indicates Group VI element (Mg^{2+}, K^+, Na^+).

(g) Test original solid for ammonium ion, NH_4^+, by heating with dil. NaOH. (NH_3 gas evolved, a pungent alkaline gas which turns moist red litmus blue.)

Properties of cations

(a) Group I

$PbCl_2$ – white ppt, sol. in hot water
AgCl – white ppt, insol. in hot water, sol. in dil. $NH_3(aq)$
Hg_2Cl_2 – white ppt, darkened by $NH_3(aq)$

Pb^{2+} – to hot solution of chloride (in hot water) add
(i) K_2CrO_4 soln: yellow ppt
(ii) KI soln: yellow ppt
(iii) pass H_2S: black ppt
(iv) add dil. NaOH: white ppt, sol in excess

Ag^+ (i) stand chloride in light: ppt darkens
(ii) to solution of chloride in dil. $NH_3(aq)$ add KI soln: yellow ppt

Hg_2^{2+} (i) to original soln add tin(II) chloride: grey ppt

(b) Group II Test solubility of ppt in hot dil. NaOH.

Ppt insoluble in dil. NaOH Add 35% HNO_3 (1 vol conc. HNO_3: 1 vol H_2O). Warm.

Cu^{2+}, black sulphide, soluble in HNO_3 to give pale blue soln.

(i) to soln add dil. NH_3(aq): pale blue ppt, sol. in excess to give dark blue soln.

(ii) to soln add 2 drops potassium hexacyanoferrate(II). Acidify with dil. ethanoic acid: red brown ppt.

Hg^{2+}, black sulphide, insoluble in HNO_3, soluble in aqua regia (3 vol conc. HCl: 1 vol conc. HNO_3) on warming.

(i) dilute 1 vol. of soln. with 3 vols. water. Add tin(II) chloride: white ppt darkening with excess $SnCl_2$.

(ii) dilute solution as for (i). Add copper turnings: metal becomes coated with grey coating (an amalgam forms).

Cd^{2+}, yellow sulphide, soluble in HNO_3 to give colourless solution.

(i) add dil. NH_3(aq): white ppt, sol. in excess.

Ppt soluble in dil. NaOH

Sn^{4+}, yellow ppt originally

(i) reprecipitate sulphide by addition of dil. HCl. Dissolve in conc. HCl. Add dil. NaOH: white ppt sol. in excess.

Sn^{2+}, brown ppt. originally

(i) add dil. HCl to give original solid. To solution add mercury(II) chloride soln: white ppt turning grey

(ii) to original solid add dil. H_2SO_4 then ammonium molybdate: blue ppt

(c) Group III

Al^{3+}, white gelatinous ppt

(i) dissolve ppt in dil. HCl. Add 1 drop aluminon then dil. NH_3(aq) till just alkaline: red lake

$Fe^{2+/3+}$, brown ppt

Prepare a solution of original solid in dil. HCl without heating

(i) add potassium hexacyanoferrate(III): dark blue ppt, Fe^{2+}; white/pale blue, ppt Fe^{3+}

(ii) add potassium hexacyanoferrate(II): brown soln, no ppt, Fe^{2+}; dark blue ppt, Fe^{3+}

(iii) add potassium thiocyanate soln: no colouration, Fe^{2+}; blood red colour, Fe^{3+}

Cr^{3+}, green ppt

(i) to some of washed ppt, add 1 cm^3 water then a little solid sodium peroxide. Warm: yellow solution

(ii) acidify yellow soln from (i) with dil. H_2SO_4. Add hydrogen peroxide and 3 drops of ether: blue colour in ether layer

(d) Group IV

Co^{2+}/Ni^{2+}, black ppt

(i) dissolve ppt in aqua regia, dilute well with distilled water: green solution, Ni^{2+}; pink soln, Co^{2+}

(ii) to soln (i) add dil $NH_3(aq)$ till just alkaline, then dimethyl glyoxime: red ppt, Ni^{2+}

(iii) to soln from (i) add solid ammonium thiocyanate then 6 drops amyl alcohol (2-methylbutan-2-ol): blue colour in upper layer, Co^{2+}

(iv) neutralize soln from (i) with dil. NaOH. Add to conc. soln of potassium nitrate(III): yellow ppt, Co^{2+}

Mn^{2+}, buff ppt

(i) dissolve some of ppt in dil HCl. Add dil. NaOH: white ppt darkens on exposure to air

(ii) dissolve rest of ppt in 35% nitric acid. Add to sodium bismuthate soln: purple colour

Zn^{2+} dirty white ppt. Dissolve ppt in dil HCl.

(i) add dil. NaOH to resultant soln: white ppt, sol. in excess

(ii) add potassium hexacyanoferrate(III): white ppt

(e) Group V Dissolve ppt in dil. ethanoic acid.

(i) add 1 to 2 drops only K_2CrO_4: yellow ppt, Ba^{2+}

(ii) if no ppt with (i) add 1 to 2 drops only dil. H_2SO_4: white ppt, Sr^{2+}

(iii) if no ppt with (ii) add ammonium ethandioate: white ppt, Ca^{2+}

Ba^{2+}

(i) to soln in ethanoic acid add dil. NaOH till neutral then ammonium ethandioate: white ppt, sol. in hot ethanoic acid

(ii) flame test: apple green

Sr^{2+}

(i) flame test: carmine red flame

Ca^{2+}

(i) flame test: brick red flame

(f) Group VI Dissolve residue in minimum of water (or if no other cations have been detected dissolve original solid in water) and to separate portions of the solution.

(i) add dil. $NH_3(aq)$, solid ammonium chloride then disodium hydrogen phosphate: white ppt, Mg^{2+}

(ii) if no ppt with (i) add sodium hexanitritocobaltate(III) then a few drops ethanoic acid: yellow ppt, K^+

(iii) if no ppt with (ii) add zinc uranyl ethanoate: yellow ppt, Na^+

Other tests

Mg^{2+}: add 1 drop dil. HCl, 1 drop magneson, 2 drops dil. NaOH: blue lake (blue coloured ppt)

K^+: flame test: lilac

Na^+: flame test: golden yellow

In recording the results of a qualitative analysis it is best to use three columns. Column 1 records briefly the test carried out; Column 2 gives the observations in the test; Column 3 gives the inference of this observation (including what ions are absent). A conclusion should be given at the end which takes into account all of the inferences.

Key terms

Quantitative analysis Analysis to determine the quantity of substance present in a sample.

Volumetric analysis Measuring volumes of reacting solutions using burette and pipette.

Molar concentration (molarity) The concentration of solution expressed in mol dm^{-3} (mol litre).

Titration The process of measuring volumes of solutions which react.

Indicator A substance generally used to indicate completion of a reaction.

Basicity of an acid is the number of moles of protons donated by 1 mole of the acid.

Acidity of a base is the number of moles of protons accepted by 1 mole of the base.

Half equation in a redox reaction gives the oxidation process alone or the reduction process alone.

Oxidizing agent An electron acceptor.

Reducing agent An electron donor.

Oxidation number The valency of the element with a sign (+ or −) indicating the relative electronegativity of the element with respect to other constituent elements.

Qualitative analysis Analysis to determine which element or ions are present.

Chapter 9
Organic Chemistry: Introduction

Organic chemistry is the study of the compounds of carbon. The simplest organic compounds are the **hydrocarbons** which are compounds containing carbon and hydrogen only. Many organic compounds may be studied as **homologous series**. These are groups of compounds which may be represented by a general formula, possess similar chemical properties, exhibit a gradation of physical properties and whose formulae differ, one from the next, by a $-CH_2-$ unit. Members of a series are termed homologues. Examples of these include the hydrocarbons in the table below.

Table 5

	Alkanes	*Alkenes*	*Alkynes*
General Formula	C_nH_{2n+2}	C_nH_{2n}	C_nH_{2n-2}
$n = 1$	CH_4 methane	–	–
$n = 2$	C_2H_6 ethane	C_2H_4 ethene	C_2H_2 ethyne
$n = 3$	C_3H_8 propane	C_3H_6 propene	C_3H_4 propyne
$n = 4$	C_4H_{10} butane	C_4H_8 butene	C_4H_6 butyne
$n = 5$	C_5H_{12} pentane	C_5H_{10} pentene	C_5H_8 pentyne
$n = 6$	C_6H_{14} hexane	C_6H_{12} hexene	C_6H_{10} hexyne
⋮	⋮	⋮	⋮

The above are examples of **aliphatic compounds**. These may have open chain or ring structures but the ring structures do not have non-localized electrons. **Aromatic compounds** (another class of hydrocarbon) contain a ring structure having non-localized orbitals, an example being benzene, C_6H_6.

When hydrogen atoms of both aliphatic and aromatic compounds are replaced by other atoms or groups of atoms the resultant compounds have certain properties in common. It is therefore more convenient to deal with organic chemistry not in terms of homologous series but in terms of **functional groups**. Those of importance at this level of study are given in the table on the next page.

Table 6 Functional Groups

Functional Group	*Structure*	*Present In*	*Systematic Name*	
			Prefix	*Suffix*
Double bond	$>C{=}C<$	Alkenes	–	ene
Triple bond	$-C{\equiv}C-$	Alkynes	–	yne
Halogen	$>C-Hal$ (Hal = Cl,Br,I)	Halogeno compounds	Halogeno	halide
Amine	$>C-NH_2$	Primary amines	Amino	amine
Hydroxyl	$>C-OH$	Alcohols or Phenols	Hydroxy	ol
Ether	$>C-O-C<$	Ethers	Alkoxy or Aroxy	–
Carbonyl	$>C{=}O$	Aldehydes Ketones	oxo oxo	al one
Carboxyl	$-C(=O)OH$	Carboxylic acids	Carboxy	oic acid
Acid chloride	$-C(=O)Cl$	Acid (acyl) chlorides	–	oyl chloride
Amide	$-C(=O)NH_2$	Acid amides	Amido	amide
Acid anhydride	$-C(=O)-O-C(=O)-$	Anhydrides	–	oic anhydride
Ester	$-C(=O)OR$	Esters	–	oate
Nitrile	$-C{\equiv}N$	Nitriles	Cyano	nitrile
Isonitrile	$-N{\equiv}C$	Isonitriles	Isocyano	isonitrile
Nitro	$-NO_2$	Nitro compounds	Nitro	–
Phenyl	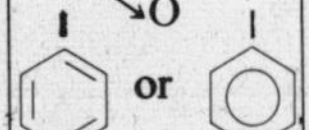	Aromatic compounds	Phenyl	

An organic compound may be represented by

(i) an **empirical formula** – this gives the simplest formula for a compound (i.e. it gives only the combining ratio).
(ii) a **molecular formula** – this gives the actual composition of a molecule of the compound.
(iii) a **structural formula** – this indicates the arrangement of atoms in a molecule.

Ethane has the empirical formula CH_3
molecular formula C_2H_6
structural formula

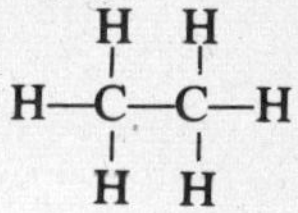

Naming of compounds

Aliphatic compounds are named according to the following rules:

(i) The longest chain containing one or more of the functional groups is noted. The name of this substance is taken as the main part of the name.
(ii) Side chains are named (a) according to the prefix in the table on p. 214 or (b) according to the number of carbon atoms. The side chain is given the name of the alkane with the same number of carbon atoms the ending being modified to -yl (e.g. CH_3– is methyl, CH_3CH_2– is ethyl etc.).
(iii) The positions of side chains and/or multiple bonds in the carbon chain are indicated by numbering the longest chain taken in (i) so that the numbers used to indicate the position of the side group/double bond are the lowest possible.

A few examples are:

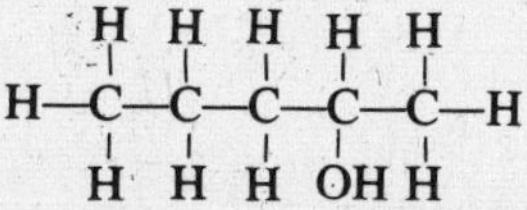

pentan-2-ol

(i) longest chain: 5 carbon atoms
(ii) functional group: hydroxyl, suffix -ol
(iii) position of functional group: on carbon atom numbers 2 (or 4)

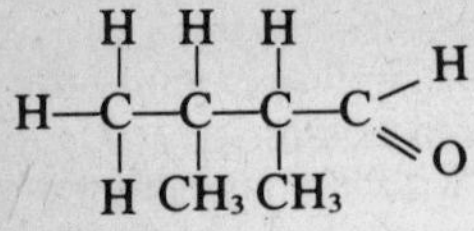

2,3-dimethyl butanal

(i) longest chain: 4 carbon atoms
(ii) functional groups: aldehyde, suffix -al, and two methyl groups
(iii) positions: aldehyde must be terminal; the carbon atom in the aldehyde group is numbered 1, the methyl groups are on carbon atoms numbers 2 and 3

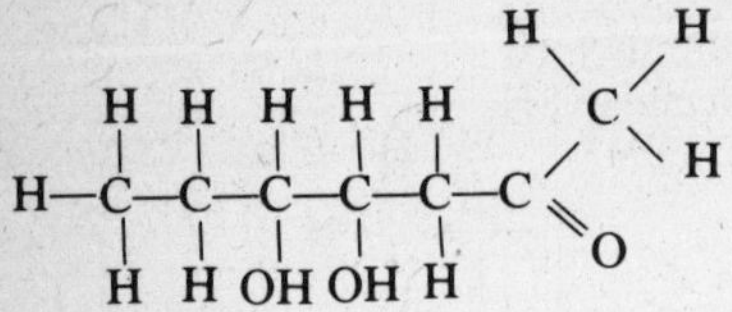

4,5-dihydroxyheptan-2-one

(i) longest chain: 7 carbon atoms
(ii) functional groups: one carbonyl, suffix -one, two hydroxyl
(iii) positions: carbonyl is on carbon atom number 2, hydroxyl groups are therefore on carbon atoms 4 and 5

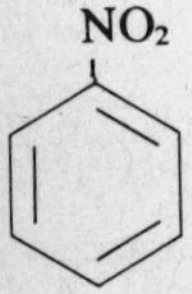

nitrobenzene

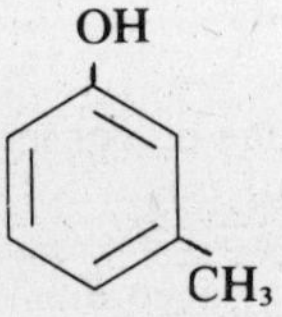

1-hydroxy-3-methylbenzene

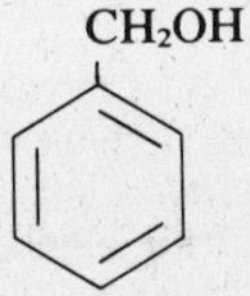

phenylmethanol (benzyl alcohol)

Aromatic compounds are generally considered a susbstituted benzene compounds, but in a few cases it may be more convenient to name them as phenyl derivatives.

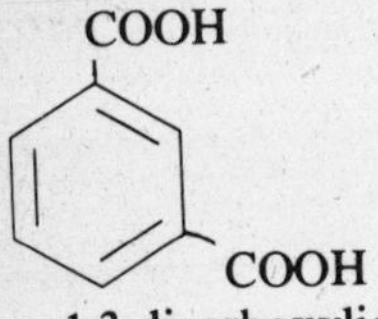

benzene-1,3-dicarboxylic acid

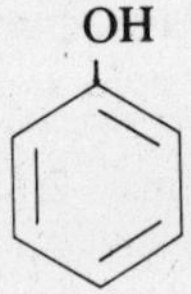

2-hydroxybenzene carboxylic acid

In naming aromatic compounds one of the groups is considered as being substituted on the first carbon atom of the six member ring, the other carbon atoms being numbered so that the remaining functional groups are indicated as being substituted on the carbon atom with the lowest possible number.

Isomerism

With increasing number of carbon atoms, it becomes possible for substances having the same molecular formula to have different structural formulae. Such compounds are known as **isomers**. There are two main types of isomerism, **structural isomerism** in which atoms are joined in different ways and **stereoisomerism** in which the same groups are attached to the same atoms but occupy different relative positions in space.

Structural isomerism can arise in a number of ways. These include (i) *Chain isomerism* in which the different structures are due to different carbon skeletons. For example, C_4H_{10} represents the two isomeric forms:

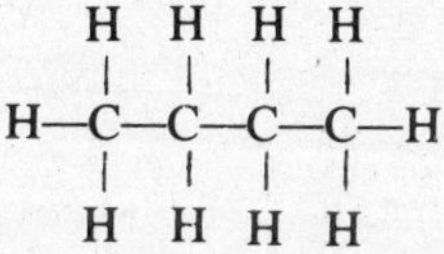

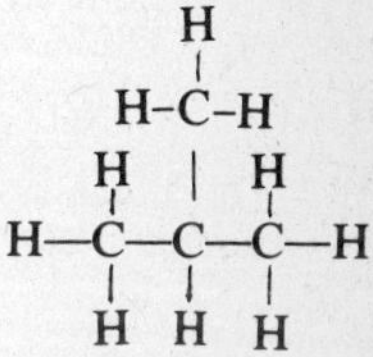

(ii) *Position isomerism* which arises in compounds in which the functional group occupies different positions on the same carbon skeleton:

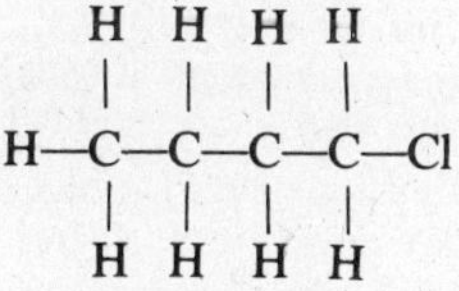

1-chlorobutane

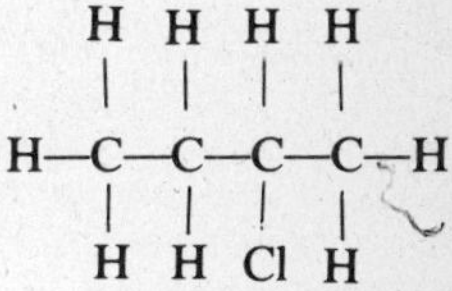

2-chlorobutane

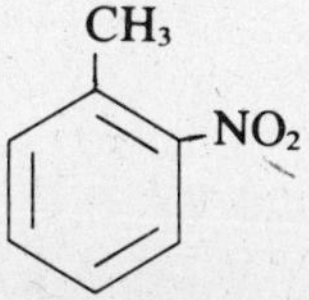

1-methyl-2-nitrobenzene

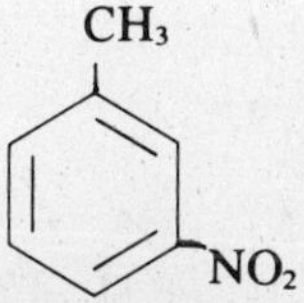

1-methyl-3-nitrobenzene

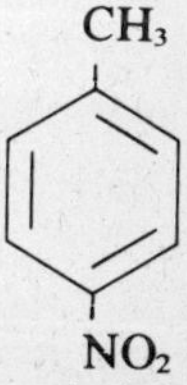

1-methyl-4-nitrobenzene

(iii) *Functional group isomerism* which is due to different functional groups:

$CH_3.CH_2OH$ — ethanol (an alcohol)

$CH_3.O.CH_3$ — methoxymethane (an ether)

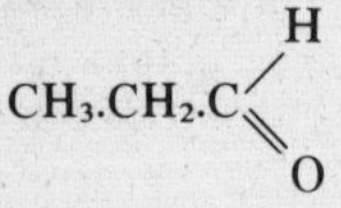

propanal (an aldehyde)

$CH_3.CO.CH_3$

propanone (a ketone)

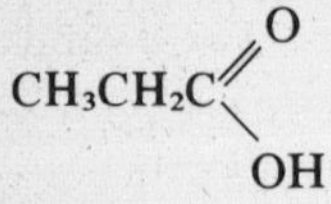

propanoic acid (an acid)

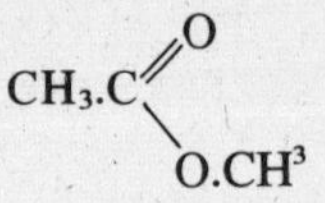

methyl ethanoate (an ester)

(iv) *Tautomerism* is a special type of isomerism in which isomers exist together in dynamic equilibrium:

$$CH_3.CO.CH_2.COO.C_2H_5 \rightleftharpoons CH_3.C(OH){=}CH.COO.C_2H_5$$

ethyl-3-oxobutanoate — ethyl-3-hydroxy-but-2-enoate

Stereoisomerism is of two types:

(i) Geometric isomerism is observed in molecules in which there is restriction to free rotation about a carbon–carbon bond and in which there are different groups attached to both the carbon atoms at the point of restriction. This restriction to rotation may be due to a double bond, to a ring structure or to steric hindrance (in which large groups may interfere with free rotation). The only type which is studied at this level is that due to a double bond.

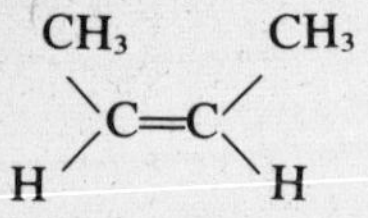

cis-but-2-ene

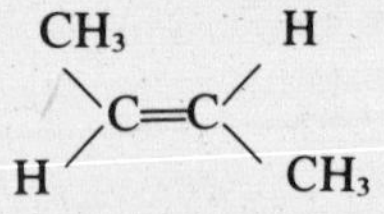

trans-but-2-ene

The isomer in which similar groups are on the same side of the double bond is referred to as the *cis*-isomer, that on which they are on opposite sides is the *trans*-isomer.

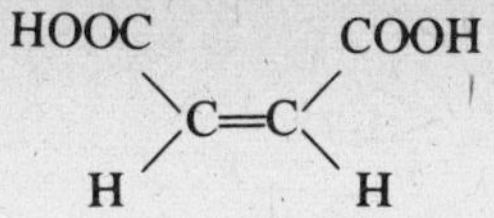

cis-but-2-endioic acid

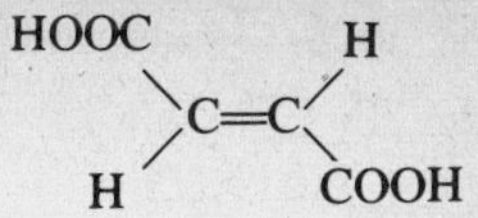

trans-but-2-endioic acid

These types of isomers have different physical properties and may also exhibit differences in chemical behaviour.

(ii) Optical isomerism is observed in compounds in which there are four different groups attached to the same carbon atom in a molecule. Molecules of this type can have these groups arranged in two ways:

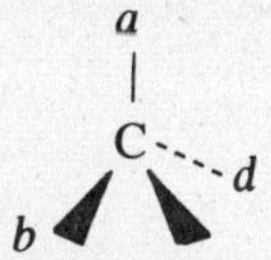

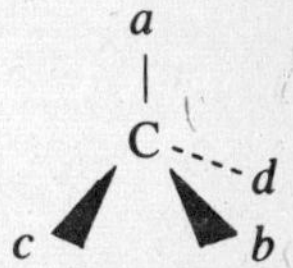

When the two molecules are compared with the groups represented by *a* and *b* aligned, the other groups are in different relative positions. The molecules are **chiral**, i.e. they bear the same relationship to each other as the left hand does to the right. One structure is the mirror image of the other. As the groups are the same distance apart in the molecules the properties of the two isomers are identical in all respects except one. Their solutions have the ability to rotate plane-polarized light (monochromatic light vibrating in one plane only), one isomer doing so by a particular angle to the right (this is called the dextrorotatory isomer, signified by the symbol (+) before the name of the compound) and the other isomer rotating the light the same amount to the left (the laevorotatory or (−) isomer).

Organic compounds of this type include

butan-2-ol

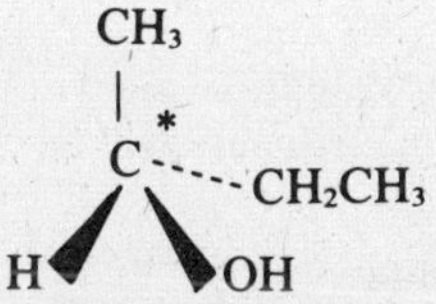

2-hydroxypropanoic acid

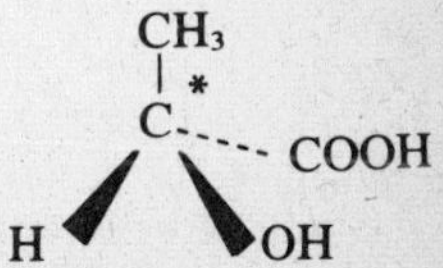

and all but one of the naturally occurring amino acids, e.g.

2-aminopropanoic acid
(alamine)

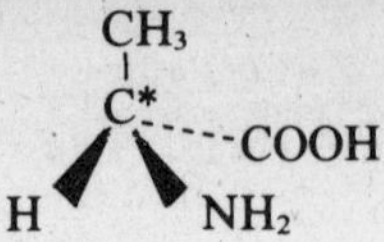

(The asymmetrically substituted carbon atoms in the molecule are indicated by an asterisk *.)

Depending on the source or method of synthesis it may be possible to obtain individual isomers or a mixture of the two in equal proportions. Such mixtures are known as **racemic mixtures** (signified as (±)). These do not rotate plane polarized light as the rotation by the (+) isomer in the mixture is cancelled out (externally compensated) by the rotation of the (−) isomer also present. Because of the similar chemical and physical properties of this type of isomer it is difficult to separate a racemic mixture into the constituent isomers and special techniques have to be employed. The original method for solid substances was to pick out individual crystals under a microscope. More refined methods are now available including preferential use as nutrient of one isomer by micro-organisms or reacting the stereoisomers with a (+) or (−) isomer of another optically active substance, the products of which are no longer mirror images. The products of reacting, for example, a (±) racemic mixture of an optically active base with the (+) isomer of an acid will be

(+) base	and	(−) base
(+) acid		(+) acid

These types of isomer are referred to as **diastereoisomers** (stereoisomers which are not mirror images).

The more the number of asymmetric carbon atoms in a molecule, the greater the number of isomers. With two dissimilar asymmetrically substituted carbons (represented as (+) or (−) A with (+) or (−) B) the possible isomers will be

(+) A		(−) A		(+) A		(−) A
|	and	|	and	|	and	|
(+) B		(−) B		(−) B		(+) B

1 pair of **enantiomers** (mirror images) — 2nd pair of **enantiomers**

Note that the isomers of pair 1 are diastereoisomers of the 2nd pair.

With two similarly substituted asymmetric carbon atoms the possibilities are more limited, the possible isomers being

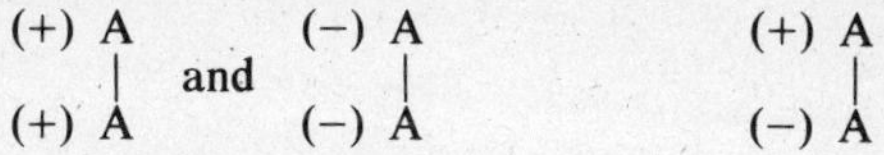

1 pair of enantiomers

one optically inactive isomer as the rotation of one atom is internally compensated by the other. This is the *meso*-isomer.

There will be four forms of acid, i.e. the (+) and (−) forms, its racemic (±) form and the *meso* form. For example, 2,3-dihydroxybutandioic acid (which is commonly known as tartaric acid)

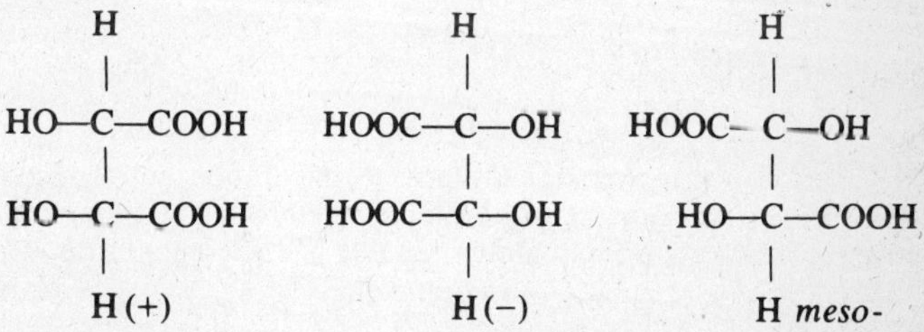

Note that with *n* (a small whole number) different asymmetric carbon atoms the total number of isomers is 2^n. As has been illustrated in the examples above when $n = 2$ there are $2^2 = 4$ isomers (2 pairs of enantiomers), when $n = 3$ the total number of isomers is $2^3 = 8$ (4 pairs of enantiomers) and when $n = 4$ the total is $2^4 = 16$ (8 pairs of enantiomers). The hexose sugars are examples of such compounds.

Glucose is one of the eight pairs of isomers of which others include galactose with the formula (i) illustrated below, whereas fructose is one of the four pairs of isomer with formula (ii):

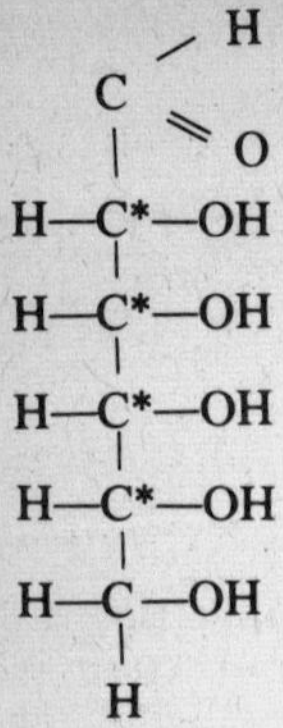

formula (i)

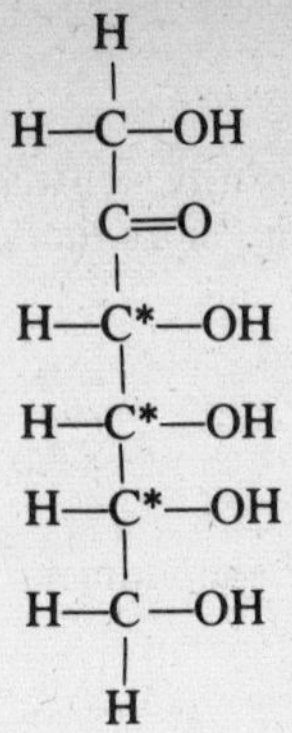

formula (ii)

Stereoisomerism (both geometric and optical) is also observed in certain inorganic complexes of the transition metals. For example, geometric isomers are found of

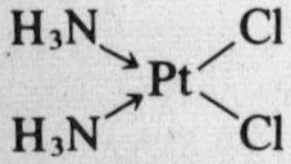

the isomer being

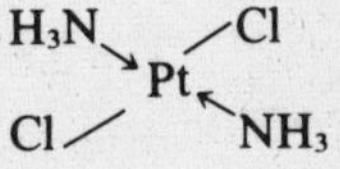

provided the complex has a planar configuration and optical isomers of certain hexacoordinate metals with bidentate ligands (ligands with two atoms capable of forming coordinate links), e.g.

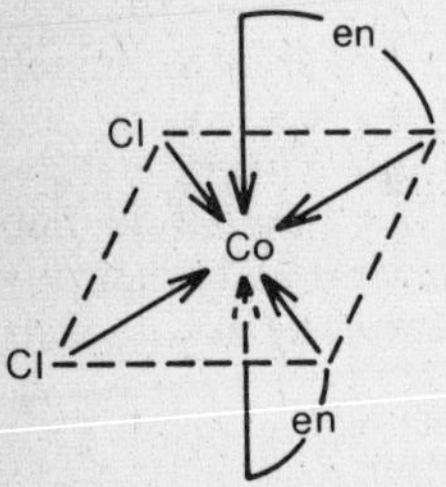

has a mirror image

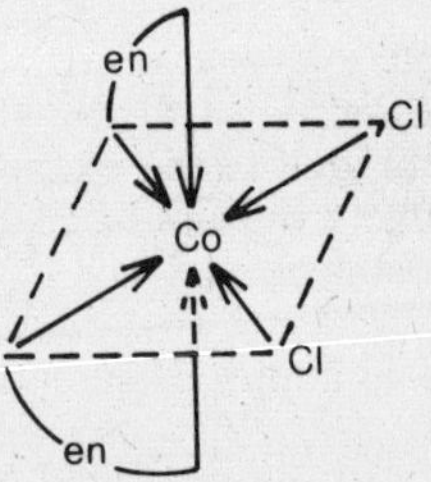

where -en- is 1,2-diaminoethane

$H_2N.CH_2.CH_2.NH_2$

Organic reaction mechanisms

Most reactions of organic compounds involve the breaking of covalent bonds followed by formation of different bonds. The breaking of a bond may take place by **homolytic fission** in which each atom retains the electron donated in forming the bond. The two particles formed are referred to as free radicals:

$$A:B \rightarrow A\cdot + B\cdot$$

The alternative type of fission is **heterolytic fission** in which one of the atoms retains both electrons of the bond, thus forming charged particles:

$$A:B \rightarrow A:^{\ominus} + B^{\oplus}$$

or

$$A:B \rightarrow A^{\oplus} + :B^{\ominus}$$

Which of these occurs depends on the relative electronegativities of A and B. The more electronegative atom or group is the part that forms the anion. This type of fission also depends on the presence of a polar solvent, e.g. water.

Reagents in reactions can be classified as (i) **electrophilic** (electron liking) if they are deficient in electrons or (ii) **nucleophilic** (nucleus, or positive charge, liking) if they can donate electrons. Examples include

Electrophilic		Nucleophilic	
$OH^{\ominus}$	hydroxide	$NO_2^{\oplus}$	nitronium ion
$Cl^{\ominus}$ etc.	halide	$H_3O^{\oplus}$	oxonium ion
$>\ddot{O}:$	e.g. CH_3OH	$Cl^{\oplus}$ etc.	halide (+ve) (halonium ion)
$-\!\!>N:$	e.g. $C_6H_5NH_2$	$-\!\!>C^{\oplus}$	carbonium ion
$CN^{\ominus}$	cyanide	$-N_2^{\oplus}$	diazonium ion

Effects which result in molecules reacting with these reagent types result from shifts of electrons in a molecule. These electron shifts are caused by

(i) the **inductive effect** which is a result of the different electronegativities of the elements joined by the bond, the electrons being attracted by the more electronegative atom, e.g.

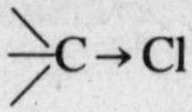

The arrow indicates the greater attraction by the more electronegative chlorine atom of the bonding electrons.
This may also be represented

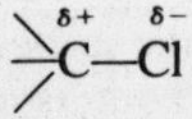

(ii) electron delocalization in which a pair of electrons (an unshared electron pair or an electron pair from a multiple bond or both) results in a similar production of slight charges on sites in the molecule, e.g.

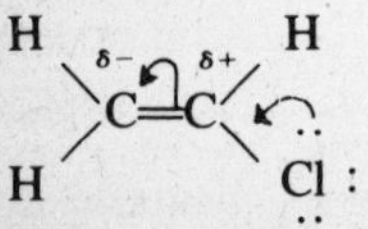

and

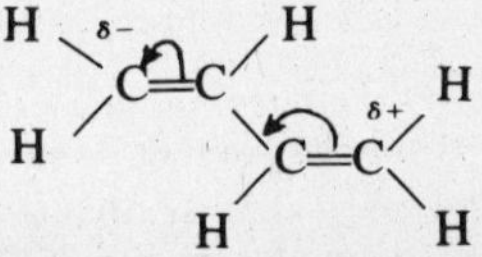

where the arrows indicate the shift of the electron pair in the molecule. As a result the atom donating the electron pair gains a slight positive charge and the atom accepting the electron pair gains a slight negative charge.

Organic reactions may be classified into a number of basic types, the main ones being

(a) Substitution, in which one atom or group of atoms in a molecule is replaced by another atom or group of atoms.

(b) Addition, in which two substances react to give a single substance.

(c) Elimination, in which a compound reacts to give two products.

(d) Condensation, a type of elimination in which a simple molecule such as water is eliminated.

(e) Polymerization, in which a compound reacts with itself to give a compound which has the same empirical formula but a molecular formula which is a multiple of that of the reactant (the monomer), e.g. ethene, C_2H_4, may be reacted under suitable conditions to give polythene $(C_2H_4)_n$ where n may have a range of values from 100 to 1000.

(f) Redox reactions, oxidation–reduction reactions in which electrons are transferred from the oxidized substance (the reducing agent) to the reduced substance (the oxidizing agent). It is possible to explain many of these reaction types by means of reaction mechanisms, which refer to the type of reagent (nucleophilic or electrophilic) and to the inductive effect or electron delocalization to show how the products are formed from the reactants. One example is the addition of a hydrogen halide to an alkene:

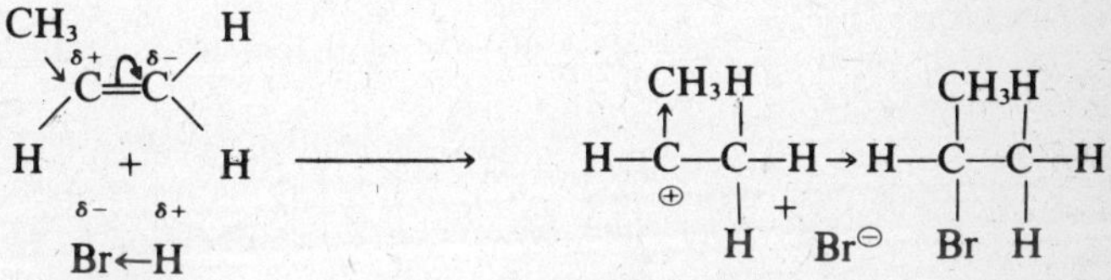

propene + hydrogen bromide

intermediate carbonium ion

2-bromopropane

In propene the inductive effect of the methyl group promotes electron delocalization towards the terminal carbon atom. The hydrogen bromide also exhibits the inductive effect as indicated and the positive hydrogen atom of this molecule is electrophilic. It adds to the negative carbon atom of the propene to form an intermediate carbonium ion. This then reacts with the bromide ion to give the addition product 2-bromopropane. As the initial addition is of the electrophilic hydrogen this reaction is referred to as **electrophilic addition**. Other reaction mechanisms are mentioned where appropriate in chapters 10 and 11.

Key terms

Organic chemistry The study of the compounds of carbon.

Hydrocarbons Compounds containing carbon and hydrogen only.
Homologous series Groups of organic compounds which may be represented by a general formula, with an increment of $-CH_2-$.
Alkanes Hydrocarbons with general formula C_nH_{2n+2}.
Alkenes Hydrocarbons with general formula C_nH_{2n}.
Alkynes Hydrocarbons with general formula C_nH_{2n-2}.
Aliphatic compounds Compounds with open chain structures, or ring structures with no non-localized electrons.
Aromatic compounds Compounds containing a ring structure with non-localized electrons.
Functional groups Groups of atoms found in organic compounds with characteristic properties.
Empirical formula The simplest formula for a substance.
Molecular formula The actual formula for a molecule of a substance.
Structural formula This indicates the arrangement of atoms in a molecule.
Isomers Substances with the same molecular formula but different structural formulae.
Structural isomerism The existence of isomers due to different arrangements of atoms in a molecule.
Stereoisomerism The existence of isomers having the same groups attached to the same atoms but occupying different relative positions in space.
Geometric isomerism Stereoisomerism due to restriction of free rotation about a carbon–carbon bond.
Optical isomerism Stereoisomerism due to asymmetrically substituted carbon atoms.
Homolytic fission Splitting of covalent bonds in which each atom joined by the bond retains one electron from the bond.
Heterolytic fission Splitting of covalent bonds in which one of the atoms joined by the bond retains both electrons so that charged particles are formed.
Electrophilic reagent A reagent which attacks molecules at a region of high electron density.
Nucleophilic reagent A reagent which attacks molecules at a region of high nuclear (positive) charge.
Inductive effect Unequal sharing of electrons in a covalent bond due to different electronegativities of atoms joined by the bond.
Electron delocalization Movement of an electron pair in a molecule.

Chapter 10
Hydrocarbons

Hydrocarbons are organic compounds containing carbon and hydrogen only. Those studied at this level are the alkanes, alkenes and alkynes (aliphatic hydrocarbons) and aromatic hydrocarbons (examples being benzene and methylbenzene).

Alkanes

Alkanes are hydrocarbons with the general formula C_nH_{2n+2}. Those with four carbon atoms or less are gases, the next higher members are liquids, their boiling points increasing with increasing molecular mass. The first solid alkanes are encountered when there are about sixteen carbon atoms in the hydrocarbon. Representative compounds are:

CH_4 methane b.p. −162°C

CH_3CH_3 ethane b.p. −89°C

$CH_3CH_2CH_3$ propane b.p. −44°C

$CH_3CH_2CH_2CH_3$ butane b.p. −0·5°C

CH_3CHCH_3 (with CH_3 on the central C) methylpropane b.p. −12°C

$CH_3CH_2CH_2CH_2CH_3$ pentane b.p. 36°C

$CH_3CH_2CHCH_3$ (with CH_3 on the third C) methylbutane b.p. 28°C

$$CH_3—\underset{CH_3}{\overset{CH_3}{|}}\!\!\!\!C—CH_3$$

$C(CH_3)_4$ dimethylpropane b.p. 9·5°C

Preparation
In the laboratory alkanes may be prepared by

(i) Decarboxylation of salts of carboxylic acids using soda lime, e.g.

$$CH_3COO^- + OH^- \rightarrow CH_4 + CO_3^{2-}$$

The hydrocarbon is driven off on heating. If gaseous it can be collected over water and if liquid it can be condensed by passing through a condenser.

(ii) Reduction of halogenoalkanes (a) using a source of nascent hydrogen (zinc/copper couple; aluminium amalgam; or sodium and alcohol)

$$CH_3I + 2[H] \rightarrow CH_4 + HI$$

or (b) via the Grignard reagent (see halogenoalkanes in chap. 11)

$$CH_3Cl + Mg \xrightarrow[\text{ether}]{\text{dry}} CH_3MgCl$$

methyl magnesium chloride (a Grignard compound)

$$CH_3MgCl \xrightarrow{H^+/H_2O} CH_4 + Mg^{2+} + Cl^-$$

Properties

Alkanes react with few other substances. They react readily with oxygen burning in excess air to produce carbon dioxide and water. In limited air carbon monoxide and even some carbon will be produced instead of the carbon dioxide. Industrially hydrocarbons are deliberately burned in a very limited air supply to obtain finely divided carbon (methane is used to obtain carbon black used in the manufacture of car tyres and other rubber products; higher alkanes give lamp black, used as a black pigment in paints etc.).

With the halogens, chlorine and bromine, substitution occurs under normal conditions, the hydrogen of the alkane being progressively substituted by the halogen:

$$CH_4 + Cl_2 \rightarrow CH_3Cl + HCl$$
$$CH_3Cl + Cl_2 \rightarrow CH_2Cl_2 + HCl$$
$$CH_2Cl_2 + Cl_2 \rightarrow CHCl_3 + HCl$$
$$CHCl_3 + Cl_2 \rightarrow CCl_4 + HCl$$

As a mixture of products is obtained, the reaction is of little commercial significance for the manufacture of halogenoalkanes except for the derivatives of methane given above. These are the only reactions taking place under laboratory conditions. Industrially other reactions are possible, particularly

pyrolysis (subjecting to strong heating). This is used to split large molecules into smaller ones as a means of increasing the useful petrol fraction from petroleum distillate. By heating under pressure with a suitable catalyst, less useful, higher boiling fractions are cracked into two or more smaller molecules. An example might be

$$C_{10}H_{22} \rightarrow C_8H_{18} + C_2H_4$$

Only one of the products is an alkane the other being an alkene. Hydrogen is also a useful by-product of this catalytic cracking.

Using different conditions and a platinum catalyst alkanes with about six carbon atoms may be converted to aromatic hydrocarbons

$$\underset{\text{hexane}}{C_6H_{14}} \rightarrow \underset{\text{benzene}}{C_6H_6} + 4H_2$$

Again, hydrogen is a valuable by-product.

Alkenes

Alkenes are hydrocarbons with the general formula C_nH_{2n}. They are examples of **unsaturated hydrocarbons**, i.e. compounds containing multiple bonds between carbon atoms. The first members are

C_2H_4

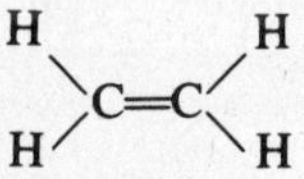

ethene

C_3H_6

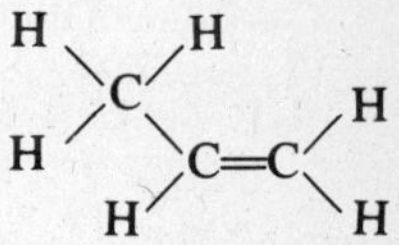

propene

C_4H_8
(4 isomers)

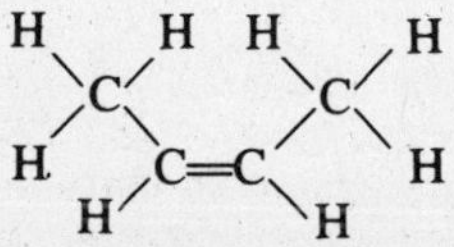

cis-but-2-ene

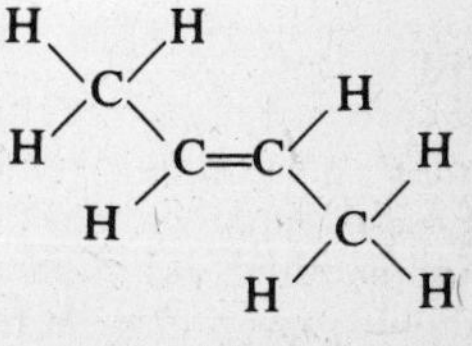

trans-but-2-ene

C_4H_8 isomers
(contd.)

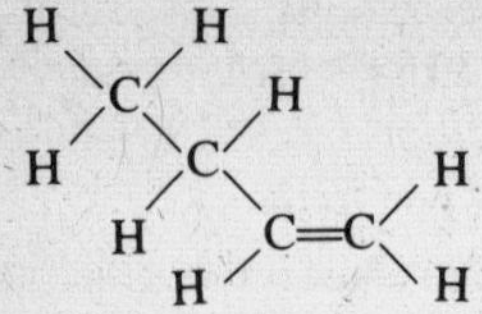

but-1-ene

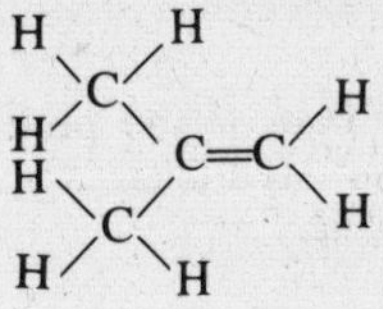

methylpropene

Preparation
They may be prepared in the laboratory by

(i) Dehydration of an alcohol, e.g.

$$CH_3CH_2OH - H_2O \rightarrow CH_2{=}CH_2$$

The alcohol may be carefully mixed with excess of either concentrated sulphuric acid or concentrated (syrupy) phosphoric acid. On heating the mixture the alkene will be evolved in the case of ethene as a gas which can be collected over water. Alternatively, alcohol vapour may be passed over a catalyst, aluminium oxide, heated to 400°C.

(ii) Dehydrohalogenation of a halogenoalkane, e.g.

$$CH_3CH_2I + KOH \rightarrow CH_2{=}CH_2 + KI + H_2O$$

The halogenoalkane is heated with a solution of the potassium hydroxide in alcohol.

The major industrial source of alkenes is from the products of cracking of hydrocarbons.

Properties
Alkenes are more reactive than the alkanes. They exhibit the typical properties of an unsaturated compound. The major reactions involve addition of substances at the site of the multiple bond. A double bond is polarized by the approach of a suitable reagent. The initial attack is electrophilic. An example is the addition of bromine to ethene:

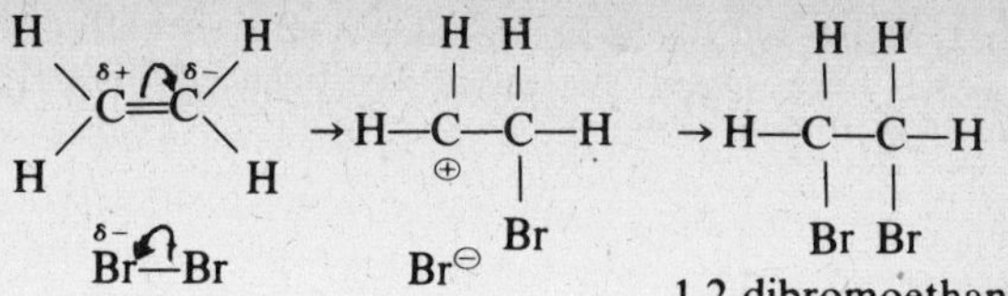

1,2-dibromoethane

The evidence for this mechanism is that if other anions are present in the mixture they compete for addition with the bromide ion. Thus if bromine water containing some sodium chloride is reacted with ethene the products will include the following

$$CH_2OH.CH_2Br \quad CH_2Cl.CH_2Br \quad CH_2Br.CH_2Br$$

but there will be no products containing two hydroxyl groups or two chlorine atoms.

The more important addition reactions are of

(a) hydrogen Reaction takes place on passing the mixed gases over a catalyst (finely divided nickel, palladium or platinum). For liquid alkenes the hydrogen is reacted under pressure at a similar temperature using a catalyst. This reaction converts the unsaturated compound to a saturated one.

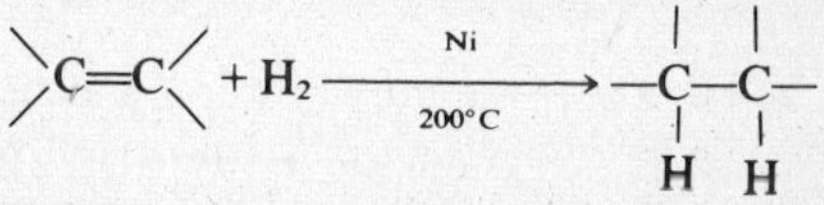

The manufacture of margarine from unsaturated oils is an example of a large scale application of this reaction.

(b) halogens Chlorine and bromine react to give dihalogenoalkanes but only if the pure halogen is used or if it is dissolved in a non polar solvent.

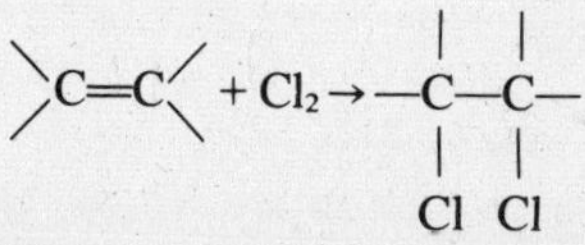

(c) hydrogen halides These add on to give halogenoalkanes. The addition obeys **Markownikow's rule** which states that the hydrogen of the hydrogen halide adds to the carbon atom of the double bond with the most hydrogen atoms already attached. This can be explained in mechanistic terms as follows:

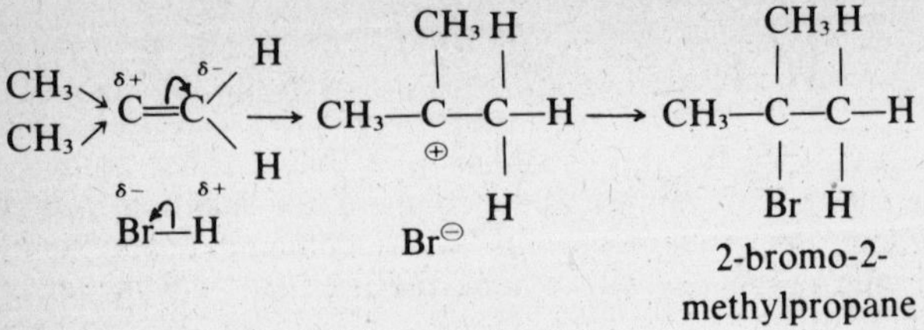

The addition of hydrogen chloride is best carried out in solution in ethanoic acid but hydrogen bromide and hydrogen iodide can be reacted in concentrated aqueous solution.

(d) concentrated sulphuric acid Addition of this also obeys Markownikow's rule. The alkene reacts with the cold concentrated acid.

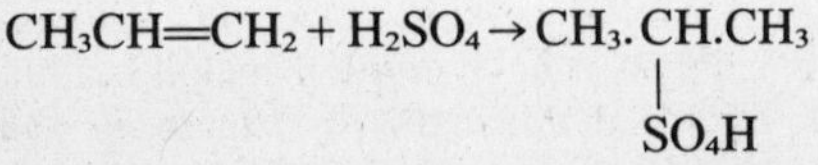

This reaction may be used to obtain alcohols from alkenes as the product may be hydrolyzed to give the corresponding alcohol.

(e) halic(I) acids These are present to a significant extent in aqueous solutions of the halogen. The reaction of alkenes with bromine and chlorine water results in the formation of halogen substituted alcohols

$$CH_3.CH{=}CH_2 + HO{-}Br \rightarrow CH_3.CH(OH).CH_2Br$$

1-bromo-propan-2-ol

(f) ozone (trioxygen) Ozonized oxygen reacts to give an addition product which can be decomposed to give two carbonyl compounds

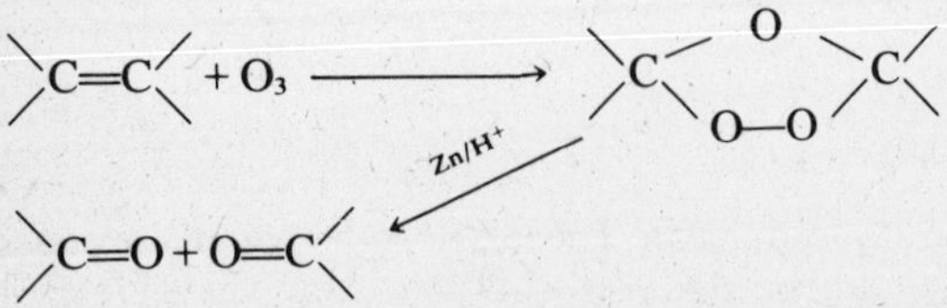

This was used, until physical methods of structure determination became available, to detect the position of a double bond in a molecule as it is possible to identify the carbonyl compounds obtained. The hydrolysis has to be carried out under reducing conditions as hydrogen peroxide is also obtained which could oxidize any aldehydes formed and make it more difficult to identify the products.

(g) potassium manganate(VII) Aqueous solutions of this reagent are rapidly decolorized, the initial product being a gem diol (i.e. a compound with two hydroxy groups, one on each of two adjacent carbon atoms). However, these are also readily oxidized so the reaction has little preparative significance, and is only used to detect the presence of an unsaturated link (i.e. double or triple bonds between carbon atoms) in an organic compound. The initial reaction may be represented:

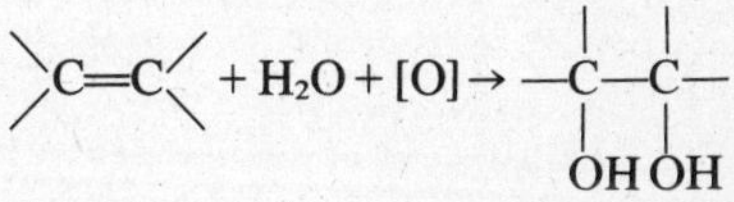

(h) polymerization This is a useful property of unsaturated compounds. In this reaction several molecules react to give a large molecule (the polymer) by a process of self addition. The conditions for polymerization vary, most involving use of a catalyst, heat and in some cases increased pressure. Examples are

monomer	*polymer*	
(a) ethene $CH_2{=}CH_2$	polythene	$(-CH_2-CH_2-)_n$
(b) propene $CH_3CH{=}CH_2$ (propylene)	polypropene (polypropylene)	$\left(\begin{array}{c}CH_3\\ \vert\\ -CH-CH_2-\end{array}\right)_n$
(c) chloroethene $Cl.CH{=}CH_2$ (vinyl chloride)	polyvinyl chloride	$\left(\begin{array}{c}Cl\\ \vert\\ -CH-CH_2-\end{array}\right)_n$
(d) phenylethene $C_6H_5.CH{=}CH_2$ (styrene)	polystyrene	$\left(\begin{array}{c}C_6H_5\\ \vert\\ -CH-CH_2-\end{array}\right)_n$

Alkynes

Alkynes are hydrocarbons with the general formula C_nH_{2n-2}. They are unsaturated hydrocarbons, containing a triple bond between carbon atoms. The compound ethyne, C_2H_2, is considered typical of the series. It has the structural formula, H—C≡C—H. Ethyne is obtained both industrially and in the laboratory by the action of water on calcium carbide (obtained by heating coke and calcium oxide in an electric furnace)

$$CaC_2 + 2H_2O \rightarrow Ca(OH)_2 + C_2H_2$$

It can also be obtained on an industrial scale from other hydrocarbons, e.g.

$$2CH_4 \xrightarrow[\text{pressure, catalyst}]{\text{heat}} C_2H_2 + 3H_2$$

and in the laboratory by dehydrohalogenation of dihalides:

$$CH_2Br.CH_2Br \xrightarrow[\text{in alcohol}]{\text{KOH}} HC{\equiv}CH + 2HBr$$

Properties

Ethyne, like ethene, is an unsaturated hydrocarbon, most of its reactions also involving addition, including reaction with hydrogen at 200°C with a nickel catalyst; **bromine** and **chlorine** can also be added the final product being 1,1,2,2-tetrahalogenoethane; **hydrogen halides** add on to give two possible products by addition of one or two molecules of the hydrogen halide:

$$H{-}C{\equiv}C{-}H + H{-}X \rightarrow CH_2{=}CHX \quad \text{halogenoethene}$$

$$CH_2{=}CHX + H{-}X \rightarrow CH_3.CHX_2 \quad \text{1,1-dihalogenoethane}$$

The order of reactivity is HI > HBr > HCl, (conc. HI and conc. HBr may be used alone; HCl requires a mercury(II) chloride catalyst). Ethyne also reacts with **dilute sulphuric acid** in the presence of a mercury(II) sulphate catalyst. The end result is the addition of water to give ethanal

$$HC{\equiv}CH + H_2O \rightarrow CH_3.CHO$$

Potassium manganate(VII) is decolorized by ethyne:

$$H{-}C{\equiv}C{-}H + 4[O] \rightarrow \underset{\text{ethandioic acid}}{HOOC.COOH}$$

Ozone reacts to give an addition product which on hydrolysis gives two separate carboxylic acids:

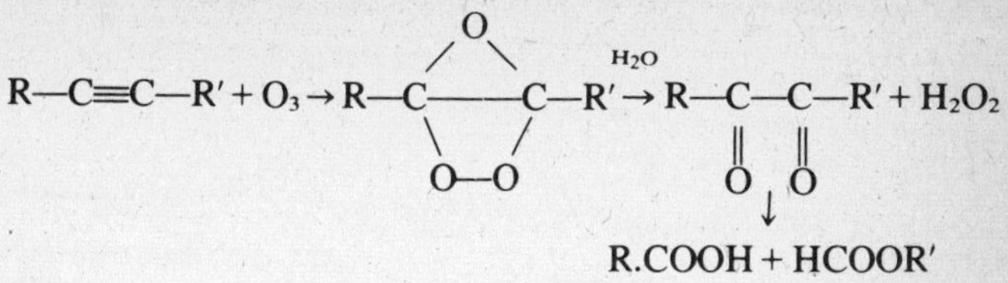

Substitution occurs with a few metals and with a few metal/ammonia complexes. With sodium (or potassium) both hydrogen atoms may be replaced by the metal either on heating the metal in a stream of the gas or with the metal dissolved in liquid ammonia. This reaction will only occur with compounds with a terminal —C≡C—H unit (if the triple bond is not terminal there is no hydrogen directly attached to the carbon atoms joined by it).

$$\mathrm{H{-}C{\equiv}C{-}H + 2Na \rightarrow Na_2[C{\equiv}C] + H_2}$$

With silver or copper(I) complexes with ammonia, a precipitate is given. On drying these detonate readily.

$$\mathrm{HC{\equiv}CH + 2[Ag(NH_3)_2]^+ \rightarrow Ag_2[C{\equiv}C] + 2NH_4^+ + 2NH_3}$$

$$\mathrm{HC{\equiv}CH + 2[Cu(NH_3)_4]^+ \rightarrow Cu_2[C{\equiv}C] + 2NH_4^+ + 6NH_3}$$

Benzene

Benzene is the simplest aromatic hydrocarbon. It has the molecular formula C_6H_6 (the empirical formula, CH is identical to that of ethyne) and although this might suggest it is highly unsaturated its properties are not typical of an unsaturated compound (it undergoes substitution reactions more readily than addition). Chemical properties and physical methods indicate benzene has a ring structure with all six carbon to carbon bonds of equal length, 0·139 nm (compared with C—C, 0·154 nm and C═C, 0·132 nm). The bond length is therefore intermediate between that of a single and double bond. The structures used to represent benzene are:

(a) Kekulé structures in which it is considered that benzene is a resonance structure (a hybrid) of several contributing structures, the main contributing ones being,

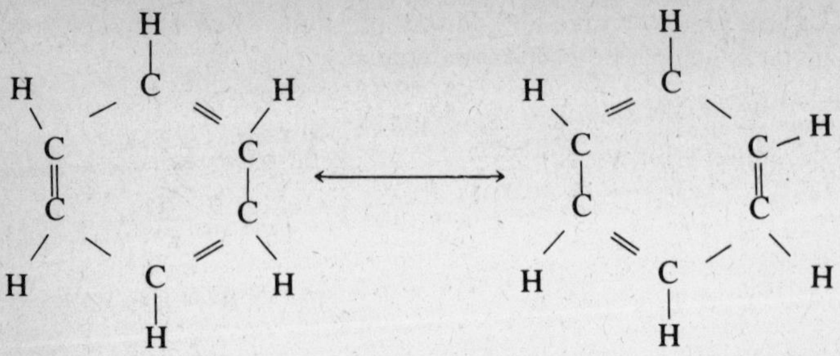

where ↔ indicates resonance. It is important to note that neither of these structures actually exists, the actual structure being a hybrid of these extreme forms.

(b) Delocalization structure in which the six carbon atoms in the ring are bonded to each other and also to one hydrogen atom by sp^2 hybridization resulting in a planar structure. The electrons in the remaining *p* orbital are then bonded by π bonding but as these can overlap with orbitals on either side the resulting orbitals result in delocalized electrons being shared around the ring:

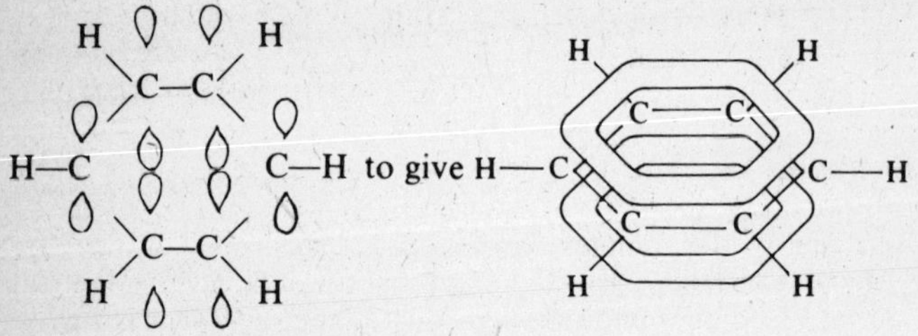

Sources of benzene

It is obtained on a large scale from two main sources, petroleum and coal. From petroleum, C_6 fractions are modified by heating under pressure with catalysts, e.g.

$$\underset{\text{hexane}}{C_6H_{14}} \rightarrow \underset{\text{benzene}}{C_6H_6} + 4H_2$$

resulting in ring closure and dehydrogenation. It is obtained from coal by destructive distillation, the major distillate containing it being the coal gas fraction which is washed to remove the volatile benzene. A small proportion, together with significant amounts of related aromatic hydrocarbons (methylbenzene, dimethylbenzene, anthracene etc.) is also obtained from the coal tar fraction.

Properties of benzene

It is a volatile liquid with a pleasant smell (the term aromatic applied to benzene and its derivatives was given because of this). It is a typical non polar liquid, being an extremely useful solvent for covalent substances. It is poisonous and can be absorbed through the skin. It should therefore be handled with care.

Substitution

Its major chemical reactions involve substitution by electrophilic reagents. These include the following electrophilic species.

(i) nitronium ion, $NO_2^{\oplus}$, formed by nitric acid accepting protons from the stronger acid, sulphuric acid:

$$\underset{\text{(conc.)}}{HNO_3} + \underset{\text{(conc.)}}{2H_2SO_4} \rightleftharpoons NO_2^{\oplus} + H_3O^{\oplus} + 2HSO_4^{\ominus}$$

(ii) halonium ion, $Cl^{\oplus}$ or $Br^{\oplus}$, formed by the pure halogens reacting with a Lewis acid (an electron pair acceptor) such as aluminium chloride or the corresponding iron(III) halide

$$:\ddot{\underset{..}{Cl}}-\ddot{\underset{..}{Cl}}: + AlCl_3 \rightleftharpoons Cl^{\oplus} + AlCl_4^{\ominus}$$

(iii) carbonium ions, CH_3^+, (and other alkonium ions) and CH_3CO^+ (and other acylonium ions) again formed by reaction of the alkyl or acyl halide with aluminium chloride

$$CH_3I + AlCl_3 \rightleftharpoons CH_3^{\oplus} + [I \rightarrow AlCl_3]^{\ominus}$$

$$CH_3COCl + AlCl_3 \rightarrow CH_3CO^{\oplus} + [Cl \rightarrow AlCl_3]^{\ominus}$$

(iv) sulphur trioxide, SO_3, present in conc. sulphuric acid and to a greater extent in fuming sulphuric acid.

An example of the reaction of benzene with an electrophilic reagent is:

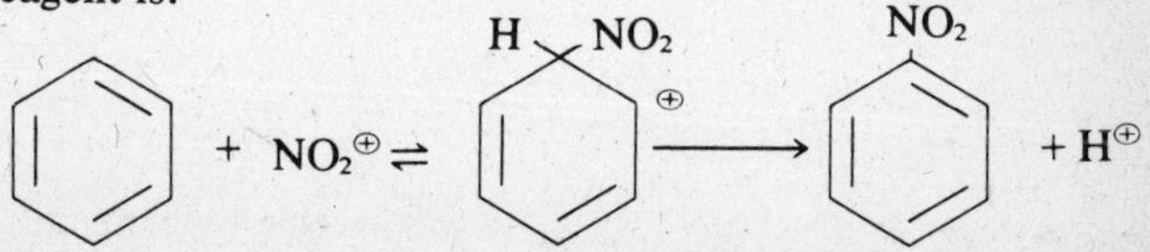

Note that the intermediate has lost the stabilization given to the nucleus by the resonance (delocalization) and although addition of a nucleophilic species might appear to be possible this does not occur as the loss of a proton by the intermediate to give the substitution product results in the end product retaining this stabilizing resonance (delocalization) energy.

The substitution reactions, with conditions are

(a) conc. nitric/conc. sulphuric acid (nitration)

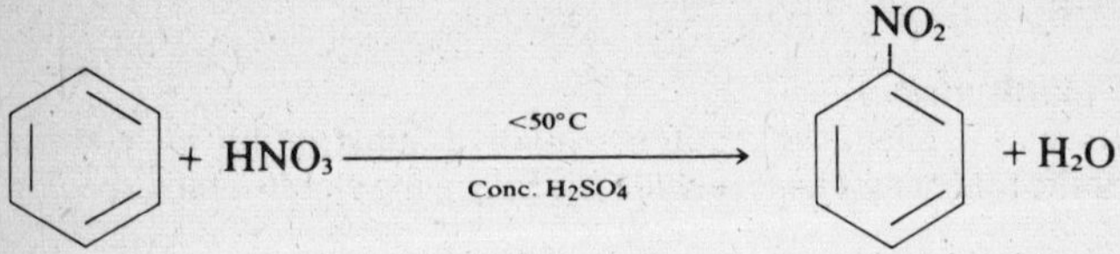

Above 50°C some of the disubstitution product will be obtained

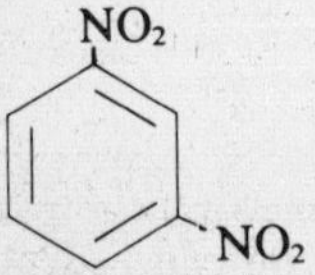

1,3-dinitrobenzene

(b) chlorine or **bromine** (halogenation)

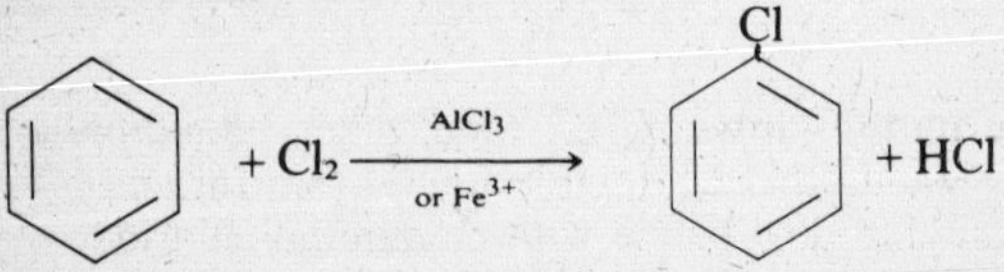

The iron(III) catalyst may be prepared in situ by adding iron filings to the benzene. Again further substitution is possible, but this can be prevented by limiting the amount of halogen used.

(c) Friedel Craft reaction
Alkyl and acyl halides react to give alkylbenzene and ketones respectively.

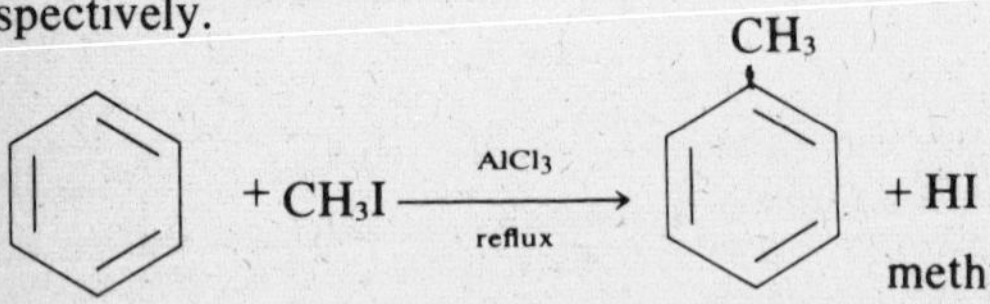

methylbenzene

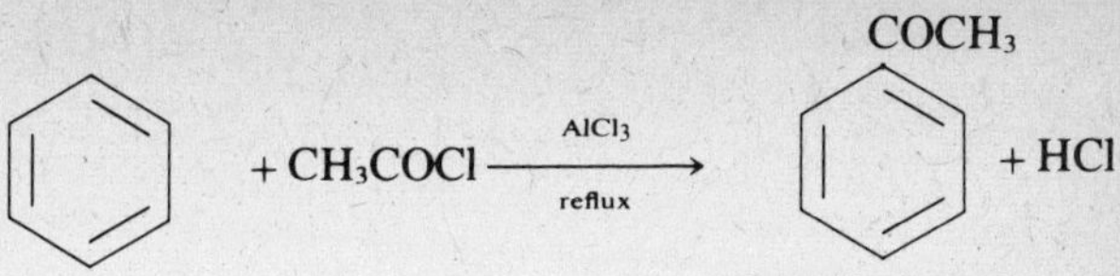

phenylethanone

(d) conc. H_2SO_4 or oleum (sulphonation)

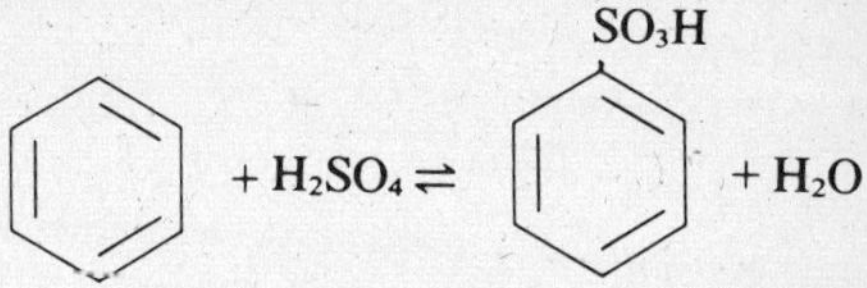

With the concentrated acid, refluxing for several hours is required, but with the fuming acid (oleum) refluxing for one to two hours only gives satisfactory yields.

Addition

Benzene will also form addition products but usually only under more severe conditions than those required for addition to typical unsaturated compounds.

(e) hydrogen

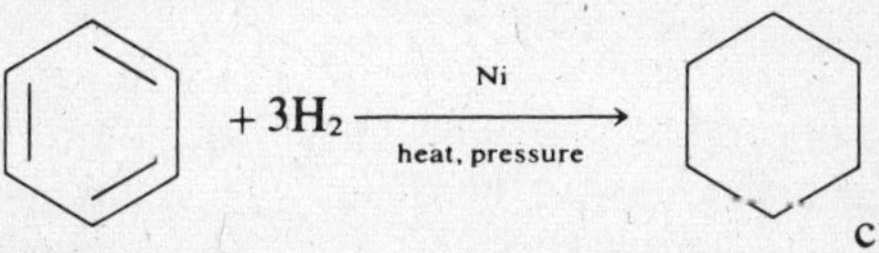

cyclohexane

(f) halogens (chlorine, bromine)

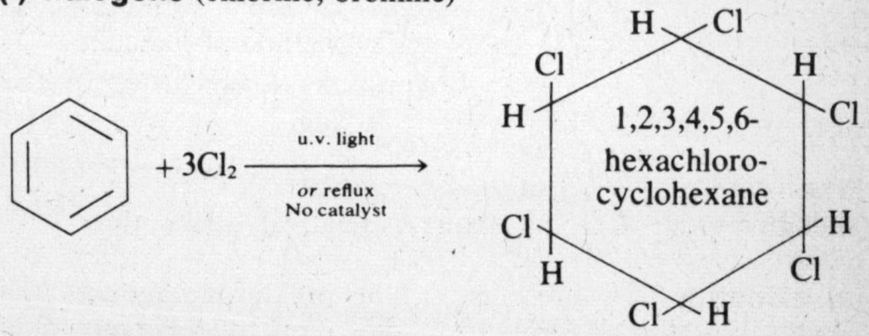

(g) ozone (trioxygen)

Ozonized oxygen will add to the molecule to give an unstable triozonide. On hydrolysis this gives 3 molecules of ethandial.

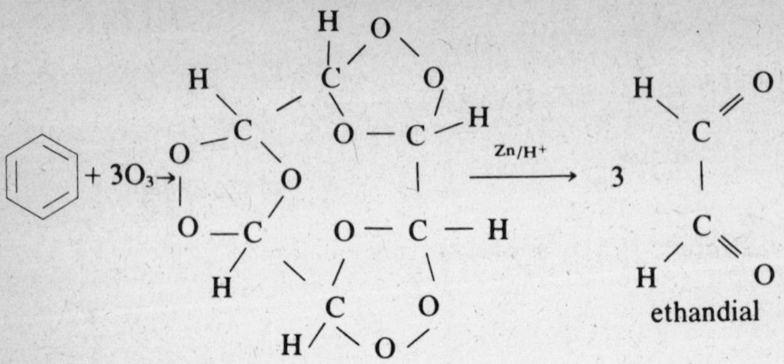

ethandial

Alkylbenzenes

Alkylbenzenes exhibit reactions typical of both the alkyl group they contain and of the aryl group. However, the presence of the alkyl group modifies the properties of the benzene (aryl) nucleus and to some extent the aryl group modifies the properties of the alkyl group.

Examples of alkylbenzenes are

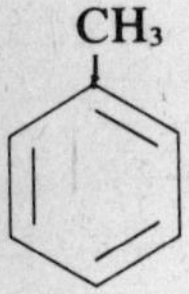

methylbenzene

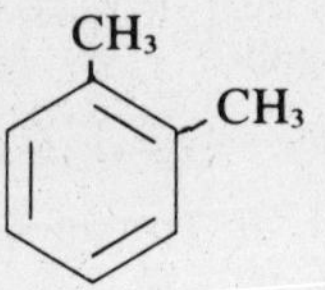

1,2-dimethylbenzene

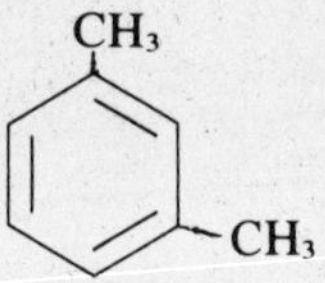

1,3-dimethylbenzene

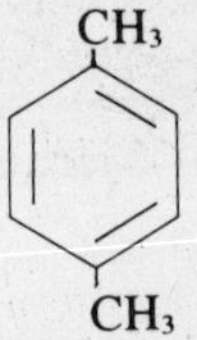

1,4-dimethylbenzene

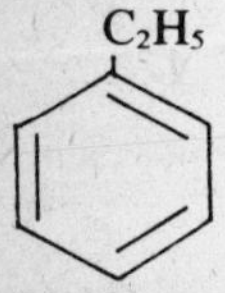

ethyl benzene

Isomers, molecular formula C_8H_{10}
Note the method of indicating the positions of two groups in the benzene ring.

Properties of alkyl group

The alkyl group, like the alkane, is relatively unreactive.

(a) oxidation The presence of the aryl group renders the alkyl side chain susceptible to oxidation by relatively mild oxidizing agents, e.g. alkaline manganate(VII). The product is always a benzene carboxylic acid (i.e. the weakness in the bond is at the carbon atom joined to the ring).

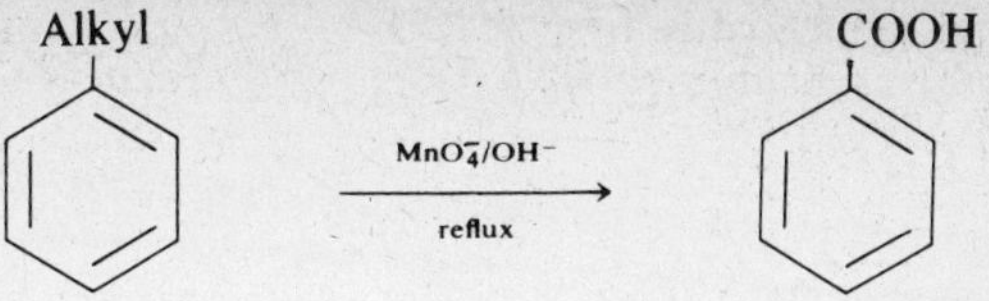

benzene carboxylic (benzoic) acid

With milder oxidizing agents it is possible to oxidize methylbenzene to benzene carbaldehyde (benzaldehyde)

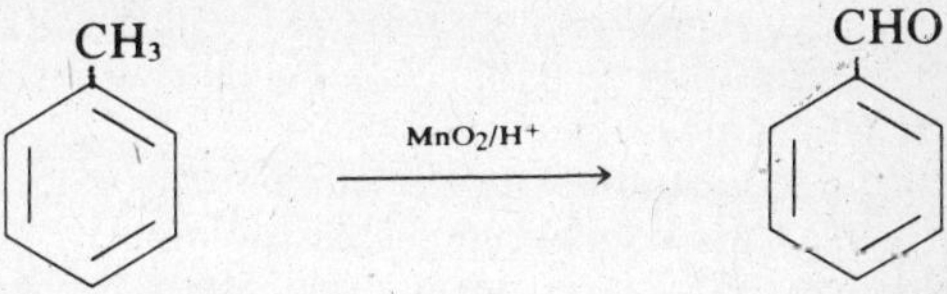

Chromium(VI) dioxide dichloride (chromyl chloride) may also be used for this oxidation.

(b) halogenation (reaction with chlorine or bromine). In the absence of a catalyst (which promotes nucleus substitution) the halogens substitute the alkyl side chain rather than add to the nucleus. This substitution occurs with the refluxing hydrocarbon or in u.v. radiation.

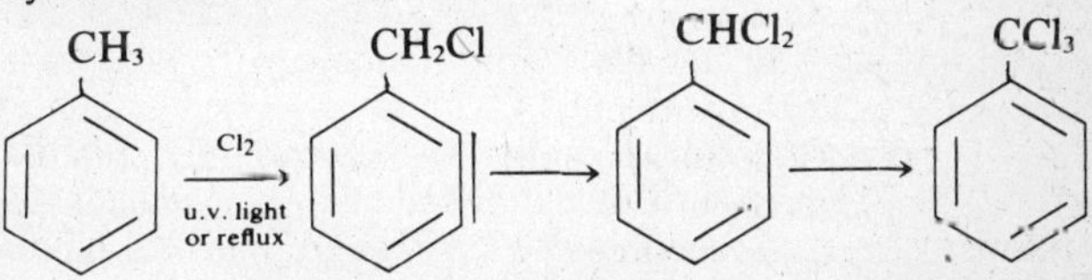

phenylchloromethane phenyldichloromethane phenyltrichloromethane

Progressive substitution is possible, as with alkanes. It is possible to control the production of the major product required by stopping the reaction when the mass gain observed for the reaction mixture is equal to the theoretical gain in mass corresponding to the formation of the particular compound.

Properties of aryl (benzene) nucleus

Apart from the reaction with chlorine already mentioned above, the major influence of the alkyl group is to direct substitution and to have an activating effect on the nucleus. Alkyl groups direct further substitution predominantly to the

2, 4 and 6 positions relative to itself and also have the effect of making further substitution occur more readily than in benzene.

Key terms

Hydrocarbons Organic compounds containing carbon and hydrogen only.
Alkanes Hydrocarbons with the general formula C_nH_{2n+2}.
Alkenes Hydrocarbons with the general formula C_nH_{2n}.
Alkynes Hydrocarbons with the general formula C_nH_{2n-2}.
Saturated compounds Organic compounds containing single bonds only between carbon atoms.
Unsaturated compounds Organic compounds with multiple (double or triple) bonds between carbon atoms.
Substitution A reaction in which one atom (or group of atoms) is replaced by another atom (or group of atoms).
Addition A reaction in which two substances react to give a single product.
Pyrolysis The breaking down of a substance by the action of heat, e.g. cracking of alkanes.
Ozonolysis The reaction of an unsaturated bond with ozone, resulting in breaking of the molecule at this point.
Markownikow's rule The addition of a compound of the type H—X to an unsaturated bond results in the addition of the hydrogen (of H—X) to the carbon atom with the most hydrogen atoms already attached.
Tests for unsaturation Unsaturated compounds rapidly decolorize both bromine water and acidified manganate(VII).
Polymerization The reaction of a compound to give a larger molecule with the same empirical formula as the starting compound, e.g. polythene $(C_2H_4)_n$ may be formed from ethene C_2H_4.
Aromatic hydrocarbons Hydrocarbons which contain a benzene (aromatic) nucleus.
Nitration The reaction of an aromatic compound with nitric acid (usually using conc. H_2SO_4 as an essential reagent) to give a nitro compound as a substitution product.
Sulphonation The reaction of an aromatic compound with sulphuric acid to give a sulphonic acid as a substitution product.

Chapter 11
Functional Groups

Halogeno compounds

Examples of these include

halogenoalkanes:

CH_3Cl	chloromethane
CH_3I	iodomethane
CH_3CH_2Br	bromoethane
CH_3CHBr_2	1,1-dibromoethane
$CH_2Br.CH_2Br$	1,2-dibromoethane

halogenoarenes: C_6H_5Cl chlorobenzene

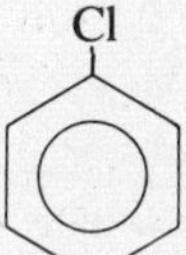

C_7H_7Br Isomers are

phenylbromomethane (benzyl bromide)

1-bromo-2-methyl benzene

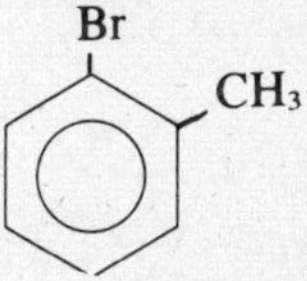

1-bromo-3-methyl benzene

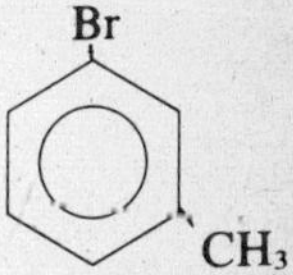

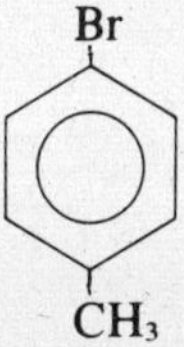

1-bromo-4-methylbenzene

Preparation

Preparation of halogenoalkanes can be by one of the following methods:

(i) Addition of hydrogen halides to alkenes

$$CH_2{=}CH_2 + HCl \rightarrow CH_3CH_2Cl$$

(ii) Substitution of alcohols using hydrogen halides or phosphorus halides (which may be prepared in situ from red phosphorus and the halogen) or sulphur dichloride oxide.

$$CH_3CH_2OH + HCl \xrightleftharpoons{ZnCl_2} CH_3CH_2Cl + H_2O$$

$$CH_3CH_2CH_2OH + PCl_5 \longrightarrow CH_3CH_2CH_2Cl + POCl_3 + HCl$$

$$CH_3.CH(OH).CH_3 \xrightarrow{\text{red P/Br}_2} CH_3.CHBr.CH_3$$

$$CH_3CH_2CH_2OH + SOCl_2 \longrightarrow CH_3CH_2CH_2Cl + SO_2 + HCl$$

Halogenoarenes are not obtained by the above methods and are best produced by
(i) direct substitution of an aromatic nucleus

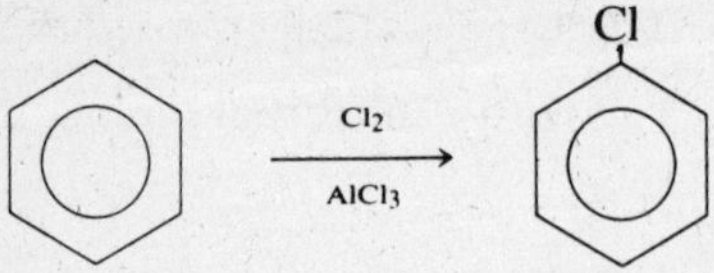

(ii) reaction of diazonium salts with conc. hydrohalic acids (HCl and HBr) or potassium iodide

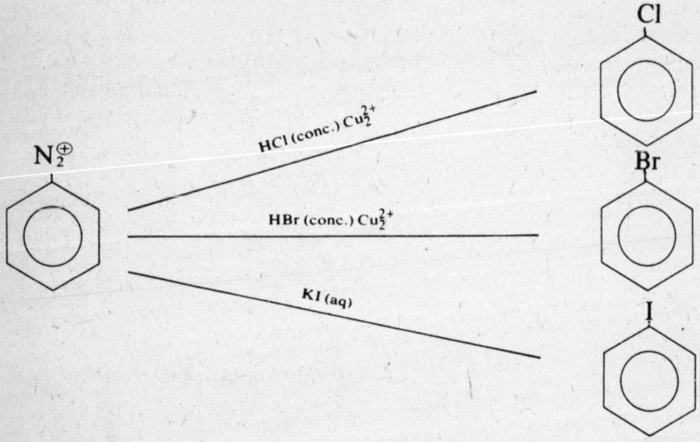

If the halogen is attached to an aliphatic side chain the compound is then obtained by one of the methods used for halogenoalkanes or by direct substitution of the side chain in the absence of a catalyst by reacting the halogen with the refluxing alkylbenzene or under irradiation with u.v. light.

$$C_6H_5CH_3 \xrightarrow[\text{u.v. light}]{Cl_2} C_6H_5CH_2Cl$$

Properties

The boiling points of halogenoalkanes are significantly higher than those of the corresponding alkanes. The order for the halogens is

$$R—Cl < R—Br < R—I$$

b.p. of halogenoalkanes				
compound	CH_4	CH_3Cl	CH_3Br	CH_3I
b.p. °C	−164	−23	3.5	44
b.p. of halogenobenzenes				
compound	C_6H_6	C_6H_5Cl	C_6H_5Br	C_6H_5I
b.p. °C	80	132	156	186

Halogenoalkanes are relatively reactive, as the carbon–halogen bond is readily substituted by nucleophiles such as the hydroxide ion, cyanide ion, ammonia etc. The ease of replacement is I > Br > Cl because of increasing bond strengths in the order

$$\begin{array}{lll} C—I < & C—Br < & C—Cl \\ 188 & 226 & 278\ kJ\ mol^{-1} \end{array}$$

The attachment of the halogen to an aromatic nucleus results in lone pairs of electrons on the halogen atom interacting with the π bonding of the ring giving greater stability to the bond. As a result halogenoarenes are much less reactive. A similar reduction in reactivity is noted if the carbon atom to which the halogen is attached is also unsaturated (for example in $CH_2{=}CHBr$, bromoethene).

Typical substitution reactions of halogenoalkanes are

(i) hydrolysis

$$CH_3CH_2Br + H_2O \rightleftharpoons CH_3CH_2OH + HBr$$

This reaction is slow and incomplete, even on refluxing. Complete hydrolysis is possible by refluxing with excess aqueous alkali, as this provides a high concentration of the nucleophilic reagent OH^-.

(ii) reaction with ammonia (and amines)
The nitrogen of ammonia and substituted ammonia compounds is nucleophilic and attacks the positive carbon atom of the carbon–halogen bond:

$$\underset{\underset{\ddot{N}H_3}{\uparrow}}{R{-}Hal} \longrightarrow H_3\overset{\oplus}{N}{-}RHal^{\ominus} \xrightarrow{NH_3} NH_4^+ + \underset{\text{primary amine}}{R\,NH_2}$$

$$\underset{\underset{\ddot{N}H_2{-}R}{\uparrow}}{R{-}Hal} \longrightarrow H_2\overset{\oplus}{N}R_2\ Hal^{\ominus} \xrightarrow{NH_3} NH_4^+ + \underset{\text{secondary amine}}{R_2NH}$$

$$\underset{\underset{\ddot{N}HR_2}{\uparrow}}{R{-}Hal} \longrightarrow H\overset{\oplus}{N}.R_3Hal^{\ominus} \xrightarrow{NH_3} NH_4^+ + \underset{\text{tertiary amine}}{R_3N}$$

$$\underset{\underset{\ddot{N}R_3}{\uparrow}}{R{-}Hal} \longrightarrow \underset{\text{quaternary ammonium compound}}{\overset{\oplus}{N}R_4Hal^{\ominus}}$$

The above reactions occur on heating with ammonia under pressure; a mixture of products may be obtained as indicated above. Note that besides reacting with ammonia, halogenoalkanes will react with primary, secondary or tertiary amines.

(iii) reaction with cyanides
Potassium cyanide reacts with halogenoalkanes to form nitriles:

$$CH_3CH_2I + KCN \rightarrow \underset{\text{propanonitrile}}{CH_3CH_2CN} + KI$$

With silver cyanide an isonitrile (isocyanide) is given

$$CH_3CH_2I + AgCN \rightarrow CH_3CH_2NC + AgI$$

isocyanoethane

In both cases the halogenoalkane should be heated with the relevant cyanide.

(iv) reaction with alcoholic potassium hydroxide

This results in elimination of the hydrogen halide to produce an alkane

$$CH_3CH_2Br \rightarrow CH_2{=}CH_2 + HBr$$

Note that elimination of hydrogen can occur from any adjacent carbon atom so that in some cases a mixture of products results:

$$CH_3CH_2CHBrCH_3 \rightarrow CH_3CH_2CH{=}CH_2$$

and

$$CH_3CH{=}CHCH_3$$

The halogenoalkane should be heated with a solution of potassium hydroxide in ethanol.

(v) halogen exchange

Heating chloro- or bromo- alkanes with potassium (or sodium) iodide in solution in propanone results in exchange of iodine for the other halogen

$$C_2H_5Br + KI \rightarrow C_2H_5I + KBr$$

Note that none of the above reactions occur readily with halogenoarenes. Hydrolysis of halogenoarenes is possible but only by heating to high temperatures under pressure with aqueous alkali

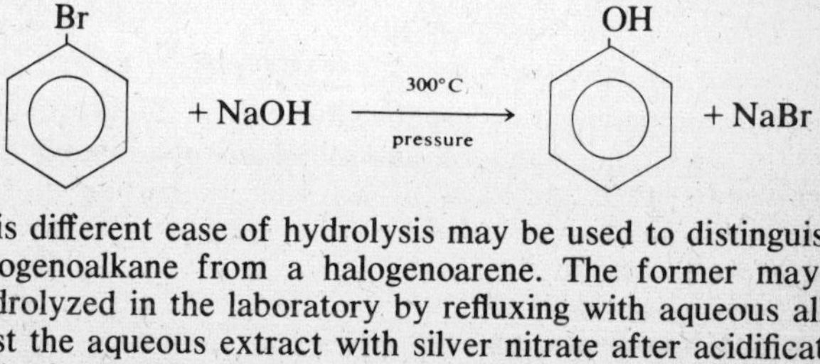

This different ease of hydrolysis may be used to distinguish a halogenoalkane from a halogenoarene. The former may be hydrolyzed in the laboratory by refluxing with aqueous alkali (test the aqueous extract with silver nitrate after acidification with nitric acid) whereas the latter does not hydrolyze under these conditions.

Reactions exhibited both by halogenoarenes as well as halogenoalkanes include the following.

(i) reaction with magnesium

On heating a halogeno compound with magnesium suspended in ether, under anhydrous conditions, an unstable compound known as a Grignard reagent, is obtained. These may then be hydrolyzed, or more usually reacted with compounds containing a carbonyl group to obtain many useful compounds:

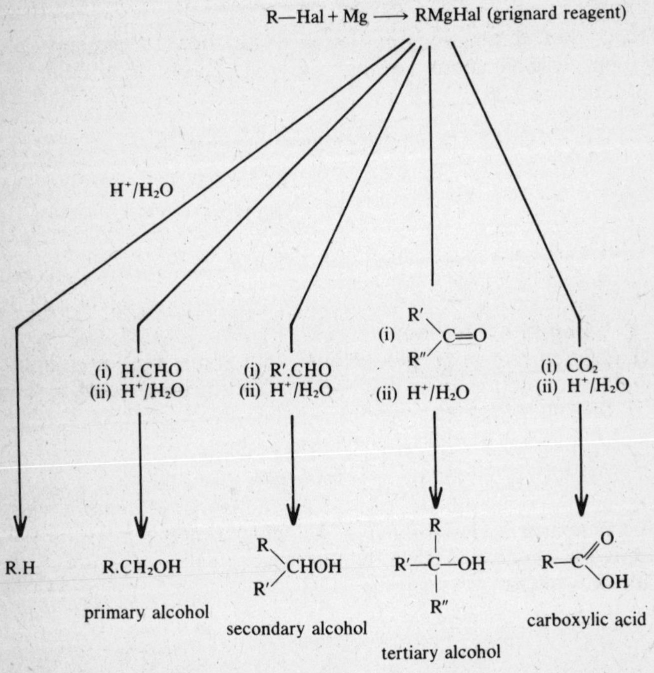

To obtain the desired end product the carbonyl compound is added to the Grignard reagent and the resultant adduct is then hydrolyzed with dilute acid. In the case of carbon dioxide either the solid may be used or the gas may be bubbled through the solution.

(ii) reaction with arenes

Halogeno compounds may be refluxed with arenes (e.g. benzene) using an aluminium chloride (anhydrous) catalyst to obtain substituted arenes:

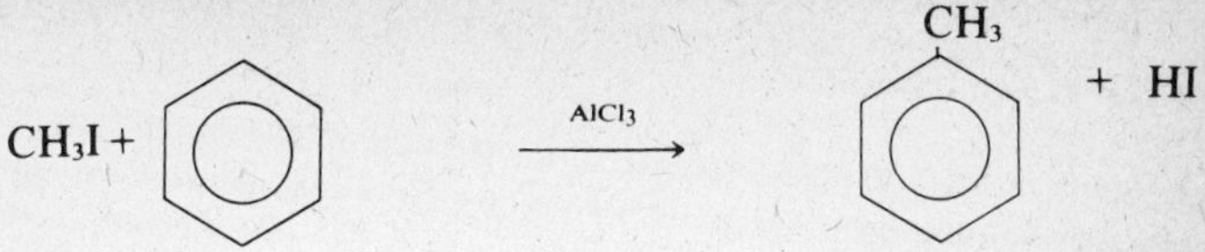

methylbenzene

(iii) reaction with silver salts of carboxylic acids

On heating together an ester is obtained:

$$CH_3COOAg + R\text{—}Hal \rightarrow CH_3COOR + AgHal$$

silver ethanoate — an ester

(iv) reaction with sodium

On heating, halogeno compounds react to produce hydrocarbons, e.g. ethyl iodide on heating with sodium produces butane.

$$2C_2H_5I + 2Na \rightarrow C_4H_{10} + 2NaI$$

$$C_6H_5Br + C_2H_5Br + 2Na \rightarrow C_6H_5C_2H_5 + 2NaBr$$

The reaction of chloromethane with a sodium lead alloy is used to manufacture lead tetraethyl, used as an anti-knock additive to petrol:

$$4CH_3Cl + Pb/4Na \rightarrow (CH_3)_4Pb + 4NaCl$$

Other reactions

The aromatic nucleus of a halogenoarene retains its characteristic properties, undergoing substitution by electrophilic reagents such as the nitronium ion. The major substitution products are the 2 and 4 derivatives. This is because halogen atoms are 2, 4, 6 directing. The halogen atoms also have a deactivating effect, the ease of substitution of the aromatic nucleus being lower than that of benzene. The directional influence is because there is a tendency for an unshared electron pair on the halogen atom to be incorporated into the delocalized electrons of the aromatic nucleus resulting in an increased electron density in the 2, 4 and 6 positions. The deactivating effect is because of the high electronegativity of the halogen which tends to reduce the electron density of the ring as a whole, making the nucleus less susceptible to attack by electrophiles.

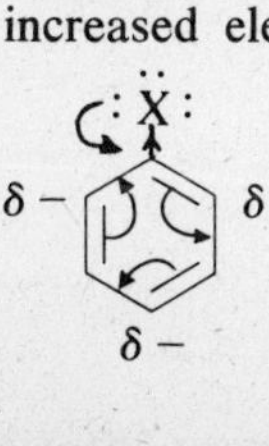

Hydroxy derivatives

Organic compounds containing hydroxy groups may be classified as alcohols (if the group is attached to an alkyl carbon atom) or phenols (if attached to a carbon atom of an aromatic nucleus). Alcohols may further be classified as primary (containing the unit —CH_2OH), secondary (containing >CHOH) and tertiary (—>C—OH) depending on the number of hydrogen atoms attached to the carbon atom with the hydroxyl group. Typical examples are:

Monohydric compounds (only one hydroxy group)

alcohols

CH_3CH_2OH
ethanol
(a primary alcohol)

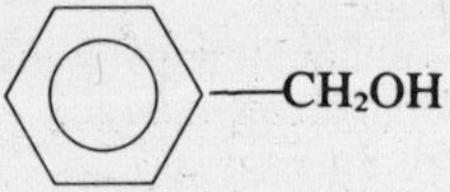

phenylmethanol
(a primary alcohol)

$CH_3CH_2CH(OH)CH_3$
butan-2-ol
(a secondary alcohol)

$(CH_3)_3COH$
2-methylpropan-2-ol
(a tertiary alcohol)

phenols

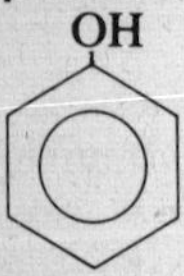

phenol

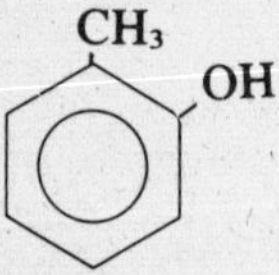

1-hydroxy-2-methylbenzene

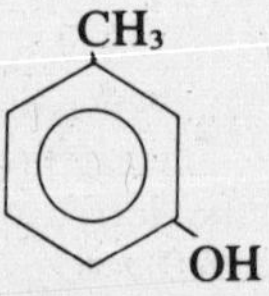

1-hydroxy-3-methylbenzene

1-hydroxy-4-methylbenzene

Polyhydric compounds (2 or more hydroxy groups)

CH_2OHCH_2OH
ethan-1,2-diol

$CH_2OHCHOHCH_2OH$
propan-1,2,3-triol (glycerol)

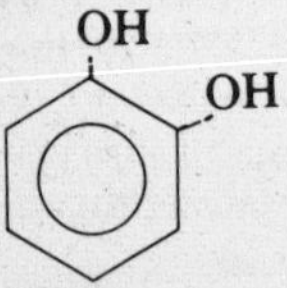

1,2-dihydroxybenzene

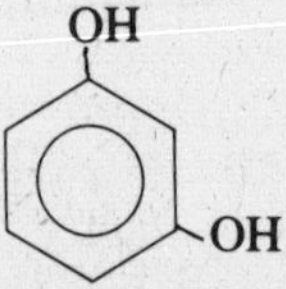

1,3-dihydroxybenzene

Preparation

Alcohols may be obtained by one or more of the following general methods:

(i) hydrolysis of halogenoalkanes

$$C_2H_5I + OH^-(aq) \rightarrow C_2H_5OH + I^-(aq)$$

(ii) from Grignard reagents (see halogeno compounds on p. 248).

$$RMgHal \xrightarrow{HCHO} RCH_2OH$$

$$RMgHal \xrightarrow{R'CHO} RR'CHOH$$

$$RMgHal \xrightarrow{R'COR''} RR'R''COH$$

(iii) hydrolysis of addition products of alkenes with sulphuric acid

$$CH_2{=}CH_2 \xrightarrow{H_2SO_4\ (conc.)} CH_3CH_2SO_4H \xrightarrow[heat]{xs.\ H_2O} CH_3CH_2OH$$

(iv) hydrolysis of esters (saponification)

$$\begin{array}{lcl} CH_2OOCC_{17}H_{35} & & CH_2OH \\ | & & | \\ CHOOCC_{17}H_{35} + 3OH^-(aq) & \rightarrow & CHOH + 3C_{17}H_{35}COO^- \\ | & & | \\ CH_2OOCC_{17}H_{35} & & CH_2OH \\ \text{(a fat)} & & \text{(a soap)} \end{array}$$

(v) reduction of aldehydes (or the corresponding acids) and ketones

$$R.COOH \xrightarrow{(a)} R.CHO \xrightarrow{(b)} RCH_2OH$$

$$R.R'CO \xrightarrow{(c)} R.R'CHOH$$

For reduction of acids, stages (a) and (b), lithium aluminium hydride in dry ethereal solution may be used, but for stages (b) or (c) alone it is possible to use reducing agents such as sodium and ethanol or hydrogen and a metal.

Phenols may be obtained by the following reactions

(i) industrially by the cumene process

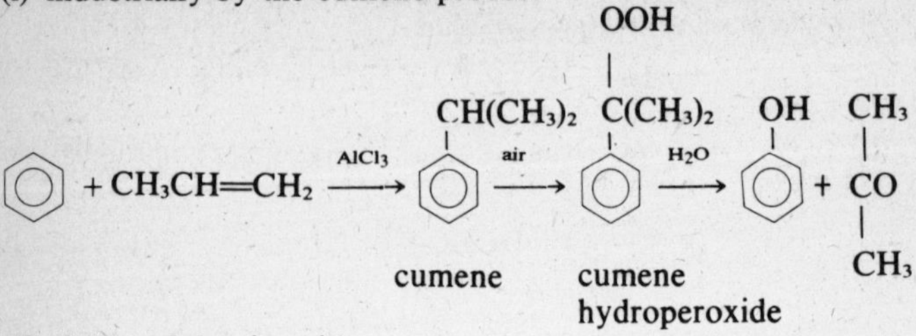

(ii) from sulphonic acids

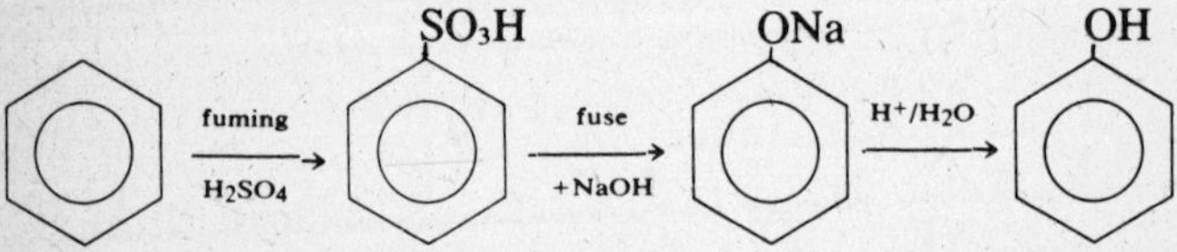

(iii) from diazonium salts

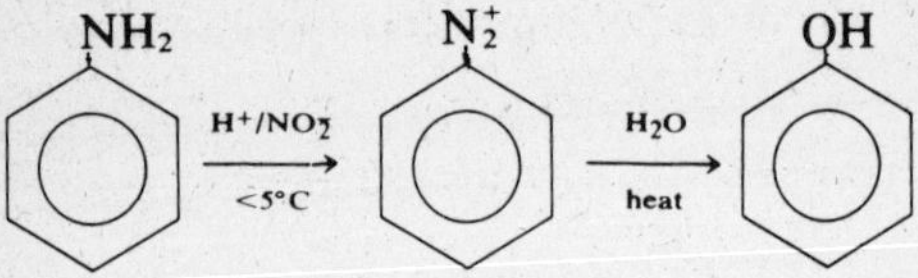

Properties

The typical properties of the carbon–OH bond are observed in alcohols. These properties are modified to some extent in phenols due to the influence of the aryl nucleus (the properties of the aryl nucleus are also influenced by the presence of the hydroxyl group).

(i) acid properties

In common with many compounds containing hydroxyl groups alcohols have acidic properties. They are less acidic than water, only reacting slowly with the reactive metals sodium and potassium:

$$2C_2H_5OH + 2Na \rightarrow 2C_2H_5ONa + H_2$$

Phenols are slightly more acidic than water and will dissolve in strong alkalis to form salts but are not sufficiently acidic to displace carbon dioxide from carbonates:

$$C_6H_5OH + NaOH \rightarrow C_6H_5O^-Na^+ + H_2O$$

(ii) replacement of OH by halogen

This is possible using halogenating agents such as phosphorus(V) chloride, phosphorus(III) chloride or sulphur dichloride oxide (thionyl chloride) or, for replacement by bromine and iodine, red phosphorus and the halogen are generally used.

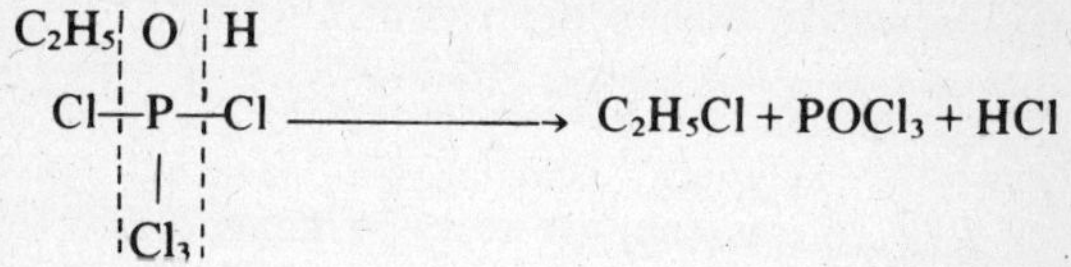

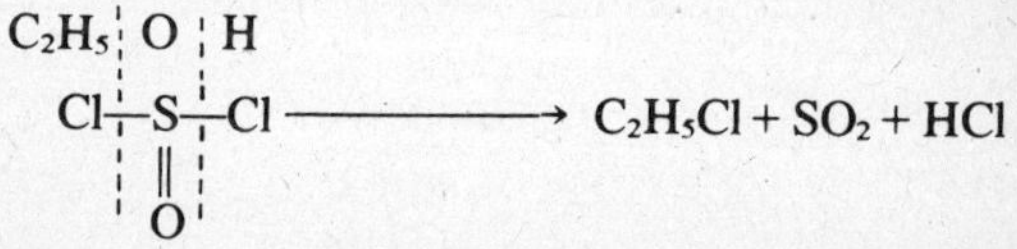

Alcohols also react with the hydrogen halides in the presence of a suitable catalyst, e.g. anhydrous $ZnCl_2$. The rate of reaction varies both with the acid used and the type of alcohol:

HI > HBr > HCl

most readily ←——————————— least readily

tertiary alcohol > secondary alcohol > primary alcohol

$$ROH + HHal \xrightleftharpoons{ZnCl_2} R\text{—}Hal + H_2O$$

Phenols do not react with the above reagents.

(iii) ester formation

With carboxylic acids, the general reaction of alcohols is

$$\text{acid} + \text{alcohol} \rightleftharpoons \text{ester} + \text{water}$$

For further details see properties of acids, p. 264.
Phenols do not react with carboxylic acids.
Both alcohols and phenols form esters with acid chlorides and acid anhydrides (see properties of acid derivatives, p. 268).

Specific reactions of alcohols

(i) oxidation

Primary alcohols may be oxidized in two stages:

$$R{-}CH_2OH \xrightarrow{(a)} R.CHO \xrightarrow{(b)} RCOOH$$

an aldehyde a carboxylic acid

The oxidation (a) can be brought about by passing alcohol vapour over a heated copper catalyst; by passing alcohol vapour and air over a heated silver catalyst; or by using a standard laboratory oxidizing mixture (usually acidified sodium dichromate is used) which is added to the alcohol, the more volatile aldehyde distilling over as it forms.

Stage (b) can be achieved by passing the aldehyde vapour and air into dilute sulphuric acid at 40°C to 50°C using a manganese(II) salt as catalyst or by refluxing either the aldehyde or the alcohol with excess oxidizing mixture.

Secondary alcohols give a single product:

$$R.R'CHOH \rightarrow RR'CO$$

a ketone

Refluxing with excess oxidizing mixture or catalytic dehydrogenation using a heated copper catalyst or passing the alcohol vapour mixed with air over a heated silver catalyst may be used. Tertiary alcohols are only oxidized under severe conditions, the oxidation involving splitting of the molecule so that the products contain fewer carbon atoms than the starting material.

(ii) dehydration

Alcohols may be dehydrated to give either ethers or alkenes. Ethers may be obtained by carefully mixing the alcohol with an equal volume of concentrated sulphuric acid, heating the mixture to 140°C and then adding the alcohol to the mixture at the same rate as the product distils:

$$C_2H_5OH + H_2SO_4 \rightleftharpoons C_2H_5OSO_3H + H_2O$$

$$C_2H_5OSO_3H + C_2H_5OH \rightleftharpoons C_2H_5OC_2H_5 + H_2SO_4$$

ethoxyethane

Alkenes may be obtained by mixing the alcohol with excess concentrated sulphuric or phosphoric acids and heating to 170°C or by passing the vapour over a heated catalyst, e.g. alumina, Al_2O_3

$$C_2H_5OH - H_2O \rightarrow CH_2{=}CH_2$$

(iii) Some alcohols will give a positive result to the **haloform reaction.** Those containing the unit CH_3.CH—OH can be both oxidized and halogenated to give the compound $CHHal_3$.

Triiodomethane is obtained if potassium iodide and sodium chlorate(I), or iodine in solution in alkali are used, crystallizing from the hot solution as yellow crystals with a characteristic smell. This reaction may be used as a test for the structural unit CH_3—C—O— in organic compounds.

Specific reactions of phenols

(i) phenols contain an enol group (the structural unit is C—OH). A characteristic of this group is the formation of a complex, with characteristic deep purple colour, on addition of neutral iron(III) chloride.

(ii) reduction
(a) Phenols may be reduced to the corresponding cyclic alcohol by heating with hydrogen under pressure using a nickel catalyst

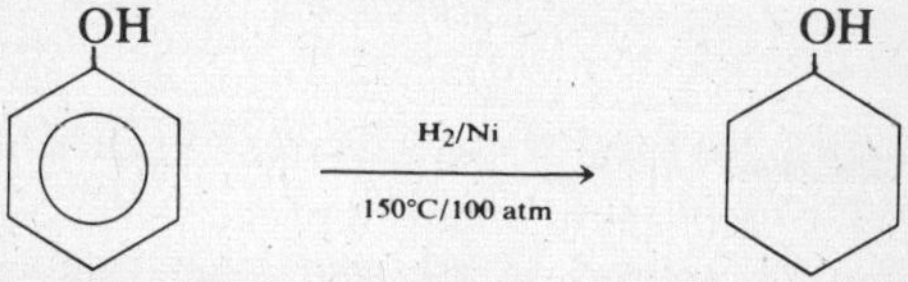

(b) When a phenol is heated with powdered zinc the oxygen is removed from the hydroxyl group:

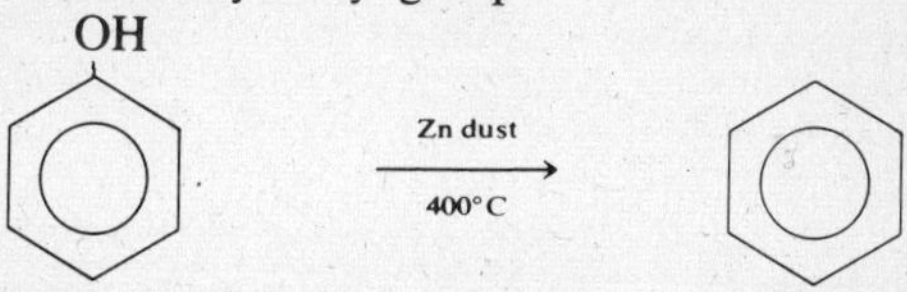

(iii) substitution of aromatic nucleus
The hydroxyl group has a strongly activating effect on the aromatic nucleus, also directing substitution to the 2, 4 and 6 positions.

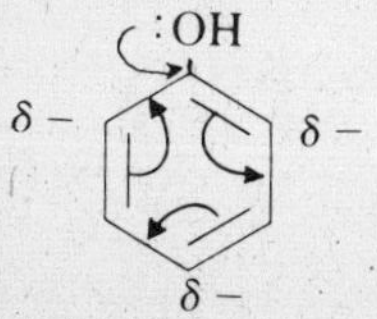

The electron density is increased in the 2, 4 and 6 positions by the tendency of the electron pair to be drawn into the nucleus.

The different ease of substitution is observed in that

(a) phenols react readily with bromine water to give a white precipitate (benzene only reacts with bromine in the presence of a catalyst)

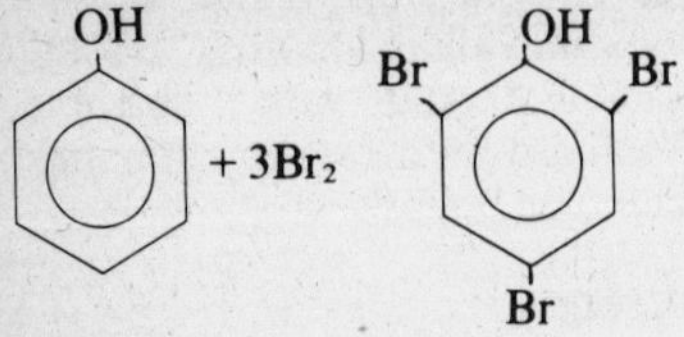

2,4,6-tribromophenol

4-bromophenol may only be obtained by using the calculated amount of bromine in a suitable non polar solvent (e.g. carbon disulphide) at low temperatures.

(b) phenols may be nitrated with dilute nitric acid

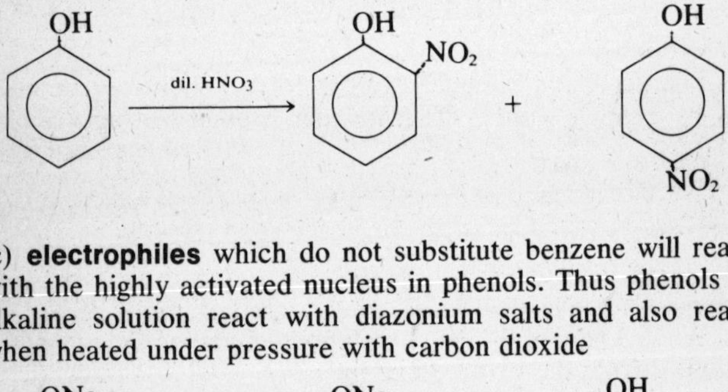

(c) **electrophiles** which do not substitute benzene will react with the highly activated nucleus in phenols. Thus phenols in alkaline solution react with diazonium salts and also react when heated under pressure with carbon dioxide

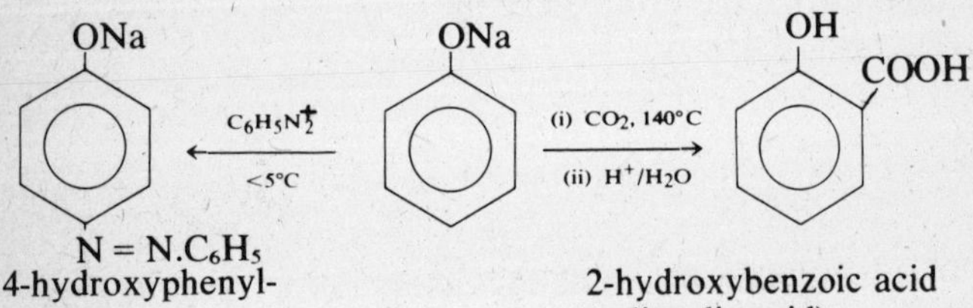

4-hydroxyphenyl-azobenzene

2-hydroxybenzoic acid (salicyclic acid)

Carbonyl compounds (Aldehydes and ketones)

These compounds contain the functional group $>C=O$.

Typical examples are:

Aldehydes **Ketones**

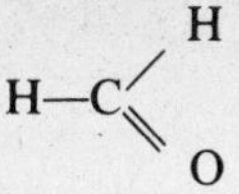
methanal

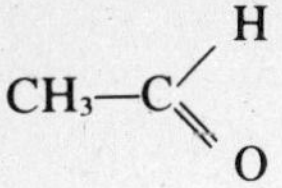
ethanal

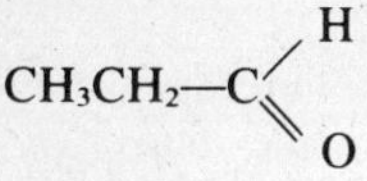
propanal

CH_3COCH_3 propanone

benzene carbonal
(benzaldehyde)

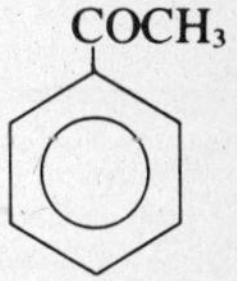
phenylethanone

Preparation

(i) A general method of preparation is the oxidation or dehydrogenation of alcohols. A primary alcohol will give an aldehyde, a secondary alcohol a ketone.

(ii) Hydrolysis of *gem*-dihalides (i.e. dihalogen compounds with both halogen atoms on the same carbon atom) may be used although strongly alkaline conditions for hydrolysis should be avoided for aldehydes, due to the reaction of aldehydes with alkalis.

$$RCHCl_2 \rightarrow RCHO$$

$$RCCl_2R' \rightarrow RCOR'$$

(iii) Ketones in which at least one of the side groups is an aryl group may be prepared by the Friedel Krafts reaction

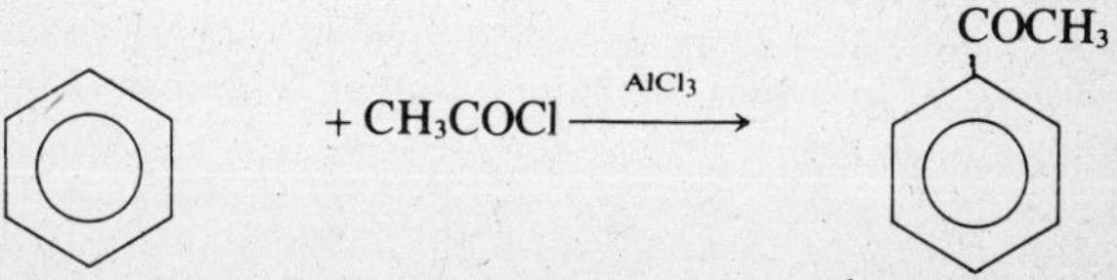

phenylethanone

Specific methods are:

ethanal may be obtained by hydration of ethyne:

$$H{-}C{\equiv}C{-}H + H_2O \xrightarrow[\text{dil. } H_2SO_4]{Hg^{2+}} CH_3CHO$$

propanone is a by-product of the manufacture of phenol by the cumene process.

benzaldehyde may be obtained by the controlled oxidation of methylbenzene, either by passing the vapour mixed with air over a vanadium(V) oxide or manganese(IV) oxide catalyst, or by heating with manganese(IV) oxide and dilute sulphuric acid.

Properties

With the exception of methanal (a gas at room temperature) the simple aldehydes and ketones are liquids. Aliphatic compounds are generally miscible with water as they contain a polar oxygen atom which can hydrogen bond with water molecules. Aromatic compounds generally have low solubility in water.

Many of the chemical properties arise because of polarization of the bond $\rangle \overset{\delta+}{C}{=}\overset{\delta-}{O}$ which results in the molecule being susceptible to attack by nucleophilic reagents:

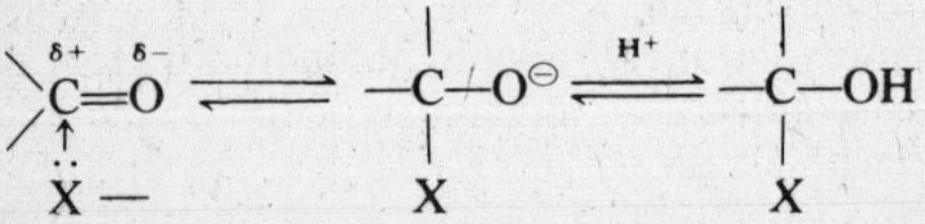

The reactions are, in some cases reversible, in which case isolation of the adduct may be difficult. In other cases elimination of water from the product may occur to give a condensation product.

Addition reactions

Typical nucleophilic reagents which give an addition reaction only are water, alcohols, ammonia, sodium hydrogen sulphite and the cyanide ion.

(i) water reacts to form a *gem*-diol, which is generally unstable as the equilibrium lies well to the left. The only carbonyl compound to form a stable hydrate is 2,2,2-trichloroethanal which is stabilized by the inductive effect of the three electronegative chlorine atoms:

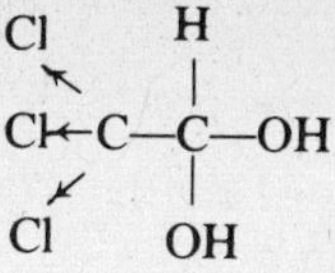

(ii) alcohols react to form 'acetals' with aldehydes only.

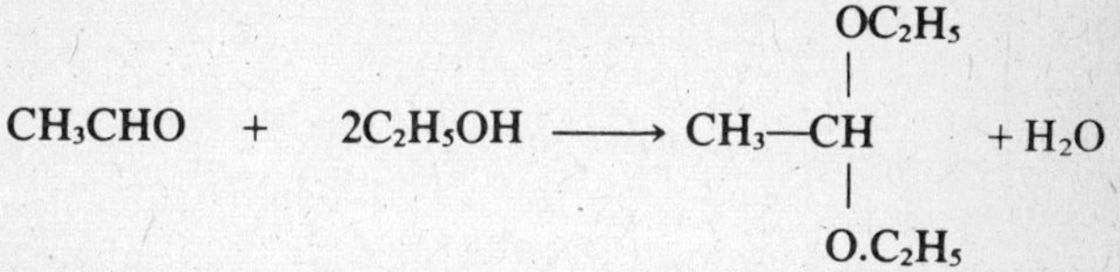

1,1-diethoxyethane

(iii) ammonia reacts to form an adduct. Those given by aldehydes are more stable than those given by ketones (these can only be obtained to any significant extent at low temperatures)

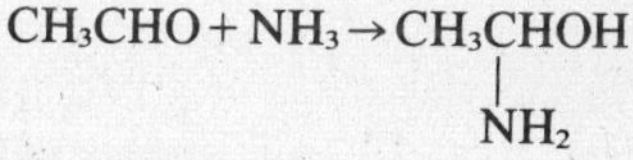

(iv) cyanides react to form addition compounds known as cyanohydrins

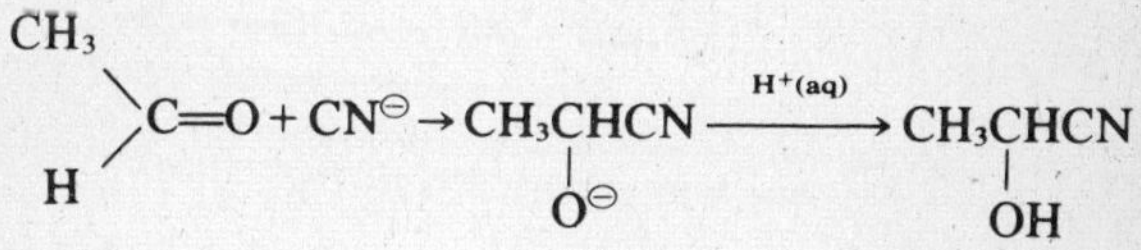

2-hydroxy-
propanonitrile

(v) sodium hydrogen sulphite reacts to form an adduct. If a saturated aqueous solution is used, this product is generally obtained as a colourless crystalline solid.

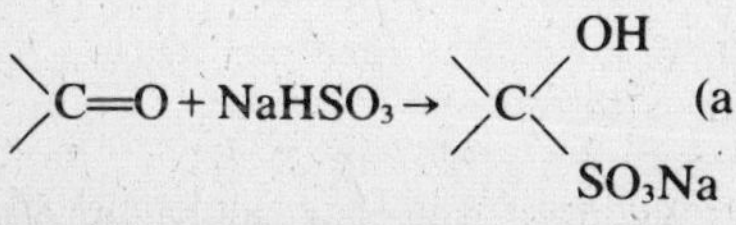

(a bisulphite compound)

Aliphatic aldehydes react so readily, as do a few ketones, that they rapidly restore the colour to Schiff's reagent (magenta bleached with sulphur dioxide) to give a magenta colour.

(vi) alkali Dimerization of many aldehydes occurs on addition of cold dilute alkali (aqueous potassium carbonate is sufficiently alkaline and is preferable to the metal hydroxide)

(a) $CH_3.CHO + OH^- \rightarrow \overset{\ominus}{C}H_2CHO + H_2O$

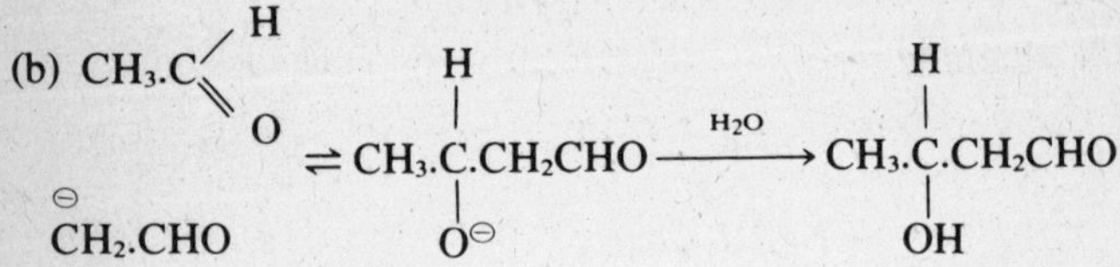

3-hydroxy-butanal

For this to occur the α carbon atom (the carbon atom adjacent to the carbonyl group) must have at least one hydrogen atom attached to it.

With dilute potassium (or sodium) hydroxide there is a tendency for the dimer to lose water to give a condensation product:

$$CH_3CH(OH)CH_2CHO \xrightarrow{\text{dil. NaOH}} CH_3CH{=}CHCHO$$

but-2-enal

Heating this product or the original aldehyde with concentrated alkali results in further polymerization and condensation, the end product being a complex yellow resin.

Ketones do not readily dimerize, although an equilibrium mixture may sometimes be given:

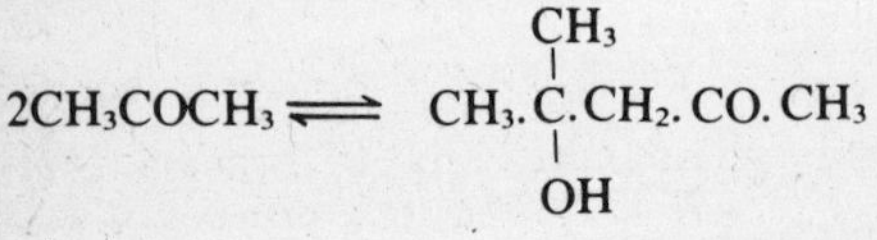

4-hydroxy-4-methylpentan-2-one

Aldehydes with no α C–H bond do not dimerize. Instead they disproportionate (are both oxidized and reduced). Two molecules of the aldehyde react to give one molecule of the corresponding alcohol (reduction) and one molecule of a carboxylic acid (oxidation). This is **Cannizzarro's reaction**:

$$2HCHO + OH^- \rightarrow CH_3OH + HCOO^-$$

$$2C_6H_5CHO + OH^- \rightarrow C_6H_5CH_2OH + C_6H_5COO^-$$

(vii) with **Grignard reagents**, carbonyl compounds form unstable adducts which hydrolyze to give alcohols (see page 248).

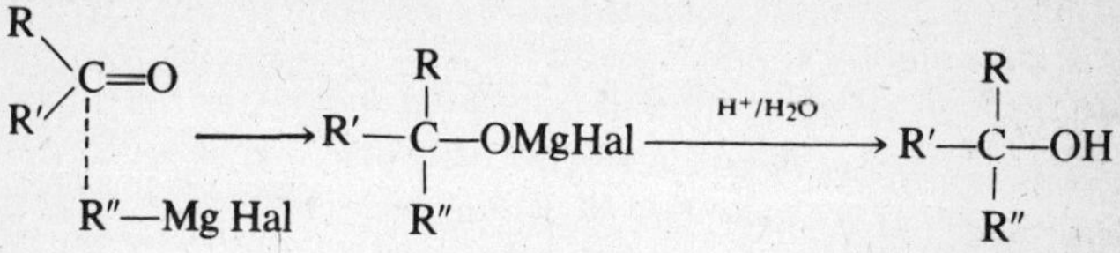

Methanal, HCHO, gives a primary alcohol, other aldehydes give secondary alcohols and ketones give tertiary alcohols.

Condensation reactions

These are given mainly on reaction with compounds of the type $R.NH_2$, including hydroxylamine, $NH_2.OH$, hydrazine NH_2NH_2, and substituted hydrazines, for example, phenylhydrazine $C_6H_5NH.NH_2$ and 2,4-dinitrophenylhydrazine, $C_6H_5NH.NH_2(NO_2)_2$.
The general reaction is:

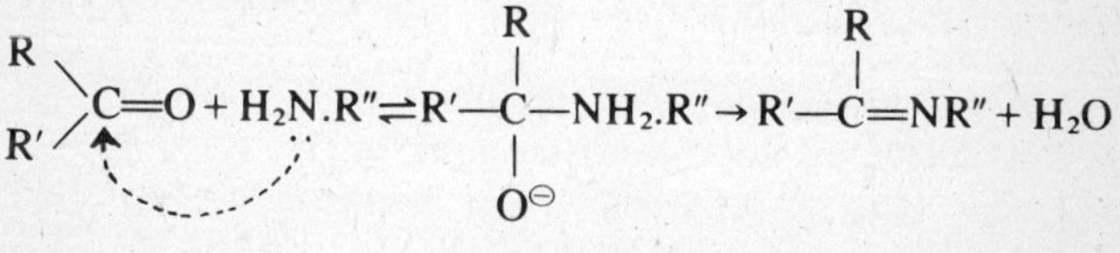

Hydroxylamine reacts to give oximes:

$$CH_3.CHO + H_2N.OH \rightarrow CH_3CH{=}N.OH + H_2O$$

ethanal oxime

Hydrazine reacts to give a hydrazone:

$$CH_3COCH_3 + H_2N.NH_2 \rightarrow CH_3.\underset{\displaystyle CH_3}{\underset{|}{C}}{=}N,NH_2 + H_2O$$

propanone hydrazone

Phenylhydrazine and **2,4-dinitrophenylhydrazine** give phenyl (or 2,4-dinitrophenyl) hydrazones.

$$CH_3CHO + H_2N.HNC_6H_5 \rightarrow CH_3.CH{=}N.NH + H_2O$$

ethanal phenyl hydrazone

$$CH_3COCH_3 + H_2N.HNC_6H_3(NO_2)_2 \rightarrow CH_3\underset{\displaystyle CH_3}{\underset{|}{C}}{=}N.NHC_6H_3(NO_2)_2$$

propanone-2,4-dinitro-
phenylhydrazone

The products are crystalline solids which may be used to identify the carbonyl compound because of their characteristic melting points. The phenyl- and 2-4-dinitrophenylhydrazones are yellow to orange solids the latter being the one most commonly used for identification purposes.

Other reactions

(i) halogenation (a) Phosphorus(V) chloride reacts to replace the oxygen atom by two chlorine atoms.

$$RR'CO + PCl_5 \rightarrow RR'CCl_2 + POCl_3$$

Note that in this reaction no hydrogen chloride is given and a *gem*-dichloro compound is obtained.
(b) chlorine also reacts to substitute the hydrogen of alkyl groups attached to the carbonyl carbon atom

$$CH_3CHO + Cl_2 \rightarrow CH_2Cl.CHO + HCl$$

Progressive substitution can occur until all hydrogens have been substituted.
(c) In **alkaline solution**, ethanal alone of the aldehydes and all methyl ketones react with **halogens** to give a haloform as these all contain the grouping $CH_3{-}\underset{|}{C}{-}O$ (see p. 254).

(ii) reduction of aldehydes and ketones is possible by either sodium and ethanol, or lithium tetrahydroaluminate in dry ethereal solution, giving a primary or secondary alcohol respectively.

(iii) oxidation Aldehydes may be oxidized by a number of oxidizing agents to the corresponding carboxylic acids. Ketones do not react. These reducing properties of aldehydes may be used to distinguish them from ketones. Test reagents commonly used are **Fehling's** or **Benedict's solutions**, both of which contain complex copper(II) salts which are reduced to copper(I) oxide as a pink/yellow precipitate; or **Tollen's reagent** (ammoniacal silver nitrate) obtained by addition of ammonia solution to silver nitrate until the original precipitate just redissolves, and is reduced to metallic silver (often forming a mirror on the inside of the test tube). For the preparation of carboxylic acids the oxidizing agents detailed under oxidation of alcohols may be used (see p. 254).

Influence of carbonyl group on aryl nucleus The carbonyl group is 3, 5 directing and deactivating. This is because the carbonyl group withdraws electrons from the ring, having the greatest effect in the 2, 4 and 6 positions:

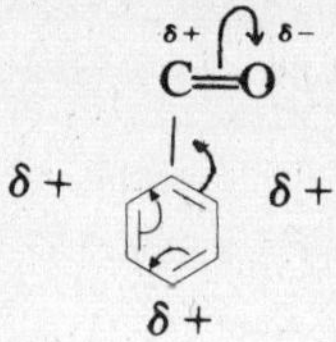

Carboxylic acids

These contain the group $-C(=O)OH$. The presence of the carbonyl group, $>C=O$, modifies the properties of the hydroxyl group, and the hydroxyl group affects the properties of the carbonyl group. Many may be obtained from natural sources examples being:

H.COOH methanoic acid

COOH
|
COOH ethandioic acid

CH_3.COOH ethanoic acid

benzenecarboxylic acid

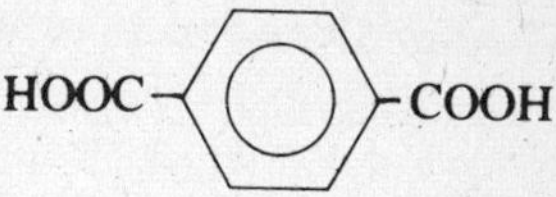

benzene-1,4-dicarboxylic acid

Preparation

(i) Oxidation of primary alcohols or aldehydes can be used to prepare carboxylic acids using the methods already described. Benzenecarboxylic (benzoic) acid may be made by oxidation of methylbenzene or other alkylbenzene

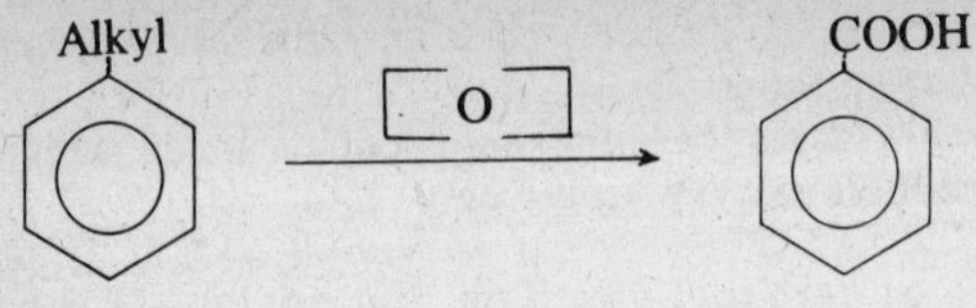

(ii) Hydrolysis of nitriles (cyanides) or esters

$$RCN + 2H_2O \xrightarrow{H^+} RCOOH + NH_4^+$$

$$RCOOR' + OH^- \longrightarrow RCOO^- + R'OH$$

(iii) Hydrolysis of 1,1,1-trichloroalkanes

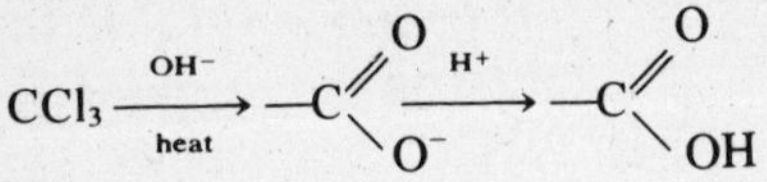

Properties
Carboxylic acids with a limited number of carbon atoms are water soluble. Those with a larger number of carbon atoms, including aromatic acids, have limited solubility. These are precipitated when acid is added to their soluble sodium salts.

(i) Acid properties These substances have properties typical of weak acids, reacting with metals more electropositive than hydrogen, with bases (including alkalis) to form salts, and with carbonates to give carbon dioxide.

(ii) With **alcohols** these acids react to give esters

$$CH_3COOH + HOC_2H_5 \rightleftharpoons CH_3COOC_2H_5 + H_2O$$

Note that use of labelled oxygen ($^{18}_{8}O$) has indicated that the oxygen of the water produced is derived from the acid, thus the reaction is not analogous to that of an acid with a base.

(iii) with halogenating reagents (phosphorus halides, sulphur dichloride oxide) the hydroxyl group is replaced by halogen

$$RCOOH + PCl_5 \rightarrow RCOCl + POCl_3 + HCl$$

(iv) with **soda lime**, acids and their salts react to give an alkane. This results due to removal of the carboxyl group, the reaction being referred to as **decarboxylation**

$$RCOO^- + OH^- \rightarrow RH + CO_3^{2-}$$

(v) Substitution by halogen results in initial attack of the alkyl carbon atom adjacent to the acid group.

$$\underset{}{CH_3CH_2COOH + Cl_2 \rightarrow} \underset{\text{2-chloropropanoic acid}}{CH_3CHClCOOH} + HCl$$

With aromatic acids, substitution of the ring occurs in the presence of a catalyst (aluminium chloride etc.). The carboxyl group is 3, 5 directing and deactivating:

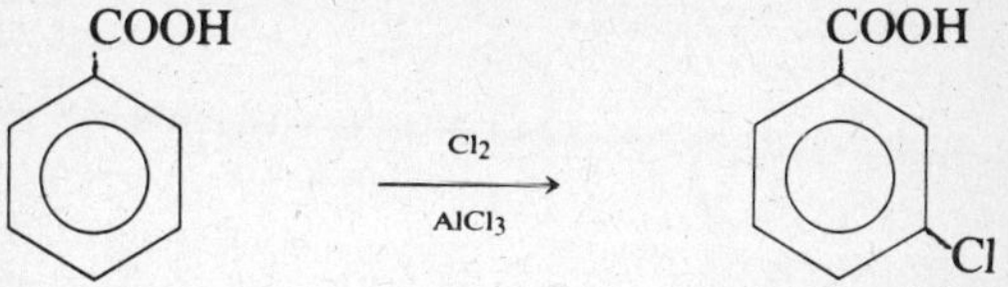

3-chlorobenzene
carboxylic acid

(vi) on heating salts decompose. Alkali and alkaline earth metal salts give carbonyl compounds

$$\begin{matrix} CH_3COO^- \\ CH_3COO^- \end{matrix} Ca^{2+} \rightarrow \begin{matrix} CH_3 \\ \diagdown \\ C{=}O \\ \diagup \\ CH_3 \end{matrix} + CaCO_3$$

Ammonium salts, in the presence of the free acid, dehydrate to give amides

$$CH_3COONH_4 \rightarrow CH_3CONH_2 + H_2O$$

The acid is required to suppress the dissociation of the ammonium salt.

(vii) Electrolysis of the acids or their salts produces a hydrocarbon at the anode (the **Kolbe synthesis**).

$$\begin{matrix} CH_3COO^- \\ \\ CH_3COO^- \end{matrix} \rightarrow \begin{matrix} CH_3 \\ | \\ CH_3 \end{matrix} + 2CO_2 + 2e^-$$

Acid derivatives

These include acid (acyl) halides, acid anhydrides, amides and esters. Examples include:

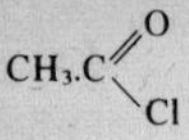

ethanoyl chloride

benzoyl chloride

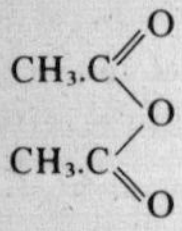

ethanoic anhydride

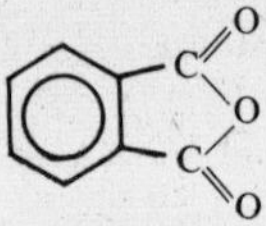

benzene-1,2-dicarboxylic anhydride

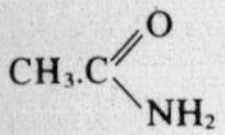

ethanamide

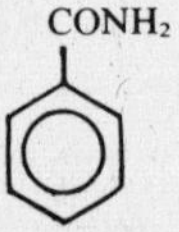

benzamide

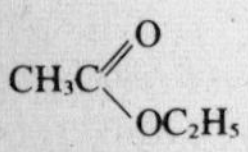

ethyl ethanoate

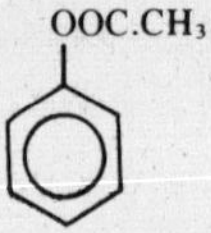

phenyl ethanoate

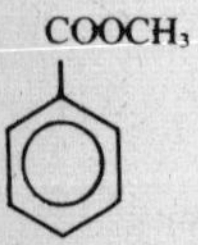

methyl benzoate

Preparation

Acid chlorides are best obtained by the reaction of the acid with either phosphorus(V) chloride or sulphur dichloride oxide (thionyl chloride)

$$CH_3COOH + PCl_5 \rightarrow CH_3COCl + POCl_3 + HCl$$

$$CH_3COOH + SOCl_2 \rightarrow CH_3COCl + SO_2 + HCl$$

Dry apparatus should be used as the product is readily hydrolyzed.

Acid anhydrides may be obtained by heating the anhydrous sodium salt of the acid with the acid chloride

$$CH_3COONa + ClOCCH_3 \rightarrow (CH_3CO)_2O + NaCl$$

Amides may be obtained by
(i) heating the ammonium salt of the acid with excess acid (to suppress dissociation of the ammonium salt), the amide distilling over

$$CH_3COONH_4 \xrightarrow[\text{excess } CH_3COOH]{\text{heat}} CH_3CONH_2 + H_2O$$

(ii) reacting either the acid chloride or the anhydride with concentrated aqueous ammonia

$$CH_3COCl + 2NH_3 \rightarrow CH_3CONH_2 + NH_4Cl$$

Esters may be prepared
(i) from the reaction of the acid with the relevant alcohol

$$CH_3COOH + C_2H_5OH \underset{}{\overset{H^+/\text{reflux}}{\rightleftharpoons}} CH_3COOC_2H_5 + H_2O$$

This reaction is acid catalyzed (conc. H_2SO_4 or gaseous HCl or anhydrous zinc chloride are generally used). An equilibrium mixture results from which the ester may be separated by cooling, addition of water, separation (the ester forms a separate layer) followed by washing with sodium hydrogen carbonate (to remove acid impurities), drying and distilling.

(ii) from the reaction of an acid chloride or anhydride with either an alcohol or phenol

$$CH_3COCl + C_2H_5OH \rightarrow CH_3COOC_2H_5 + HCl$$

(iii) from the reaction of a silver salt of the acid with an alkyl halide

$$CH_3COOAg + BrC_2H_5 \rightarrow CH_3COOC_2H_5 + AgBr$$

Properties
Common properties of these acid derivatives are

(i) Hydrolysis All are hydrolyzed to the acid

(a) $$CH_3COCl + H_2O \rightarrow CH_3COOH + HCl$$

The acid chloride fumes in moist air and reacts vigorously with water

(b) $$(CH_3CO)_2O + H_2O \rightarrow 2CH_3COOH$$

Acid anhydrides react slowly with cold water, more rapidly on warming

(c) $$CH_3CONH_2 + OH^-(aq) \rightarrow CH_3COO^- + NH_3$$

Amides only react on heating with aqueous alkali (they may be distinguished from the ammonium salt of an acid by this reaction as the salt gives ammonia on gentle warming whereas the amide has to be heated quite strongly before ammonia is produced).

(d) Esters are hydrolyzed by heating with acids (giving an equilibrium mixture) or aqueous alkali

$$CH_3COOC_2H_5 + H_2O \rightleftharpoons CH_3COOH + C_2H_5OH$$

$$CH_3COOC_2H_5 + OH^- \rightarrow CH_3COO^- + C_2H_5OH$$

(ii) reaction with ammonia All acid derivatives with the exception of amides react, to give the amide

(a) $$CH_3COCl + 2NH_3 \rightarrow CH_3CONH_2 + NH_4Cl$$

(b) $$(CH_3CO)_2O + 2NH_3 \rightarrow CH_3CONH_2 + CH_3COONH_4$$

(c) $$CH_3COOC_2H_5 + NH_3 \rightarrow CH_3CONH_2 + C_2H_5OH$$

Conc. ammonia solution should be added to the reagent.

(iii) reaction with alcohols and phenols Acid chlorides and anhydrides react to form esters when added to an alcohol. Phenols are best reacted either in alkaline solution or by refluxing with a solution of the acid chloride or anhydride in the corresponding acid

(a) $$CH_3COCl + C_2H_5OH \longrightarrow CH_3COOC_2H_5 + HCl$$

(b) $(CH_3CO)_2O$ +

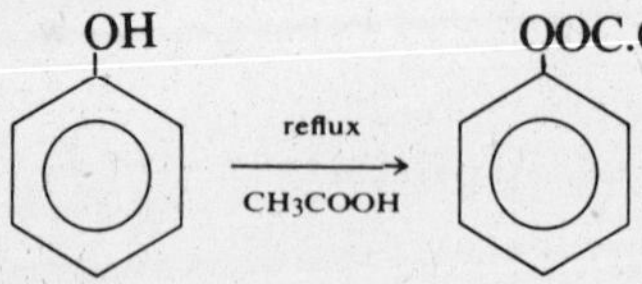

$+ CH_3COOH$

(c) Amides do not react.

(d) Esters may undergo alcohol exchange on refluxing (a volatile alcohol is generally displaced by a less volatile one), e.g. in the production of terylene

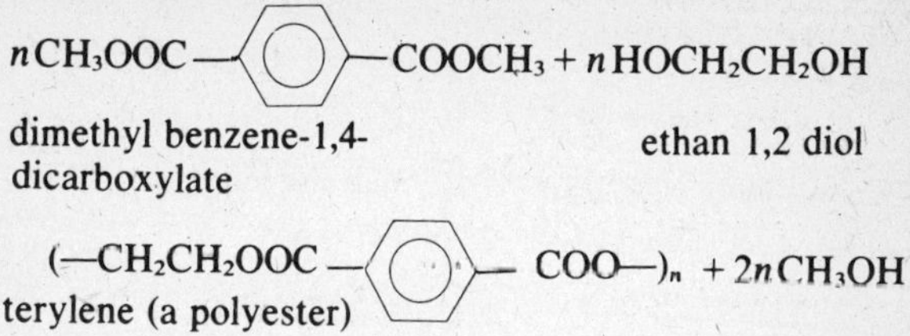

There is no reaction with phenols.

(iv) reaction with amines Only acid chlorides and anhydrides react to give substituted amides:
(a) addition of an acid chloride to an amine results in formation of an amide with an alkyl (or aryl) group substituted for the hydrogen on the nitrogen atom

$$CH_3COCl + H_2NC_2H_5 \rightarrow CH_3CONHC_2H_5 + HCl$$

N-ethylethanamide

(b) refluxing of the amine with the acid anhydride in solution in the corresponding acid also gives a substituted amide

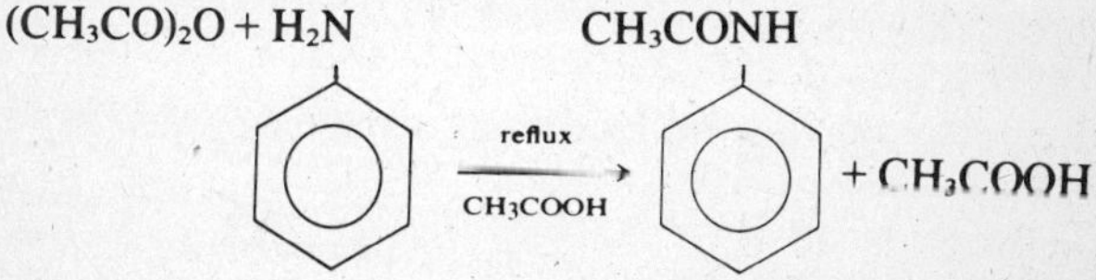

N-phenylethanamide

Neither amides nor esters react.

(v) reaction with benzene Again only acid chlorides and anhydrides react to give ketones. Refluxing with an aluminium chloride catalyst is required:

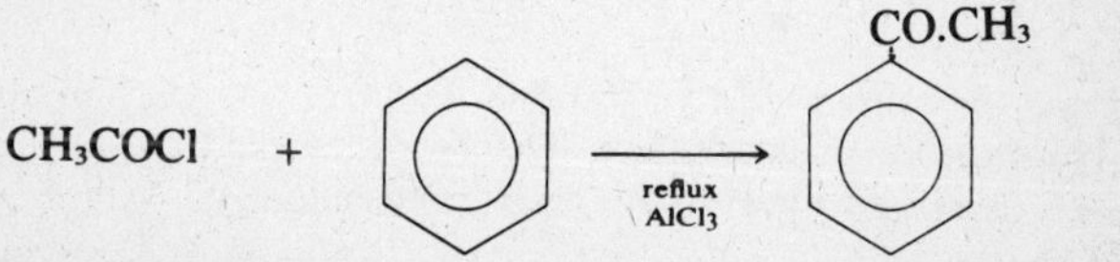

(or $(CH_3CO)_2O$) phenylethanone

Specific reactions

Acid chlorides

(i) may be **reduced** by hydrogen, using a palladium catalyst to give the corresponding alcohol.

$$CH_3COCl + 2H_2 \xrightarrow{Pd} CH_3CH_2OH + HCl$$

If the catalyst is poisoned with barium sulphate, reduction then only occurs to give the aldehyde

$$CH_3COCl + H_2 \xrightarrow{Pd/BaSO_4} CH_3CHO + HCl$$

(ii) react with **anhydrous sodium salts** of acids to form anhydrides (see preparation of anhydrides)

Acid anhydrides

(i) may be **reduced** by sodium amalgam to the corresponding aldehyde

$$(CH_3CO)_2O + 4[H] \rightarrow 2CH_3CHO + H_2O$$

Amides

(i) have **weakly basic properties**, reacting only with strong acids to form unstable salts.

(ii) may be **dehydrated** by heating with phosphorus(V) oxide

$$CH_3CONH_2 - H_2O \rightarrow \underset{\text{ethanonitrile}}{CH_3CN}$$

(iii) because the —NH_2 group is present will react with **nitrous acid** (this is prepared in situ by adding aqueous sodium nitrate(III) (nitrite) to a solution of the amide in a strong acid, e.g. hydrochloric acid) the result being replacement of —NH_2 by —OH

$$CH_3CONH_2 + H^+ + NO_2^- \rightarrow CH_3COOH + N_2 + H_2O$$

(iv) may be converted to an amine with one less carbon atom by **Hofmann's degradation**. The reagents used are bromine and an **aqueous alkali** (sodium or potassium hydroxide)

$$CH_3CONH_2 + Br_2 + 4OH^- \xrightarrow{heat} CH_3NH_2 + 2Br^- + CO_3^{2-} + 2H_2O$$

This is a useful reaction as it provides a way of reducing the number of carbon atoms in a compound whilst still retaining a functional group.

Esters

(i) may be **reduced** by lithium tetrahydroaluminate (used in calculated amount in dry ethereal solution) to the corresponding alcohols

$$R.COOR' + 4[H] \rightarrow RCH_2OH + R'OH$$

(ii) react with **hydroxylamine** to give a hydroxamic acid

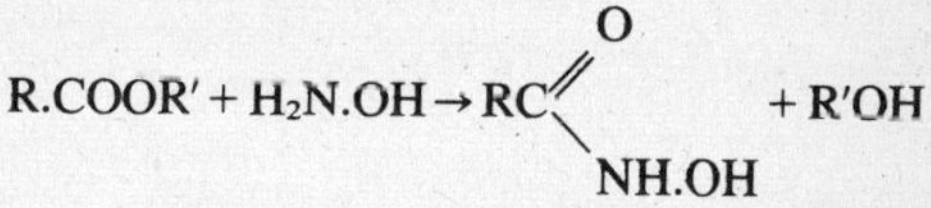

a hydroxamic acid

(iii) react with **Grignard reagents** to give tertiary alcohols:

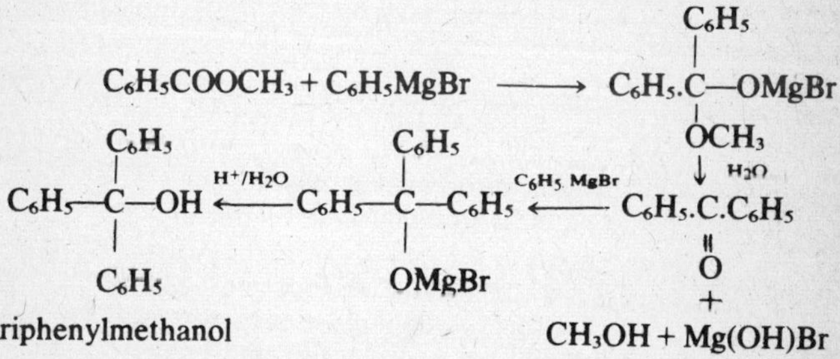

triphenylmethanol

Amino Compounds

These contain the group $-NH_2$. Examples are:

CH_3NH_2 methylamine
$C_2H_5NH_2$ ethylamine

phenylamine

Preparation
General methods of preparation include

(i) Hofmann degradation of an amide using bromine and alkali

$$CH_3CONH_2 + Br_2 + 4OH^- \rightarrow CH_3NH_2 + 2Br^- + CO_3^{2-} + 2H_2O$$

(ii) Reduction of other nitrogen containing compounds:

$$CH_3CN \xrightarrow{Na/C_2H_5OH} CH_3CH_2NH_2$$

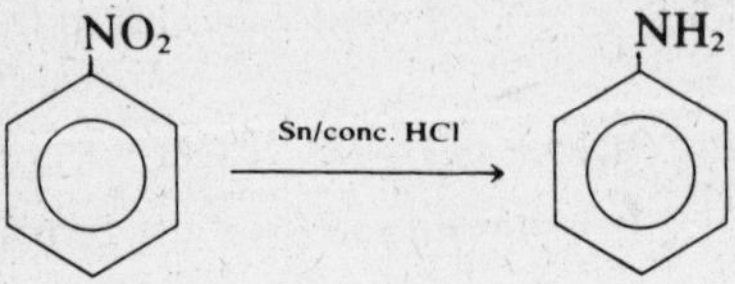

Properties

Methyl- and ethylamines are gases, others being volatile liquids. Amines can be considered as a substituted ammonia and they share many properties with ammonia.

(i) Basic properties

Relative to ammonia, alkylamines are slightly stronger bases due to the electron repelling nature of alkyl groups increasing the availability of the electron pair on the nitrogen atom to attract a proton

$$R\rightarrow\ddot{N}H_2 + H^{\oplus} \rightarrow RNH_3^{\oplus}$$

Arylamines are significantly weaker bases than ammonia due to the electron pair interacting with the delocalized electrons of the aromatic nucleus:

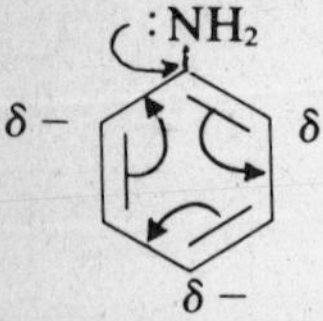

This reduces the electron density on the nitrogen, reducing the attraction for a proton and hence reducing the basicity. Alkylamines therefore form salts with most acids, giving characteristic white fumes with hydrogen chloride, are extremely soluble in water and form coloured complexes with transition metal salts. Arylamines on the other hand only form salts with strong acids (hydrochloric, sulphuric acids). As amines are weak bases they are displaced from their salts by addition of aqueous alkalis.

(ii) With nitrous acid alkylamines react in a similar way to ammonia:

$$\begin{matrix} R{-}NH_2 \\ HO{-}N{=}O \end{matrix} \longrightarrow \begin{matrix} R \\ | \\ OH \end{matrix} + N_2 + H_2O$$

As nitrous acid is unstable, sodium nitrite is added to an acid solution of the amine. The product of the reaction is an alcohol, the hydroxyl group replacing the amino group of the amine. Arylamines react to give an intermediate compound which is only stable in cold solution (below 10°C). When solutions of the amine in excess dilute acid (hydrochloric or sulphuric) and of sodium nitrite are both cooled in ice, and the latter then added daily to the former, to ensure the temperature is kept below 5°C, a diazonium salt is obtained:

$$C_6H_5NH_3^{\oplus} + HNO_2 \rightarrow C_6H_5\overset{\oplus}{N}{\equiv}N + 2H_2O$$

Diazonium salts are valuable intermediates in the synthesis of other aromatic compounds.

(a) heating gives the usual product of reaction of an amino compound with nitrous acid:

$$C_6H_5N_2^+ + H_2O \rightarrow C_6H_5OH + N_2 + H^+$$

(b) heating the chloride with copper powder or with copper(I) chloride and conc. hydrochloric acid gives chlorobenzene:

$$C_6H_5N_2^+ + Cl^- \rightarrow C_6H_5Cl + N_2$$

If copper(I) bromide and concentrated hydrobromic acid are used, bromobenzene is obtained:

$$C_6H_5N_2^+ + Br^- \rightarrow C_6H_5Br + N_2$$

Iodobenzene is given if the diazonium salt is heated with potassium iodide solution. No catalyst is needed for this reaction:

$$C_6H_5N_2^+ + I^- \rightarrow C_6H_5I + N_2$$

Heating with potassium cyanide and copper(I) cyanide as a catalyst on warming gives a nitrile:

$$C_6H_5N_2^+ + CN^- \rightarrow \underset{\text{benzonitrile}}{C_6H_5CN} + N_2$$

(c) **reduction** of diazonium salts can result in either elimination of the nitrogen, by using ethanol or phosphinic acid, or with sodium sulphite then dilute acid to phenylhydrazine.

$$C_6H_5\overset{+}{N}{\equiv}N + 4[H] \rightarrow \underset{\text{phenylhydrazine}}{C_6H_5NH.NH_2} + H^+$$

(d) the diazonium salts are weak electrophiles and will attack strongly activated aromatic nuclei preferably in the -4 position if this is available.

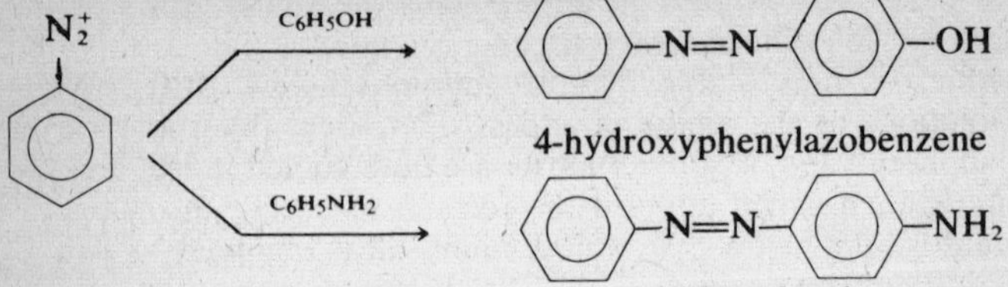

4-hydroxyphenylazobenzene

4-aminophenylazobenzene

Only the hydroxy, amino and N alkyl substituted amino groups have a sufficiently activating effect to promote this reaction. The reaction is referred to as coupling. The products are coloured (the –N=N– group is a chromophore group , i.e. it imparts colour when part of a system containing delocalized electrons) and are used as dyes.

(iii) Alkylhalides react with amines to form secondary tertiary amines and quaternary ammonium salts (see properties of halogeno compounds).

$$CH_3I + CH_3NH_2 \xrightarrow[\text{pressure}]{\text{heat}} (CH_3)_2NH_2I$$

(iv) Acid halides and anhydrides react with both alkyl and arylamines to form substituted amides (see properties of acid derivatives).

$$R.NH_2 + R'COCl \rightarrow R'CONH.R + HCl$$

(v) With trichloromethane and **potassium hydroxide** dissolved in ethanol an isocyanide is obtained which can be recognised by its unpleasant smell. This is a characteristic property of a primary amine.

$$R{-}NH_2 + CHCl_3 + 3OH^- \rightarrow RN{\equiv}C + 3H_2O + 3Cl^-$$

(vi) The amino group has a strongly activating effect on the aromatic nucleus and directs further substitution to the 2,4,6 positions.

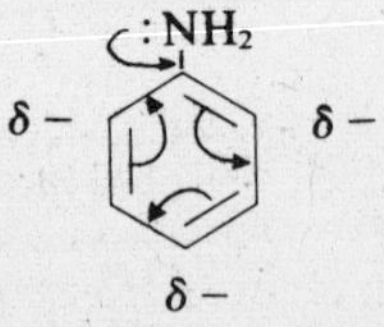

Phenylamine thus reacts readily with bromine water to give a white precipitate of the 2,4,6-tribromophenylamine (benzene requires pure bromine and a catalyst).

However phenylamine is readily oxidised, giving complex coloured products – this is used as a test for phenylamine which is oxidised by dichromate(VI), hydrogen peroxide and by iron(III) salts to dark coloured products. Because of this ease of oxidation phenylamine cannot be substituted by reagents with oxidizing properties. Nitration of phenylamine is not possible with nitric acid due to its oxidizing properties. However, if the amino group is protected by acylation, substitution is then possible using the usual nitrating mixture (conc. nitric and sulphuric acids). Once the product has been obtained, the protecting group can be removed by heating with aqueous alkali:

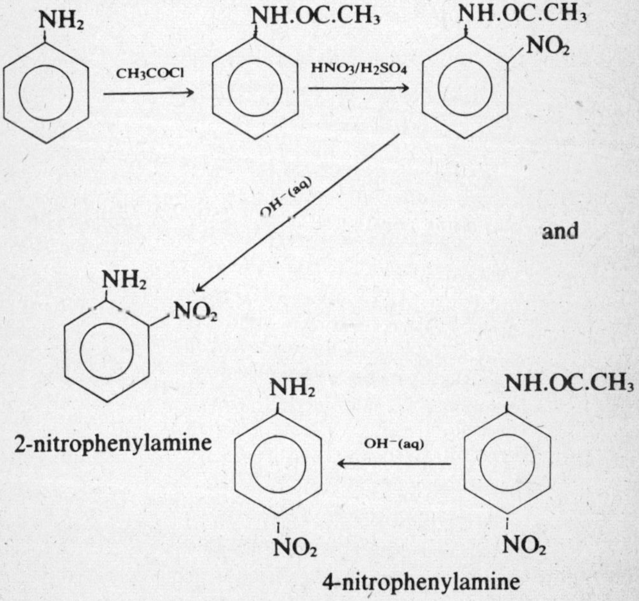

Nitriles and Iso-nitriles (isocyanides)

These are isomeric compounds. Nitriles contain the group —C≡N, isocyanides the group —N⇄C.

CH_3CN ethanonitrile (methyl cyanide)
CH_3NC isocyanomethane (methyl isocyanide)

Preparation
Nitriles may be prepared by
(i) dehydration of amides, heating with phosphorus(V) oxide:

$$CH_3CONH_2 - H_2O \rightarrow CH_3CN$$

(ii) heating alkyl halides with potassium cyanide:

$$CH_3I + KCN \rightarrow CH_3CN + KI$$

Isocyanides are prepared by
(i) the isocyanide (carbylamine) reaction in which a primary amine is heated with trichloromethane and alcoholic potassium hydroxide

$$CH_3NH_2 + Cl_3HC + 3OH^- \rightarrow CH_3NC + 3Cl^- + 3H_2O$$

(ii) heating an alkyl halide with silver cyanide

$$CH_3I + AgCN \rightarrow CH_3CN + AgI$$

Properties

(i) Hydrolysis of both compounds can be brought about by heating with aqueous acid.

$$CH_3CN \xrightarrow[\text{heat}]{H^+(aq)} CH_3COOH + NH_4^+$$

$$CH_3NC \xrightarrow[\text{heat}]{H^+(aq)} CH_3NH_3^+ + HCOOH$$

Nitriles, but not isocyanides, are also hydrolyzed on heating with aqueous alkali.

(ii) Reduction Nitriles may be reduced by sodium and ethanol to the primary amine:

$$CH_3CN + 4[H] \rightarrow \underset{\text{ethylamine}}{CH_3CH_2NH_2}$$

Isocyanides are reduced by hydrogen, using a platinum or nickel catalyst:

$$CH_3NC + 2H_2 \xrightarrow{\text{Ni/heat}} \underset{\text{dimethylamine}}{CH_3NHCH_3}$$

The product is a secondary amine, one of the alkyl groups present always being a methyl group.

Ethers

These are compounds containing a C–O–C linkage. The oxygen may be the link between two alkyl, two aryl or one alkyl and one aryl groups. Examples are:

CH_3OCH_3 methoxymethane

$CH_3OCH_2CH_3$ methoxyethane

$CH_3O.CH_2CH_2CH_3$ 1-methoxypropane

$CH_3O.CH(CH_3)_2$ 2-methoxypropane

$CH_3.O.C_6H_5$ methoxybenzene

$C_6H_5O.C_6H_5$ phenoxybenzene

These compounds are isomeric with alcohols but have significantly lower boiling points (methoxymethane bp −24°C, ethanol bp 78°C) than the corresponding alcohols. This is because hydrogen bonding is not possible in ethers but does occur in alcohols.

Preparation

Ethers may be prepared by

(i) dehydration of alcohols, mixing the alcohol and conc. sulphuric acid in equal volumes, warming to 140°C and adding the alcohol at the same rate as the product distils:

$$2C_2H_5OH \xrightarrow{\text{conc. } H_2SO_4} C_2H_5OC_2H_5 + H_2O$$

(ii) reaction of a halogenoalkane with the sodium salt of an alcohol or phenol:

$$R\text{—}I + NaOR' \xrightarrow{\text{heat}} R.O.R' + NaI$$

Properties

Ethers are relatively unreactive due to the stability of the C–O–C linkage. They are volatile, flammable compounds. The only chemical reaction of note other than combustion is with hot concentrated solutions of hydrogen halides.

$$CH_3O.CH_2CH_3 + 2HI \rightarrow CH_3I + C_2H_5I + H_2O$$

This reaction may be used to distinguish between two ethers as the products may be identified by boiling points.

Chapter 12
Organic Syntheses and Analysis

Syntheses

Synthesis of one organic compound from another is a common question in examinations. There are a number of standard sequences which may be used for many of these problems. An essential point is to limit the number of steps involved to a maximum of four due to the limited yield in many organic reactions. Also, it is important to note the number of carbon atoms in the starting and finishing materials as this can indicate which of the following general or specific methods apply.

An **increase** in the **number of carbon atoms** can be achieved by (i) the reaction of a halogenoalkane with potassium cyanide, a typical sequence being

$$ROH \xrightarrow{\text{red } P/I_2} RI \xrightarrow{KCN} RCN \xrightarrow{H^+/H_2O} RCOOH$$

$$RCN \xrightarrow{Na/C_2H_5OH} RCH_2NH_2$$

(ii) preparation and use of a Grignard reagent

$$ROH \xrightarrow{\text{red } P/I_2} RI \xrightarrow[\text{in dry ether}]{Mg} RMgI \xrightarrow[\text{(b) } H^+/H_2O]{\text{(a) H.CHO then}} R.CH_2OH$$

$$RMgI \xrightarrow[\text{(b) } H^+/H_2O]{\text{(a) } CO_2 \text{ then}} R.COOH$$

(iii) use of a special compound, diethylpropandioate, $CH_2(COOC_2H_5)_2$. This has a hydrogen atom which can be replaced by sodium and the resultant compound will react with halogenoalkanes. Hydrolysis of this product gives a carboxylic acid with two more carbon atoms than the halogenoalkane.

$$CH_2(COOC_2H_5)_2 \xrightarrow{Na} Na.CH.(COOC_2H_5)_2$$

$$Na.CH.(COOC_2H_5)_2 \xrightarrow{RI} R.CH.(COOC_2H_5)_2$$

$$R.CH_2.COOH \xleftarrow[\text{(b) } H^+/H_2O]{\text{(a) } OH^-/H_2O \text{ then}} R.CH.(COOC_2H_5)_2$$

The halogenoalkane may be prepared from the corresponding alcohol as in (i) or (ii) above.

(iv) heating calcium salts of carboxylic acids on their own gives a ketone (except when R = H)

$$\begin{matrix} RCOO^- \\ \\ RCOO^- \end{matrix} Ca^{2+} \xrightarrow{\text{heat}} \begin{matrix} R \\ \\ R \end{matrix}\!\!>\!C{=}O + CaCO_3$$

Alternatively, heating a mixture of the calcium salts of methanoic acid and a second carboxylic acid the major product is an aldehyde with one more carbon atom than the carboxylate used

$$\begin{matrix} RCOO^- \\ \\ HCOO^- \end{matrix} Ca^{2+} \xrightarrow{\text{heat}} \begin{matrix} R \\ \\ H \end{matrix}\!\!>\!C{=}O + CaCO_3$$

(v) reacting an aldehyde or ketone with potassium cyanide followed by addition of acid and heating

$$R.CHO + HCN \longrightarrow \underset{\displaystyle OH}{R.\underset{|}{CH}.CN} \xrightarrow{H^+/H_2O} \underset{\displaystyle OH}{R.\underset{|}{CH}.COOH}$$

An α-hydroxycarboxylic acid is obtained having one more carbon atom than the starting material.

(vi) dimerization of aldehydes with an αC–H bond, e.g.

$$2CH_3.CHO \xrightarrow{Na_2CO_3} CH_3.\underset{\displaystyle OH}{\underset{|}{CH}}.CH_2CHO \xrightarrow{OH^-(aq)} CH_3CH{=}CHCHO$$

A **decrease** in the **number of carbon atoms** is possible by two reactions, only one of which is of any general application. This is using the Hofmann degradation which might, for example, be used in the following sequence.

$$\mathrm{R.COOH} \xrightarrow{\mathrm{PCl_5}} \mathrm{RCOCl} \xrightarrow{\mathrm{NH_3}} \mathrm{RCONH_2}$$

$$\mathrm{RCONH_2} \xrightarrow{\mathrm{Br_2/OH^-}} \mathrm{RNH_2}$$

$$\mathrm{R.OH} \xleftarrow{\mathrm{H^+/NO_2^-}} \mathrm{RNH_2}$$

The second method is limited as the end product is an alkane from which it is difficult to obtain any further product. The reaction involved is decarboxylation by heating the sodium salt of a carboxylic acid with soda lime

$$\mathrm{R.COO^-} + \mathrm{OH^-} \rightarrow \mathrm{R.H} + \mathrm{CO_3^{2-}}$$

Specific reactions in which the **number of carbon atoms is not changed** include:

Propan-1-ol to **propanone** (this cannot be achieved directly as oxidation of propan-1-ol gives an aldehyde) can be brought about by dehydration of the alcohol to propene, hydration of this (addition obeys Markownikow's rule) and oxidation of the propan-2-ol thus obtained

$$\mathrm{CH_3.CH_2.CH_2OH} \xrightarrow[\mathrm{400°\,C}]{\mathrm{Al_2O_3}} \mathrm{CH_3{-}CH{=}CH_2}$$

$$\mathrm{CH_3{-}CH{=}CH_2} \xrightarrow{\mathrm{conc.\ H_2SO_4}} \mathrm{CH_3CH(SO_4H).CH_3}$$

$$\mathrm{CH_3.CO.CH_3} \xleftarrow{\mathrm{Cr_2O_7^{2-}/H^+}} \mathrm{CH_3.CH(OH).CH_3} \xleftarrow[\mathrm{heat}]{\mathrm{H_2O}} \mathrm{CH_3CH(SO_4H).CH_3}$$

To convert **ethanol**, C_2H_5OH, to **ethandioic acid**, $(COOH)_2$, the following sequence may be used

$$\mathrm{CH_3.CH_2OH} \xrightarrow[\mathrm{400°\,C}]{\mathrm{Al_2O_3}} \mathrm{CH_2{=}CH_2} \xrightarrow{\mathrm{Br_2}} \mathrm{CH_2Br.CH_2Br}$$

$$\mathrm{CH_2Br.CH_2Br} \xrightarrow[\mathrm{heat}]{\mathrm{OH^-/H_2O}} \mathrm{CH_2OH.CH_2OH}$$

$$\mathrm{(COOH)_2} \xleftarrow{\mathrm{Cr_2O_7^{2-}/H^+}} \mathrm{CH_2OH.CH_2OH}$$

Ethyne may be converted to **ethanoic acid**

$$\mathrm{HC{\equiv}CH} + \mathrm{H_2O} \xrightarrow{\mathrm{Hg^{2+}/H^+}} \mathrm{CH_3.CHO} \xrightarrow{\mathrm{Cr_2O_7^{2-}/H^+}} \mathrm{CH_3COOH}$$

Useful reaction schemes involving benzene derivatives include methylbenzene, aminobenzene and diazonium salts:

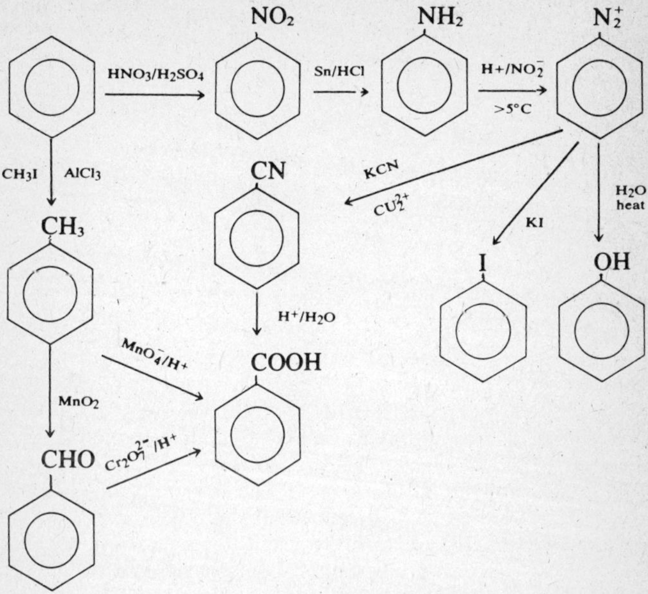

Note that a compound of the type RCONHR′ may be obtained as the end product of a synthesis by reacting an acid chloride with a primary amine. For example, to obtain the compound $CH_3.C_6H_4NH.CO.CH_3$ from iodomethane and benzene as the only starting materials the sequence used might be:

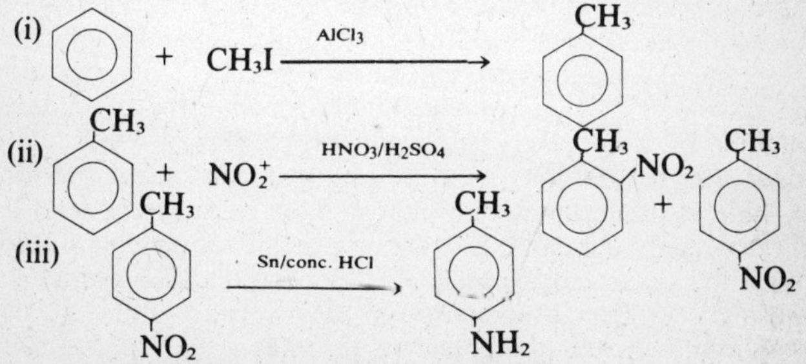

(iv) $CH_3I + KCN \longrightarrow CH_3CN$

(v) $CH_3CN \xrightarrow{H^+/H_2O} CH_3COOH$

(vi) $CH_3COOH \xrightarrow{PCl_5} CH_3COCl$

(vii) 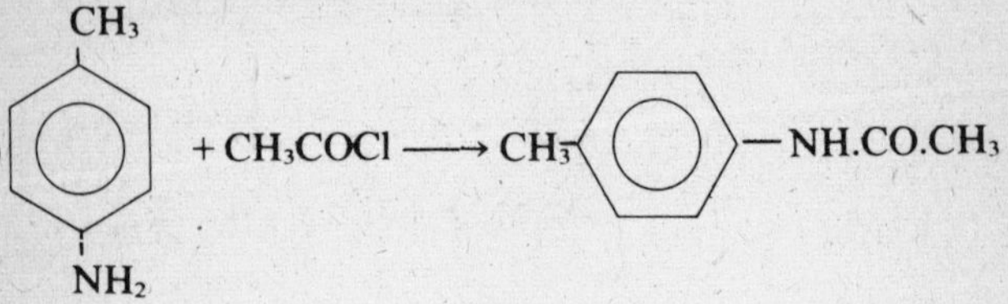

Organic analysis

Elements may be detected in organic compounds by

(i) heating with copper(II) oxide. The carbon in the compound is oxidized to carbon dioxide and the hydrogen to water.

(ii) the **Lassaigne sodium test**. The organic compound is heated with sodium which reduces (a) nitrogen, if present to sodium cyanide, (b) sulphur, if present to sodium sulphide and (c) halogen, if present to sodium halide. These sodium salts are water soluble and the aqueous extract of the reaction mixture is then tested for the relevant ions. Cyanide ions are detected by heating part of the aqueous extract with freshly prepared iron(II) sulphate and dilute sodium hydroxide. This converts the cyanide to hexacyanoferrate(II) which on acidification gives a green to dark blue colouration with iron(III) ions. Sulphide ions are detected by addition of freshly prepared sodium pentacyano-nitrosylferrate(II), $Na_4Fe(CN)_5NO_2$ to some of the aqueous extract. A purple colour is given if sulphide ions are present. Halide may be detected by acidifying the aqueous solution, heating to decompose cyanide or sulphide (if either nitrogen or sulphur are present) and adding silver nitrate solution. A white precipitate of silver chloride (soluble in dilute ammonia) indicates the presence of chlorine in the organic compound. A cream precipitate (soluble only in concentrated ammonia) indicates the presence of bromine and and a pale yellow precipitate (insoluble even in concentrated ammonia) indicates the presence of iodine.

Functional groups may be detected by making use of their characteristic properties. Most examining boards include a qualitative organic exercise in the practical exam. Many of those commonly met in examinations are given below, including typical observations and the inferences which may be made from such observations.

Test	*Observation*	*Indication*
1. Add water	(a) soluble giving	
	(i) neutral soln.	lower alcohols
	(ii) acid soln.	lower aliphatic acid or anhydride or salt of amine
	(iii) alkaline soln.	salt of acid or salt of phenol
	(b) partially soluble	
	(i) sl. acid soln.	phenol/aromatic acid
	(ii) sl. alkaline	aromatic amine
	(iii) neutral soln.	higher alcohols
	(c) reacts to give fumes of HCl	acid chloride
2. Add dil. HCl	(a) soluble	weak base (aromatic amine)
	(b) white solid crystallizes from solution (soluble in (1))	salt of higher aliphatic or aromatic acid or of phenol
3. Add conc. H_2SO_4 to solid (or pure compound)	(a) CO evolved (odourless neutral gas with blue flame)	methanoate (formate)
	(b) CO and CO_2 evolved	ethandioate (oxalate)
	(c) ethanoic acid evolved	ethanoate
4. Add dil. NaOH (warming may be necessary)	(a) soluble (partly soluble in (1))	aromatic or higher aliphatic acid or phenol
	(b) (i) substance separates from solution	salt of aromatic acid
	(ii) heat gently—NH_3 evolved	ammonium salt
	(iii) heat strongly—NH_3	amide (or nitride)
	(iv) yellow resin	aldehyde with αC–H bond
	(v) alcohol and acid given (acid separates on acidification)	aldehyde with no αC–H bond, or ester

Test	*Observation*	*Indication*
5. Mix with solid NaOH or soda-lime. Heat strongly	(a) H_2 evolved (ignites with pop) (b) alkane evolved (c) benzene or other aromatic compound (smoky flame)	methanoic acid or salt aliphatic acid or salt aromatic acid or salt
6. Bromine water	(a) decolorized, no ppt (b) decolorized, white ppt	unsaturated compound phenol or aromatic amine
7. Bromine and dil. alkali. Warm	(a) amine evolved (pungent, alkaline)	amide
8. Manganate(VII) usually in acid solution	(a) decolorized in cold (b) decolorized on warming (c) coloured oxidation product	unsaturated compound alcohol, or aldehyde, or ethandioic acid or its salt, or methanoic acid or its salt aromatic amine
9. Dichromate in acid solution	(a) turns green on warming (b) coloured oxidation product (also given by other oxidizing agents, MnO_4^-/H^+, Fe^{3+}, H_2O_2, bleaching powder, NaClO, (sodium chlorate(I)) etc.)	as 8(b) above aromatic amine, e.g. phenylamine
10. Add iron(III) chloride solution	(a) coloured oxidation product (b) characteristic colour given (usually in neutral solution) and sometimes a precipitate (especially on heating)	aromatic amine carboxylic acids or salts, or phenols or salts
11. Silver nitrate solution	(a) reduced to silver mirror on warming (b) white ppt, (i) sol. in dil. HNO_3 (ii) insol. in HNO_3	aldehyde ethandioic acid or its salt chloride
12. Fehling's or Benedict's soln.	reduced to copper(I) oxide (yellow to brown ppt)	aldehyde or methanoic acid

Test	*Observation*	*Indication*
13. Phenylhydrazine or 2,4-dinitro compound	yellow precipitate	aldehyde or ketone
14. Sodium meta-bisulphite	colourless crystalline ppt or exothermic reaction	aldehyde or ketone
15. Hydroxy-ammonium chloride	white ppt	aldehyde or ketone
16. Schiff's reagent	magenta colour restored rapidly	aldehyde
17 Ethanol + test substance + conc. H_2SO_4. Heat	ester formed (characteristic smell, especially when poured into water)	acid or salt of acid
18. Add ethanoyl chloride or anhydreid. Warm	(a) liquid with characteristic odour, especially when poured into water	alcohol
	(b) white solid given when cooled mixture is poured into water	phenol or aromatic amine
19. Heat with phthalic anhydreid and a few drops conc. H_2SO_4. Pour carefully into dil. NaOH	coloured product given. pink colour (phenolphthalein)	phenol
	yellow/green fluroescein	resorcinol (1,3-dihydroxybenzene).
20. To solution in excess dil. acid add sodium nitrate(III) (nitrite)	(a) N_2 evolved	aliphatic amine or amide
	(b) N_2 evolved, phenol smell on warming	aromatic amine
	(c) if ice cold solution used,yellow oil or solid	aromatic amine
21. To yellow oil from 20(c) add		
(i) KI soln.,	iodobenzene given	aromatic amine
(ii) phenol, or naphthol in alkali	yellow/orange solid or solution	aromatic amine
(iii) an aromatic amine	yellow/orange solid or solution	aromatic amine
22. Heat dry solid alone	(a) methanal given	methanoate
	(b) a ketone given	salt of carboxylic acid

Test	*Observation*	*Indication*
23. Heat with phosphorus(V) oxide	alkyl cyanide given	amide
24. Add trichloromethane and alkali. Warm	unpleasant odour of isocyanide	primary amine
25. Add phosphorus(V) chloride	(a) reacts giving HCl fumes (b) reacts, little or no HCl fumes	alcohol aldehyde or ketone
26. Add a little sodium to dry test substance	hydrogen given slowly	alcohol
27. Add sodium carbonate solution. Warm	CO_2 evolved	aliphatic or aromatic acid, not a phenol
28. Carefully add 1:1 mixture conc. HNO_3, conc. H_2SO_4. Warm gently. Pour into water	nitro derivative (often yellow) separates out. Many are solids	aromatic compound

Quantitative analysis

Quantitative analysis of organic compounds can be carried out to determine the empirical and molecular formula of a compound. The carbon content is determined by weighing a sample of the compound and measuring the mass of carbon dioxide produced on complete combustion. The hydrogen content may be obtained at the same time by determining the mass of water produced. Nitrogen is determined by using a second sample and converting the element either to ammonia or to nitrogen gas. Sulphur may be estimated as $BaSO_4$ and halogens as the silver halide. The oxygen content can only be determined by calculating the difference between the mass of sample and the masses of the elements determined.

Examples

1. A compound has the percentage composition by mass, C = 60%, H = 13·3%, O = 26·7%. Its vapour density is 30.

Determine its empirical and molecular formulae, and suggest possible structural formulae (C = 12, H = 1, O = 16).

Solution

$$\text{Ratio } C:H:O = \frac{60}{12} : \frac{13{\cdot}3}{1} : \frac{26{\cdot}7}{16}$$

(Divide % by relevant relative atomic masses) = 5 : 13·3 : 1·67
(Divide by smallest no. in ratio) = 3 : 8 : 1
Empirical formula is C_3H_8O
Relative molecular mass = vapour density × 2 = 30 × 2 = 60
Empirical formula mass = (3 × 12) + (8 × 1) + (1 × 16) = 60
∴ Empirical formula = molecular formula
Molecular formula is C_3H_8O
Structures are

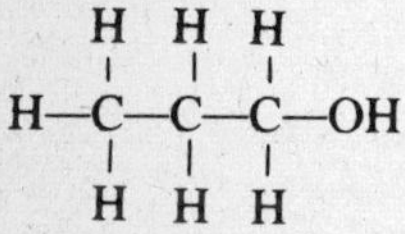

propan-1-ol

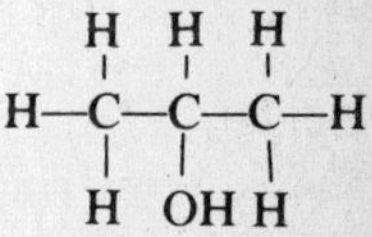

propan-2-ol

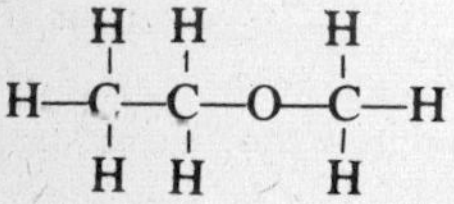

methoxyethane

Chapter 13
Macromolecules

Macromolecules are large molecules, most of which are carbon compounds. Naturally occurring compounds of this type are of great significance in nature, including carbohydrates, lipids (fats), proteins and nucleic acids. Many synthetic compounds of industrial importance are macromolecules, including the plastics, both thermoplastics such as polythene, terylene, nylon etc. and thermosetting materials such as bakelite, melamine and some polyester resins.

Carbohydrates are of prime importance to living organisms. They are the product of photosynthesis by plants and are an essential for respiration of all living organisms. All carbohydrates contain a potential carbonyl group and also several hydroxyl groups. All of these compounds contain the elements carbon, hydrogen and oxygen, in most the ratio of hydrogen to oxygen being 2:1, the same as in water. However, there are some important compounds belonging to this class which do not have this ratio of hydrogen to oxygen.

Monosaccharides are the building units for carbohydrates.

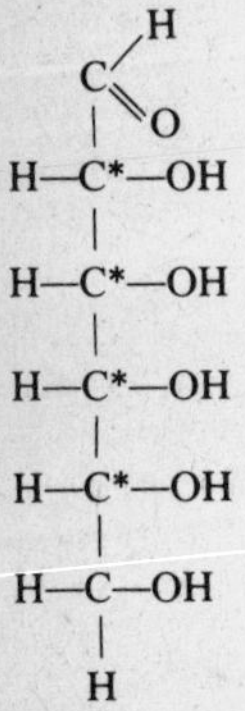

I

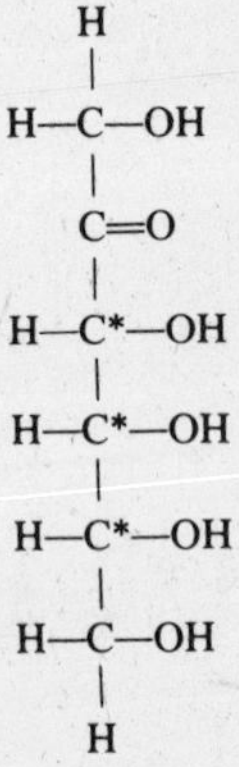

II

The most commonly distributed monosaccharides are the **hexose sugars** (soluble carbohydrates with six carbon atoms), although monosaccharides may have from three to seven carbon atoms. A simple representation of typical hexoses is given above.

Note that I, an aldehyde, has 4 asymmetrically substituted carbon atoms, indicated by ∗, so that $2^4 = 16$ optical isomers (8 pairs of enantiomers) are possible, whereas II, a ketone, has only 3 asymmetric carbon atoms so that this structure has $2^3 = 8$ optical isomers (4 pairs of enantiomers). Compounds with structures based on I include glucose and galactose.

Glucose has the structural formula given below.

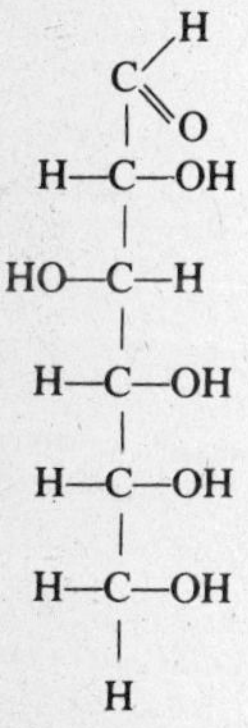

D(+) glucose

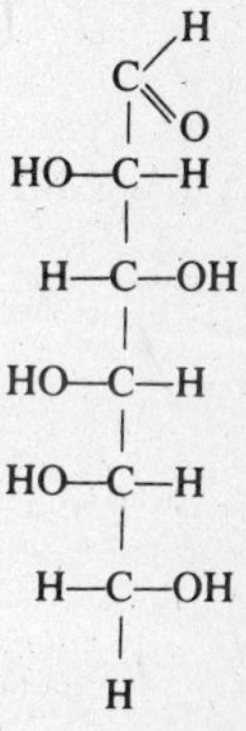

L(−) glucose

However, hexose sugars normally exist as ring structures formed by the aldehyde group linking to the hydroxyl group of the 4th or 5th carbon atom of the chain. The rings thus formed are either five or six membered rings. In glucose a six membered ring is the one generally formed. The aldehyde carbon atom of the straight chain structure in the ring becomes a further asymmetric carbon atom so that each glucose isomer has two possible structures, designated α and β, shown overleaf.

The three structures are in equilibrium with each other in

aqueous solution so that the open form is always present allowing for glucose to show many properties typical of aldehydes, including the reduction of Fehling's and Benedict's solutions. It is therefore termed a reducing sugar, (sugars are soluble carbohydrates).

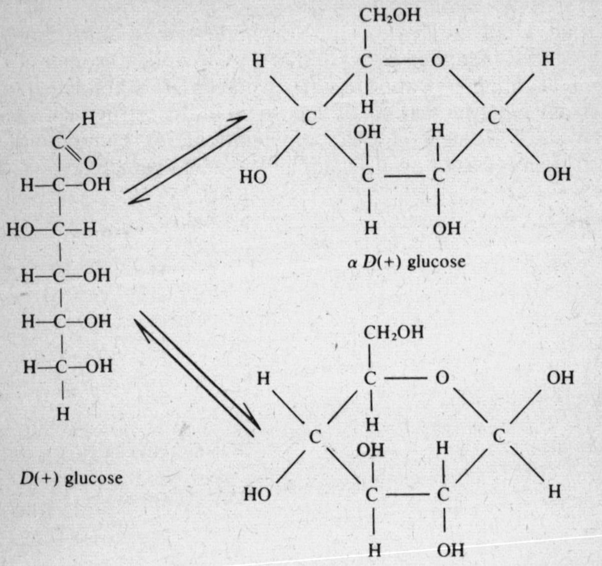

α D(+) glucose

D(+) glucose

β D(+) glucose

Fructose is another hexose sugar, but instead of being an aldehyde it has a ketone grouping. Apart from the resultant

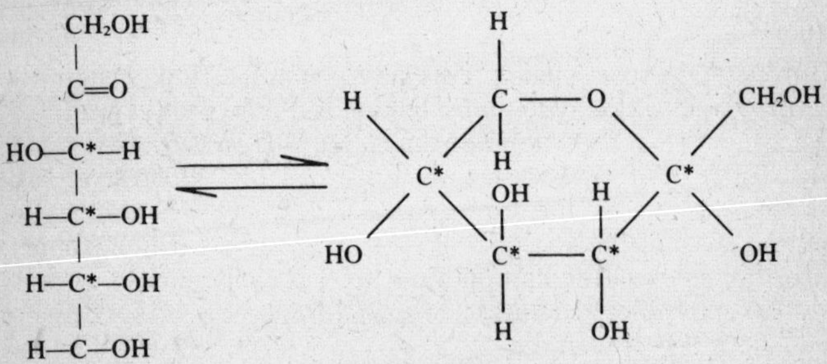

(* asymmetric carbon atoms)

different arrangement on carbon atoms 1 and 2, the arrangement on atoms 3 to 6 is identical to that in glucose. Also like glucose in aqueous solution it exists as a ring structure. However a five membered ring as well as a six membered ring is possible, although the former is found only in fructose derivatives such as the 1,6-diphosphate.

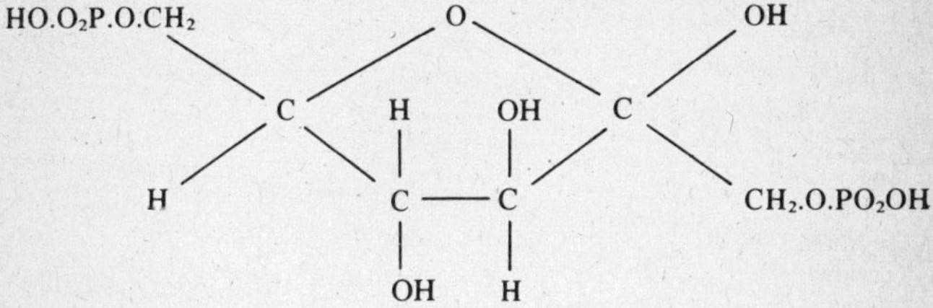

The above are examples of monosaccharides, the building units of all carbohydrates. Three carbon, triose (glyceraldehyde, or 2,3-dihydroxypropanal) and five carbon, pentose (particularly ribose $C_5H_{10}O_5$, and deoxyribose $C_5H_{10}O_4$) monosaccharides are also important. The former is an intermediate in the process of photosynthesis, the pentose sugars are constituents of the nucleic acids, ribonucleic and deoxyribonucleic acids.

Disaccharides are formed from two monosaccharides by a condensation reaction (removal of one molecule of water). The synthesis of a disaccharide is catalyzed by enzymes in living organisms. Examples of disaccharides are maltose (glucose + glucose), sucrose or cane sugar (glucose + fructose) and lactose or milk sugar (glucose + galactose). In some disaccharides the aldehyde group of one of the monosaccharides may not be involved in the linkage, in which case the resultant disaccharide retains the reducing properties of the aldehyde group and is a reducing sugar. **Maltose** and **lactose** are examples.

Sucrose is probably present in all green plants being commercially extracted from sugar-beet and sugar cane. It is dextrorotatory, the angle of rotation being +66·5°. **Maltose** is produced in germinating barley by enzyme hydrolysis of starch, but does not occur widely in the free state. It is a dextrorotatory sugar, its angle of rotation being +137·5°.

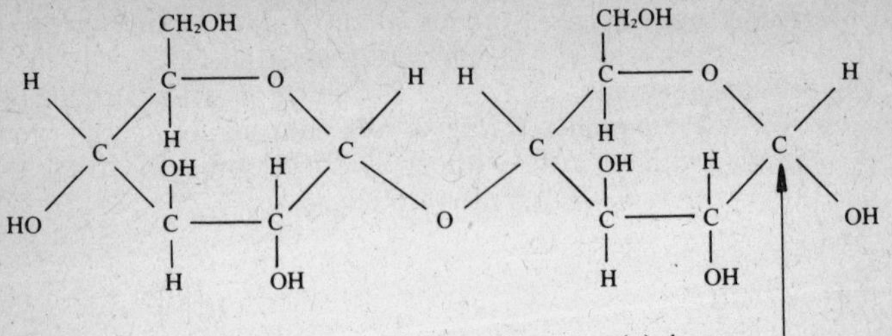

If, on the other hand, the aldehyde group is used in the linkage of a reducing sugar (glucose) to a non reducing sugar (fructose) the disaccharide formed has no reducing properties and is a non reducing sugar (**sucrose**).

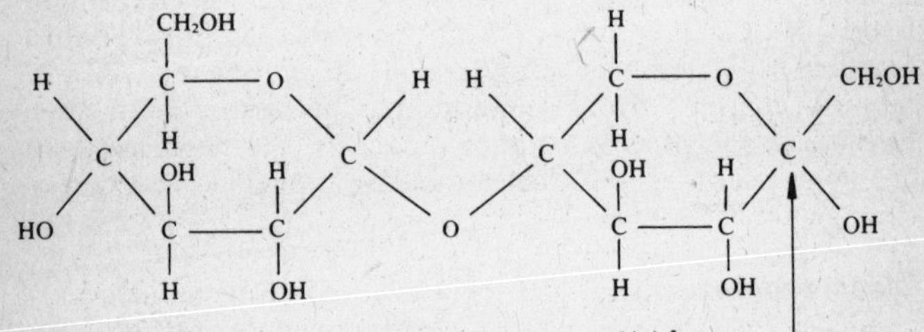

Polysaccharides are macromolecules (large molecules) formed by condensation of large numbers of monosaccharides. The three of significance in living organisms are starch (a food reserve in plants), cellulose (of structural importance in plants) and glycogen (a temporary food store in animals, found especially in the liver and in muscles). These differ only in the nature of the glucose units from which they are built up and in the position of linkage between the units. **Cellulose**, for instance, consists of β(+) glucose units linked exclusively by condensation between the 1-carbon atom of one glucose molecule and the 4-carbon atom of the next, as indicated on the next page.

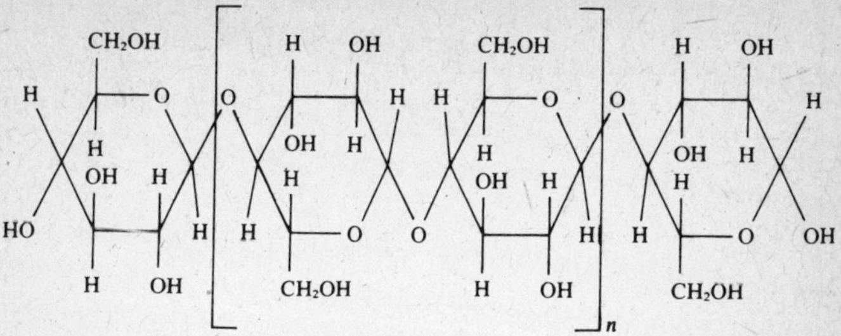

cellulose

Starch, on the other hand, consists of $\alpha(+)$ glucose units linked by the 1 and 4 carbon atoms.

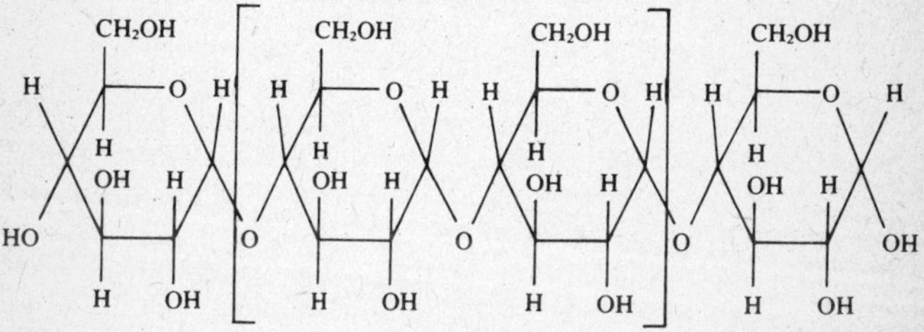

Glycogen is also made from glucose but in this case the 1,4-linkage and the 1,6-linkage both occur resulting in a high degree of branching.

In living organisms, the building up and breakdown of disaccharides and polysaccharides is enzyme controlled. These are so specific in their action that the digestive enzymes which catalyze the breakdown of starch cannot catalyze the hydrolysis of cellulose. As a result only certain animals are able to fully digest grasses and other plants and these generally rely on intestinal bacteria to produce the cellulase for digestion of the cellulose.

The relationship between mono-, di- and polysaccharides is:

$$n\,C_6H_{12}O_6 \underset{+H_2O}{\overset{-H_2O}{\rightleftharpoons}} \frac{n}{2}\,C_{12}H_{22}O_{11} \underset{+H_2O}{\overset{-H_2O}{\rightleftharpoons}} (C_6H_{10}O_5)_n$$

The enzymes for these reactions are named after the substance either acted on or formed, the ending being changed to -ase.

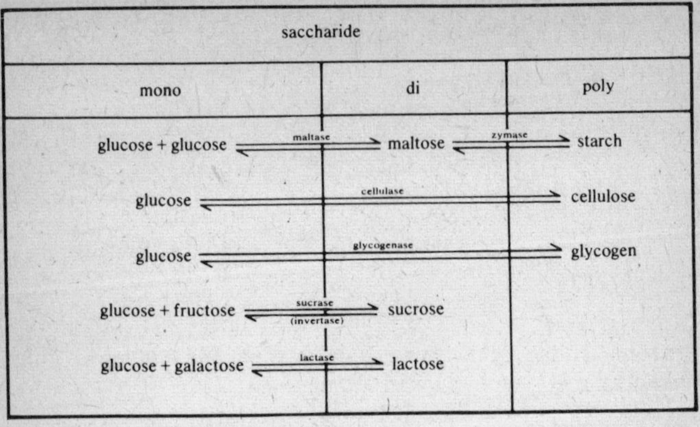

The properties of carbohydrates are the properties of the alcohol and carbonyl groups present in the compounds. Thus esters can be formed. Ethanoic anhydride reacts to produce polyethanoates enabling the positions of the hydroxyl groups and also of the carbon atoms joined by the ether link in the ring systems to be determined. Esterification of cellulose-containing materials is important industrially. Nitrate derivatives are used as explosives and also as the base for cellulose paints. Cellulose ethanoate (acetate) and ethanoate/butanoate (acetate/butyrate) co-polymers are plastics used as packaging material (films, bottles) etc. Esters with phosphoric acid are important in living organisms, being formed during respiration and being important constituents of nucleotides and nucleic acids.

Carbohydrates may also be oxidized. Concentrated sulphuric acid removes water from all carbohydrates.

Sugars also react with some reagents which typically react with the carbonyl group. Thus oximes are formed with hydroxylamine. Phenylhydrazine initially forms a phenylhydrazone but further reaction follows due to oxidation of the adjacent hydroxyl group and a double hydrazone (called an osazone) is then formed. These may be used to identify sugars as the osazone of a particular sugar has a characteristic shape and often a particular period for crystallization.

Proteins are other natural macromolecules of significance. These are made of **amino acids**, compounds which contain both an amino group, $-NH_2$ and a carboxylic acid group, $-COOH$. In proteins there are about twenty amino acids and with one exception these are optically active with the *L* relative configuration. The exception is aminoethanoic acid (glycine) which does not have an asymmetric carbon atom. The names and formulae of a number of these amino acids are given in table 7.

Table 7

Systematic Name	*Common Name*	*Formula*
aminoethanoic acid	glycine	$H.CH.COOH$ NH_2
2-aminopropanoic acid	alanine	$CH_3.CH.COOH$ NH_2
2-amino-3-hydroxy-propanoic acid	serine	$HO.CH_2.CH.COOH$ NH_2
2-amino-4-methyl-pentanoic acid	leucine	$(CH_3)_2.CH.CH_2.CH.COOH$ NH_2
2,6-diamino-hexanoic acid	lysine	$H_2N.(CH_2)_4.CH.COOH$ NH_2
2-amino-3-phenyl-propanoic acid	phenylalanine	$C_6H_5.CH_2.CH.COOH$ NH_2
2-amino-3-methyl-butanoic acid	valine	$(CH_3)_2.CH.CH.COOH$ NH_2
2-amino-3-hydro-sulphurylpropanoic acid	cysteine	$HS.CH_2.CH.COOH$ NH_2
2-aminopentan-dioic acid	glutamic acid	$HOOC.(CH_2)_2.CH.COOH$ NH_2
2-amino-3-(4-hydroxy-phenyl)-propanoic acid	tyrosine	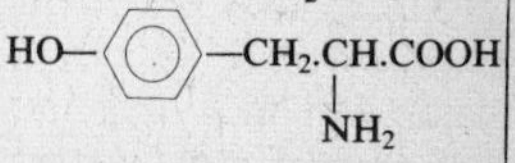
2-amino-3-hydroxy-butanoic acid	threonine	$CH_3.CH.CH.COOH$ OH NH_2

As the formulae indicate, all naturally occurring amino acids have the amino group in the 2-position relative to the carboxylic acid group. The **amino group** has most of the **properties** associated with it, as does the **carboxylic acid group**. For example, the amino group has basic properties, forming a salt with acids:

$$\mathrm{H_2N.\overset{R}{\overset{|}{C}}H.COOH + H^+ \rightarrow H_3N^+.\overset{R}{\overset{|}{C}}H.COOH}$$

With bases the acid group reacts:

$$\mathrm{H_2N.\overset{R}{\overset{|}{C}}H.COOH + OH^- \rightarrow H_2N.\overset{R}{\overset{|}{C}}H.COO^- + H_2O}$$

At a particular pH the acid can exist in the form in which the amino group has gained a proton from the acid group:

$$\mathrm{H_3N^+.\underset{\underset{R}{|}}{C}H.COO^-}$$

This is known as a **zwitterion**, which probably predominates both in aqueous solution and in the solid state. The melting point of 2-aminoethanoic acid (glycine) is 236°C (with some decomposition) which is significantly greater than that of ethanoic acid (17°C) indicating that electrostatic attraction occurs in the amino acids, which can only be explained by the zwitterion structure.

Other properties of the amino group are reactions with nitrous acid (sodium nitrate(III) (nitrite) in acid solution), acid chlorides, anhydrides and with trichloromethane and alkali (the carbylamine reaction). The carboxylic acid group reacts with phosphorus(V) chloride and with alcohols.

Proteins are formed from amino acids by condensation (elimination of water) resulting from the reaction of the amino group of one acid with the carboxylic acid group of a second acid forming an amide (or peptide) link. The reaction is catalyzed in living organisms by enzymes. The stages in the build up of proteins are given on the following page.

Although the difference between various proteins arises mainly from the type of amino acids present, it is also affected by the proportion in which these are present and the sequence in which they are linked. Simple proteins contain relatively few amino acids whereas more complex ones have several thousand amino acid units. In many structures another compound is joined to the protein unit, forming a conjugated protein, typical non protein components being phosphoric acid, carbohydrate, haem units and even nucleic acids. The final structure has a characteristic shape depending on cross linking of the amino acid chain, involving hydrogen bonding, sulphur links etc.

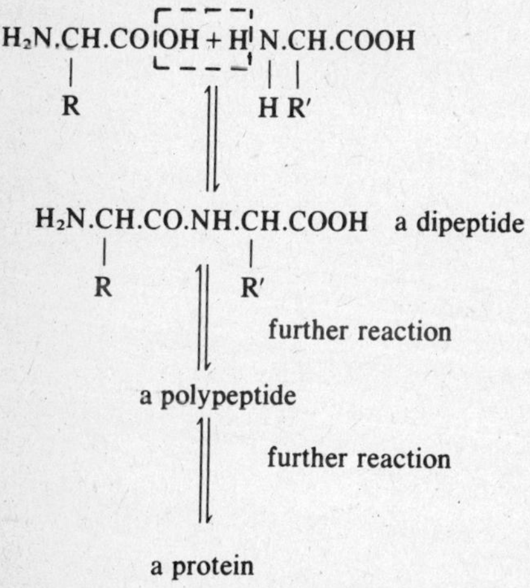

The properties of proteins relate to the presence of excess acid and basic groups, and to the nature of the cross linking in the structure. The addition of acid or alkali will break down the structure due to reaction with these acid and basic groups and denature the protein. Similar breakdown of the structure occurs on heating, as this provides energy to break the hydrogen bonds, and on addition of other substances which interfere with the hydrogen bonding, such as alcohols and many metal ions particularly transition metals such as copper.

Proteins are hydrolyzed on heating with acids. The individual amino acids obtained may be identified by chromatography. The sequence of amino acids in a protein can be determined by more specific means, using enzymes for hydrolysis of terminal acids or of the peptide link between particular amino acids.

Lipids (including fats and oils) are naturally occurring esters mostly containing the triol, propan-1,2,3-triol (glycerol). This is esterified with carboxylic acids containing an even number of carbon atoms. The physical state of the ester depends on the degree of unsaturation of the acids present. A high proportion of saturated acids results in a solid (a fat) whereas a high proportion of unsaturated acids results in a liquid (oil).

The manufacture of margarine, mostly from blends of vegetable oils although originally an animal oil, whale oil, was used, is carried out by saturation of the oil by reacting with hydrogen under pressure using a nickel catalyst.

Exposure of oils to air also results in saturation of oils by reaction with oxygen. This property has resulted in the use of some oils, for example linseed oil, as a constituent of paints and putty and as a wood treatment. The oil gradually hardens to a solid on exposure to air.

Lipids are hydrolyzed in living organisms by the action of the enzyme lipase, and under laboratory conditions by the action of aqueous alkali:

$$\begin{array}{lcl} CH_2.OOC.C_{17}H_{35} & & CH_2.OH \\ | & & | \\ CH.OOC.C_{17}H_{35} & \underset{-H_2O}{\overset{+H_2O}{\rightleftharpoons}} & CH.OH + 3C_{17}H_{35}COOH \\ | & & | \\ CH_2.OOC.C_{17}H_{35} & & CH_2.OH \end{array}$$

a fat	propan-1,2,3-triol (glycerol)	octadecanoic acid (stearic acid)

The salt of the carboxylic acid is a soap, having detergent properties. Addition of salt to the reaction mixture results in the soap separating out as a solid. The process is known as **saponification** (soap making).

Lipids are important in living organisms as food reserves,

particularly in animals and in seeds of plants. Esters containing other acids as well as the carboxylic (fatty) acids are also important, particularly phospholipids, containing phosphoric acid, which are constituents of cell membranes.

Key terms

Carbohydrate A compound containing carbon, hydrogen and oxygen only; in most the ratio of hydrogen to oxygen is 2:1.
Sugar A soluble carbohydrate.
Monosaccharide A simple sugar with general formula $C_nH_{2n}O_n$ where $n = 3$ to 7.
Disaccharide A sugar consisting of two monosaccharides joined by elimination of water.
Polysaccharide Insoluble carbohydrates formed from large numbers of monosaccharide molecules.
Reducing sugar A sugar which reduces Fehling's and Benedict's solutions due to the presence of a free aldehyde group.
Protein A compound containing carbon, hydrogen, oxygen and nitrogen and often sulphur. They consist of large numbers of amino acids linked by peptide links.
Amino acids The building units of proteins, containing both an amino ($-NH_2$) and carboxylic acid ($-COOH$) group, the amino group being on the -2-(α) carbon atom relative.
Denaturing The breakdown of a protein by the action of heat, or acid or alkali or other chemical such as alcohol or transition elements.
Lipid An ester of propan-1,2,3-triol with carboxylic or other acids such as phosphoric acid.
Fat A solid lipid containing a high proportion of saturated fatty acids.
Oil A liquid lipid containing a high proportion of unsaturated fatty acids.

Chapter 14
Industrial Aspects of Organic Chemistry

Organic chemicals are all derived, directly or indirectly, from living organisms. The sources are:

1. Petroleum
2. Natural gas
3. Coal
4. Plant and animal sources

Of these, petroleum and natural gas are of the greatest importance in terms of the amount and range of compounds obtained. The initial products from the refining of petroleum are indicated below.

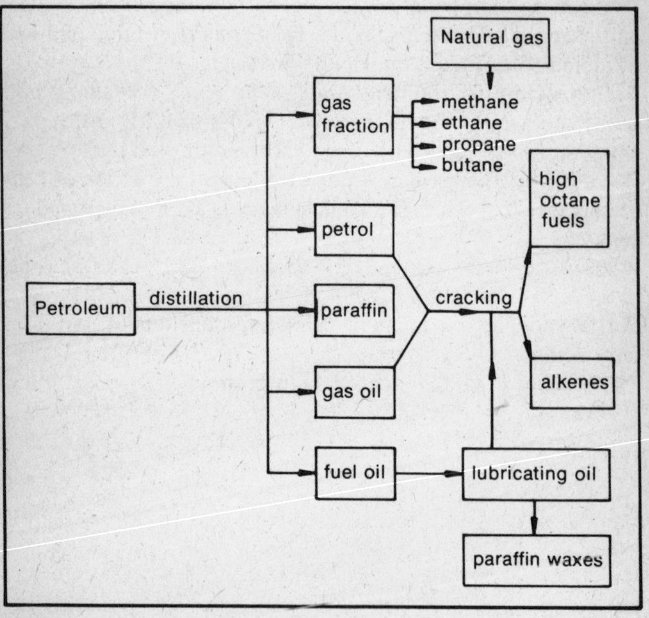

Figure 50

Catalytic and thermal cracking are important in producing an increased yield of the petrol fraction but they also give a significant yield of alkenes and hydrogen as by-products.

Alkenes obtained include **ethene**, **propene** and **butene**, these being an important source of a large number of materials. Some of these are indicated in figs. 51, and 53.

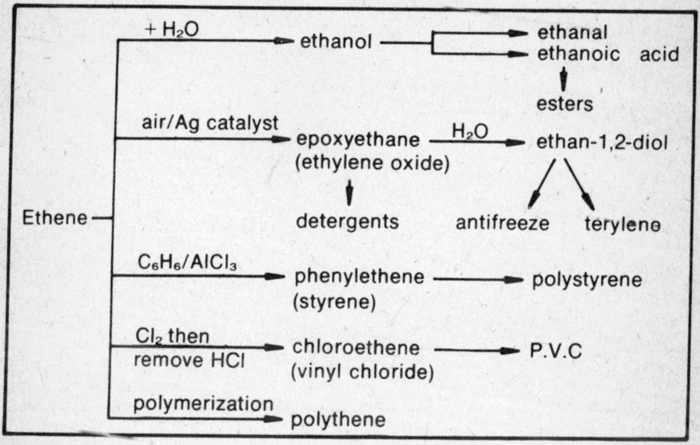

Figure 51

Methane is an important source of organic compounds, as it can be converted to a mixture of carbon monoxide and hydrogen (syntheses gas) as can other hydrocarbons; it can also be converted to ethyne and hydrogen by pyrolysis.

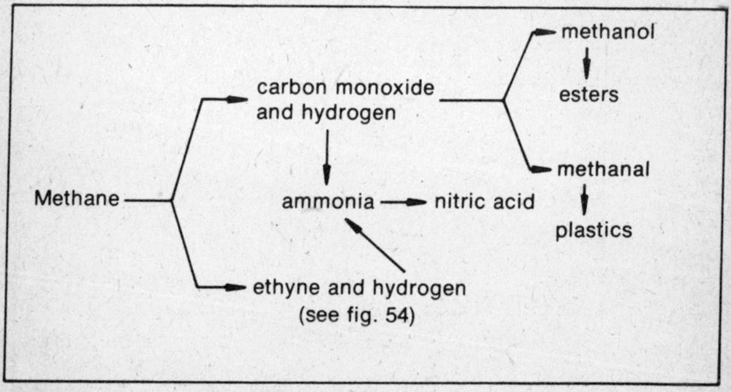

Figure 52

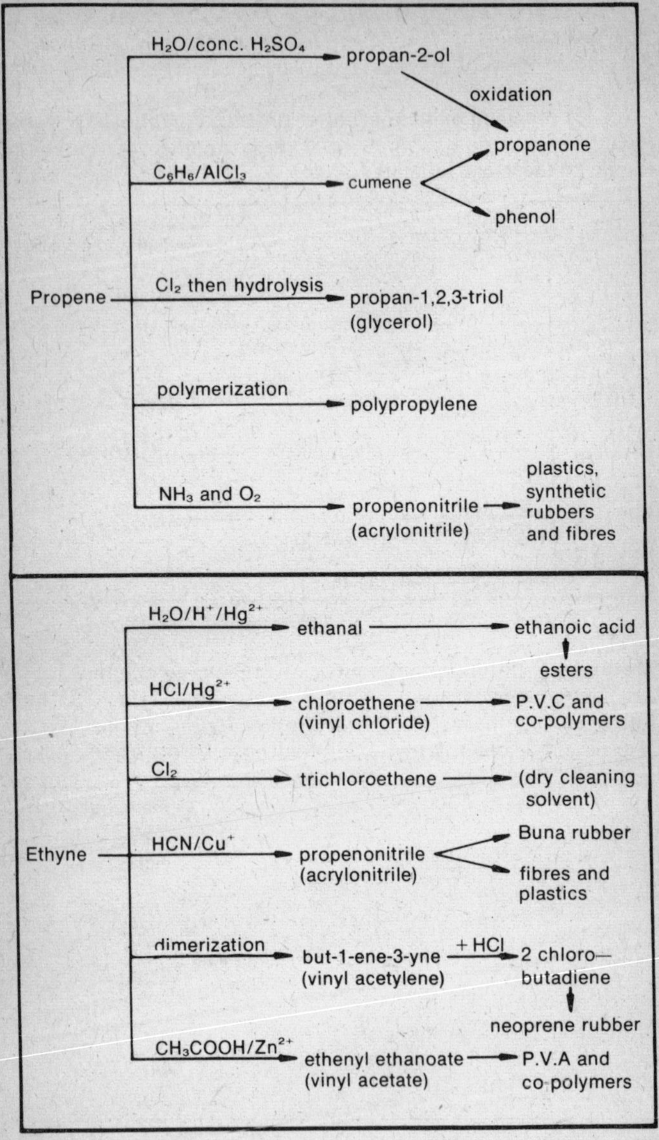

Propene
H₂O/conc. H₂SO₄
propan-2-ol
oxidation
propanone
C₆H₆/AlCl₃
cumene
phenol
Cl₂ then hydrolysis
propan-1,2,3-triol (glycerol)
polymerization
polypropylene
NH₃ and O₂
propenonitrile (acrylonitrile)
plastics, synthetic rubbers and fibres
Ethyne
H₂O/H⁺/Hg²⁺
ethanal
ethanoic acid
esters
HCl/Hg²⁺
chloroethene (vinyl chloride)
P.V.C and co-polymers
Cl₂
trichloroethene
(dry cleaning solvent)
HCN/Cu⁺
propenonitrile (acrylonitrile)
Buna rubber
fibres and plastics
dimerization
but-1-ene-3-yne (vinyl acetylene)
+ HCl
2 chloro—butadiene
neoprene rubber
CH₃COOH/Zn²⁺
ethenyl ethanoate (vinyl acetate)
P.V.A and co-polymers

Figure 53

Petroleum is also a major source of aromatic organic compounds. Benzene and its homologues may be obtained from fractions containing six or more carbon atoms by catalytic dehydrogenation.

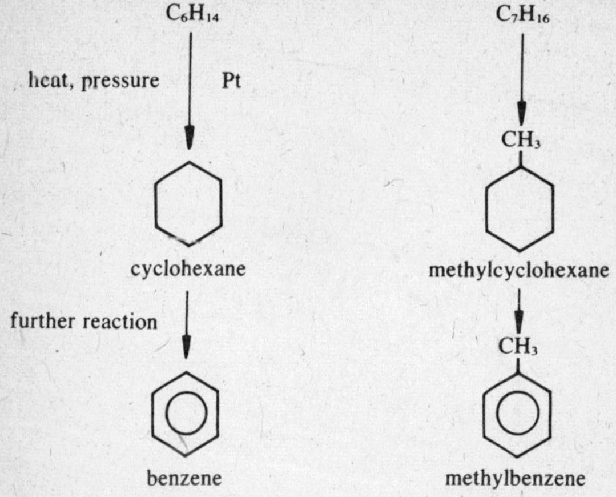

Coal has been used as a source of coal gas since the early nineteenth century. When first discovered the other products had no useful application. After some time crude distillation of the coal tar enabled the separation of it into light oil, creosote and pitch. The light oil found use in the manufacture of waterproof cloth because of its property as a solvent for natural rubber. Creosote was used as a wood preservative particularly for ships hulls (until the increased use of iron for shipbuilding reduced the demand) and for railway sleepers. The pitch was initially used to make coal briquettes from coal dust and later in road making.

The rapid expansion of the chemical industry based on coal tar followed the discovery by Perkins in 1856 of aniline dyes. The discovery of pharmaceuticals, explosives and a variety of other chemicals followed this resulting in increased use of coal. As petroleum has become an increasing source of chemicals, together with decreased demand for coke by the steel industry and for coal gas as a fuel so coal has reduced in importance as a source of chemicals. Even so, coal is still used as an important source of organic chemicals. Figure 54 gives an indication of the products obtained on destructive distillation of coal (heating coal to high temperatures in the absence of air).

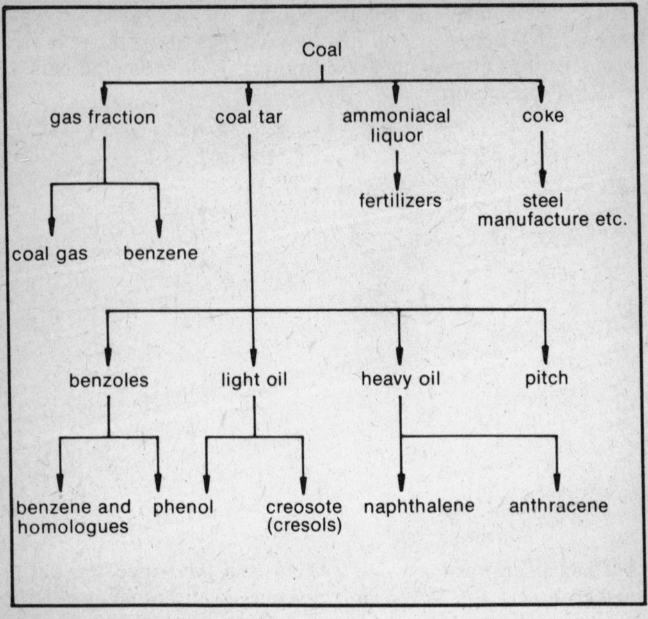

Figure 54

Plants and animals remain a valuable source of many chemicals, not necessarily in terms of quantity, but more in terms of the value of the substances which may be obtained. Plants provide a source of, amongst other materials, carbohydrates (including sugars, starch), natural rubbers, vegetable oils, natural flavourings and essences, vitamins and pharmaceuticals.

Carbohydrates, in particular are further used to obtain many other chemicals (fig. 55).

Materials obtained from animal sources include oils, fats and hormones. The oils and fats from both vegetable and animal sources are used to manufacture soap and margarine.

The above materials are the source of the wide range of substances increasingly used by modern society. **Plastics** and fibres have become increasingly important materials in industry and in everyday life. Plastics are substances which at some stage during the processing can be moulded. They can be

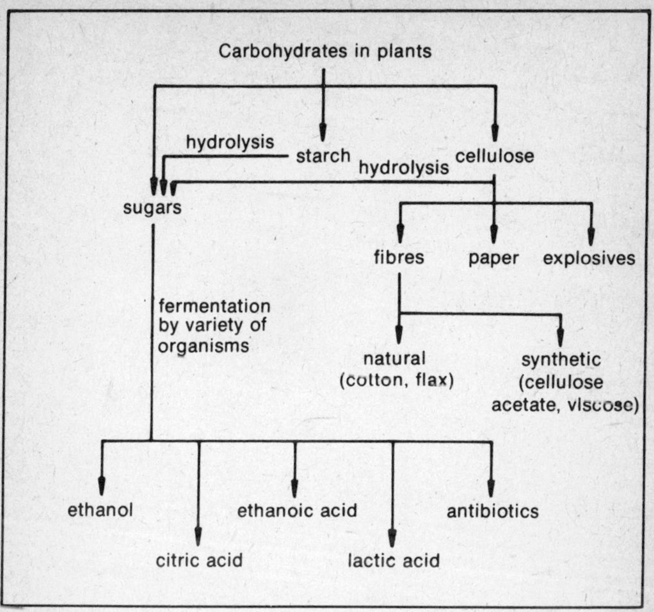

Figure 55

broadly classified into two main types. **Thermoplastics** are those substances which retain their plastic properties. **Thermosetting plastics** are only plastic during the processing, which often involves heating under pressure or in the presence of a catalyst. Once moulded into a particular shape the plastic properties are lost.

Many thermoplastics are addition polymers of unsaturated compounds, including co-polymers which are made from mixtures of two different unsaturated compounds. Substances of this type include polythene, obtained by polymerization of ethene, polystyrene, polyvinyl chloride, perspex, polytetrafluoroethene and others. These are listed, with some condensation polymers in table 8, which also gives the building units and states their main uses. Condensation polymers are formed from substances each containing two or more reacting groups by elimination of a simple substance, often water. **Nylon** is made from either a diamine and a dicarboxylic acid or from a cyclic amide, caprolactam.

Table 8 Thermoplastics

Monomer(s)	*Polymer*	*Uses*
ethene $CH_2{=}CH_2$	polythene	Packaging (film, bottles); Industrial and building uses (electrical insulation, chemical resistant drums); Household goods
propene $CH_3.CH{=}CH_2$	polypropylene	Car components; Plastic film; Sterilizable vessels; Ropes
phenylethene $C_6H_5.CH{=}CH_2$ (styrene)	polystyrene	Packaging (jars, cartons, bottle closures); Expanded material used for packaging delicate equipment and for thermal insulation
chloroethene $Cl.CH{=}CH_2$ (vinyl chloride)	polyvinyl chloride (P.V.C.)	Packaging; Fabrics; Electric cable insulation; Plumbing (pipes, guttering); Chemical plant; Records; Floor coverings (tiles etc.)
ethenyl ethanoate (vinyl acetate) $CH_3COOCH{=}CH_2$	polyvinyl acetate (P.V.A.)	Emulsion adhesives and emulsion paints
phenylethene } propenonitrile }	styrene-acrylonitrile co-polymer (S.A.N.)	Kitchen equipment; Crockery (cups, plates, saucers etc.)

Table 9 Thermoplastics contd.

Monomer(s)	*Polymer*	*Uses*
tetrafluoroethene $F_2C{=}CF_2$	polytetrafluoroethene (P.T.F.E. Fluon, Teflon)	Coating for surfaces requiring low friction and/or resistance to high temperatures and/or chemicals, e.g. chemical plant, baking tins etc.
methyl-2-methyl-propenoate (methylmethacrylate) $CH_2{=}C(CH_3).COOCH_3$	polymethylmethacrylate (Perspex etc.)	Alternative to glass; Also decorative signs
methanal, H.CHO (formaldehyde)	polyacetal	Light engineering
phenylethene propenonitrile butadiene	styrene, acrylonitrile butadiene co-polymer (A.B.S.)	Car and light engineering components
2-methylpropene 2-methylbutadiene	Butyl rubber	Synthetic rubber

Terylene, another condensation polymer, is made by reacting dimethyl benzene-1,4-dicarboxylate (dimethyl terephthalate) with ethan-1,2-diol (ethylene glycol). It finds application mainly as a fibre.

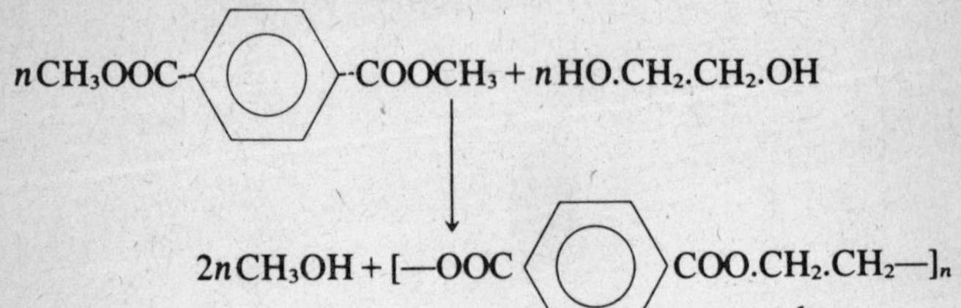

terylene

Synthetic rubbers are polymers which have a high degree of elasticity (it can be stretched by application of an extending force but returns to its original shape when the force is removed). This property is due to the presence of some cross linkage between the main chains – the more cross linkage the less elastic the material. Natural rubber is a thermoplastic and is unsuitable as an elastic material until it is processed. The natural rubber has the basic unit 2-methylbuta-1,3-diene (isoprene)

$$CH_2{=}\underset{\displaystyle CH_3}{\underset{|}{C}}.CH{=}CH_2$$

but the polymer has little cross linking. The required degree of cross linking is promoted by adding a calculated amount of an agent (a vulcanizing agent) such as sulphur or sulphur compounds. The cross linking results from formation of sulphur bridges between the chains of the polymer. Usually other additives are also compounded with the rubber to improve certain properties. These additives include carbon black (particularly in car tyres where it improves the wear resistance), pigments, anti-oxidants and materials to reduce degradation by chemicals, ultraviolet radiation and other agents.

Synthetic rubbers have been developed and these are now an important class of materials due to their special properties. Buna rubbers are based on butadiene giving materials with similar characteristics to natural rubber except they have improved resistance to the action of oils and some solvents. Neoprene, based on 2-chlorobutadiene and generally vulcanized by zinc oxide, is less elastic than natural rubber. It has greatly increased resistance to chemicals, including solvents, to heat and to abrasion. It is used to manufacture seals for machinery, for conveyor belts and for footwear. Butyl rubber is less elastic than natural rubber but has high strength. It is used for electrical insulation and for high speed tyres.

Silicone rubbers have a degree of organic content although the important links in the structure involve silicon–oxygen–silicon bonds. These are generally made from a mixture of alkyl and aryl silicon halides.

Chain forming compounds are of the type:

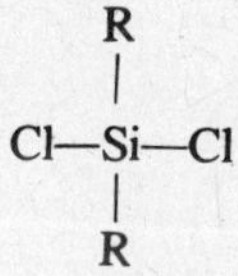

cross linking compounds of the type:

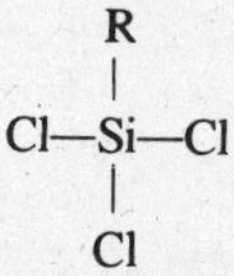

and chain ending compounds of the type:

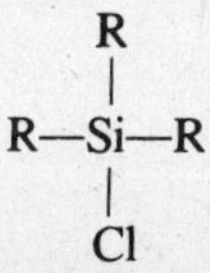

The properties of the end product depend on the nature of the radicals, 'R', and on the ratio of the 3 types of compound used. The more of the first two used, the more solid the end product; the higher the proportion of the last of these compounds, the more likely the material is to be a liquid. Liquid silicones are important as water proofing materials for cloth etc.; for mould release agents particularly in the plastics industry; for treatment of conveyor belts in frozen food factories to prevent the material to be packed from sticking to the belt; as a constituent of wood glass and metal polishes and as hydraulic fluids because of their small change in viscosity over a range of temperatures. Solid silicones are used as synthetic rubbers mainly as sealing or waterproofing materials and as electrical insulators for applications where their special properties warrant the expense. The way in which the above compounds may react to form a silicone is given below.

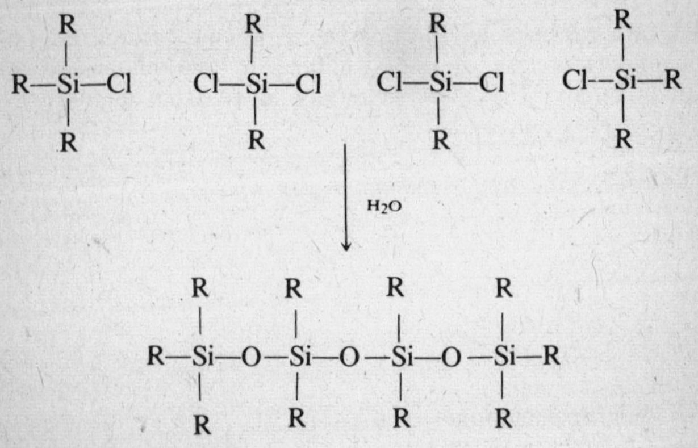

Thermosetting polymers owe their final properties to the degree of cross linking present in the final structure. Some materials are initially only partially reacted, the final hardening being completed during the moulding or by the addition of a catalyst or other chemical. Some of these thermosetting polymers are listed in table 10 and for some of these further details are given below.

Bakelite is one of the earliest discovered thermoplastics. The reaction of the two reactants (phenol and methanal) is either acid or alkali catalyzed. Industrially the phenol is heated with formalin (50% aqueous methanal) and a little sulphuric acid. A brown solid results probably consisting of a chain structure

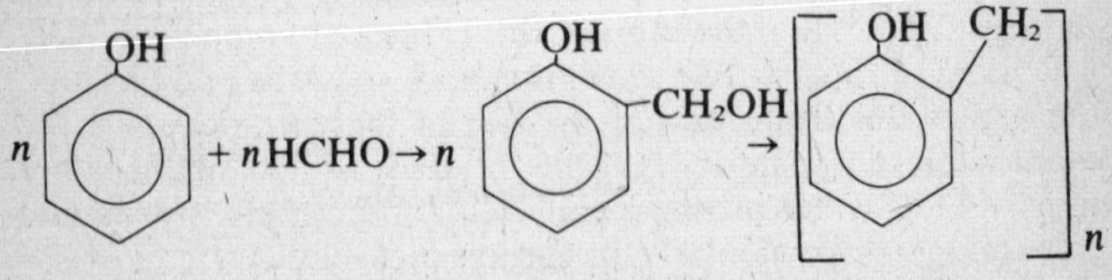

Table 10 Thermosetting plastics

Monomers	*Polymer*	*Uses*
phenols methanal (formaldehyde)	phenol-formaldehyde resins (Bakelite)	Electrical components; Laminated plastics; Brake linings; Adhesives
urea methanal	urea-formaldehyde resins	Electrical components; Cavity wall insulation; Bottle closures; Adhesives
melamine methanal	melamine-formaldehyde resins	Laminated plastics; Melaware cups and other crockery
isocyanates poly -ols	polyurethanes	Paints; Adhesives; In foam form in furniture etc.
propan-1,2,3-triol (glycerol) benzene-1,2-dicarboxylic acid anhydride (phthalic anhydride)	alkyd or glyptal (polyester) resin	Paint, varnish and lacquer bases; Adhesives
bisphenol A epichlorhydrin	epoxide resins	Adhesives; Protective internal lacquer for cans; Encapsulation of eng. and elect. components

This is then mixed with filler (ground rags, sawdust or other cheap materials), pigment (to mask the dark colour of the final product – the final colour is limited because of this) and any other additive. This mixture can then be heated under pressure in suitable moulds causing it to fuse to a hard infusible solid, due to cross linking as indicated below.

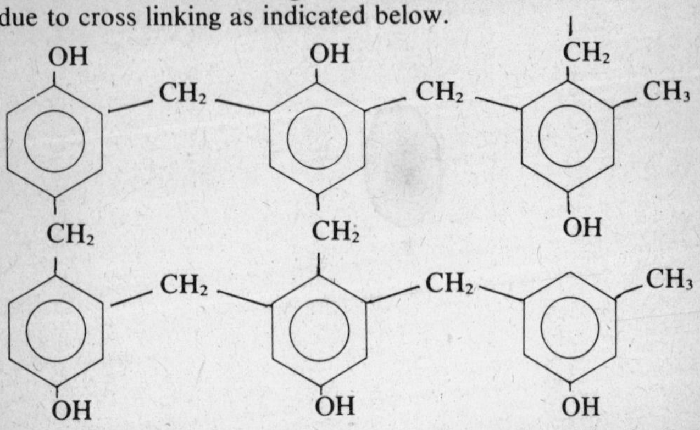

Polyester resins are obtained by heating polyhydric alcohols with polycarboxylic acids or their anhydrides. The cross linking necessary to produce a resin is brought about either by using propan-1,2,3-triol (a trihydric alcohol) as the alcohol or by adding sufficient cross linking additive, such as phenylethene, to a mixture of a dihydric alcohol and a dicarboxylic acid. An alkyl resin results in the former case. When propan-1,2,3-triol is heated with benzene-1,2-dicarboxylic acid anhydride, using a trace of acid catalyst the probable initial product is

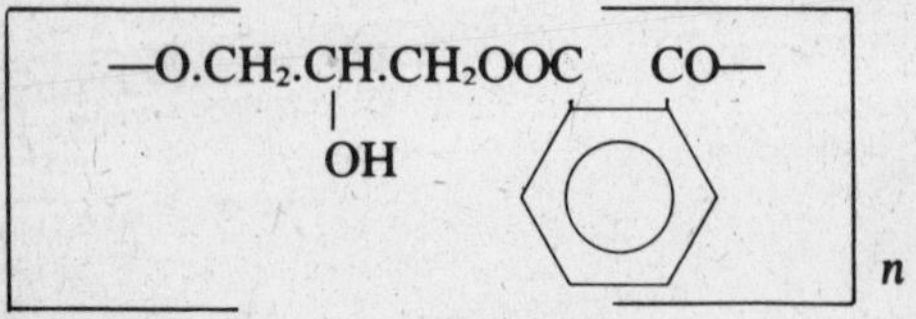

Further heating results in cross linking, which involves the free hydroxyl group in the above structure.

If a cross linking agent is used a polyester resin suitable for use in fibreglass manufacture is obtained. A viscous liquid is obtained by heating, for example, ethan-1,2-diol with butenedioic acid anhydride with the cross linking agent. This sets as a hard resin on addition of a suitable catalyst (the hardener) in most cases no further heating being necessary.

Organic compounds also find significant use as **solvents**. This includes their use as solvents during manufacturing processes, for example as a reaction medium or for extraction and purification of the products of a reaction. When used for these purposes, the solvent is often recovered as completely as possible to prevent problems with disposal due to the flammable or toxic character of many solvents. Solvents also find application in end products including paints and lacquers, many cosmetics, insecticides and other sprays and concentrates. Other uses are in cleaning (particularly dry cleaning) and in analytical techniques, particularly chromatography.

Surface active agents are another class of important organic compounds. These owe their cleaning properties to the presence of a hydrophilic (water liking) group and a hydrophobic (water hating) group. Hydrophilic groups may be charged, as in the carboxyl (COO^-), the sulphonate ($-SO_3^-$), and quaternary ammonium (NR_4^+) groups, or have some polar character, particularly the hydroxyl group. These owe their hydrophilic character to their ability to attract polar water molecules. Hydrophobic groups are long chain aliphatic or aliphatic/aromatic groups. These, having nonpolar character, have an affinity for oil (which holds dirt to materials). The presence of these two types of group allows the mixing of water with non polar substances such as oil by bringing them into closer contact. Surface active agents find use as detergents and soaps; as emulsifying agents, in foods, cosmetics and other creams and lotions; and in industry as constituents of cutting oils.

Soaps are the sodium (or potassium) salts of long chain aliphatic carboxylic acids. Soap is generally represented as being the octadecanoate (stearate) $C_{17}H_{35}COO^-Na^+$, although it probably contains a mixture of acids. It has the disadvantages (i) that the calcium and magnesium salts of these acids are insoluble so that a wasteful scum is formed with hard water (ii) that in acid conditions the acid is displaced from the salt and hence it loses its surface active properties (iii) that soaps are precipitated by addition of salts, due to their colloidal character and hence they do not work efficiently in salt water.

Detergents are generally of three types, **anionic**, **cationic** and **non ionic**.

Neither liquid nor powder detergents are the pure surface active agent as best cleaning action is attained by using a mixture of surface active agents (nowadays this is chosen to avoid damage to the ecology of lakes and rivers). Other additives are also included, particularly builders, which assist the surfactant agents, examples being sodium tripolyphosphate, sodium silicate and sodium carboxymethylcellulose; bleaches such as sodium borate and brighteners which produce the 'whiter than white' effect; bulking agent, usually sodium sulphate, which increases the amount of inert material present and also the concentration of ions in solution and, finally, colour and perfume which have no practical use other than to make the product more attractive to the customer.

Key terms

Sources of organic compounds are petroleum, natural gas, coal and natural (plant and animal) products.
Thermoplastics are materials which retain their plastic property after moulding.
Thermosetting plastics are materials which are only plastic at some stage during the manufacturing process and which do not retain this plastic property once moulded to shape.
Rubbers are elastic plastics.
Vulcanizing agents are chemicals which promote cross linking in natural and synthetic rubbers.
Surfactants are substances which reduce the surface tension of water.
Detergents are surfactants used as cleaning agents.
Cationic detergents are surfactants in which the hydrophilic group has a negative charge.
Anionic detergents have a hydrophilic group with positive charge.
Non ionic detergents have polar groups which impart hydrophilic character.

Index